Mo[illegible] and Idaho's Continental Divide Trail

THE OFFICIAL GUIDE

TEXT BY
LYNNA HOWARD

PHOTOGRAPHY BY
LELAND HOWARD

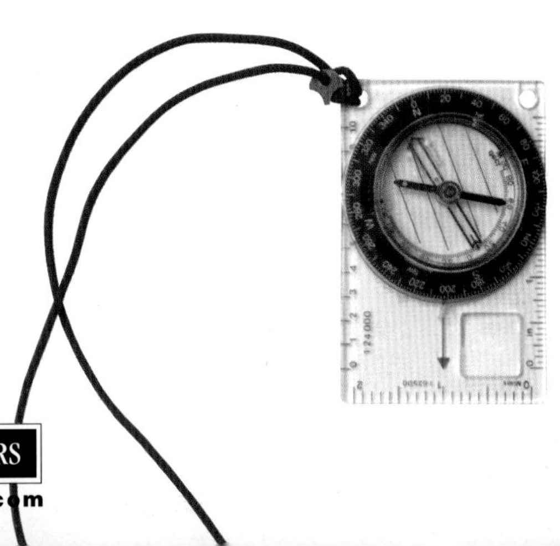

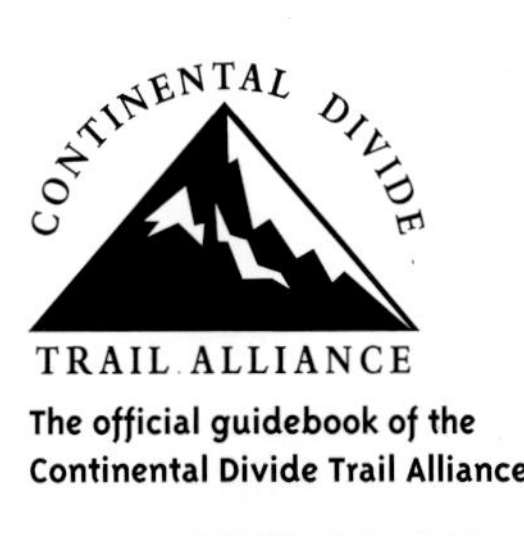

The official guidebook of the Continental Divide Trail Alliance.

www.westcliffepublishers.com

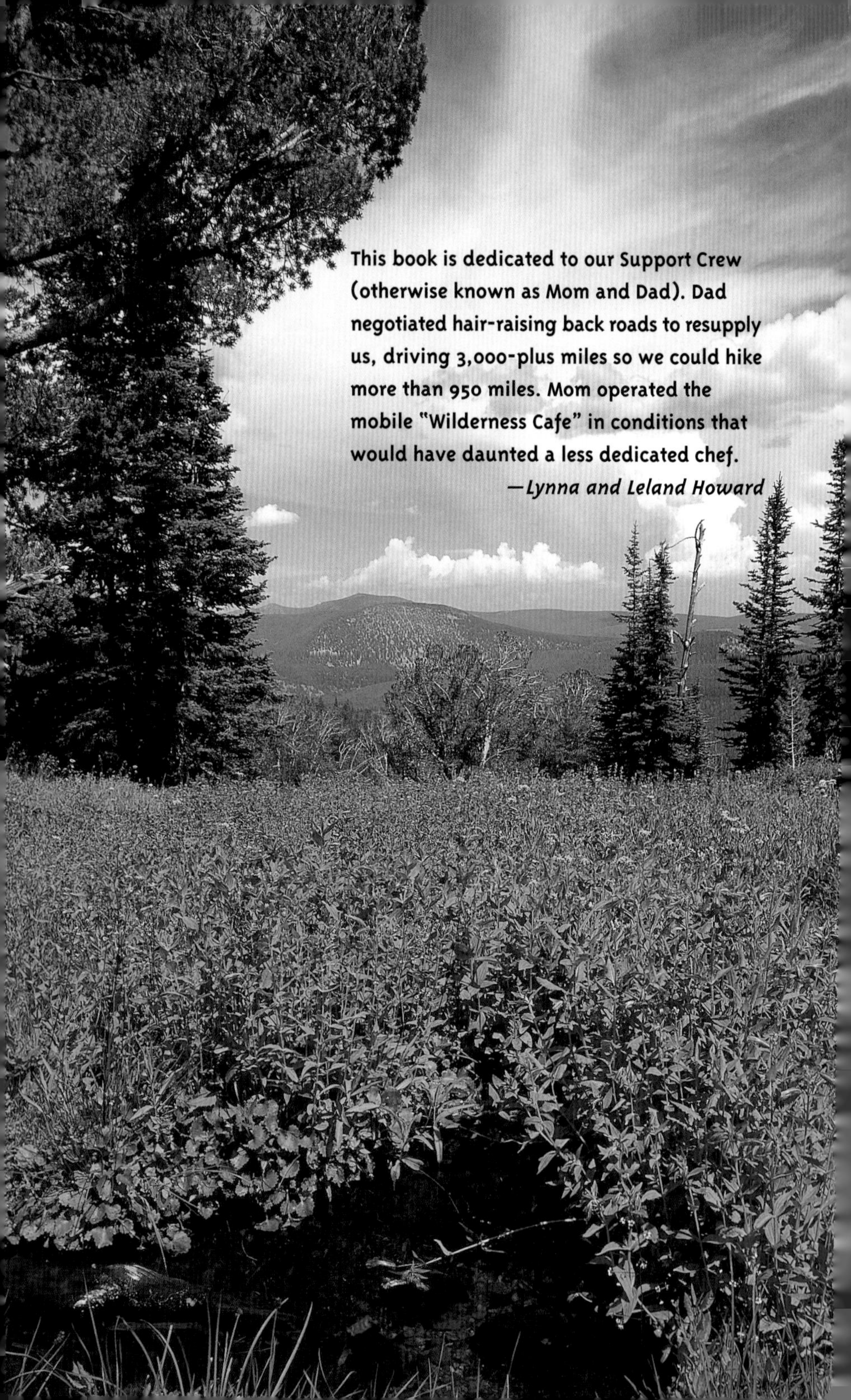

This book is dedicated to our Support Crew (otherwise known as Mom and Dad). Dad negotiated hair-raising back roads to resupply us, driving 3,000-plus miles so we could hike more than 950 miles. Mom operated the mobile "Wilderness Cafe" in conditions that would have daunted a less dedicated chef.

—*Lynna and Leland Howard*

Preface

by Lynna Howard

On the Continental Divide, summer is a chimera whose light hand quickly releases its hold, and the high country slips into autumn just as the long-distance trekker is getting warmed up. In September, cottonwood and aspen groves along the rivers pave the trails with gold. In Glacier National Park's highest meadows, "spring" flowers emerge in August, bravely showing their colors through a coat of morning frost.

It is this fleeting beauty, the changeable nature of the land and the weather—and the threat of danger behind it—that defines the Continental Divide National Scenic Trail (CDT). It takes your breath away in more ways than one.

In an age when science has measured the neurons in our brain down to the submicron level and the distance to the Eagle Nebula with astounding accuracy, we couldn't find anyone who knew for sure how many miles we'd have to hike to complete the Montana/Idaho portion of the Continental Divide Trail. We got estimates from other long-distance trekkers. Some sources pretended to know, quoting distances that turned out to be inaccurate. Several forest rangers gave us good estimates, and some admitted that they just didn't know. The estimates were usually low. We've filled in all the blanks to the best of our ability.

The bottom line is that the season is short and the trail is long. Even with this guidebook in hand, I'm willing to bet that some of you will get a little lost, though not as often as we did. Leave room in your hiking schedule for some wandering around, either for fun or out of necessity.

Ponds and streams along the approach route to Goldstone Pass from the Montana side of the Continental Divide water a profusion of wildflowers in July and August.

Table of Contents

Evening light on snowdrifts along the ridge near Goldstone Mountain in the Beaverhead Mountains of the Bitterroot Range

For more information about other fine books and calendars from Westcliffe Publishers, please contact your local bookstore, call us at 1-800-523-3692, write for our free color catalog, or visit us on the Web at ***www.westcliffepublishers.com****.*

PLEASE NOTE:
Risk is always a factor in backcountry and high-mountain travel. Many of the activities described in this book can be dangerous, especially when weather is adverse or unpredictable, and when unforeseen events or conditions create a hazardous situation. The author has done her best to provide the reader with accurate information about backcountry travel, as well as to point out some of its potential hazards. It is the responsibility of the users of this guide to learn the necessary skills for safe backcountry travel, and to exercise caution in potentially hazardous areas, especially on glaciers and avalanche-prone terrain. The author and publisher disclaim any liability for injury or other damage caused by backcountry traveling, mountain biking, or performing any other activity described in this book.

COVER PHOTO:
Hiker on the traditional route of the CDT in Glacier National Park, near Fifty Mountain.

OPPOSITE:
Indian paintbrush covers the ground beneath the north section of the Chinese Wall in the Bob Marshall Wilderness.

INTERNATIONAL STANDARD BOOK NUMBER:
1-56579-330-7

EDITOR:
Kristen Iversen
DESIGN AND PRODUCTION:
Rebecca Finkel, F + P Graphic Design, Inc.; Boulder, CO
PRODUCTION MANAGER:
Craig Keyzer

PUBLISHED BY:
Westcliffe Publishers, Inc.
P.O. Box 1261
Englewood, Colorado 80150
www.westcliffepublishers.com

Printed in Hong Kong
through World Print

LIBRARY OF CONGRESS CATALOGING-IN-PUBLICATION DATA
Howard, Lynna Prue.
Montana and Idaho's Continental Divide Trail : the official guide / text by Lynna Prue Howard ; photography by Leland Howard.
p. cm.
Includes bibliographical references (p.) and index.
ISBN: 1-56579-330-7

1. Hiking—Continental Divide National Scenic Trail—Guidebooks. 2. Continental Divide National Scenic Trail—Guidebooks. 3. Idaho—Guidebooks. 4. Montana—Guidebooks. I. Howard, Leland, 1953– II. Title.
GV199.42.C833H69 2000 98-49511
917.8604'33—dc21 CIP

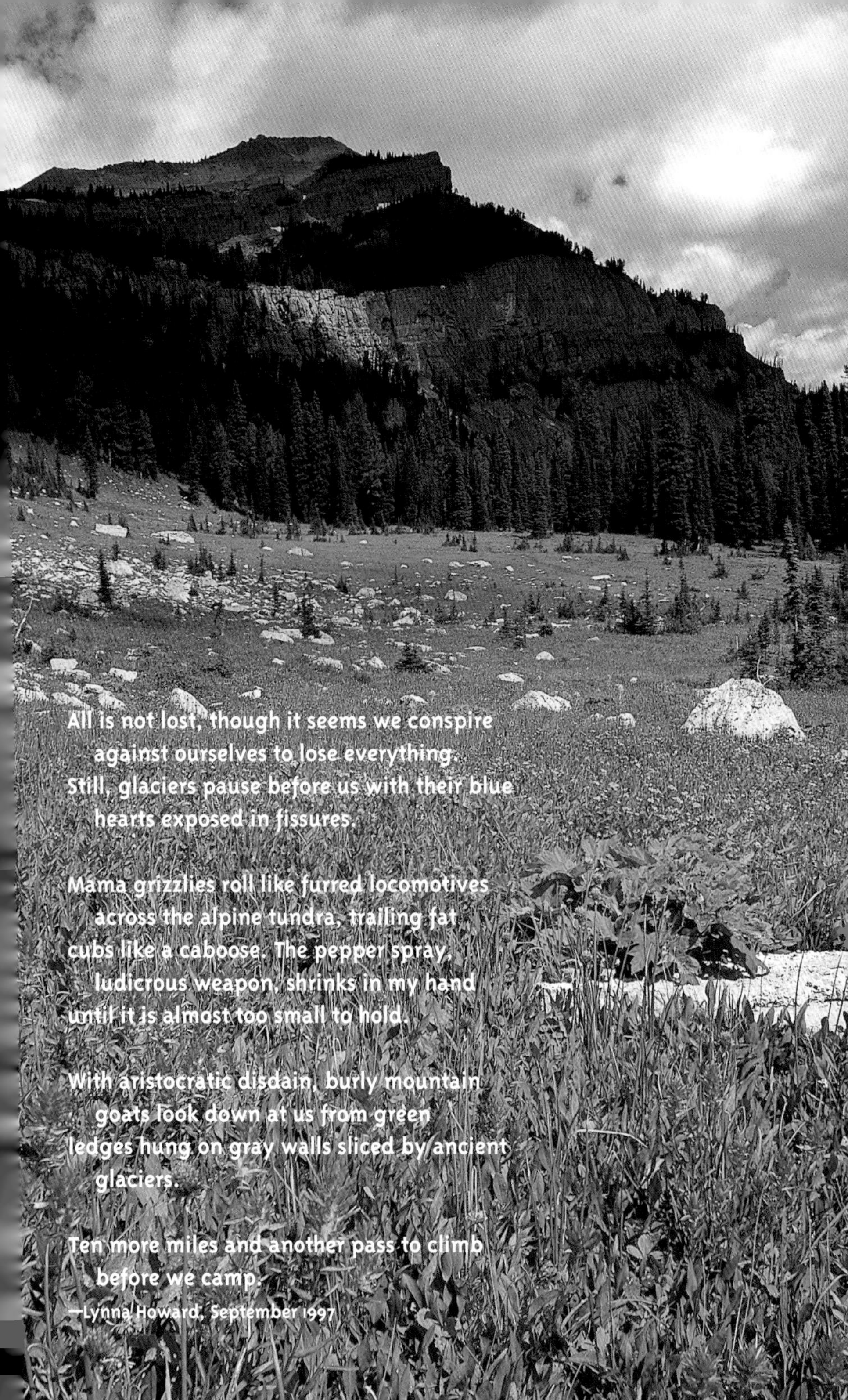

All is not lost, though it seems we conspire
against ourselves to lose everything.
Still, glaciers pause before us with their blue
hearts exposed in fissures.

Mama grizzlies roll like furred locomotives
across the alpine tundra, trailing fat
cubs like a caboose. The pepper spray,
ludicrous weapon, shrinks in my hand
until it is almost too small to hold.

With aristocratic disdain, burly mountain
goats look down at us from green
ledges hung on gray walls sliced by ancient
glaciers.

Ten more miles and another pass to climb
before we camp.

—Lynna Howard, September 1997

Acknowledgements

My brother and I owe special thanks to our father and mother, Calvin and Edna Howard, for their unfailing support and their spirit of adventure.

Thanks to our big brother, Robert, who taught us the ways of bears and helped us get through Glacier National Park safely. Thanks to Steve and Jerry Howard, who gave us support and hiked with us when they could.

Forest Service employees in Montana and Idaho took time out of their busy schedules to go over the route of the trail with us—sometimes more than once. Special recognition goes to Patricia Johnston, who helped us plan for the most difficult sections of our trek, the Scapegoat and Bob Marshall Wilderness areas. Gene Hardin showed the patience of a saint in answering many questions about the route through the Targhee and Gallatin National Forests. Larry Jordan of the Bureau of Land Management added not only his expert knowledge of the trail, but his enthusiastic support of the CDNST project. Roger Simlar, wilderness manager for Glacier National Park, helped us with the logistics of hiking in a National Park. Olie Olsen showed us the way through the Anaconda-Pintler Wilderness in meticulous detail. Eric Tolf shared his own journeys on the trail and resorted to drawing pictures when we got lost. Both Salmon and Dillon Ranger District personnel took the time to pore over topographical maps with us. Countless others gave of their time and expertise. *We thank them all.*

The following companies generously supplied gear or discounts for our expedition:

REI provided overall expedition support, including rain gear, sleeping bags, trekking poles, and backpacks. We highly recommend REI's "Down Time Dryloft" sleeping bags—they saved our lives more than once.

JANSPORT provided both day and expedition packs that withstood hundreds of miles of hard use.

LOWEPRO provided Leland's "Pro Trekker" and "Nature Trekker" specialty backpacks for professional camera gear.

VASQUE Super Hiker II boots. Those boots are tough as nails.

CLIF BAR, INC. Clif™ Bars and Clif™ Shot.

EARLY WINTERS expedition-worthy clothing.

TUBBS SNOWSHOE COMPANY snowshoes.

SWEETWATER Guardian water filter.

U-DIG-IT trowels for leaving no trace.

N.E.O.S. Ridgerunner overshoes.

TRAILS ILLUSTRATED Glacier/Waterton maps.

ATWATER CAREY Backpacker First Aid kits.

SPORTLINE mechanical pedometers.

Special thanks to the Continental Divide Trail Alliance and Westcliffe Publishers for believing in our ability to get the job done.

—LYNNA AND LELAND HOWARD

Part of the proceeds from the sale of this book benefits the Continental Divide Trail Alliance.

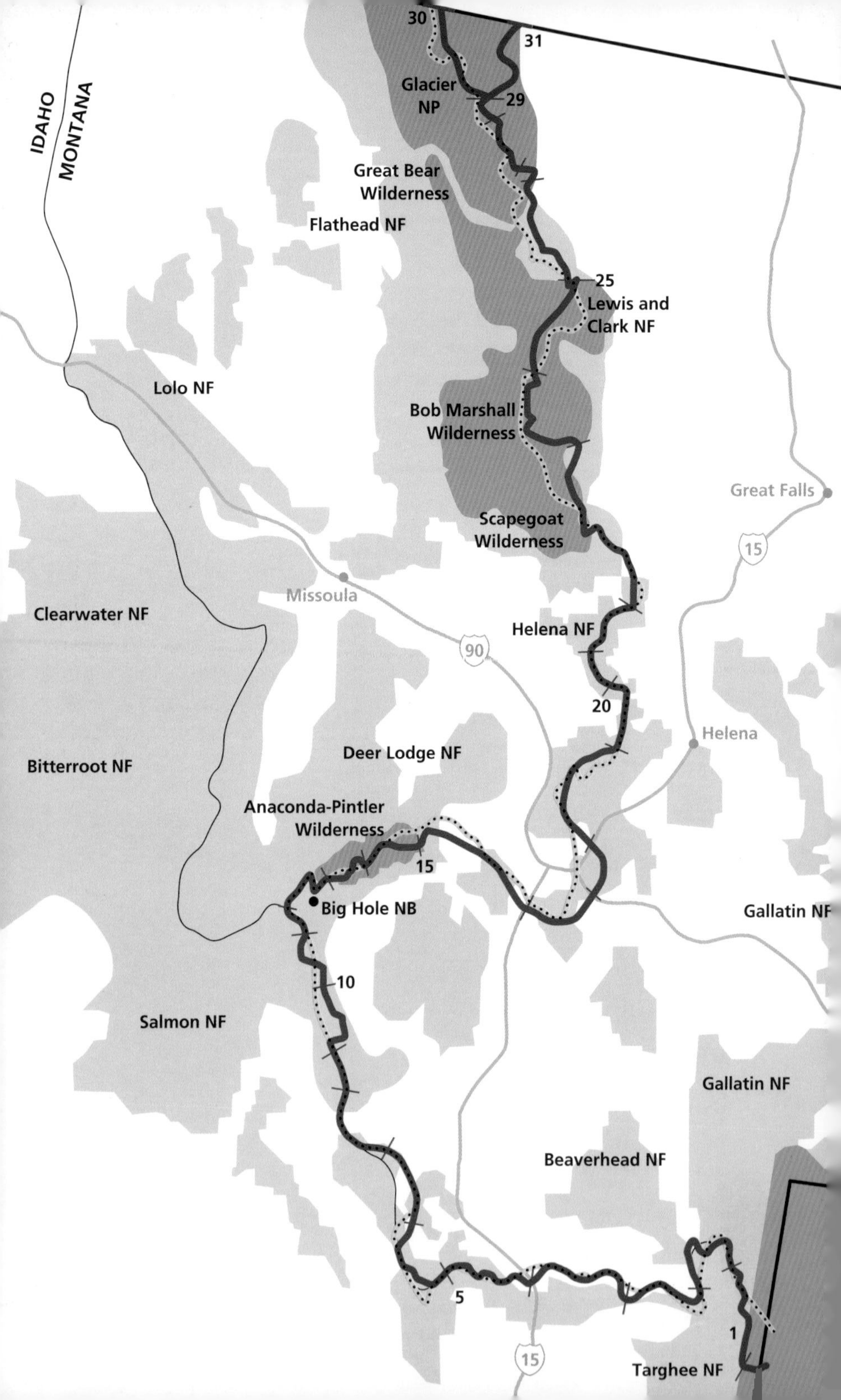

IDAHO
MONTANA
30
31
Glacier NP
29
Great Bear Wilderness
Flathead NF
25
Lewis and Clark NF
Lolo NF
Bob Marshall Wilderness
Great Falls
Scapegoat Wilderness
15
Missoula
Clearwater NF
Helena NF
90
20
Helena
Deer Lodge NF
Bitterroot NF
Anaconda-Pintler Wilderness
15
Big Hole NB
Gallatin NF
10
Salmon NF
Gallatin NF
Beaverhead NF
5
1
15
Targhee NF

CANADA
MONTANA
Lewis and
Clark NF

CONTINENTAL DIVIDE TRAIL
SEGMENTS 1–31
5
Continental Divide Trail
(segments)
Continental Divide
Road
City or Town
Wilderness Area
or National Park
National Forest

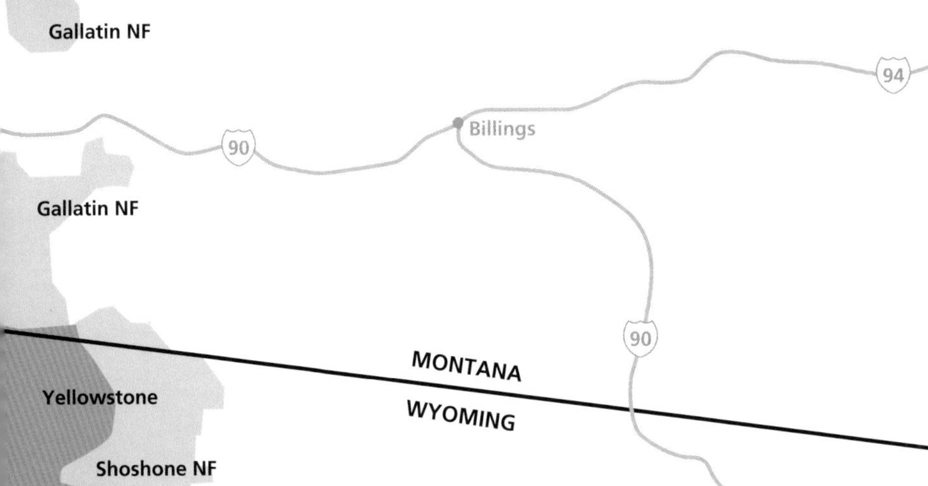
Gallatin NF
94
Billings
90
Gallatin NF
90
MONTANA
WYOMING
Yellowstone
Shoshone NF

Segments Chart

Total miles on designated route: 980.7
Total elevation gain on designated route: 134,724 feet

Total miles on alternate route: 967.5
Total elevation gain on alternate route: 134,396 feet

SEGMENT	STARTING POINT	ENDING POINT	DIFFICULTY
1	Yellowstone N. P. border	Targhee Pass	easy
2	Targhee Pass	Red Rock Pass	moderate
3	Red Rock Pass	Aldous Lake	strenuous
4	Aldous Lake	I-15 / Modoc Access	moderate
5	I-15 / Modoc Access	Bannack Pass	moderate
6	Bannack Pass	Morrison Lake	strenuous
7	Morrison Lake	Bannock Pass	moderate
8	Bannock Pass	Lemhi Pass	moderate
9	Lemhi Pass	Goldstone Pass	moderate
10	Goldstone Pass	Miner Lakes TRHD	moderate
11	Miner Lakes TRHD	Big Hole Pass	strenuous
12	Big Hole Pass	Chief Joseph Pass	moderate
13	Chief Joseph Pass	Schultz Saddle	easy
14	Schultz Saddle	Johnson Lake	moderate
15	Johnson Lake	Lower Seymour Lake	strenuous
16	Lower Seymour Lake	I-15 / Deer Lodge Pass	easy
17	I-15 / Deer Lodge Pass	Homestake Pass	easy
18	Homestake Pass	I-15 at Elk Park	easy
19	I-15 at Elk Park	MacDonald Pass	moderate
20	MacDonald Pass	Dana Spring	easy
21	Dana Spring	Stemple Pass	strenuous
22	Stemple Pass	Rogers Pass	moderate
23	Rogers Pass	Benchmark / S. Fork TRHD	strenuous
24	Benchmark / S. Fork TRHD	Badger Pass	strenuous
25	Badger Pass	Marias Pass	moderate
26	Marias Pass	East Glacier Park	easy
27	East Glacier Park	Two Medicine Campground	moderate
28	Two Medicine Campground	St. Mary Falls	strenuous
29	St. Mary Falls	Many Glacier	strenuous
30	Swiftcurrent Pass TRHD	Waterton Townsite	strenuous
31	Many Glacier	Chief Mountain	strenuous

MILEAGE	TOTAL ELEV. GAIN (FEET)	TRAILHEAD ACCESS	PAGE	SEGMENT
35.6	2,564	bumpy road, hike	52	1
33.9	4,914	paved road	62	2
30.1	4,890	bumpy road	70	3
30.7	4,540	bumpy road	80	4
42.0	5,951	paved road	88	5
32.8	5,179	bumpy road, 4WD	98	6
22.8	5,577	bumpy road, extreme 4WD	106	7
27.6	4,027	bumpy road	114	8
19.8	3,940	bumpy road	120	9
26.6	2,667	bumpy road, extreme 4WD	126	10
32.7	5,707	bumpy road, 4WD	134	11
16.8	2,700	bumpy road	144	12
18.7	2,028	paved road	150	13
26.9	4,398	bumpy road	154	14
33.5	7,372	bumpy road, hike	162	15
45.2	3,775	bumpy road	170	16
39.3	4,072	paved road	178	17
27.7	2,949	paved road	184	18
65.5	8,904	paved road	190	19
24.4	3,713	paved road	204	20
18.1	3,513	bumpy road	214	21
22.8	4,851	bumpy road	220	22
65.3	9,245	paved road	226	23
88.3	7,861	bumpy road	238	24
34.3	4,111	bumpy road, hike	250	25
15.2	1,190	paved road	258	26
10.5	2,605	paved road	266	27
38.7	4,394	paved road	270	28
15.6	3,060	paved road, hike	278	29
39.3	4,027	paved road	284	30
26.1	3,699	paved road	292	31

Introduction

My brother, Leland, and I were hiking against a fierce headwind in the Beaverhead Mountains when an eagle came over the ridge, flying from Montana into Idaho across the Continental Divide. Something about the moment fixed it in my memory, where it remains fresh and resonant with a significance I have been trying to plumb ever since. In part, it was the unexpected closeness with a wild creature—the eagle not knowing I was there, clearing the ridge by about 10 feet and flying past me at near eye level, adjusting its flight path with a deft swerve, a startled look about its head and eyes at seeing humans in such an unlikely spot.

But there was more to that moment than just surprise. It was the gift of a moment without boundaries, devolving very simply from the fact that the eagle crossed the state line without knowing it was there. The Divide suddenly became part of a much larger picture. The Continental Divide exists without reference to political boundaries—it makes state lines and the borders between nations look very temporary. Walking the Divide, one walks in a world concerned with other things, a world that transcends the thin carapace of names, of lines on maps.

This 8,000-mile geological uplift is the backbone of the North American continent, running from Alaska to the Panama Canal. It separates the land mass into the major watersheds of the Atlantic, Pacific, and Arctic oceans. About 3,200 miles of the Divide make up the Continental Divide National Scenic Trail as it meanders through the lower 48 states, from the Mexican border to the Canadian border. At Triple Divide in Glacier National Park, waters flow to the Atlantic via the Missouri River drainage system, to the Pacific via the Columbia River, and to the Arctic via the Saskatchewan River and Hudson Bay. Water, weather, elevation changes—these are the important factors to humans, animals, and plants on the Continental Divide.

The eagle riding an updraft over the Divide was only one of a legion of wild creatures we met on our journey. At one point, we had hiked over 200 miles without encountering any other humans on the trail; but elk, deer, moose, black bears, and coyotes were much in evidence. We joked that the CDT was a good game trail. Animal prints outnumbered human sign by many orders of magnitude. On Glacier National Park trails, we saw about an even mix of humans and bears. In this respect, the Montana/Idaho CDT is unique. It crosses the only wilderness areas in the lower 48 states that are prime grizzly bear habitat, and human traffic is virtually nil in some sections. On most of the Montana/Idaho CDT, you are alone as soon as you leave the trailhead.

Old-fashioned self-reliance and wilderness survival skills are more important here than on more well-known and better-traveled trails. You'll find some areas little changed since Lewis and Clark passed this way in 1805. So hone your skills, choose your equipment carefully, and read the preparatory information in this book before you begin. When you're ready to hit the trail, there's only one last instruction to heed—enjoy! There is no better way to transcend the boundaries of time and space than by hiking the Continental Divide.

By taking a short detour off the Continental Divide Trail, hikers can discover Hidden Falls, located south of Swiftcurrent Lake on Cataract Creek in Glacier National Park.

How to Use This Guide

Most people don't like to read instructions. You're probably one of them. But if you take the time to go over this introductory material, you'll not only find this book easier to use, you'll increase your chances of a safe journey.

This book is equally useful for the day hiker, overnight camper, through-hiker, or mountain biker who wants to experience the wonders of the Continental Divide National Scenic Trail. The heart of this book is divided into 31 chapters that correspond to the 31 segments of the CDT in Montana and Idaho. Each segment represents a distinct section of the trail, with starting and ending points on or near highways, dirt roads, and, in some cases, foot trails.

The segments chart lists segments by difficulty, mileage, total elevation gain, and trailhead access, allowing you to quickly choose segments that suit your abilities and goals. However, you should read the corresponding segment chapters before you make up your mind, as the chart is not set up to reflect other difficulties you might encounter. Please note that "elevation gain" is just that — gain only. It tells you how many feet you have to climb when hiking south to north, but it doesn't tell you the elevation loss or descent. As all experienced hikers know, those steep descents can be difficult, too. The elevation chart at the beginning of each chapter will show you the descents as well as the gains. To see the trail in its entirety, refer to the overview map.

The segments are in geographical order from south to north, and a through-hiker can use the book start to finish. The trail begins in Idaho at the western border of Yellowstone National Park and wends its often devious way to the Canadian border about 980 miles later. Your mileage may vary depending on which of the official, alternate, or proposed routes you choose. This book is written to carry on where Westcliffe Publishers' *Wyoming's Continental Divide Trail: The Official Guide* leaves off. (Westcliffe publishes Colorado and New Mexico guides as well.)

It is difficult to hike the Montana/Idaho portion of the CDT from north to south, but some hardy souls have done it. Bear in mind that there are campgrounds in Glacier National Park that routinely do not clear of snow until August 1. You might need an ice ax, and the ability to ford deep, icy rivers, to get through Glacier earlier in the season. The Chinese Wall in the Bob Marshall Wilderness is often snowed-in until mid-July, as are sections of the Beaverhead Mountains. You'll increase your chances of success if you hike from south to north and plan on reaching the Yellowstone border in July, the Scapegoat/Bob Marshall in August, and Glacier Park in September. If you're not convinced and still feel that you want to hike north to south, look for important information marked with this "southbound" symbol: S

Each segment is a chapter in this book. Introductory information at the beginning of each chapter summarizes the important aspects of the segment. The first items you will see are the segment's distance in miles and a difficulty rating: easy, moderate, and strenuous. The background color of each segment's introductory page also corresponds to difficulty: green for easy, blue for moderate, and red for strenuous. Note that these ratings are highly subjective, and what is easy for the seasoned hiker may be quite strenuous for someone else. Also, "difficulty" could include access problems that force hikers to plan for longer trips. If you have to carry food for 10 days, the hike will be difficult even if the trail is only moderately strenuous.

A graphic elevation profile at the bottom of each segment's introductory page illustrates elevation gain and loss, and also notes an estimate of the total elevation gain over the entire segment. The profile box indicates the trail mileage from Wyoming to Canada. These figures are based on each segment's starting point.

WHAT YOU NEED TO KNOW

After the elevation profile, several paragraphs describe the segment and contain information about water, camping, highlights and pitfalls, and some local history.

This icon appears in segment chapters where hikers can expect to encounter bears. Grizzly bears are a serious hazard in some areas. Please read the "Safety Concerns" chapter before you begin your expedition.

The last paragraph, titled "Mountain Bike Notes," tells you whether you may ride bikes on the trail, accompanied by the following symbols:

Most of the terrain is non-technical, but there may be some elevation gain. Check the segment's elevation profile.

You will find steep or technical riding on most of the segment, and you may have to carry your bike in spots. These segments are not recommended for novice cyclists.

Some or all of the terrain on the segment is not ridable due to rocks, steepness, lack of a trail, environmental sensitivity, etc.

The segment passes through a designated wilderness area, National Park, or some other area where bikes are prohibited by law.

The last item you will find here are the names of the ranger districts through which the trail passes. For management purposes, the U.S. Forest Service and Bureau of Land Management (BLM) divide forests into distinct jurisdictions. If you have questions about the trail, you should contact the appropriate districts. You will find their addresses and phone numbers in Appendix A.

MAPS

Each chapter has a list of the maps that cover the segment. There are three kinds of maps: United States Geological Survey (USGS) quadrangles, U.S. Forest Service, and Trails Illustrated®.

Forest Service maps provide a good overview of a segment's location, surroundings, and accessibility, but they do not lend themselves to precise navigation. The best

Arrowleaf balsamroot grows on the east side of the Rocky Mountain Front Range, near the Dearborn River access to the Scapegoat Wilderness.

maps for that purpose are the 7.5-minute topographical quadrangles put out by the USGS. The scale for these USGS maps is 1:24,000, and the detail is excellent for navigation. Please note that in this book, the maps depicting the trail are USGS 30 x 60 minute quadrangles. These maps are great for planning purposes, but not detailed enough for use on the trail. For most of the Montana/Idaho CDT, you need to carry the 7.5-minute USGS maps, Forest Service maps, and a compass.

There are 117 USGS 7.5-minute topographical maps for the Montana/Idaho CDT, plus 12 more topos that are recommended for access information. As I write this, these maps cost $4 each. You can cut down on the expense by eliminating the quadrangles for Glacier National Park, the Anaconda-Pintler Wilderness, and the Bob Marshall Wilderness. The trails are more clearly marked in these areas, and other, detailed maps are available (see the maps listed for each segment). However, your understanding and appreciation of the terrain will be enhanced if you carry the USGS maps. USGS maps are accurate in regard to terrain, but are out-of-date with respect to trails and roads.

There is only one Trails Illustrated map available for the Montana/Idaho CDT: Glacier National Park. It is an excellent value as it is waterproof, tear-proof, and more up-to-date than the USGS topos. The Trails Illustrated map uses a smaller scale than the USGS maps but it is sufficient for hiking the CDT.

See Appendix C for a list of map sources and Appendix D for lists of the maps required for the Montana/Idaho CDT. It can be very time consuming to order the correct quadrangles and then align them from south to north when planning an expedition, so two lists are provided here. The first list is alphabetical—that's the one you'll need for placing your map order. The second list is in order from south to north— that's the list you'll need for planning your expedition and marking your route.

Sometimes it helps to just put the topographical map down and look for the Continental Divide. Where is the water flowing? To the Columbia River or to the Missouri River? The CDT is somewhere in the middle. I was often reminded of Lewis Carroll's opinion of large-scale maps.

> *"We actually made a map of the country, on a scale of a mile to a mile!"*
> *"Have you used it much?" I inquired.*
> *"It has never been spread out, yet," said Mein Herr. "The farmers objected. They said it would cover the whole country and shut out the sunlight! So we now use the country itself, as its own map, and I assure you it does nearly as well."*
>
> — Lewis Carroll

ACCESS TO TRAILHEADS

After the map information, you'll find detailed directions for driving or hiking to the segments' trailheads.

The segments are divided logically so you can reach their beginning and ending points, whenever possible, on good roads. Alternate access points are also mentioned to give you some options for planning shorter hikes, and to give friends or support crews the information they need to meet you on the trail. Because the Continental Divide is in the middle of some of the most remote land in Idaho and Montana, there are many segments where you may have to take dirt roads or four-wheel-drive (4WD) roads to reach the trailheads. Four-wheel-drive "roads" may be mere tracks in some instances—please note where short-wheel-based, high-clearance vehicles (not full-size 4WD) are required. If you do not have access to such a vehicle, and the experience to drive it well, you should hike the access route instead. To give you a quick visual reference of what kind of terrain to expect, the following symbols precede each set of driving directions:

The trailhead is accessible with a normal passenger car. The road is either paved or well-graded dirt.

A normal passenger car can get to the trailhead, but the road is not paved and may be quite rough. Adverse weather conditions may make these routes impassable.

You will need a four-wheel-drive vehicle.

You will need a short-wheel-based, high-clearance, four-wheel-drive vehicle, nerves of steel, and considerable driving experience.

A hike is required to reach the Continental Divide Trail.

The symbols may be used in combination, and mileage is given for each one. In the following example, you would drive 3.4 miles over bumpy or rough roads and hike an additional 0.7 mile to reach the CDT:

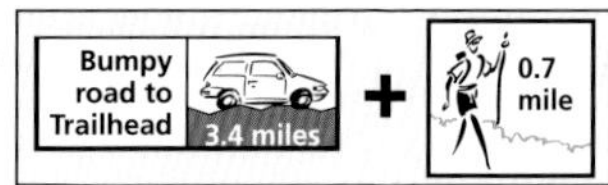

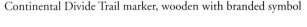

TRAIL MARKERS

These markers are regular features on the trail, and the book refers to them frequently:

Continental Divide Trail marker, wooden with branded symbol

Continental Divide Trail marker, blue and white

tree blaze
(a cut in the tree that is shaped like a crude, lowercase "i")

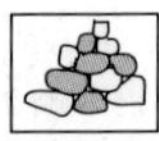

rock cairn

SUPPLIES, SERVICES, AND ACCOMMODATIONS

Through-hikers as well as segment hikers will find this section useful for planning an itinerary. The names of towns near the trail are provided as well as the names, addresses, and phone numbers of important businesses such as grocery stores, outdoor-gear shops, motels, and the post office. If you plan to send boxes of supplies ahead to post offices along the route before you depart, it's a good idea to give them a call first to check on business hours and to make sure they can accommodate general delivery.

OTHER EXCURSIONS

After the detailed segment description, which makes up the bulk of each chapter, you'll find information on other activities near or on the trail segment. Most, but not all, of the segment chapters end with information for other excursions. These descriptions are not as detailed as the regular segment descriptions, so you should supplement this information with a good map and additional information from local sources.

An alpine spruce stump tells the tale of a battle lost against the weather on Pintler Pass in the Anaconda-Pintler Wilderness.

DIRECTIONS AND THE COMPASS

People understand directions in one of two ways: one, using the cardinal directions (east, south) and compass bearings (145°); and two, using directions like up, down, left, and right, and cues such as landmarks, trail markers, and terrain variations. Both methods are employed in this book.

A compass and a basic understanding of how it works are invaluable. When you shop for a compass, look for a rotating dial with the degrees ticked off around it. For very precise or serious orienteering, an attached mirror is useful.

Particularly confusing or obscure areas in the trail description are marked with this symbol: 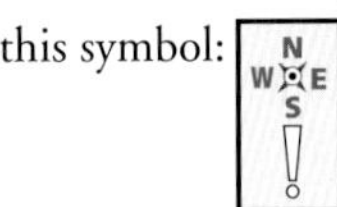

The circular compass dial is divided into 360 equal units called degrees, which are numbered starting with 0° at due north and increasing in a clockwise direction. Due east is at 90°, south is at 180°, and west is at 270°.

A compass may be affected by its surroundings; for example, you may not get an accurate reading from inside your car. Electric motors can demagnetize or disorient the compass needle. Women hikers should avoid underwire bras as they may affect the compass reading. Take your compass readings out in the open, well away from possible interference.

The compass needle always points toward magnetic north, but maps are based on "true north." The difference between the two, which varies with location, is called "magnetic declination." The magnetic declination for the Montana/Idaho CDT varies from 15° to 17° east. That is, your compass will actually point 15° to 17° east of true north. Most compasses come with instructions for adjusting for declination, so that the compass you use will indicate true north for the location in which you are hiking.

Phrases such as "westerly" or "northerly" appear frequently in this book. These directions are given where exact compass readings in degrees are not required for route finding. For example, "westerly" may indicate that the hiker should look or walk in a westerly direction (260° to 280° on the compass) for a short distance, until the next obvious landmark or trail marker is visible. Sometimes a general direction like "northerly" is given to indicate which trail to take at an intersection. A winding trail may take the hiker north, but not adhere strictly to a 0° heading.

Bearings provided in this book are based on true north and have a margin of error of ±10°.

MEASURING DISTANCE: HOW FAR IS IT?

Mileage in this book may not match U.S. Forest Service signs. The Forest Service sometimes rounds distances off to the nearest mile, a practice that can add up to quite a bit of mileage difference. Also, land administrators sometimes leave an old sign up after changes in the trail, such as the addition of switchbacks or rerouting, have significantly changed the mileage. In 1989, the Forest Service approved a proposed route for the

CDT through Idaho and Montana and estimated the mileage at 795 miles. We now know that the actual distance is more than 980 miles.

How did we determine the distance covered in each segment? Where we had them, we began with Forest Service estimates and then checked those by using a map-rolling device on USGS topographical maps. The device can be calibrated to the scale of the map, and with the addition of elevation information, gives a reasonable estimate of the distance between two points. It is not accurate on tight switchbacks and where there are frequent changes in elevation.

As we hiked the trail, we averaged the output from two pedometers and compared that to our previous estimates. Where the trail crosses civilized areas, it follows roads, even paved highways. In those areas, our support crew often helped us out by mileaging the motorized sections.

Before we began hiking, I met with land administrators in each district and drew the approximate route of the CDT on all the topographical maps. As we hiked the trail, I corrected this approximation by drawing the actual trail on the maps. I even resorted to counting switchbacks and putting them on the map. (There are exactly 50 switchbacks between Targhee Divide and the trailhead near Highway 87.) Once the trail was drawn more accurately, I carefully placed a string along the route, accounting for each twist, turn, and switchback. The string was then measured against the map's scale guide. Where necessary, elevation changes were added, although an accurate representation of switchbacks usually accounts for most elevation changes. With this method, trail mileage can be represented as accurate to within about three-tenths of a mile for every 10 miles. Our method is not 100 percent accurate, but it is very close to correct. We applied the same method to the approach routes.

The Continental Divide Trail is a work in progress. In some places it is like "The Emperor's New Clothes." Those who believe, claim that they can see it. The CDT route appears on maps, but when you try to hike it, sometimes it can't be found. As a result, U.S. Forest Service, BLM, and National Park administrators, along with an army of volunteers, have been working to improve the trail. Significant improvements have been made in the past two years and the pace of change is accelerating as interest in the trail increases. Sections of the trail have changed since we hiked them; more will change in the future.

PLANNING A THROUGH-HIKE

Take time to plan thoroughly. After you have selected the segments you want to hike, order the maps you'll need and mark your route on them. For the first two weeks of your hike, plan to do less mileage per day, allowing for water sources. Water will determine where you camp or stop for a rest. Plan frequent food resupply points so that you won't have to carry as much weight. Recruit all your friends and relatives to help in the resupply effort. Even the most physically fit will find backpacking all day in such rough terrain to be difficult. Work into longer treks slowly, planning to make more mileage later in your trip. We met several long-distance trekkers on the trail who had already hiked the Appalachian Trail and/or the Pacific Crest Trail—all of them found the CDNST to be more difficult, and most of them were not meeting their planned mileage goals. Even experienced trekkers should modify their goals for the Montana/Idaho CDT. We saw some hikers who gave up on the hard-to-find trail and were hiking dirt roads in the valleys so they could make their planned 25 miles per day. They missed the entire Continental Divide experience. Better to plan for shorter segments done over several seasons of hiking than to miss the trail entirely. We were taking photos and notes for the book, so we carried more equipment and stopped much more frequently. Our average was 10 miles per day, and we planned for a day off about every five days.

FOOD. Measure and count your food supplies carefully. You may want to make several practice runs beforehand to determine your food needs. According to *Backpacker* magazine, the average 200-pound man needs about 3,600 calories in day-to-day life, but will require an additional 3,000 calories or more to hike carrying a heavy pack at high altitude. Carbohydrates should account for 60 to 70 percent of calories, protein 10 to 15 percent, and fat 20 to 25 percent. Plan to eat a nutritious snack about every 90 minutes as you hike, and drink a lot of water, or water mixed with sport drinks.

RESUPPLY. You can make resupply boxes to be picked up at post offices along the way, or better yet, have friends and relatives bring the resupplies to you. Most post offices along the Montana/Idaho CDT are far off this remote route, so it will add considerable time and miles to your trek to collect supplies that you have mailed to yourself. However, if you do mail boxes ahead to yourself, write "General Delivery" and your name above the post office address and include instructions to "Hold for Continental Divide Trail hiker." Post office addresses and phone numbers are listed in the town information boxes in this book. We've added a list of outfitters to Segment 24, the Bob Marshall Wilderness, where access is so limited that you may wish to pay an outfitter to pack in your resupplies.

If people are meeting you for resupply, you will have to stick to a more precise itinerary, but you should still leave room for delays due to bad weather, getting lost, and slowdowns from minor injuries like blisters and sprains. We gave our support crew approximate days and times that we expected to arrive at a meeting point, based on mileage and elevation changes.

PACKING. Make a detailed checklist, and check off things to take as well as things to do. Practice by using a shorter, local backpacking trip to make sure it all works. See Appendix B for a gear checklist. In general, your pack should not weigh more than 30 percent of your body weight. If you weigh 120 pounds, your pack should be 40 pounds or less—less is better. Keep your pack as light as possible. This involves mostly common sense, but here are some suggestions:

- If you have a cook set with several pots, leave all but one pot at home. Use the lid as a plate. Hike with a buddy and bring only one cooking pot to share.
- Avoid heavy food. Fresh fruit is nice, but it weighs much more than its dried counterparts. For dinners, freeze-dried food is light, and with some experimentation you'll find selections you actually like.

Early October brings snowfall to Red Rock Pass and the Centennial Mountains, the range that forms the Montana/Idaho border for more than 40 miles.

- Get rid of excess packaging. Pack food and condiments in small, plastic bottles or baggies. Bring only as much as you need for the days you will be on the trail, plus one day more of emergency supplies. Include your first-aid supplies, toiletries, insect repellent, sunscreen, etc., in this "only as much as you need for X number of days" selective process.
- Avoid unnecessary luxuries like a chair, shower, cassette tape player, etc. None of this will feel like a luxury when you have to carry it uphill.
- Take lightweight, high-tech clothing that retains its warmth when wet and that can be worn in layers, adjusting for changes in temperature. Don't bring clean clothes, except for a change of socks.
- Use food drops for more than just food. Put fresh clothes in your resupply boxes. If the same person will be meeting you at several resupply points, give him or her one box with refill items in it to take to each point, such as that tube of toothpaste, fresh batteries, or stove fuel.
- You can get by without a ground cloth for your tent if you choose your campsites carefully. The exception is Glacier National Park, where you must camp in assigned spots that are often wet, muddy, and rocky.

Test all of your equipment before you leave, including stove, tent, water filter, and pack. Give yourself plenty of time before the hike to break in new boots. Boots that will give you the kind of support you need to hike 500 miles may take as many as 60 miles to break in. Don't take a chance on this. Blisters are painful beyond belief. We met a limping hiker near Monida Pass who begged us for ibuprofen. We met hikers in Glacier who were carrying too much weight and their blisters looked like fresh volcanic calderas.

GET IN SHAPE. Most of us have other obligations like work, school, and families that limit the time we can give to physical fitness. Even a small amount of regular exercise starting four to six months before your trip can make a big difference in your comfort and performance on the trail. Stress aerobic activity and leg-strengthening exercises. The truth is that whatever you do, it won't be enough. Backpacking Idaho and Montana's CDT is a humbling experience. Start slow and work your way up to bigger and longer challenges.

On the Trail

Be sure to keep the following important things in mind as you hike the Montana/Idaho CDT.

LEAVE NO TRACE (see Appendix E)

When you hike the Montana/Idaho Continental Divide you will cross Forest Service lands, Bureau of Land Management areas, state-owned land, and some private land. Most of the land along the Divide is public. It belongs to all of us and is in our care. When we set foot there, we should respect these places in their natural state, and strive to leave no trace of our passing. The Forest Service has developed the principle of "Leave No Trace," which should govern the behavior of every backcountry visitor.

PLAN AHEAD. Proper planning, especially for long-distance hikes, will make it easier for you to stick to Leave No Trace guidelines. Your gear, clothing, and food should be chosen to lessen your impact.

HIKE SINGLE FILE. Hiking single file and staying on the trail help to avoid trampling fragile plants and soft ground. Never cut switchbacks. In places where there is no trail, or where it is necessary to leave the trail, choose the most durable surfaces to walk on, such as rocks, dry ground, or a carpet of pine needles. In the absence of a trail, groups should fan out to disperse their impact.

BE COURTEOUS. When meeting other trail users such as mountain bikers and horse packers, give them room to pass. The current standard is that bikers and hikers yield to horses, and bikers yield to hikers, but the prudent hiker will make room for a mountain biker.

CONCENTRATE IMPACT IN HIGH-USE AREAS. In well-traveled areas, select an established campsite that has already seen a lot of use. This reflects the philosophy that certain spots are sacrificed to be used again and again without the intention of restoring them to a natural state. Choose hard, dry ground with the least amount of vegetation for a tent site. Make sure your camp is at least 200 feet from streams, lakes, and trails, and be aware of "visual pollution"—how visible your tent and camp are to other visitors seeking a remote backcountry experience.

DISPERSE IMPACT IN LOW-USE AREAS. If you are in an area that has seen less human impact, try not to use the same route each time you travel around camp so that no single area becomes worn. The cooking area should be situated on a durable surface, such as a large, flat rock. If you have them, wear light shoes instead of heavy, hard-soled hiking boots once you arrive at camp.

CAMPFIRES. Campfires are a traditional source of warmth, comfort, and safety in backcountry areas. However, fire does impact the environment, leaving scars and other signs of human impact. A small backpacking stove provides a quicker and more efficient way to cook. In Glacier National Park, fires are prohibited in some campgrounds. If you must build a fire, make sure you are below timberline (not in an alpine area) and are in an area where there is an abundant supply of dead and downed wood. Use an existing fire ring or build a "mound fire"—never build a new fire ring. A mound fire is built by finding a source of mineral soil, such as a streambed during low water or the hole left by a tree that has blown over. Use a stuff sack to carry a large amount of this soil to the fire site, lay down a ground cloth, and use the soil to build a flat-topped mound 6 to 8 inches thick on top of the cloth. Build the fire on the mound. When it is time to break camp, scatter the few ashes, and then use the ground cloth to return the soil to its source.

PACK IT IN, PACK IT OUT. With the exception of human waste, nothing should be left in the woods that wasn't there before. Everything else, including toilet paper, personal hygiene items, and uneaten food, should be packed out. Never feed a wild animal. Long-distance hikers should not use food caches in their planning strategy.

PROPERLY DISPOSE OF WHAT YOU CAN'T PACK OUT. The best way to dispose of solid human waste is via the "cat hole" method. Dig a hole 6 to 8 inches deep and fill it in after use. An alternative to packing out toilet paper is forgoing its use and trying "natural" alternatives. Snow works well, and you can experiment to find out what will work best for you, including smooth stones or pine cones. Feminine hygiene products should be packed out. Tea bags or baking soda in a baggie or container will lessen odors. Masking odors is especially important in bear country, which is most of the Montana/Idaho CDT.

LESSEN THE IMPACT FROM PACK ANIMALS. At camp, all stock should be hitched to a highline. Select access to water where they will cause the least amount of erosion to stream banks and lake shores. Avoid tethering stock in a small area, such as at the base of a tree, where the ground will be devastated and unable to sustain any vegetation in the future. Horse packers can get more information on responsible practices by calling the Leave No Trace number, 1-800-332-4100. Request the "Backcountry Horse Use" publication.

RESPONSIBLE BIKE RIDING. Mountain bikes are permitted on all parts of the CDT except where it passes through designated wilderness areas and in Glacier National Park, but bikers should consult with local Forest Service representatives before heading out for a ride. Some sections of the trail are not suitable for mountain biking for a variety of reasons. Mountain bikers are reminded that it is their responsibility to ride in control and yield to all other users, and to conscientiously minimize their impact on the land. The Adventure Cycling Association in Missoula, Montana, is currently working to create a Great Divide Mountain Bike Route. They can be contacted at (406) 721-1776. Or contact the International Mountain Bike Association in Boulder, Colorado, at (303) 545-9011.

SAFETY CONCERNS

BEAR AVOIDANCE. One of the most pressing concerns of land administrators along the Continental Divide in Idaho and Montana is the protection and recovery of *Ursus arctos horribilis*—the grizzly bear. CDT trekkers will often be hiking in the "grizzly corridor" as they make their way along the Divide. In the text of this book, segments of the trail that cross grizzly territory are marked with a bear icon to alert hikers. Read this "Bear Avoidance" section before you venture into bear country.

The author map reading at Little Lake in the Beaverhead Mountains of the Bitterroot Range

When you are issued a backcountry permit in Glacier National Park, you will be required to watch a video full of do's and don'ts. This video tells hikers that seeing a bear in the wild is a "rare privilege" and that bears will usually run from humans. We were privileged to see a total of 13 bears on the Montana/Idaho CDT. Two of those bears ran from us, one ambled away, and the rest stood their ground or came toward us, forcing us to retreat or get off the trail. On the basis of our limited experience, I would guess that bears are no longer frightened of humans, and that grizzly bears in particular have resumed their place at the top of the food chain. Near our camp at St. Mary Lake, a hiker was mauled through his tent by a grizzly. He survived. The following spring, a hiker was killed by a grizzly bear near Two Medicine Lake. Please take seriously these tips on avoiding bears.

DON'T WEAR A BACON NECKLACE IN BEAR COUNTRY. In other words, don't smell like food. Carry freeze-dried foods and limit cooking as much as possible. Use only fragrance-free soap. This means no perfumed deodorants, shampoos, laundry soap, or lotions. Female hikers should be careful to pack feminine hygiene products in odor-masking containers. The addition of baking powder, tea bags, or aspirin to containers or baggies will help. Bears are omnivorous. They'll eat anything—sometimes this includes members of their own species. The only creature along the CDNST who thinks about food more than a backpacker does is a grizzly bear. A mature grizzly consumes about 20,000 calories per day.

DON'T RUN FROM A BEAR. In other words, don't look like food. If you run from a bear, you are acting like prey. On the other hand, if you encounter a bear near or on the trail, don't challenge it either. Grizzly bears interpret direct eye contact as a challenge, so avert your eyes. Don't shout, but speak in a soft monotone and back slowly away. Most bears will take a few moments to figure out that you are human and probably not worth the bother. Some bears will bluff charge, making a run at you but stopping short of an attack. Don't run from a bluff charge. Most bears will retreat after they have made their point. Black bears can sprint up to 35 miles per hour, twice as fast as even the most macho backpacker. Don't count on climbing a tree. Mature grizzlies don't like to climb trees, but they can. Black bears, especially younger ones, climb trees all the time. Bears are also excellent swimmers.

DON'T GIVE A BEAR A SURPRISE PARTY. Surprising a bear is not good animal kingdom etiquette and they are likely to take offense. When you are hiking in bear country, talk loudly, clap your hands, bang your trekking poles together, or sing (assuming your hiking buddies can stand it). Most bears will leave the area if they hear you coming. Be especially careful when terrain limits your view, when crossing avalanche chutes, and when approaching water courses. A recent study in Glacier Park revealed that grizzly bears spend 50 to 60 percent of their time in avalanche chutes. Running water or strong winds can mask the sound of your approach. Those little bells that are sold to hikers are completely inadequate. The sound of the human voice or clapping your hands carries further.

DON'T CAMP IN A BEAR'S DINING ROOM. Don't pitch your tent in a berry patch or in a stand of white bark pines when the pine nuts are ripe. Set your tent up well away from your intended food preparation area. Don't store food, or any other items that a bear might consider food, in your tent. Hang all your food, trash and other smelly items at least 10 feet above ground and 4 feet away from any vertical support. We carried a light, strong rope and waterproof bags for hanging our food. Tie one end of the rope around a rock or piece of wood and throw it over a high limb. Then tie the food bags to the rope and pull them up out of reach. There have been some reports that bears are associating white ropes with food, so it might be better to choose a different color. Your food-hanging tree should be 100 yards away from the sleeping area.

CARRY PEPPER SPRAY. Get the big can and make sure it is oleoresin capsicum spray meant to deter bears. Sprays designed to deter humans are not good enough. Pepper spray will stop most bears. However—and this is important—you must take wind direction or rain into account. The spray will only work if it is sprayed in the bear's eyes, nose, or mouth. If you use the spray incorrectly, it will act as a strong attractor, sort of like catnip for bears. You cannot use pepper spray like mosquito repellent. If you get pepper spray on your clothing, skin, or gear, wash immediately with water and soap or get out of the backcountry as quickly as possible. Pepper spray is illegal in Canada.

FIREARMS ARE NOT ALLOWED in Glacier National Park, and that's where most of the bears are. Guns are not the best idea for most hikers anyway. Even a large-caliber gun may not stop a bear, and wounding a bear will put you in far greater danger.

PEPPER SPRAY AND WEAPONS ARE BOTH LAST RESORTS. If you come upon a bear on the trail, and the encounter is a close one, drop something like your hat on the trail and slowly back away, talking softly. The bear may stand on its hind legs to get a better view or smell of you. Standing is not an aggressive display. Bears show agitation and aggression by swaying their heads, huffing, clacking their teeth, lowering their heads, and laying back their ears. If a bear charges you, remain standing at first. The charge may be a bluff charge. Don't run. If the bear actually attacks, use your pepper spray. If the bear does not retreat, assume a cannonball position on the ground, with your arms and hands covering your head and neck. Leave your backpack on to protect your back; curl up to protect your stomach.

DO NOT HIKE ALONE IN BEAR COUNTRY. We constantly watched for bear trails that intersected human trails, determining the relative freshness of bear scat and bear prints, noting claw marks on trees, and checking for movement in avalanche chutes. On one trail we came upon bear scat and prints that were relatively fresh, then more recent, then fresh. We were making noise, but the bear would not be hurried. We slowed our hiking pace until we finally came to a point where the bear left the human trail, heading up slope on a bear trail. You need this level of awareness and skill to ensure your own safety. See the bibliography for reference books to increase your knowledge and help you learn to distinguish grizzlies from black bears.

Note that there are no photos of bears to illustrate this text. If you are close enough to photograph a bear, you are too close. If you are getting your camera out instead of taking the safety off your pepper spray, you've seriously confused your priorities.

AVOIDING OTHER ANIMALS. Many of the bear avoidance techniques will work for other large animals as well. Be particularly wary of females with young. A cow moose will charge you to protect her young. Unlike grizzly bears, you can fend off other animals by fighting back. Put up a fight if a mountain lion, cow elk, or moose attacks you. Experts suggest standing tall, waving your arms, making noise, and slowly backing up. Throwing rocks or using a trekking pole against attackers may also be effective. Children and small adults are more vulnerable to attack. Avoid direct contact with any wild animal, regardless of its size.

LIGHTNING. This serious hazard kills several hikers each year, and it is of particular concern on the high, exposed ridges of the Continental Divide. Although a strike can occur anywhere at any time, there are certain rules of thumb that can help hikers avoid a shocking experience in the backcountry. Lightning tends to seek the shortest path from earth to sky, so you should avoid high points of land or lone trees when a storm comes in. Experts recommend seeking out a low, treeless point in the terrain and squatting there until the storm passes. For those who are as concerned about getting drenched as they are about a lightning strike, taking shelter in a low-elevation stand of trees of uniform height may be preferable. Hiding in caves is not recommended.

WATER. The low-moisture content of the air along the Divide, combined with the greater respiration rate required for hiking at altitude, may result in dehydration, a potentially dangerous condition. Hikers should be prepared to filter or purify water. Introductions to the trail segments in this guidebook provide information on water availability. Where it is critical that you not hike past a water source, a water icon appears in the text.

The greatest peril concerning drinking water in the high country is a small parasite called *Giardia lamblia,* which is transmitted via the fecal matter of animals, survives in very cold water at high altitudes, and causes severe intestinal discomfort in humans. Three methods of water treatment are recommended: boiling for three to five minutes; treating with iodine tablets; or using a filter. Filters are lightweight and easy to use, and they provide water that is immediately drinkable. Check the manufacturer's guidelines to make sure a filter is suitable for removing *Giardia.* Iodine tablets require time to work, and leave a mild aftertaste.

WEATHER. Mountain weather can change at any time, and its effects are magnified at the higher elevations of the Continental Divide. We were on the CDT from late May to October and it snowed on us at least once each month, even in August. Hikers should carry the proper clothing for snow, rain, high winds, or a combination of these. While a thunderstorm portends the danger of lightning, remember that rain accompanied by wind can cause hypothermia. The sun's radiation is more intense at high altitude, making sunscreen, lip protection, and a hat essential gear.

HYPOTHERMIA. Hypothermia is the lowering of the body's core temperature to dangerous levels, and is most common when wet skin and clothing are exposed to heat-depleting winds. Symptoms include a loss of coordination, shivering, and exhaustion. Hypothermia victims need to be warmed and protected from the elements immediately.

The author filters water from the inlet to Little Lake in the Beaverhead Mountains.

They should be sheltered in a tent and given many layers of dry clothes as well as hot liquids (but no alcohol!). Surrounding a victim with the warm bodies of stripped-down fellow hikers is also recommended. Victims will need plenty of water, high-energy food, and rest. Prevention is the best medicine. Be prepared with clothing that retains heat even when wet, and with a waterproof outer layer. Some of the specific clothing we used is listed in the acknowledgments.

ACUTE MOUNTAIN SICKNESS. This most common of high-altitude maladies can strike anyone at any time, but visitors from lower elevations are more susceptible. Prevention, in the form of a few days of rest on arrival at altitude, is recommended. Symptoms of acute mountain sickness include headache, nausea, dizziness, shortness of breath, loss of appetite, and insomnia. The best treatment is to descend to a lower altitude, drink plenty of water, and rest. The CDT in Idaho and Montana seldom climbs above 10,000 feet, so it is unlikely that more serious conditions like pulmonary edema, the buildup of fluid in the lungs, will occur. If hikers develop a dry cough, difficulty in breathing, and gurgling sounds, descend immediately to a lower altitude, and/or administer oxygen to the victim.

SNAGS. Snags are dead trees that are still standing, but whose root structures may be decayed to the point that the tree is ready to topple over at any moment. Be aware of the proximity of such danger when choosing a campsite.

FORDING RIVERS AND STREAMS. Early in the hiking season, many streams are swollen with snowmelt. A pair of river sandals or water shoes, combined with trekking poles, are helpful in keeping your balance. The water flow decreases dramatically as the season progresses, making it much easier to ford water courses in August and early September. Unless you are expert at water crossings, and have more than one person in your hiking group who can help to establish a rope across deep water, you should not attempt to hike through Glacier National Park or the Bob Marshall Wilderness early in the season. Rangers put up seasonal bridges in Glacier that eliminate most of the river fords, but these bridges will not be up in many areas until late June or even mid-July. Rangers begin removing bridges in mid to late September. To prevent hypothermia, put on dry clothes after crossing a deep water course.

CLIMATE AND SEASONS

The summer season on the Continental Divide is a short one, generally lasting from early July to mid-September. The trail's accessibility is mostly a function of the amount of snow that fell during the preceding winter. Snow continues to fall in May and June. Here's a generalized look at the Montana/Idaho CDT from south to north: From the Island Park area near Yellowstone, through the Henrys Lake Mountains and most of the Centennials, snowfall is heavy. You'll find trails do not melt out until July 4 or later. From Monida Pass to Goldstone Pass you'll find lesser amounts of snow, so this section can be accessed by mid-June. From Goldstone Pass to Big Hole Pass the trail receives heavy snowfall and the snow lingers until mid-July, and sometimes later. Big Hole Pass to Schultz Saddle may be open by late June, but some passes north of there in the Anaconda-Pintler Wilderness do not clear until mid-July, and sometimes later. East of the Anaconda-Pintler Wilderness, the CDT curves like a scythe as it goes around Butte, Montana, mostly through lower-elevation mountain ranges. This section can be hiked by mid-June if you don't mind crossing infrequent snowfields. Most of the area north of Lowland Campground, in the Boulder Mountains, is clear of snow by late June all the way to Black Mountain below Stemple Pass. The exception is the CDT near the ghost town of Leadville and near Thunderbolt Mountain—they will not be clear of snow until early to mid-July. From Black Mountain northward, including Rogers Pass, the Scapegoat Wilderness, the Bob Marshall Wilderness, and Glacier National Park, you can encounter snow at any time of the year.

Most trails are clear by mid-July. However, in Glacier National Park we traversed old snowfields in September. They never completely melted. You will need an ice ax and the ability to self-arrest if you hike through Glacier National Park in June. Using the elevation profiles in this book, you can select trail segments that can be hiked in June and in late September or early October. Gentler segments, with good road access, may be traversed with snowshoes or backcountry skis from November to March or April. Avalanche dangers are extreme along most of the CDT, so winter enthusiasts may want to limit their excursions to officially designated cross-country ski trails.

Unusually high or low snowfall will affect trail conditions and the dates that trails melt out. The Forest Service monitors the snowpack, so a quick call to the right district can help you plan. Be prepared for snow and freezing cold, even in the height of summer. Nighttime temperatures during summer routinely dip into the low 30s, so make sure your sleeping bag can handle freezing conditions.

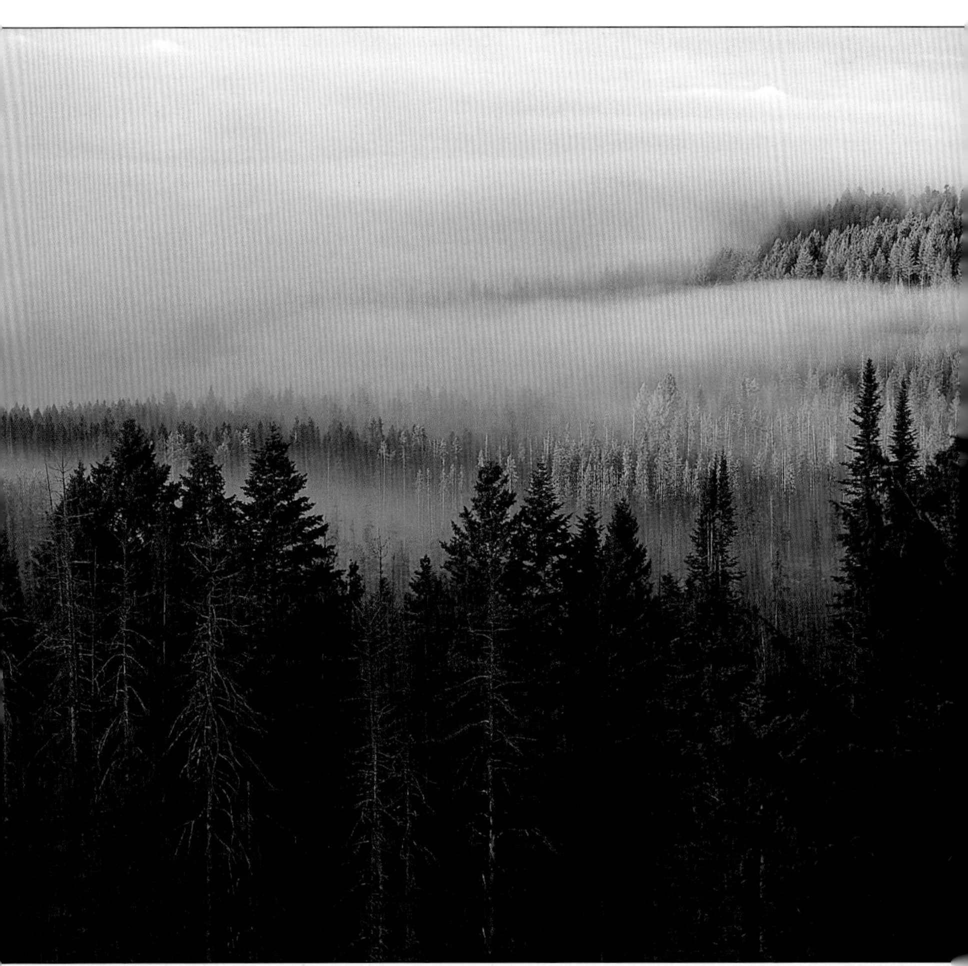

Fog blankets a mixed conifer forest at sunrise on the Moose Creek Plateau, where the CDT leaves Yellowstone National Park and turns north along the Idaho border.

History of the Continental Divide National Scenic Trail

The Continental Divide National Scenic Trail (CDNST) began in 1966 as the dream of Benton MacKaye, an 87-year-old man who had already devoted much of his life to seeing the Appalachian Trail come to fruition. MacKaye's idea was to create a trail that would connect a series of wilderness areas along the Divide from Montana's border with Canada to New Mexico's border with Mexico.

MacKaye (rhymes with "deny") proposed his idea to Congress, which soon authorized a study of the trail under the National Trails Act of 1968. At around the same time, a Baltimore attorney by the name of Jim Wolf was hiking the 2,000-mile-long Appalachian Trail, which he completed in 1971. Inspired to seek out a new hiking challenge further afield, Wolf walked the Divide Trail from the Canadian border to Rogers Pass, Montana, in 1973. He soon published a guidebook covering that section of the trail and devoted much of his time to advocating its official designation. After a 1976 study by the Bureau of Outdoor Recreation found the scenic quality of the trail to surpass anything available anywhere else in the country, the Congressional Oversight Committee of the National Trail System held hearings on the trail in 1978, at which Wolf testified. The CDNST received official recognition from Congress later that year under the National Parks and Recreation Act.

In that same year, Wolf founded the Continental Divide Trail Society (CDTS) to garner publicity for the trail and involve the public in work surrounding its construction, particularly its route selection. Wolf continued to hike portions of the trail each summer, and by the mid-'80s he had completed all of its 3,100 miles. The CDTS has grown to a membership of 250 from 46 states and several foreign countries.

The United States Forest Service is responsible for managing most of the land through which the trail passes. In the 1980s, its work on the trail progressed at different rates in different areas, but it suffered in general from a lack of public involvement. In 1994, two trail advocates began working under the auspices of a group called the Fausel Foundation to raise funds and build support for the trail. By 1995, their efforts evolved into the Continental Divide Trail Alliance (CDTA), a nonprofit organization devoted to fund-raising, publicity, education about the trail, and grassroots volunteer coordination. The CDTA founders were Bruce Ward, formerly the president of the American Hiking Society, and his wife, Paula, a landscape architect. The CDTA is based in Pine, Colorado.

In its first year, the CDTA grew to include 425 individuals or families, 20 corporate sponsors, and a budget of $400,000. Estimates suggest the Alliance coordinated volunteer work worth $70,000 in that first year. However, trail advocates are quick to point out that there is much work yet to be done. Completion and maintenance of the trail will require funding and volunteer coordination throughout the 21st century. For more information about joining the CDTA, see Appendix E.

Generously contributed by Tom Lorang Jones

Revised from *Colorado's Continental Divide Trail: The Official Guide*

History of Montana and Idaho's Continental Divide by Lynna Howard

For centuries, humans and animals have sought ways across or around the Continental Divide. The Divide once determined the range of vast herds of buffalo, and still demarcates the paths of everything from wind and clouds to human travel. Only long-distance trekkers are crazy enough to hike along the Divide instead of just crossing it at its low points, as common sense would dictate.

Long before self-closing baggies, waterproof fabrics, and guidebooks, Native Americans were crossing the Montana/Idaho Continental Divide to hunt buffalo, fish for salmon, dig camas bulbs, or engage in trading or fighting with other tribes. The Shoshone, Nez Perce, Hidatsa, Blackfeet, and Flathead tribes were just some of the Native Americans that Lewis and Clark met on their "Voyage of Discovery" from 1804 to 1806. The Indians had created many trails along and across the Continental Divide, some so well-defined that Lewis referred to them as "roads"—and a good thing too, since the expedition carried enough spare parts to give a backpacker nightmares. How would you like to include "9 chisels, 2 adzes, 2 hand saws, 6 augers, 2 hatchets, 1 whetstone, and 4 dozen awls" in your equipment list?

Despite the Indian roads, Lewis and Clark got lost, hence "Lost Trail Pass" near where the CDT crosses Montana's Highway 43. As you wander around looking for the Continental Divide National Scenic Trail, you're bound to feel a certain kinship with these early explorers. They explored so many dead ends and got lost so often that the present-day CDT crosses their path many times. North of Rogers Pass, a dilapidated and weathered sign announces "Lewis and Clark Pass." In a nice display of poetic justice, the CDT disappears where it is supposed to head north from Lewis and Clark Pass (Helena Forest Service rangers, Lincoln District, had plans to finish this section of the trail, so it may exist by the time this book is printed). Sometimes I wonder if it's true that forest service rangers don't have the time and the funds to complete the trail—or if they've merely developed a fine sense of irony and black humor.

Our support crew said that we ought to hire those Lewis and Clark guys, because it was obvious they'd already been everywhere we needed to go.

Lewis and Clark thought that many centuries would pass before the wild country they passed through was settled. They were wrong. It didn't take long before a succession of trappers, miners, loggers, stockmen, soldiers, ne'er-do-wells, and do-gooders flooded the West. Trappers were first on the scene, responding to Lewis's report that "the portion of the continent watered by the Missouri and all its branches is richer in beaver and otter than any country on earth." Railroads built in the 1860s greatly hastened settlement on both sides of the Divide, and Native American tribes were nearly swept away by the flood of new settlers. One of the most famous battles that resulted was the "war" of 1877, actually a series of skirmishes between the Nez Perce and U.S. forces.

Lewis and Clark were the first white men the Nez Perce met, and the Indians befriended the explorers, saving them from starvation and beginning a tradition of friendly relations that lasted for a generation. Chief Joseph tried to keep the friendship

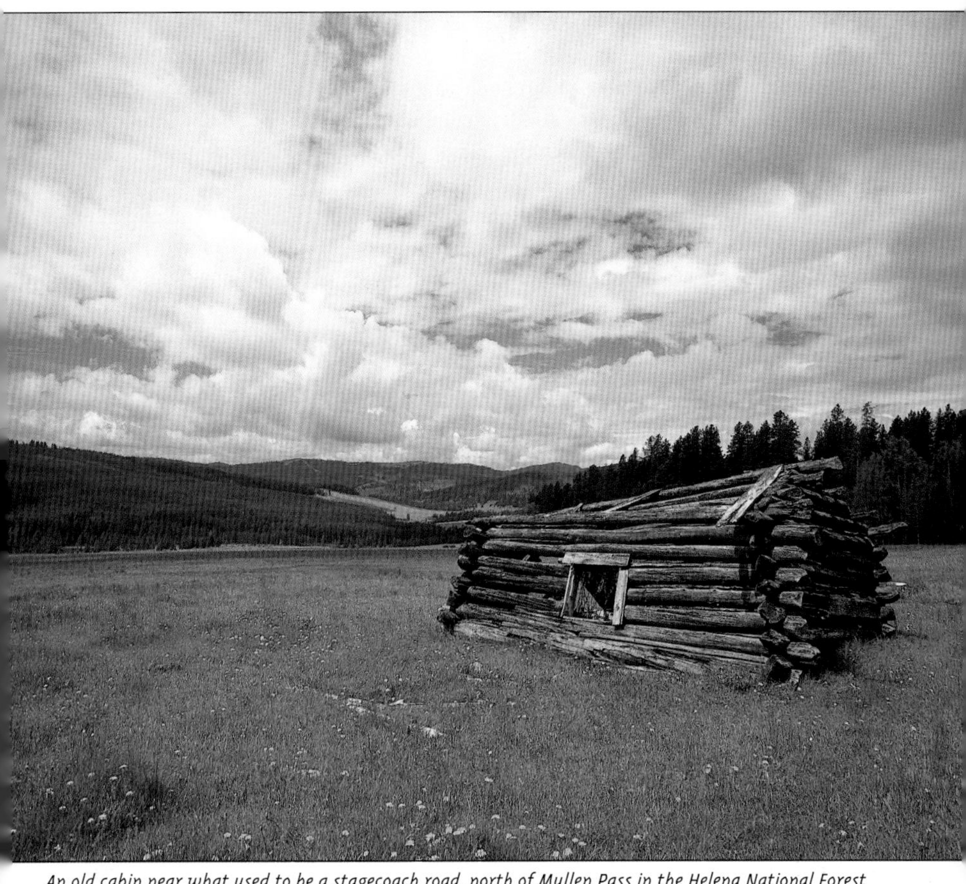

An old cabin near what used to be a stagecoach road, north of Mullen Pass in the Helena National Forest

intact, but the odds, and some members of his own tribe, were against him. In 1877, he led his people in a desperate search for sanctuary, crossing the Divide several times, including at what is now Chief Joseph Pass, and again at Bannock Pass. Chief Joseph's route from Walla Walla, Washington, to Canada was even more convoluted than Lewis and Clark's wanderings. CDT trekkers will cross the Nez Perce trail many times, and will circle the Big Hole Battlefield, where Colonel John Gibbon's forces attacked the tribe in August of 1877. "The air was heavy with sorrow I would not want to hear, I would not want to see, again," recalled tribal member Yellow Wolf. Forty miles short of the Canadian border, Chief Joseph surrendered and the conflict ended. Gibbons Pass, which is also on the route of the CDT, is named for the U.S. colonel.

Thanks to the railroads, the great herds of buffalo had been hunted to near extinction by the early 1880s, and that was the final blow to many Native American tribes. Today, the Montana/Idaho portion of the CDT crosses about five miles of the Blackfeet Indian Reservation near Glacier National Park, a small remnant of the Indian cultures that once dominated the area. Railroad tracks laid in the late 1800s and early 1900s still bring visitors to East Glacier, a town on reservation land that expresses its split personality with multiple espresso stands and shops selling Indian art and crafts.

Railroads also played a role in developing mining, logging, and cattle ranching along the Continental Divide. Montana's and Idaho's gold, silver, and copper mines are now inactive for the most part, but CDT trekkers will walk among their ghostly ruins. It seems that every road and track that leads to the Divide from Montana's Big Hole Valley ends at the remains of some prospector's dream (Segments 10 and 11). Their disintegrating pack trails and roads are the basis of much of the CDT route. The "Mule Ranch" at the eastern edge of the Anaconda-Pintler Wilderness was a sort of Betty Ford Clinic for hardworking mules that worked underground in the Anaconda copper mines. Periodically, the mules were sent to the ranch to recover from their labors and from the toxic fumes in the mining area. There are still active mines in the Mount Haggin area, and CDT hikers who take a wrong turn at the Hungry Hill Mine will end up at a nasty sign warning them about "Industrial Areas," mining and private property (Segment 16). The largest concentration of mining relics directly on the Montana/Idaho CDT is in the Marysville area, between Mullen Pass and Dana Spring (Segment 20), where the legendary Drumlummon mine yielded $16 million in gold and silver.

Stockmen followed the gold strikes, providing fresh meat to the burgeoning population. Ranching is still big business in Montana, and CDT trekkers will see both cattle and sheep grazed along the Divide. Sheep are grazed on the U.S. Sheep Experimental Station in the Centennial Mountains, mostly on BLM lands (Segments 3 and 4). In the Beaverhead Mountains of the Bitterroot Range, cattle are grazed on some National Forest lands, with especially heavy use in the Lima Peaks and Red Conglomerate Peaks areas (Segment 6). Cattle are not permitted in the Anaconda-Pintler Wilderness area, but hikers will encounter grazed areas again when they leave the Wilderness and enter the Deerlodge National Forest. As hikers proceed northward on the CDT, a combination of logging and grazing will be evident at lower elevations in most of the National Forest lands that have not been designated as wilderness areas.

Fur trade along the Divide was given a boost when John Jacob Astor's American Fur Company established a trading post on the Missouri River. Rocky Mountain fur traders in Montana shipped their furs from this post from the 1830s to the Civil War.

The period following the Civil War was characterized by more domestic pursuits, including an influx of "sod busters" who plowed the plains right up to the Rocky Mountain Front. Some of them were marginally successful until "The Great Die-Up" of the winter of 1887–1888. All across the northern plains, snow and wind battered farms and cattle ranches for months. A survivor wrote, "It seemed as if all the world's ice from Time's beginnings had come on a wind which howled and screamed with the fury of demons." The truth was and is that the winter of The Great Die-Up was not an anomaly, but a fairly common occurrence in Montana, east of the Continental Divide. When we crossed the Blackfeet Indian Reservation in October, we saw two semi-trucks lying on their sides where the vicious winds had blown them off the roads.

There is still some dry-land farming, mostly of wheat, east of the Divide, but many modern-day ranchers stick to cattle and have backup plans to handle the worst of the winter weather. Cheat grass and Russian Thistle (tumbleweeds) are legacies of seeds brought over by Russian immigrant farmers. Their wheat was highly successful in the arid plains of the West, but so were the unwelcome weeds. Today's Forest Service management plans have to include strategies for limiting these and other noxious weeds.

CDT hikers will see some of the nation's richest ranch lands in Montana's Big Hole Basin. In the Big Hole, conditions are perfect for hay to grow wild, and the 50-mile long basin is known as the "valley of 10,000 haystacks." Four access routes in this guidebook take hikers through the Big Hole: those leading to Goldstone Pass, Miner Lakes Trailhead, Chief Joseph Pass, and Schultz Saddle.

Theodore Roosevelt was a rancher/entrepreneur of the late 1800s, and those early experiences set the stage for his lasting romance with the West. As president, Roosevelt asked Congress to pass the Forest Transfer Act in 1905, placing forest lands under the jurisdiction of the Department of Agriculture and setting the stage for the creation of the U.S. Forest Service. CDT trekkers will pass by a memorial to Roosevelt where the trail crosses Marias Pass (Segments 25 and 26).

Robert Marshall was another legendary figure who altered the administration of lands along the Continental Divide. Marshall worked for the Forest Service in the 1920s and '30s and was famous for his long trips into what is now his namesake, the Bob Marshall Wilderness. Largely in response to Marshall's lobbying, wilderness areas where a hiker could "spend at least a week or two of travel without crossing his own tracks" were set aside. Together, The Bob, Great Bear, and Scapegoat add up to more than 1.5 million acres of wilderness—that's 2,400 square miles (6,215 sq km) that is known collectively as Bob Marshall Country. (See Segment 24.)

In the early 1900s, the Great Northern Railway advertised what is now Glacier National Park as "the Switzerland of America." Some of the lodges and chalets built during that era still reflect that romantic vision. Another oft-quoted description of Glacier is "the crown of the continent." Blackfeet Indians call it "the backbone of the world." After you've hiked the route of the CDNST through the park, you will agree with all of these superlatives and think that perhaps they are not enough. Glacier is one of those rare places that actually lives up to any hyperbole, any purple prose, that writers have come up with over the past hundred years. In 1932, Canada and the United States agreed to create the "Glacier-Waterton International Peace Park." The Peace Park status signifies that management and conservation of this remarkable ecosystem require international cooperation. The park was also designated a World Heritage Site in 1995, an honor meant to recognize Glacier/Waterton as being of outstanding value to all of humanity. Glacier's international fame is partially responsible for bringing more than two million visitors to the park every summer. CDT through-hikers must plan far in advance to obtain one of the limited backcountry permits that are issued each season. Permits are particularly difficult to obtain for the month of August. They are issued on a 50/50 basis, with 50 percent of the campsites held for those with advance reservations and 50 percent held for walk-ins. If you cannot reserve the itinerary you want, you may be able to obtain it as a walk-in. (See Segments 26-31.)

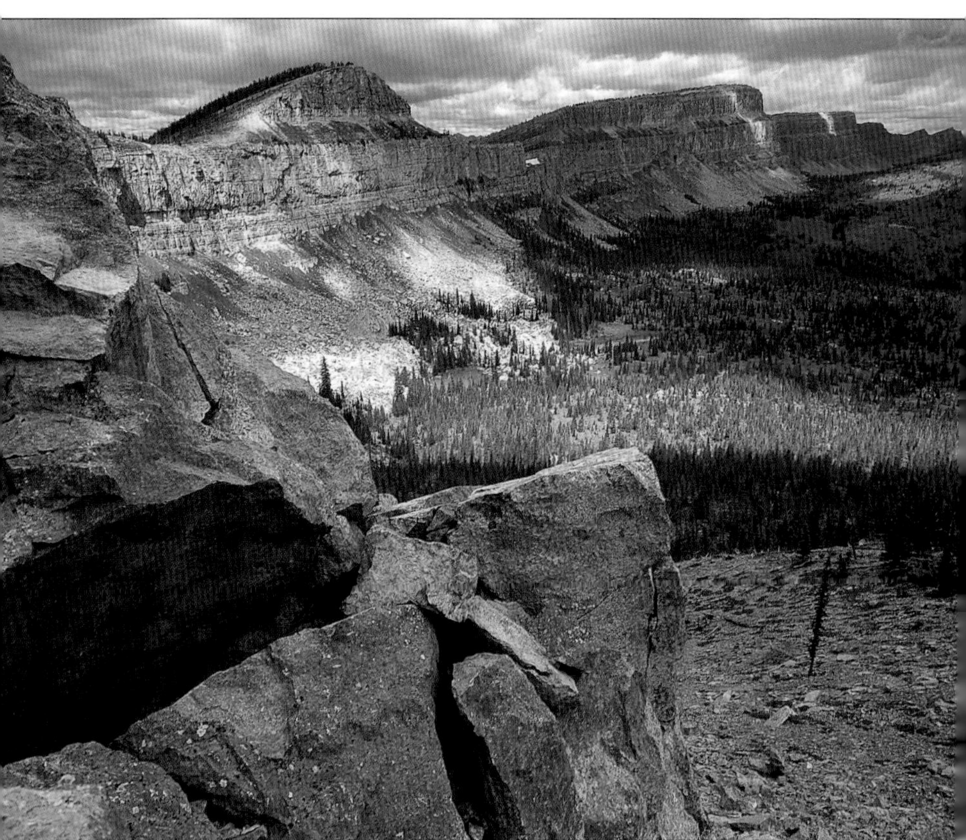

The Chinese Wall, a 1,000-foot-high escarpment that marks the Continental Divide, wends its sinuous way northward in the Bob Marshall Wilderness.

All along Montana and Idaho's Continental Divide, the concerns of residents and land administrators are much the same as they were in the early 1900s. Depending on what segment of the population is doing the talking, cattle grazing, logging, fishing, hunting, mining, exploration by motor or horseback, preservation, and "getting away from it all" are sacred pursuits. Balancing the needs and concerns of these diverse groups is not easy. Forest rangers are practically drawn and quartered as they try to follow mandates from Washington, allow for local needs, preserve ecosystems, and support recreational opportunities. Hiking the CDNST will bring people to a greater appreciation of what is needed to manage our public lands. That word "public" is important. It means that you—as an individual—have a say in how things go and what the history books will say 50 years from now. So go for a really long walk and think things over. See Appendix E for like-minded groups you may want to support.

The Natural Environment

The Montana and Idaho sections of the Continental Divide are home to a large expanse of what ecologists call "Rocky Mountain montane forest." Lodgepole pine, ponderosa pine, Douglas-fir, and quaking aspen are common in this middle-elevation forest. Alpine larch, western white pine, Engelmann spruce, and limber pine are evident in lesser quantities.

Segments 1–25

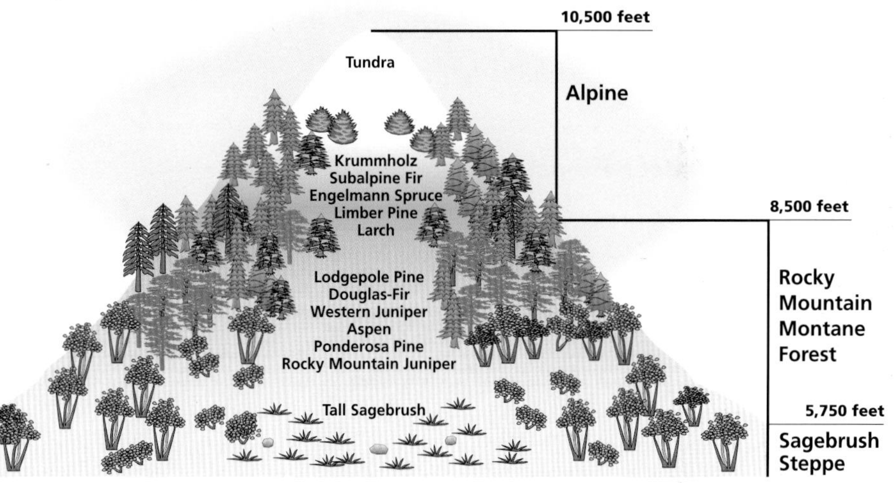

Montana and Idaho's Life Zones

The middle-elevation montane forest occupies a zone from about 6,000 to 8,000 feet in southwestern Montana and eastern Idaho; and from about 4,000 to 5,500 feet along the trail in Glacier National Park. From region to region, the upper and lower limits will vary, depending largely on water availability and exposure to the harsh, drying winds of winter.

Below the montane forest, grasslands and sagebrush steppes are dominant, with some areas also supporting juniper woodlands. Above the montane forest, subalpine forests, and then treeless alpine zones, complete the picture.

Along the Montana/Idaho border, desert conditions threaten the lower reaches of the forest while extreme cold limits the upper reaches. This region lies in the Sierra/Cascade rain shadow, with western coastal ranges catching most of the moisture from the Pacific. To complicate the situation, many individual mountain ranges cast lesser rain shadows. You won't see moisture-loving trees like California's redwoods and Alaska's Sitka spruce here.

Segments 26–31

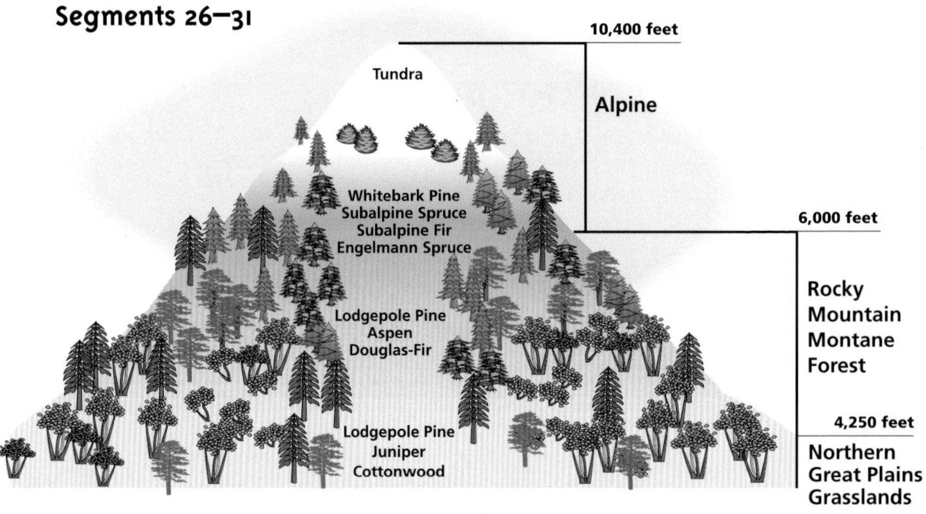

Glacier National Park Life Zones

Glacier National Park is a partial exception. Moisture-laden clouds make their way to the Continental Divide much more frequently in the Glacier area of the Rockies because the mountain ranges west of the park are lower and don't create enough uplift to capture the Pacific moisture. In the park, the average annual snowfall along the Divide is 800 to 1,000 inches—more than 80 feet of snow. It's no wonder that Fifty Mountain campground often doesn't melt out until the first week of August, and the Going-to-the-Sun Road closes in winter because no amount of snowplowing can keep it open. Still, the growing season is short, so the cold limits the number of species that flourish along the Divide. The ample snowfall does make for more lakes, streams, rivers, and waterfalls than you will see anywhere else along the Montana/Idaho Continental Divide.

Where there is more moisture, the coniferous forest exhibits a diverse mix of pine, fir, cedar, hemlock, and spruce trees. As they enter Glacier National Park, CDT hikers would experience a more dramatic change in the ecosystem were it not for the fact that the route of the trail stays mainly to the east of the Divide. The east side is known for the sudden appearance of warm winds in the winter months and for frequent, dry summer winds. These winds desiccate both soil and plants, leaving us with more drought-resistant trees like the Douglas-fir, limber pine, and lodgepole pine; and with fewer red cedar and hemlock.

Locals call the warm winter winds that sometimes accompany low-pressure systems "chinooks," an Athabascan Indian word that means "snow eater." Like Jekyll and Hyde, the snow eater is balanced by frigid Arctic air that flows down the eastern front, dropping temperatures to 50° below zero. Such wild extremes in the weather can result in temperatures that rise or drop 40 degrees in a few minutes' time, and in hurricane-force winds. Ponderosa pines cannot survive these harsh conditions; Douglas-fir and limber pine grow in dwarfed versions; while lodgepole pine and aspen trees fare quite well.

Let's take a closer look at the ecosystems that CDNST hikers will pass through on the Idaho and Montana Continental Divide.

SAGEBRUSH STEPPE

On both sides of the Divide, sagebrush steppes dominate the lower elevations from the Yellowstone Park border to near Rogers Pass and the southern border of the Scapegoat Wilderness. Isolated instances of sagebrush steppe are encountered further north, but hikers do cross the northern limit of this ecosystem in Montana as they make their way toward Glacier National Park. Sagebrush steppe areas have been called "cold deserts," but they are really quite different from what we normally associate with the words "desert" and even "sagebrush."

The high sagebrush plains along the Divide are dotted with meadows that plainly outline drainage patterns. Sedges, grasses, flowering plants, and willows fill the meadows. Tall sagebrush (*Artemisia tridentata*) and grasses prevail from the meadow's edges to forest treelines. Lupines, balsam roots, bitterbrush, buckwheat, Indian paintbrush, penstemon, daisies and other flowering plants are common companions in this sagebrush community. Monkey flowers and shooting stars join the sagebrush community where seeps keep the ground more moist.

JUNIPER WOODLAND

Rocky Mountain juniper and western juniper grow further north than do their cousins in Colorado, Wyoming, and Utah. These drought-resistant junipers sometimes form a transition zone between sagebrush communities and montane forests, mingling with both. Rocky Mountain juniper is often used for fence posts, and the aromatic wood is used for cedar chests. Its cones are tiny (1/4 inch) blue "berries" with a whitish coat, one of the most beguiling trees you'll see, especially when low light or dew outlines the berries.

Antelope, mule deer, sage grouse, coyote, jackrabbits, and ground squirrels are common both in sagebrush communities and in the lower edges of forest ecozones.

PONDEROSA PINE

Stands of ponderosa pine often adjoin grasslands, sagebrush, and juniper woodlands. Ponderosas flourish in the warmest, driest forest sites, so as you travel north, or up in elevation, this pine tree becomes a marginal species and then disappears altogether. Douglas-fir, lodgepole pine, quaking aspen, and limber pine are dominant where the ponderosa's domain ends. There are beautiful, park-like stands of ponderosa pines on the approach road from Gibbonsville, Idaho, to Big Hole Pass. Their thick, red trunks are fire resistant and the understory around them is sparse because the trees monopolize the soil resources.

QUAKING ASPEN

Because of their remarkable ability to adapt to different ecological conditions, quaking aspen are the most widely distributed of any tree in North America. Their extensive range has made them an emblem of the beauty we associate with the Rockies. CDNST hikers will see aspen stands from New Mexico to Canada. Its fine, saw-toothed leaves "quake" in the slightest breeze, and leaf movement is emphasized by the disparity between the bright green on top and the dull gray/green on the bottom of the leaf. As if a master painter were working toward a perfect but minimalist effect, the leaves go from green to gold to nothing in the autumn, leaving the aspens' black twigs and papery white trunks outlined against the sky. Aspen trees will grow in diverse soil types, but they reach their full glory in porous soils where lime is plentiful. It is estimated that some 500 species of animals and plants, from elk and bear to the lowly fungi, utilize aspen trees. The larger animals browse on them and they are a particularly important food source for beaver. Birds, including grouse and quail, devour the buds, catkins, and seeds. Aspen trees occupy the lower elevations of mid-elevation montane forest, often mixing with lodgepole pines. Aspen groves diminish as you climb to higher altitudes. The CDT passes through many aspen parklands on the eastern edge of Glacier. The aspen grove on Two Dog Flat, near the area where the Red Gap Pass trail approaches Swiftcurrent Ridge Lake, shows a distinct browse line where elk have gnawed the bark.

LODGEPOLE PINE

Of all the pines, lodgepoles are the most ubiquitous on the Montana/Idaho CDT. This opportunistic tree often takes over after a fire, relying on the heat from the flames to melt the resin seal on its cones, releasing its seeds in an open, non-competitive environment. Pure stands of lodgepole pine cover acre after acre in the northern Rockies. In many areas, lodgepoles have replaced Douglas-fir. Normally, lodgepoles would colonize a burned area, and then slowly give way to Douglas-fir, but along the Montana/Idaho Divide, lodgepoles often become the climax species. Their staying power is a result of their ability to tolerate a broader range of conditions. Areas that are too hot, too cold, too wet, or too dry for other trees will support a lodgepole forest. Mature lodgepole forests are subject to insect infestations. Lodgepoles have been logged in parts of Idaho's Targhee National Forest to prevent the spread of insects. Lodgepoles look like the weeds of the pine family, growing so close together that they form a gloomy, impenetrable fence of skinny trunks. They grow so close together that they form what is called "dog hair" forests. Just north of Bison Mountain, in the Helena National Forest (Segment 19) the CDT passes through young lodgepoles that are so thick you could not walk between them without a trail. They make you feel like an ant in a patch of tall grass.

DOUGLAS-FIR

Along the Montana/Idaho CDT, Douglas-fir is usually mixed with lodgepole pines. It is a bit too cold and too dry for Douglas-fir in most areas east of the Divide, so you're more likely to encounter fir-dominated stands wherever you cross to the west side of the Divide. These tall, large trees are important to the lumber industry. In sharp contrast to the more open yellow-green pine forests, Douglas-fir forests are cooler, darker, and blue-green in color. CDT hikers pass through fir and lodgepole combination forests in the Bob Marshall Wilderness as the zigzag trail makes its way along creek drainages.

SUBALPINE FOREST

Subalpine forests in the Montana/Idaho Rocky Mountains are dominated by Engelmann spruce (sometimes called subalpine spruce), subalpine fir, whitebark pine, and limber pine. Below these trees lie the mid-elevation montane forests; above them is the treeless alpine zone.

Subalpine trees will work their way up slope as far as possible, battling strong winds and cold temperatures. Dwarf, twisted versions known as "krummholz" cling to life at the higher elevations (above 8,500 feet along most of the Divide, and above 6,000 feet in Glacier National Park). "Krummholz" is a German word meaning "crooked wood." The wind prunes krummholz into fantastic, beautiful, and desperate shapes that are a living metaphor for struggle and life in the face of overwhelming odds. Above Two Medicine Lake in Glacier National Park, near Scenic Point, krummholz snakes along the ground, seldom rising more than a foot high. We empathized when gusty winds almost forced us to a crawl as we crossed the ridge west of Scenic Point.

ALPINE ZONE

Elk Mountain in the Beaverhead Mountains, and Targhee Divide in the Henrys Lake Mountains, are good examples of alpine areas. Above the treeline, the ground is festooned with hardy grasses and thousands of miniature flowers that vibrate like tuning forks in the ever-present wind. Most of the terrain above 9,000 feet is alpine on the Montana/Idaho CDT. Once again, Glacier National Park is an exception, with the alpine zone beginning at about 6,000 feet.

High-elevation plant communities are very sensitive. Stay on the trail or on rocky surfaces as much as possible, to avoid damaging plants that may have taken as long as two decades to mature and blossom. Buttercups, moss campion, cushion phlox, forget-me-nots, and yellow stonecrop are common flowering plants. Some of their blooms are only 1/4-inch across, and in places they seem to spring from rock itself with no apparent requirement for soil.

Unlike plants, animals can move about to escape bad weather. Mountain goats, bighorn sheep, elk, and deer may all browse in alpine areas, but will seek shelter at treeline during the worst weather. Alpine grouse, coyotes, hawks, and other smaller birds and animals will hunker down in the krummholz to evade the weather. If you look closely, you can see that they have worn paths in and out of the low cover.

Grizzly bears prefer parklands and alpine areas to closed forests. In Glacier National Park, we saw grizzlies foraging above the timberline and in avalanche chutes, while black bears were more common in the mid-elevation forests.

For many hikers, the alpine areas are the most enjoyable because they offer commanding views of the surrounding terrain. In good weather, you can see the topography of the Continental Divide for 50 miles or more. On the sometimes ill-defined route of the CDT, it is a relief to see all that topographical relief, to see where you're going— or at least where you're supposed to end up. Be wary of camping in alpine areas, though. Lightning and windstorms can come up with little or no warning. If you do set up in an alpine area, look for rocks or krummholz that will give you some protection from the wind. You can often find rocky or barren soil large enough to hold your tent even in alpine areas that are thick with flowers.

ALONG STREAMS AND RIVERS

Willows, alders, water birch, Rocky Mountain maple, and western serviceberry are just some of the shrubs and small trees that line the banks of mountain streams and rivers, anchoring riparian ecosystems. CDT hikers will know they've reached lower elevations when narrowleaf cottonwoods also line the riverbanks. Lewis and Clark discovered this tree in 1805 and noted in their journals the narrow, willowlike leaves. Narrowleaf cottonwood is the most common cottonwood of the northern Rockies. The extensive root systems play a large part in erosion control. The tree's name derives from the cloud of cottony seeds that it releases in spring and summer. Although it is surprising to see them so far north, there are cottonwoods along the CDT where it crosses Red Eagle Creek in Glacier National Park.

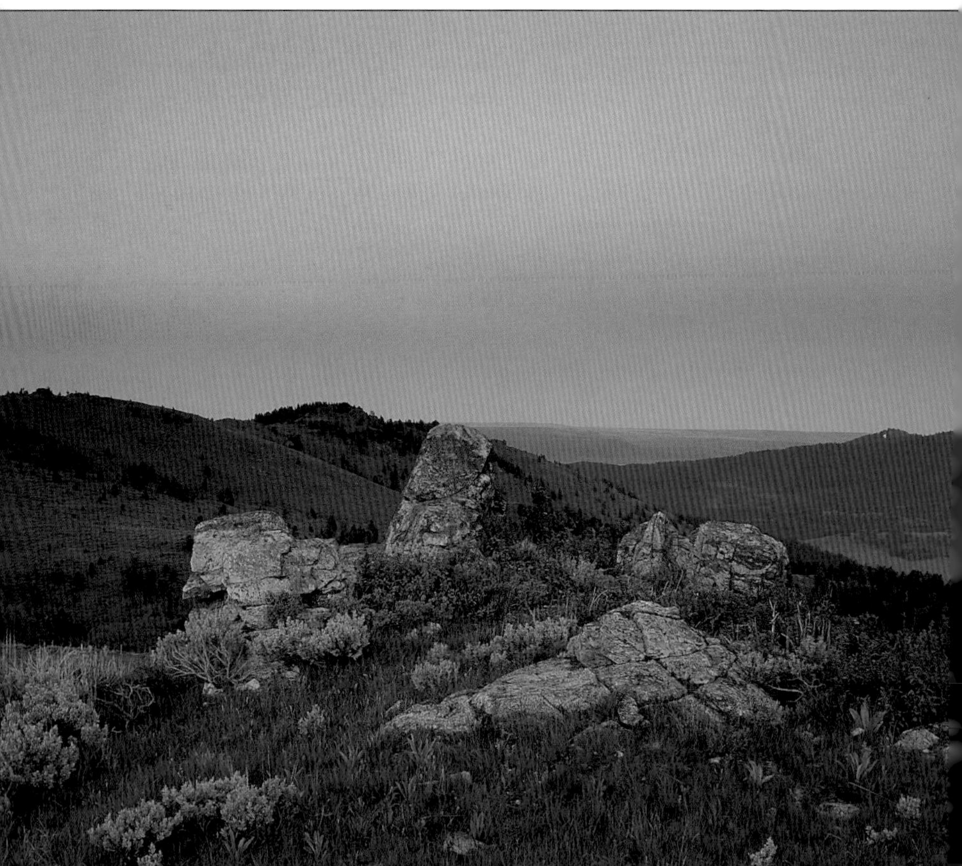

Approaching Red Rock Pass, where the CDT follows the southward curve of the Henrys Lake Mountains, hikers pass through open areas and islands of sagebrush.

Geology

Even a brief dunk in the river of time represented by the Divide's geological history will flood you with information. Mountain ranges rise and crumble, only to rise again. Tectonic plates collide and coastlines are subsumed, reformed, extended. A brief overview of regional geology and plate tectonics will enhance your appreciation of the varied landforms that make you huff and puff from Yellowstone to Canada.

The outer skin of the earth's mantle is relatively rigid compared to the hotter rocks below it. This outer skin, approximately 60 miles thick, is called the lithosphere, and the upper portions of it can be roughly divided into oceanic crust and continental crust. Oceanic crust is mostly basalt (common black lava) several miles thick. Continental crust is about 25 miles thick and is composed of lighter rocks, mostly granite.

Plate tectonics envisions the lithosphere as broken into rafts of rock, like pieces of a giant puzzle, that cover the earth's surface. In some places the puzzle pieces are moving away from each other; in others they collide; and in still others they are sliding past each other. The movement of these tectonic plates helped to create the Continental Divide.

About 175 million years ago, the plate bearing the North American continent moved west and collided with the Pacific Ocean plate. This collision compressed the western edge of the continent, creating a broad highland. The heavier oceanic crust had no place to go but down, and the edge of it slid under the continental plate and was pushed downward into the hot mantle. In the way of most things geological, change was slower than slow. About 90 to 70 million years ago, enough basalt of the oceanic crust had melted in the intense heat that it, in turn, melted the granite of the continental crust above it. Melted granite (magma) rose because it was lighter and could crystallize beneath the surface like a giant, granite bubble. This bubble is called a batholith. The Idaho batholith extends to the Bitterroot Range of southwestern Montana. The Boulder Batholith formed between Butte and Helena, Montana. Some of the Boulder Batholith erupted to form the Elkhorn Mountains.

It is easy to imagine the earth bulging upward above these and other batholiths. Sedimentary veneer slid off the high bulges and, in places, huge slabs broke off and moved eastward. Some of the slabs were 1,000 feet thick, and when they came to rest, they were stacked against each other. Stacked-up slabs of overthrust rock are what tourists see as they drive along the east front of the Rockies from Helena to the Canadian border. In the Bob Marshall Wilderness, hikers along the CDNST walk behind the eastward-most slab and on the slab that forms the Continental Divide.

Overthrusts can push younger rocks over the top of older rocks, and older rocks over younger rocks, complicating the picture that geologists try to decipher. Rocks along the eastern edges of the overthrusts are crumpled and tightly folded. The Anaconda-Pintler Wilderness is a prime example. You can blame events 70 million years ago for the fact that you have to climb up, over, and down as many as three steep passes in a single day of hiking in the Anaconda Range.

The peaks in Glacier National Park were formed, in part, by the Lewis Overthrust, a slab of Precambrian Belt rocks about 2 miles thick. The slab thrust eastward, burying sedimentary rocks only 65 to 100 million years old under Precambrian rocks a billion years old.

There are many examples of glaciation along the Montana/Idaho CDT, but none as spectacular as Glacier National Park. Geologists argue about the number of ice ages, with estimates ranging from a high of 20 to a low of four, but we are concerned with the glaciers of the Pinedale ice age. These most recent glaciers reached their zenith about 15,000 years ago and began melting only 10,000 years ago—the blink of an eye in geological time. The glaciers straightened the valleys and carved them into the classic "U" shape, giving us the long, magnificent views for which the park is justly famous. Ice that formed, melted, and reformed chewed up the bedrock at the heads of valleys, creating "cirques," the big, ice-cream-scoop-shaped bowls that hold some of Glacier National Park's most beautiful lakes. When two glaciers gnawed at a mountain from both sides, an "arête" was formed—a knife-edged ridge like "The Garden Wall" that CDT hikers see from Piegan Pass. When three or more glaciers work away at a peak, a "horn" or pinnacle is formed, with cirques below the horn.

Although much of the activity that formed the Rocky Mountains seems to have slowed down, the Continental Divide is still an active geological zone. The Island Park area that abuts Yellowstone is affected by the Yellowstone volcano that still shows off today. The Yellowstone volcano is a resurgent caldera. It erupts, collapses into a giant caldron-shaped cavity, erupts again, collapses again, and so on. So far, it has erupted three times, with the eruptions about 600,000 years apart. If it is periodic, we are due for another one just about now. When CDT hikers exit Yellowstone Park and enter Idaho, they walk across the Moose Creek and Madison Plateaus, part of the rim between the Island Park Caldera and the Yellowstone Caldera.

Most of the mountains along the Montana/Idaho border are still active. The Centennials and the Beaverheads are rising along active faults. In another 10,000 years, I may have to adjust the elevation figures in this book. In the meantime, enjoy all the ups and downs as you hike the Continental Divide—there are a lot of them. This trail is rougher and more challenging than the Pacific Crest Trail or the Appalachian Trail—a spirit of adventure is the best thing you can pack.

The route of the CDT follows the south shore of Saint Mary Lake in Glacier National Park; Wild Goose Island rises in its center.

Segment 1
Yellowstone National Park to Targhee Pass

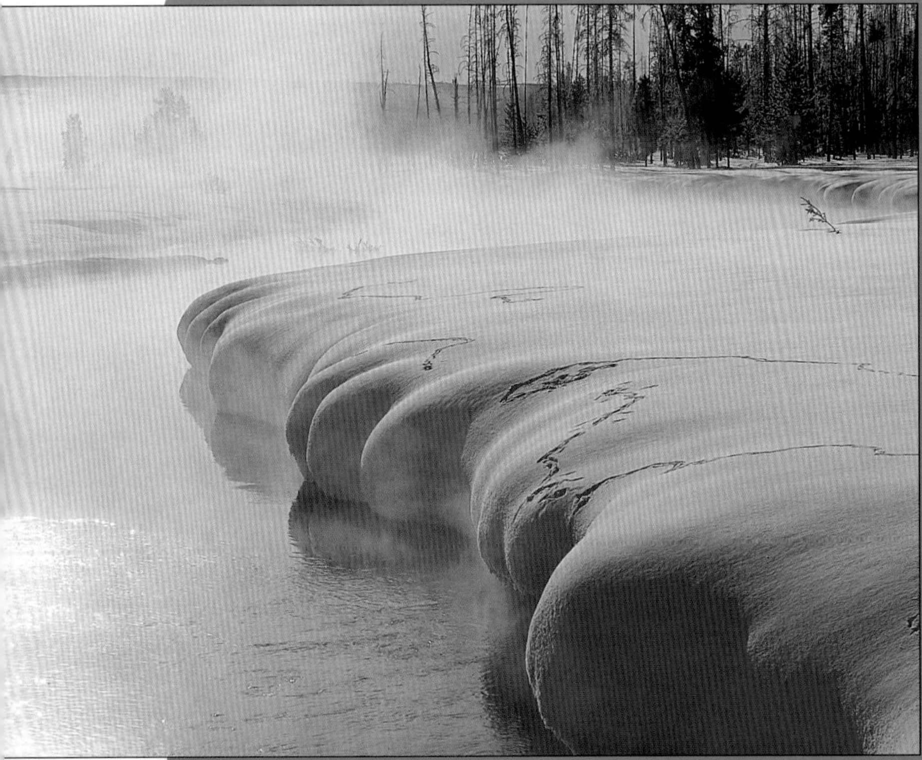

Winter on the Buffalo River near Macks Inn, Idaho, a traditional resupply point for many Continental Divide trekkers

35.6 miles
Difficulty: Easy

Segment 1 **Total Elevation Gain:** 2,564 feet
From Wyoming 0 miles
To Canada 980.7 miles

CONTINENTAL DIVIDE TRAIL ALLIANCE

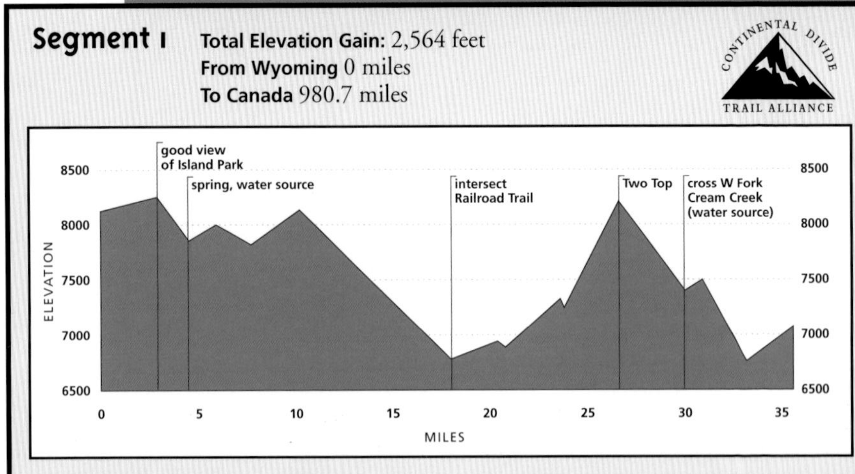

TRAIL OVERVIEW This segment begins at the western border of Yellowstone National Park, where the Continental Divide Trail enters Idaho's Island Park area. "Island Park" was reportedly named by early settlers for islands of timber on the high sagebrush plain. It looks quite different today due to tourism and forestry.

Island Park is the world's largest recognized caldera, a collapsed volcanic chamber about 18 to 23 miles in diameter, shaped like an enormous shallow bowl. Roughly half-a-million years ago, a large shield volcano erupted in what is now eastern Idaho. After the eruption, the volcano's magma chamber collapsed to form the caldera. The Continental Divide National Scenic Trail (CDNST) traverses the high plateaus that form the eastern edge of the Island Park Caldera. As far as we know, the Yellowstone and Island Park volcanoes will remain docile while you walk their edges, but there are no guarantees.

Water percolates westward from the Yellowstone Plateau, ending up in Island Park. CDT trekkers will see their first instance of such springs about 4.5 miles west of the Yellowstone Park border, near the trailhead where the Montana/Idaho CDNST begins.

Speaking of trailheads . . . well, actually there isn't one. Trekkers planning to hike the Montana/Idaho portion of the Continental Divide Trail really have no place to start. In one way, it is entirely appropriate that even finding a trailhead should be difficult—the search for a place to begin will be your initiation into the prevailing character of the Continental Divide Trail's northern sections. The skills you use to find the trail in Island Park will come in handy for the next 900-plus miles as you hike this work-in-progress, the Continental Divide National Scenic Dream of a Trail, that will someday be a completed reality.

Most of the trail in this segment follows snowmobile routes that, in the summer months, look like roads or what I call "trodes"—trails that used to be roads. Hikers will find the trek relatively easy, with only a few steep climbs in mellow terrain. Two Top, in the Henrys Lake Mountains near the end of the segment, offers the best views. Trail crews have recently signed most of the intersections with wooden CD placards. If any of the signs are missing, it is easy to get lost in the maze of trails. Make sure you have all the suggested maps, and this guide.

This is the only portion of the Montana/Idaho CDT that has speed limit signs posted along the trail. I hope you obey them. We wouldn't want any hikers getting tickets! (Of course, these signs apply to snowmobiles.)

Winter recreation is a big industry in Island Park, where hundreds of miles of snowmobile trails crisscross the terrain and snow often exceeds 20 feet. Those speed limit signs are barely high enough. The snow doesn't completely melt out of the trails until mid-July, though it is possible to hike them earlier if you don't mind crossing some packed snowfields. Trails are wide and gentle, with very little summer traffic. A snowmobile map will help you find all the trails (see Maps on next page).

When we hiked the trail, we were entertained by a huge black bear that resembled Orson Welles. This bear ran from us, churning up a cloud of old ash and dust on the trail, his bulk not deterring him in the least. At the time we thought, "Oh yeah, that's what they're supposed to do. They run from humans." We were naive.

As it turned out, that black bear was one of the few, the proud, and the swift. Eleven out of the thirteen bears we met on the CDT stood their ground or pressured us off the trail. Read the bear and animal avoidance tips in "Safety Concerns" before hiking this segment.

Water is a problem for about 13 miles of this segment. Most of the water courses shown on the topographical maps are now dry, in part due to the 1988 fires. (This is also true of the trail where it enters Yellowstone National Park. Going east into the park, it is nine miles to the next water source at Summit Lake.) Don't pass up the spring in the newly constructed portion of the trail (see trail description) near the park border. Water is adequate, but not plentiful in the remainder of this segment. Notes in the trail description direct hikers to water sources.

MOUNTAIN BIKE NOTES: This trail is open to mountain bikes and is generally considered "easy," but areas of fine gravel and cinders several inches deep make it like riding through sand. The trail requires maximum effort but offers few technical challenges. The ride up Two Top is the steepest and most challenging section.

LAND ADMINISTRATORS (SEE APPENDIX A)

Targhee National Forest, Island Park Ranger District
Gallatin National Forest, Hebgen Lake Ranger District

MAPS

USGS QUADRANGLES: Buffalo Lake NE, Latham Spring, Reas Pass, Madison Arm, Targhee Pass

USFS: Targhee National Forest, Island Park/Ashton; Gallatin National Forest, West Half

OTHER: Winter Guide to Yellowstone Country: West Yellowstone Snowmobile Trails (free from most West Yellowstone businesses) Targhee National Forest Island Park Ranger District Travel Map (free from the Forest Service)

IMPORTANT NOTE: All of the Forest Service maps show the CDT crossing US-20 *east* of Targhee Pass. This is not correct. The FS maps do not even show a trail going south from Targhee Pass where the CDT is actually located. Only the snowmobile map shows that trail, but of course the CDT is not mentioned on a snowmobile map. Forest Service maps also show the CDT descending into Tygee Creek Basin north of Two Top. The trail has been rerouted around this sensitive riparian area—it now stays on the Divide briefly and then descends on the Montana side instead. The trail is signed correctly on the ground, and if you combine information from all the maps, you can find it.

BEGINNING ACCESS POINT

This approach begins on US Highway 20, south of the small town of Island Park/Ponds Lodge. From US-20 go east on Chick Creek Road 291 for 14 miles. The road climbs to a high plateau and ends at an intersection with Forest Service Road 082. Turn left (north) on 082 and drive 0.4 mile to an intersection with Forest Service Road 078. It is 0.3 mile east on 078 to a locked gate that blocks motorized travel. There is no place to park at this gate and barely room for hikers to squeeze by in the young lodgepole pines that grow close to the gate. Hike another 2.4 miles eastward and uphill on Road 078 to intercept the Continental Divide Trail. A blue and white CD sign marks the entrance to newly constructed tread that leads north. To actually begin at the beginning of this segment, hikers must proceed south 3.9 miles on 078 to reach the western border of Yellowstone National Park, then turn around and hike back along the same trail.

Consequently, you begin with no place to begin on your long trek to Canada. Rangers are hoping to get enough funds to establish a trailhead here in the future.

If you have a support or shuttle crew, supply them with a Forest Service map and a "Travel Map" (see maps). On the ground, road signs that look like regulation street signs show the miles and direction to other intersections, but many of these roads cannot be accessed by motorized vehicles in the summer. It can be extremely frustrating if you plan an access route that is blocked by locked gates. Get a Travel Map so you can easily see all the gates that close approaches to the route of the CDT.

ENDING ACCESS POINT

This segment ends at Targhee Pass on US-20. Lionshead Resort is 1 mile east on the highway, and the town of West Yellowstone is 9 miles east. Macks Inn is about 15 miles southwest on US-20.

TRAIL DESCRIPTION

Where the Continental Divide Trail exits Yellowstone National Park and enters the Targhee National Forest, the trail is not actually signed as the CDT. However, it is easy to find for both north- and southbound hikers. As soon as it crosses the park border, the CDT turns north on Trail 078.

S **SOUTHBOUND HIKERS** should take care that they don't go too far south on 078. To find the correct turn eastward into the park, look for an orange, fluorescent piece of metal hung on a tree. Near the metal, there is a Yellowstone National Park sign on the ground listing park regulations.

There are excellent views from Trail 078 of the Island Park Caldera at mile 2.6, where hikers can see the Island Park Reservoir and the Centennial Mountains. Both Targhee and Gallatin Forest Service maps show this first section as Trail 078, but hikers on the ground will not see a trail number unless they walk out to the approach road. The "trail" looks like a road that has not been used in a while.

Trail 078 passes through a combination of new growth, some unburned sections, and areas that were burned in the 1988 fires. In fact, it was here, about 50 feet from the Continental Divide Trail, that a firewood cutter started the 1988 North Fork fires with a cigarette.

It is 3.9 miles from the Yellowstone border to new trail construction built to connect 078 to 066, the Black Canyon Loop Road. The new trail leaves 078 at an intersection that is marked with a large blue and white CD sign. However, the sign is turned

SUPPLIES, SERVICES, AND ACCOMMODATIONS

WEST YELLOWSTONE, MT, is on US-20. The traditional but unofficial route of the CDT used to depart from the Divide and go through Macks Inn. This is no longer true. West Yellowstone is recommended for supplies because it has all services; the town can be accessed from several spur trails that connect with the CDT (see trail description); and north-to-south hikers need to stop there to pick up backcountry permits before entering Yellowstone Park. If you wish to use Macks Inn for resupplies, see Segment 3 for more information. Supplies are also available at Ponds Lodge on US-20.

Distance from Trail: 44 road miles to trailhead, 11.2 trail miles to intersect the CDT near Reas Pass

Zip Code: 59758

Bank:	First Security Bank, at Conference Hotel	406-646-7646
	First Security Bank, at Stage Coach Inn	800-823-7646
Bus:	Greyhound, Yellowstone Office Services	406-646-0001
Camping:	KOA Kampgrounds, west of West Yellowstone	406-646-7606
	Yellowstone Grizzly Park, 210 S. Electric Street	406-646-4466
	Buffalo and Box Canyon FS campgrounds near Ponds Lodge	
Dining:	Ernie's Bighorn Deli, 406 Highway Avenue	406-646-9467
	Cappy's Bistro & Coffeebar, 108 Canyon Street	406-646-9537
	Running Bear Pancake House, Madison Ave. & Hayden St.	406-646-7703
Gear:	Freeheel & Wheel, 40 Yellowstone Avenue	406-646-7744
Groceries:	Food Roundup Supermarket, 107 Dunraven Street	406-646-7501
	Market Place, 22 Madison Avenue	406-646-9600
Information:	West Yellowstone Chamber of Commerce, 30 Yellowstone Avenue	406-646-7701
	Yellowstone National Park, West District	406-646-7332
	Yellowstone National Park Backcountry Office, Mammoth Hot Springs, WY	307-344-2160
Laundry:	Canyon Street Laundry, 312 Canyon Street	406-646-9733
	Econ-Mart & Laundromat, 307 Firehole	406-646-7887
Lodging:	Big Western Pine Motel, 234 Firehole, $65	406-646-7622
	One Horse Motel, 216 Dunraven Street, $59–$65	406-646-7677
	Pony Express Motel, 4 Firehole, $69	406-646-7644
	Stage Coach Inn, 209 Madison Avenue, $75–$120	406-646-7381
Medical:	The Clinic at West Yellowstone, 236 Yellowstone Avenue	406-646-7668
Outfitters:	Jacklin's Outfitters, 105 Yellowstone Avenue	406-646-7336
	Madison River Outfitters, 117 Canyon Street	406-646-9644
Post Office:	U.S. Post Office, 209 Grizzly Bear Loop, 59758	406-646-7704
Showers:	See "Camping" above.	

Special Notes: Limited services are available 1 mile east of Targhee Pass at the Lionshead Resort, 1545 Targhee Pass Hwy., West Yellowstone, MT 59758. Alice's Restaurant, 406-646-7296. Super 8 Lodge, 406-646-9584. Laundromat, gas station, mail drop, maps.

so that it is most visible only from the approach to the trail, and not for either north- or southbound hikers. Someone has used a marker to write CDT on the back of the sign for southbound hikers to see, but you have to watch carefully to see this sign and the trail intersection.

The new trail is 446, a number that appears on the Travel Map, but not on any of the other maps. One mile long, it boasts three bog bridges. When we hiked the trail, only one of the bog bridges crossed running water, and that was a trickle. The section of planking furthest north has a spring that runs all season.

As was mentioned in the Trail Overview, every other water course shown on the topographical map is dry except for a short period of time during spring runoff. Don't pass this spring up, you'll need the water. It's about 13 miles to the next reliable water source on the trail. Mountain bikers are likely to encounter some deadfall near the spring.

At its northern end, Trail 446 climbs to meet Road 066. There is a CD sign at the intersection. An intersection with a spur trail on the east side, 075, is also signed with a CD symbol.

This 6.1-mile section of Black Canyon Loop Road (066) is closed to motorized traffic during the summer months. The trail crosses Thirsty Creek at mile 7.7, but it is not a reliable water source. Spur trails that enter Black Canyon Loop Road can be ignored—the road is the trail for about 13 miles. There is a gate on Road 066 at mile 11. North of the gate, the road is open to motorized traffic.

The higher elevations (8,135 feet) of Black Canyon Loop Road remain snowed in until mid-July, but the drifts have been packed hard by snowmobiles and are easy to walk over. Once hikers pass the gate, there is a 7-mile-long downhill section that loses enough altitude to leave the snow behind (see elevation chart). At the next CDT intersection, Railroad Trail, the closest water source is 0.5 mile off the trail, in Reas Pass Creek. For water, continue on the road toward Big Springs, which is also the access road to Macks Inn. There is a culvert where the road crosses the creek. The next water source is about 3 miles east, over Reas Pass, at the Madison River.

At mile 18 for this segment, hikers turn east on "Railroad Trail" to cross the Divide at Reas Pass. Northbound hikers will not be able to read the sign until they walk around to the other side, but there are two CD signs where you turn onto Railroad Trail off of Black Canyon Loop Road. This is the best access/exit point for the town of West Yellowstone. From this intersection it is 14 miles to the town, and 2.8 of those miles are on the CDT.

From the turn east on Railroad Trail, it is 1.8 miles to the first CD sign and another trail intersection. Watch for the speed limit sign that says 45 mph, and bear left (northeast). At mile 20.4 for this segment, the trail crosses the Divide at 6,941 feet elevation, so low that it is not really noticeable.

East of the Divide, and 2.8 miles from Black Canyon Loop Road, the CDT turns left (west) on Road 1727. The turn is well-marked with CD signs. A right-hand turn here will take you to water about 500 yards away on the South Fork of the Madison

River. This is also where hikers can leave the CDT and continue northeast to West Yellowstone. Look for the bridge over the Madison River for the route to town.

Road 1727 bends from west to northwest. An intersection signed only as "Jct. 17" is reached at mile 21.4. CDT trekkers continue straight ahead (northwest). Continue northwest at another unsigned intersection at mile 23.6 (5.6 miles from Black Canyon Loop Road). This intersection is gated, and has a CD post from which the signs were missing.

The trail turns left (west) to climb back up to the Divide at mile 23.8 (5.8 miles from Black Canyon Loop Road). Watch for a much rougher track that leads steeply uphill and is marked with a wooden CD symbol. Three miles of relatively steep climbing brings the trail back to the Divide.

Two Top, reached at mile 26.6, is the highlight of this segment. The 8,208-foot knoll offers a panoramic view of the Grand Tetons in Wyoming, the Centennial Mountains to the northwest, and miles of the Yellowstone and Island Park areas. The topographical map shows Mount Two Top west of, and higher than, this "Two Top," which is signed as being part of the National Recreational Trail System.

At the Two Top sign, northbound hikers take a right-hand turn, following the Divide northeast. It looks tempting to continue uphill on a jeep track that climbs higher, but the Divide turns downhill. This is one of the few places in this segment where there were no CDT signs or posts to keep us on the right track.

1.4 miles northeast of Two Top, a Y-shaped intersection is marked with a CD sign and a motorcycle trail symbol. Northbound hikers take the right fork. This is where the reroute begins that takes hikers on the Montana side of the Divide to protect Idaho's Tygee Creek Basin from summer traffic that would damage the riparian area.

An intersection that looks like a meeting of four rough jeep tracks is reached at mile 29.1. There is no four-way intersection on the maps, but there is a gate symbol on the Gallatin Forest Service map. The gate was open when we were there. A CD sign shows the trail continuing straight ahead.

The trail crosses the West Fork of Cream Creek and a culvert at mile 30. The stream is a good water source that runs all summer. The two-track you are now on is shown best on the Gallatin FS map—it does not exist on the topo.

The next intersection, at mile 30.9 (12.9 miles from Black Canyon Loop Road) is marked with CD symbols and directional arrows, but no road numbers. Continue downhill and more or less straight ahead (north/northeasterly). On the FS maps, this road is identified as 1703, but it was not signed on the ground when we were there.

Intersect Forest Service Road 1720 at mile 32.2. This road crosses Buttermilk Creek and is shown as the CDNST on the Gallatin FS map. Stay on 1720 as it trends northwest and continues downhill toward US-20.

Near US-20, watch carefully for the intersection with snowmobile Trail 1710. The CDT makes a sharp left here, turning more than 90° at a gate that functions as a "closed to motorized" barrier. On the topographical maps and on the Forest Service maps, 1710 appears to dead-end before it reaches Targhee Pass. Only the snowmobile trail map shows a trail continuing to the pass.

With many twists and turns, 1710 passes by some private property and climbs about 300 feet to the highway. From the "closed to motorized" gate at the intersection of 1710 and 1720, it is 2.4 miles to Targhee Pass (mile 35.6 for this segment). When we were there, the CD signs had been ripped off the posts south of the parking lot at Targhee Pass. The parking lot is next to a historical marker and elevation signs for the pass. Better and safer parking can be found north of the pass about 0.5 mile up the 4WD road.

Arrowleaf balsamroot blooms in open meadows along the CDT in Idaho's Island Park area, near Two Top Mountain.

Segment I
1:100,000 MAPS: HEBGEN LAKE and ASHTON
SCALE: 5/8 INCH = 1 MILE
1 CM = 1 KM
Continental Divide
Continental Divide Trail (current segment)
Continental Divide Trail (previous and next segments)
River or stream
Lake or pond
Marsh or swamp
Primary highway
Secondary highway
Light duty road
Unimproved road
Trail
Quarry or open mine pit
good water source
good water source
water here
Targhee Pass
Howard Spring Wayside
TARGHEE
NATIONAL FOREST BOUNDARY
MOUNTAINS
NATIONAL
FOREST
CONTINENTAL
DIVIDE
MONTANA
IDAHO
Tygee Creek Basin
Mount Two Top
Mosquito
Gulch
Madison
River
Black Sand Spring
Buttermilk
Yellowstone Airport
Heliport
Radio Facility
Landing Strips
HENRYS
LAKE
FLAT
Gaging Sta
Garner Springs
Reas Pass
Radio Facility
NATIONAL FOREST BOUNDARY
NATIONAL PARK BOUNDARY
Rocky
Draw
Jack Straw Basin
Meadow
MONTANA
WYOMING
MADISON
Canyon
Dry
RAILROAD
GRADE
Ski Lift
DIVIDE
BOUNDARY

USGS: HEBGEN LAKE
USGS: ASHTON
Dry, no water
Dry, no water
Dry, no water
Bog bridges
New trail construction
Big Springs
Macks Inn
Landing Strips
Gravel Pits
Trude
Black Canyon
Moose Creek Plateau
Echo Canyon
Black Canyon
GALLATIN CO
FREMONT CO
CONTINENTAL
MONTANA
IDAHO
GALLATIN NAT FOR
Meadows
4 WD

Segment 2
Targhee Pass to Red Rock Pass: Henrys Lake Mtns.

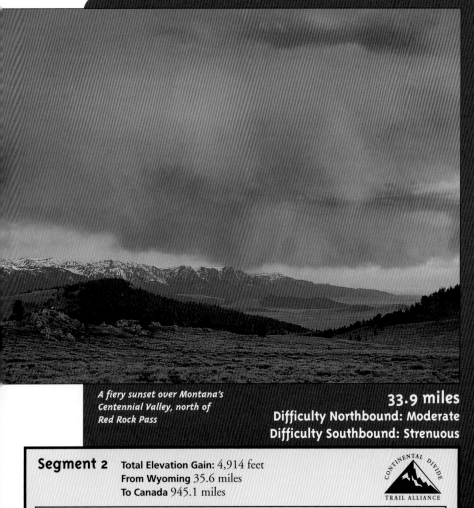

A fiery sunset over Montana's Centennial Valley, north of Red Rock Pass

33.9 miles
Difficulty Northbound: Moderate
Difficulty Southbound: Strenuous

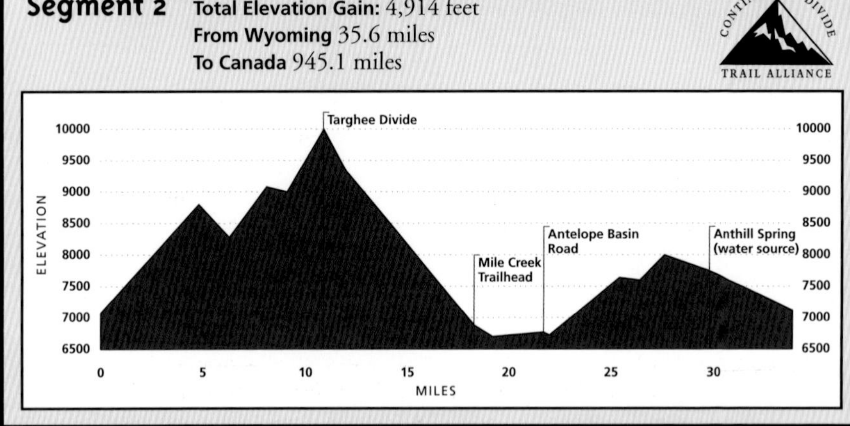

TRAIL OVERVIEW The Henrys Lake Mountains dominate this segment of the Continental Divide Trail. This small range is shaped like an arch that connects the Centennial Mountains to the Madison Plateau. The terrain is steep, with dramatic elevation differences between Henrys Lake below and the plus 10,000-foot peaks above. The trail crawls over the shoulder of Targhee Peak at 10,000 feet. The distinctive, resting-lion shape of Lionhead Peak, 9,574 feet, lends its name to the recreation area, "Lionshead Resort."

This section of trail is quite different from the CDT in Island Park to the south. Mixed conifer forests replace the repetitive lodgepole pines. The northern Henrys Lake Mountains were not burned in the 1988 fires, so the landscape is not as dreary. Impressive rock cliffs in Mile Creek Canyon are a distinct contrast to the rounded plateaus of Island Park.

New trail has recently been constructed from near Lionhead Peak to a saddle northwest of Targhee Peak. The new route is shown on the Gallatin Forest Service map, but does not appear on any other maps. In fact, the topographical map will mislead hikers because it shows the route of an old pack trail that used to cross the Continental Divide at a higher point.

We camped on the Targhee Divide at 10,000 feet and then dayhiked to 10,500 feet above Edwards Lake, a shallow tarn. This is the highest section of the Montana/Idaho Continental Divide that is easily accessible to hikers, and it also provides an awe-inspiring look at the Lee Metcalf Wilderness, the Grand Tetons, and the entire length of the Centennial Mountains.

Sawtell Peak (9,866 ft) in the Centennials can be identified by its radio towers. The peak is named for Gilman Sawtell, who ranched in the area in 1868. He was so driven to distraction by mosquitoes and horseflies that he gave up ranching and switched to fishing on Henrys Lake. Mosquitoes and flies still bedevil residents and visitors—carry plenty of insect repellent. When we were there in late July, a herd of cows at the Mile Creek Trailhead brought with them a swarm of flies that bit repeatedly and were not deterred by repellent. The only escape was in climbing above their preferred altitude.

Southbound hikers face a more strenuous climb in this segment. There are a total of 50 switchbacks between the Mile Creek Trailhead and the shoulder of Targhee Peak—that's 7 miles of strenuous climbing, and a gain of 3,112 feet. Northbound hikers will have an easier time of it, with the approach from Targhee Pass being more gentle.

There are special orders for food storage within this "Grizzly Bear Recovery Area." To provide for public safety and protection of the grizzly bear, several regulations apply:

Human food and beverages, horse food, and dog food must be kept unavailable to grizzly bears unless it is being consumed, prepared for consumption, or transported. Items are considered unavailable if they are stored in a closed, bear-resistant container, enclosed within a vehicle constructed of solid, non-pliable material, or suspended at least 10 feet clear of the ground and 4 feet horizontally from any supporting tree or pole. Food should be hung at least 100 yards from any sleeping area. Violation is punishable by a fine of $500. Review the bear avoidance techniques in "Safety Concerns."

There is no water at the beginning and ending points of this segment, but water is available in small stream crossings close by. There is only one water source in

the 50-switchback segment, and it is unreliable. Plan to refill water bottles before tackling the switchbacks. Water sources are adequate, but not frequent, from Highway 87 to Red Rock Pass. See the trail description for specifics.

MOUNTAIN BIKE NOTES

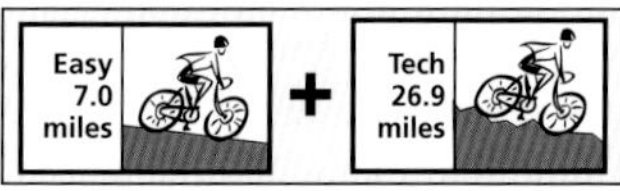

This segment is open to mountain bikes. It is much easier to ride the segment from south to north, avoiding the torture of riding up 50 switchbacks from the Mile Creek Trailhead. A short jaunt along Highway 87 is easy, as well as a few miles of 4WD road—the remainder of the segment requires technical riding skills.

LAND ADMINISTRATORS (SEE APPENDIX A)

Gallatin National Forest, Hebgen Lake Ranger District
Beaverhead National Forest, Madison Ranger District

MAPS

USGS QUADRANGLES: Targhee Pass, Targhee Peak, Earthquake Lake, Hidden Lake Bench, Mount Jefferson

USFS: Gallatin National Forest, West Half; Winter Guide to Yellowstone Country, West Yellowstone Snowmobile Map

BEGINNING ACCESS POINT

TARGHEE PASS: Targhee Pass is on US-20, at the Montana/Idaho border.

ENDING ACCESS POINT

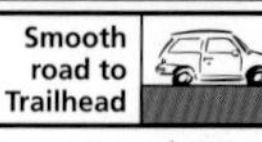

RED ROCK PASS: Take US-20 to Forest Service Road 053. Turn west on Road 053 and continue about 7 miles west/northwest to Red Rock Pass Road. Turn left (south, southwest) on the Red Rock Pass Road and continue about 4.5 miles west to the pass. There is room to park and unimproved camping both south and north of the road. The Red Rock Pass road may be downgraded to 4WD due to bumps and ruts during spring rains.

SUPPLIES, SERVICES, AND ACCOMMODATIONS

The town of **WEST YELLOWSTONE, MT,** is on US-20, at the Yellowstone National Park border. Southbound hikers need to stop there to pick up backcountry permits before entering Yellowstone National Park. See Segment 1 for supplies and services details.

Distance from Trail: 9 miles

Special Notes: Limited services are available 1 mile east of Targhee Pass at the Lionshead Resort, 1545 Targhee Pass Hwy., West Yellowstone, MT 59758. Alice's Restaurant, 406-646-7296. Super 8 Lodge, 406-646-9584. Laundromat, gas station, mail drop, maps.

TRAIL DESCRIPTION This segment begins at Targhee Pass (7,072 feet) on the Montana/Idaho border. The pass is named after the Bannock Indian chief Tahgee, who died in 1871. The pass was also used by Shoshone Indians as the easiest route to buffalo hunting grounds between the Musselshell and Yellowstone Rivers.

From US-20, turn north on a 4WD road at Targhee Pass. The road is marked as a snowmobile trail. Hikers will see the first CDT sign at 0.1 mile. There is room to park past the sign, and again farther up the road.

A gate on the trail at mile 0.5 is designed to restrict motorized traffic in the summer months. Continue past the gate to a defunct ski area and an intersection of jeep tracks at mile 2.0. Hike northwest on Trail 114, which is shown correctly on the FS map as the CDNST.

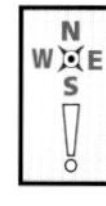

The Gallatin Forest Service map depicts the CDNST incorrectly near the intersection with trail 114. A right (west) turn is shown on the map, but the trail continues on a snowmobile trail in a northwesterly direction to meet Trail 114. See the "Lionhead Loop" on the snowmobile map.

Cross a tributary of the West Fork of Denny Creek at mile 5.1. Lionhead Peak is the high point in the cliffs of the Divide to the west. Less than a mile past the creek crossing, the CDT joins Trail 217 at an intersection of two trails. The CDT still looks like a rough road at this point. Turn left (west) on Trail 217. The CDT is on Trail 217 for 0.5 mile before newly constructed tread diverges to the west (another left turn for northbound hikers) on Trail 027. The newly constructed trail is wide and all of the switchbacks are graded for stock animals.

Descend to cross two tributaries of Watkins Creek at mile 6.4, then begin an uphill slog to the Divide. Bald Peak (10,180 feet) lies to the south, and this peak is also called "Lionhead"—there are two Lionhead peaks within a mile of each other on the Divide.

The new trail crosses the Divide at mile 8.2, elevation 9,080 feet. This is the first of two crossings of the Divide, effectively cutting off the higher portion of the Divide that looms to the north. In a bowl of subalpine trees, marshy ground, and stream tributaries, the CDT traverses the terrain near Clark Lake, and below Edwards Lake. Depending upon the time of year and the past season's snowfall, there may be good camping spots in the bowl. In wetter seasons, hikers may have to climb out of the bowl to find a dry camp.

Cross two tributaries of Targhee Creek at mile 8.6 and mile 8.7, then turn south, still following the new tread toward Clark Lake. An almost level walk brings hikers to Clark Lake at mile 9.2. From the lake, the trail trends southwest and begins to climb again as it heads for a saddle on the shoulder of Targhee Peak. A series of short switchbacks mounts the talus slope on the east side of Targhee Divide, which is not the Continental Divide, but a dividing ridge between two forks of Targhee Creek.

The trail crosses Targhee Divide at mile 10.8 at an elevation of 10,000 feet, the highest point on the trail for this segment. In two steep-sided canyons, Targhee Creek and the West Fork of Targhee Creek wrap their arms around the peak itself. A combination of springs and snowmelt provides water on the west side of Targhee Divide. The water source is not shown on the topo, but it usually runs all year.

More switchbacks, some of them with very long legs, lead down from Targhee Divide to a saddle on the Continental Divide, north of Black Mountain. Snow lingers on this section of trail until late July. The trail crosses the Divide at 9,333 feet at a signed intersection. CDT trekkers turn right (north) at the saddle on Mile Creek Trail 214 to contour around the slopes of the Divide to yet another set of switchbacks.

The trail switchbacks down the steep west-facing slope of the Divide for 3 miles. At mile 14.8 it reaches the banks of Mile Creek, a good water source. There are ample camping spots along Mile Creek, and the area closer to the head of the canyon is preferable because it is farther from grazing cattle.

Follow CD poles and visible tread through a grassy area to reach the trailhead on Mile Creek at mile 18.3. There are several signs at the trailhead, including the warning about the grizzly recovery area. A map shows the route of the CDT. The small parking area outlined with rocks is next to a ford of Mile Creek.

Ford Mile Creek and continue on a dirt road, suitable for 2WD traffic, to Montana State Highway 87 (mile 19.2 for this segment). Turn south on the highway and walk 2.5 miles to Antelope Basin Road. There is no way to get off the highway, so one must walk on the shoulder. At Antelope Basin Road (mile 21.7), turn west. A CD sign on a pole corral confirms the route.

If you come to a sign for Raynolds Pass on Hwy. 87, you have gone too far south.

Antelope Basin Road looks suitable for 2WD vehicles, but soon disintegrates into a 4WD track. Hike 1.2 miles on the road to a trail intersection marked with a blue and white CD sign. The trail turns south and starts uphill just past a cattle guard. Visible tread doesn't appear until shortly after the trail tops the first low hill. The trail becomes easy to follow when it enters a stand of trees both blazed and occasionally marked with CD symbols.

There is a pretty view of Henrys Lake 0.7 mile south of Antelope Basin Road. All of these terrain features that apparently belong to "Henry" were named after Major Andrew Henry, a U.S. army officer who built Fort Henry in 1810. The fort was situated five miles southwest of what is now St. Anthony, Idaho, on (of course) Henrys Fork of the Snake River.

The footpath ends and road-walking begins at mile 24.9. (At this intersection, north-to-south hikers look for a CD sign and dim tread that descends slightly through a grassy meadow and a stand of aspen trees.) When I was on this trail in July, I disturbed a moose that was snoozing next to the trail in a spot shaded by pine and spruce trees.

Most of the trail from Antelope Basin Road to Red Rock Pass is from 7,000 to 8,000 feet in elevation on a high sagebrush steppe dotted with trees. The wide-open spaces allow for long-distance views of the Henrys Lake Mountains and of the Centennial Mountains. Northbound hikers find themselves walking south for 12 miles, with the forbidding northern face of the Centennials before them. Grazing cattle mix with antelope and deer on the plateau.

Wildflowers surround an aspen trunk where the CDT approaches Red Rock Pass in the Henrys Lake Mountains.

At mile 29.7, near the intersection of two 4WD roads, Anthill Spring offers an opportunity to refill water bottles. Look for an area where a log fence has been erected to keep the cattle out. The trail is somewhat boggy near Anthill Spring. CDT hikers continue south on Road 056 to Red Rock Pass.

Red Rock Pass (mile 33.9 for this segment) is well-signed, and there is ample camping in grassy, wooded areas south of the pass, though you will have to hike to Cole Creek for water. The creek can be accessed on either Red Rock Pass Road (one mile west), or on the continuation of the CDT (1.1 miles).

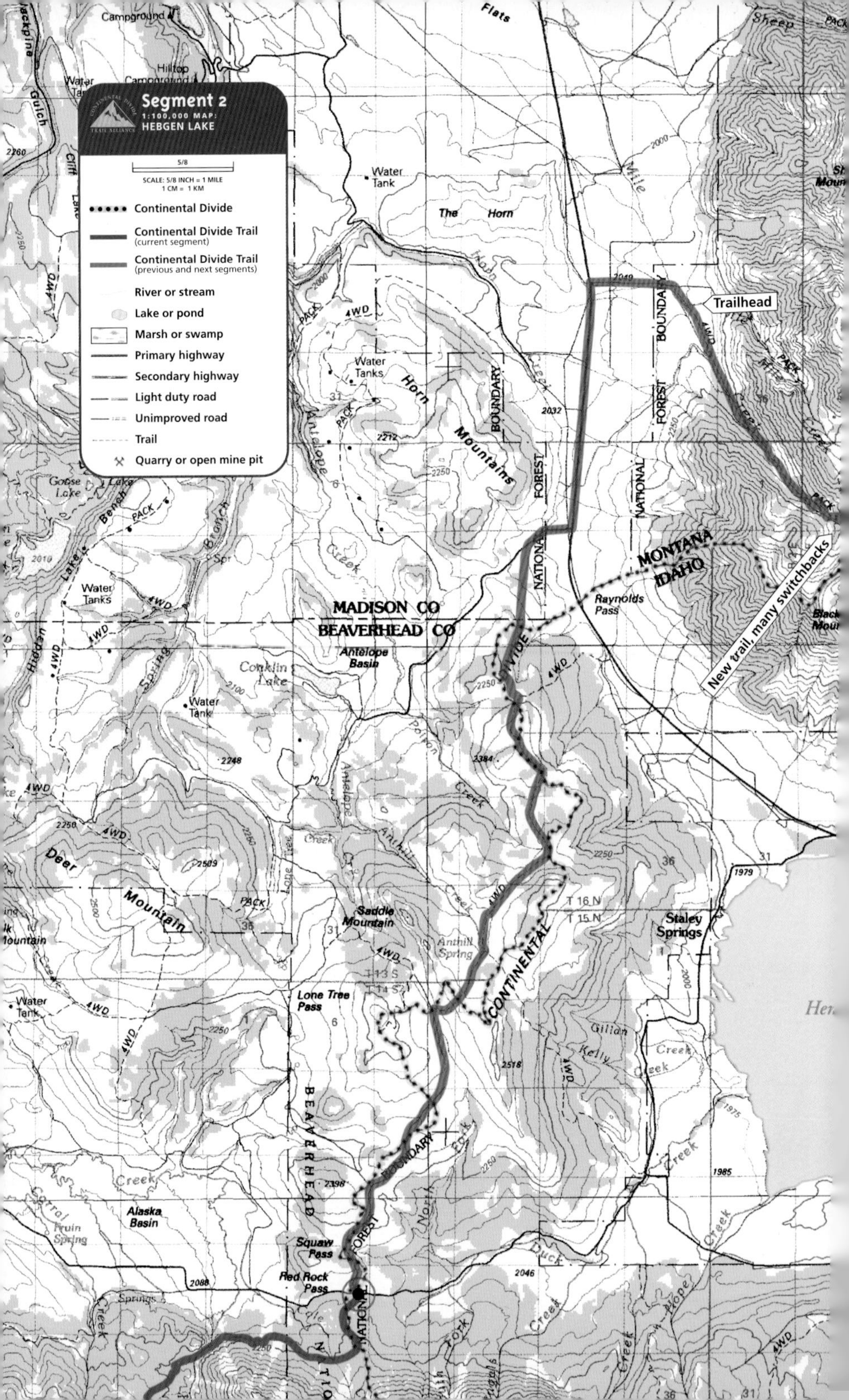
Segment 2
1:100,000 MAP: HEBGEN LAKE
5/8
SCALE: 5/8 INCH = 1 MILE
1 CM = 1 KM
Continental Divide
Continental Divide Trail (current segment)
Continental Divide Trail (previous and next segments)
River or stream
Lake or pond
Marsh or swamp
Primary highway
Secondary highway
Light duty road
Unimproved road
Trail
Quarry or open mine pit
Trailhead
New trail, many switchbacks
MONTANA
IDAHO
MADISON CO
BEAVERHEAD CO
Raynolds Pass
The Horn
Horn Mountains
Antelope Basin
Conklin Lake
Saddle Mountain
Lone Tree Pass
Deer Mountain
Staley Springs
Alaska Basin
Squaw Pass
Red Rock Pass
Goose Lake
Hilltop Campground
Campground
Water Tank
Water Tanks
NATIONAL FOREST BOUNDARY
BEAVERHEAD
CONTINENTAL DIVIDE
Anthill Spring
Gillan
Kelly Creek
Duck Creek
Hope Creek
Flats
Sheep

Campground
Gray
Hebgen Lake
Spring Creek Campground
Rumbaugh Campground
Campground
Campground
Horse Butte Peninsula
Lookout Tower
Coffin Mountain
Upper Coffin Lake
MADISON CO
GALLATIN CO
FREMONT CO
New trail construction
West Fork
Watkins Creek
Rumbaugh Creek
Cherry Creek
Lionhead
Bald Peak
HENRYS LAKE MOUNTAINS
CONTINENTAL DIVIDE
NATIONAL FOREST BOUNDARY
TARGHEE NATIONAL FOREST
Ski Lift
Targhee Pass
Howard Spring Wayside
Basin Cabin Spring
Denny Creek
Buttermilk
Cream Cr
T 16 N
T 15 N
Landing Strips
HENRYS LAKE
Tygee Creek Basin
Mount Two Top
MONTANA
IDAHO
Gaging Sta
Jesse Creek
Garner Canyon
Mosquito

Segment 3
Red Rock Pass to Aldous Lake: Centennial Mtns.

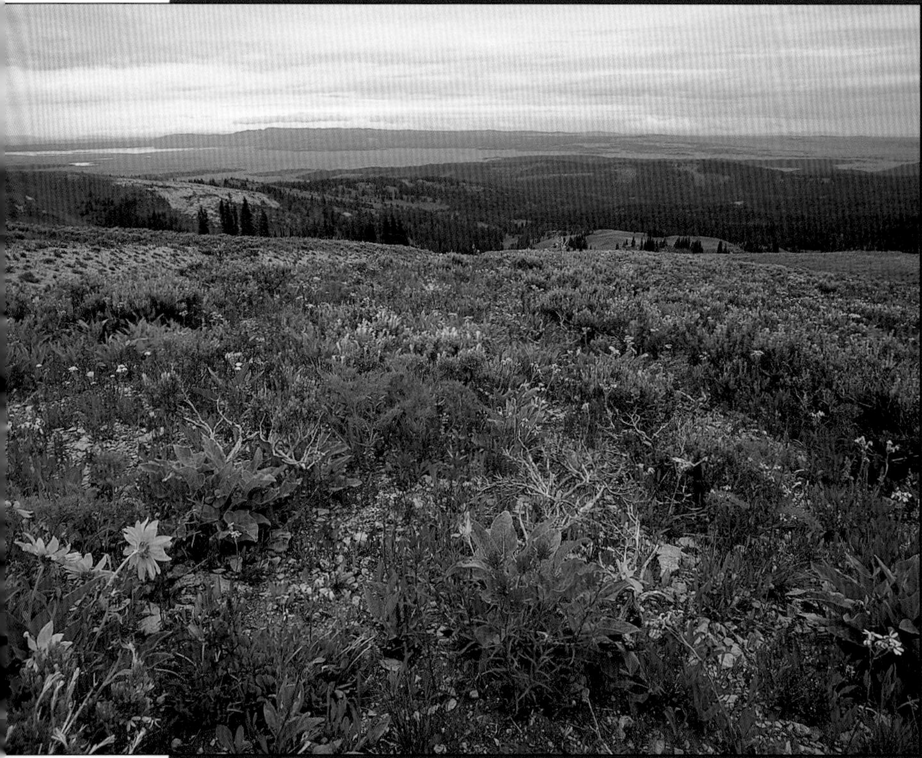

Arrowleaf balsamroot, Indian paintbrush, and other wildflowers on a ridge above Blair Lake in the Centennial Mountains, on the approach to Taylor Mountain.

30.1 miles
Difficulty: Strenuous

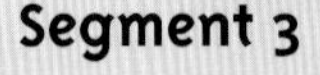

Total Elevation Gain: 4,890 feet
From Wyoming 69.5 miles
To Canada 911.2 miles

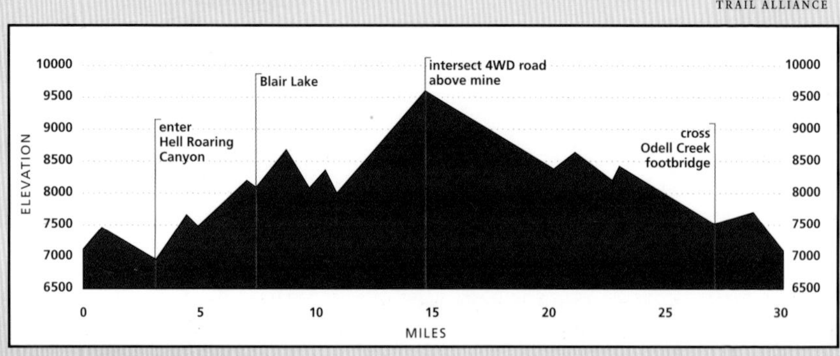

TRAIL OVERVIEW This segment of the Continental Divide Trail leads hikers into the rugged Centennial Mountains, an east/west range that forms the border between Idaho and Montana for about 40 miles. Hikers cross Hell Roaring Creek, the most distant headwater of the Missouri River. The creek's waters end up in the Gulf of Mexico, some 4,200 miles downstream as the kayaker paddles.

Near the trailhead on the south side of Red Rock Pass, you'll find newly constructed tread and new CDT signs. As the trail skirts the northern base of Nemesis Mountain, there are some open views into the ranchlands of the Centennial Valley and over a basin dotted with stands of aspen trees. The trail turns southwest into Hell Roaring Canyon and climbs through thick pine, spruce, and fir forests with only occasional clearings before it reaches the Blair Lake cirque. If you like to fish, bring your rod and Montana license—Blair Lake is famous for trout fishing.

This segment of the trail is narrow but relatively easy to negotiate, with switchbacks on the steeper slopes. It is suitable for pack animals if the deadfall has been cleared. Deadfall normally chokes the trail and has to be cleared every year. Local horsemen offer guided rides to Blair Lake and to Lillian Lake, and their side trails can lead away from the CDT. Keep to the trail marked with wooden CD signs. The "finger" of the Continental Divide that jabs east toward Red Rock Mountain and Sawtell Peak is cut off by this new trail.

Review the precautions and safety guidelines for hiking and camping in bear country. This trail is near lands managed as prime grizzly bear habitat. Both grizzly and black bears are rare here, but may be encountered throughout the Centennial Mountains. (See "Safety Concerns.")

Before you hike this section, check the status of the bridge over Hell Roaring Creek by calling the BLM Dillon Resource Area office at 406-683-2337. The creek can be forded at low water but is not passable at high water (May and June). If the bridge is out, you may have to take the Nemesis Mountain Trail Detour described at the end of this segment.

Be aware of avalanche danger in the spring. The entire northern front of the Centennial Mountains and all of Hell Roaring Canyon are subject to avalanches. One avalanche chute crosses Hell Roaring Creek above the site of the bridge and flows up the other side of the canyon, leaving the creek to tunnel under it. Hikers are tempted to cross on the resultant snow bridge, a practice which is extremely dangerous. Do not cross on the snow bridge. Avalanche danger diminishes by July. Depending on weather conditions, the trail is usually impassable in early June.

If you are camping at Red Rock Pass, the closest water is in Cole and Hell Roaring Creeks where they cross the road about a mile west of the pass. On the trail, there is water at the Cole and Hell Roaring crossings, and in three tributaries that flow east from the ridge above Hell Roaring Creek. Blair Lake is a good water source and camping spot. The trail crosses a tributary of Schneider Creek about 5 miles west of the lake.

MAKE SURE YOU GET WATER at Blair Lake or at the Schneider tributary. There are 12 dry miles before a spring that feeds the West Fork of Sheridan Creek. There are frequent water sources from East Dry Creek (which is not dry) to Aldous Lake.

MOUNTAIN BIKE NOTES: Experienced mountain bikers will find this segment very difficult, but possible, with many hairpin turns and quite a few steep climbs. Deadfall may make the trail impassable earlier in the season.

LAND ADMINISTRATORS (SEE APPENDIX A)

BLM, Dillon Resource Area
Targhee National Forest, Dubois Ranger District
U.S. Sheep Experiment Station, Dubois, ID

MAPS

USGS QUADRANGLE: Mount Jefferson, Upper Red Rock Lake, Slide Mountain (Antelope Valley recommended for access)

USFS: Targhee National Forest: Island Park/Ashton

BEGINNING ACCESS POINT

TO RED ROCK PASS TRAILHEAD FROM US-20: Take US-20 to Forest Service Road 053. Turn west on Road 053 and continue about 7 miles west/northwest to Red Rock Pass Road. Turn left (south, southwest) on the Red Rock Pass Road and continue about 4.5 miles west to the pass. Red Rock Pass is well marked with an elevation sign (7,120 feet), Montana/Idaho border, and Forest Service signs. There is room to park and unimproved camping both south and north of the road. The Red Rock Pass road may be downgraded to 4WD due to bumps and ruts during spring rains.

ENDING ACCESS POINT

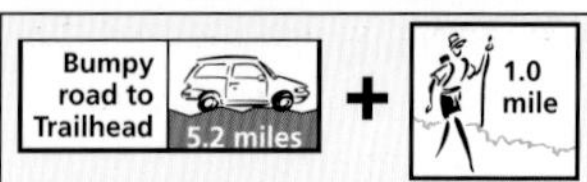

ALDOUS LAKE TRAILHEAD: Take US-20 to Forest Service Road 030, the Kilgore/Yale Road, and proceed west to the small town of Kilgore, making a right-hand (north) turn on Road 026 (Cottonwood Road). Follow 026 north 6.3 miles to a junction with 027, which is signed as leading to Aldous Lake. Turn right (southeast) on 027, which leads, with many twists and turns, to the trailhead. Hike 1 mile to Aldous Lake to intercept the CDNST.

TRAIL DESCRIPTION

On the south side of Red Rock Road, at Red Rock Pass, follow a two-track and a faded, wooden CD sign into the trees. In less than 0.25 mile, you'll come to a new sign that says "Continental Divide Trail, Blair Lake 7½ mi., Hell Roaring Canyon 3½ mi." New signs are courtesy of the Bureau of Land Management (BLM), so they differ a little in style from Forest Service signs. At 0.2 mile there is a no-motorized sign and new tread begins a gentle climb. The trail climbs steadily for 1 mile and closely parallels the geographical Divide. At 1.1 miles, the trail crosses Cole Creek and heads westerly, contouring around the base of Nemesis Mountain. For the next 1.5 miles, the trail rolls up and down, with 200- to 300-foot elevation changes and one short series of switchbacks, before it turns southwest and enters Hell Roaring Canyon.

In Hell Roaring Canyon, the trail follows the left (east) bank of the creek for 0.4 mile before it crosses at 3.3 miles on a man-made bridge. The bridge has washed out in the past, so it may be there and it may not (see Detour). The BLM has plans to construct a new bridge. At 3.5 miles, the trail forks. Avoid the left fork that leads to Lillian Lake; turn right and go only a few steps north of the Lillian Lake sign to find the CDT as it continues steeply uphill and almost directly west. (The branch of the trail that continues north here is the Nemesis Mountain Trail, which leads back to Red Rock Pass Road.)

For about 0.9 mile the CDT climbs, via a series of switchbacks, onto the ridge west of Hell Roaring Canyon. At 4.4 miles the trail intersects the Corral Creek Trail, another trail leading back to the Red Rock Pass Road. Turn left (south/southeast) at the intersection and continue along the ridge, climbing toward a rocky knoll (7,800 feet).

At about 6.3 miles, you will top the knoll and can look back into Hell Roaring Canyon, which looks as wild as any wilderness can get. The loop trail to Lillian Lake reenters the CDT here, coming in from the left (east). Bear right (westerly) on a trail that climbs steeply, with some switchbacks, for about 0.75 mile before it crests the ridge (8,200 feet) overlooking the Blair Lake cirque.

From the ridge, the trail descends through forested slopes to Blair Lake (mile 7.4, 8,090 feet). In the summer, the lake is surrounded by grasses and wildflowers and is a draw for deer, elk, and other wildlife. The CDT crosses the lake's outlet on the northeastern shore. There are ample camping spots on a rise above the lake's northern shore. When we were there, a particularly heavy snow season, coupled with high winds, had snapped the tops off hundreds of trees and downed many more, which blocked the CDT where it climbed from the cirque. (Horsemen have since cleared the trail from Blair Lake to the Nemesis Mountain Trail, but not from Hell Roaring Creek to Red Rock Pass.)

At Blair Lake's western edge, the trail climbs for 300 feet to a ridge and then intersects a 4WD road (now closed to motorized vehicles) that leads to the Keg Spring Road. Keep left where another, little-used 4WD track leads downhill. At 1.6 miles from the lake, large signs explain the U.S. Sheep Experiment Station. New trail construction begins near here. It is all too easy to continue on the road. No visible tread led up onto the ridge above the road when we were there, but rangers assure me that they have since improved this intersection with cut tread and CD signs. Watch for posts with wooden CD signs. Once you're through the grassy area and into rocks and trees, the tread is easier to see.

About 2.3 miles from Blair Lake, the 4WD road turns south onto the unimproved but easily negotiated Keg Spring Road, a good exit point for a 4WD shuttle car or for friends to deliver supplies. From this intersection, it is about 1 mile south on the road to good water, and 5 miles to the Yale/Kilgore Road, which leads east to US-20 (about 13 miles).

Five miles of new trail heads westerly from the big signs around the sheep pastures, putting hikers close to, and sometimes on, the Divide. Where the trail crosses briefly to the Montana side of the Divide, north-facing areas may have ice and snowfields well into July. However, hikers enjoy excellent views of Montana's Centennial Valley and the impressive cliffs lining the north face of the Centennial Mountains.

Just east of Carrot Canyon, the trail contours around some steep terrain, coming down from the Divide on the Idaho side. Anytime you lose altitude, you know you're going to have to climb back up again, and sure enough, the trail switchbacks up to 9,200 feet above the Carrot Canyon drainage. It continues to climb to 9,600 feet as it crosses below the Divide to intercept what used to be a 4WD road (now closed) near an open pit mine east of Taylor Mountain (mile 14.7 for this segment). This section of trail now looks like a wide cat cut, with some vegetation beginning to fill in the cut.

This closed mining road skirts the Divide on the Idaho (south) side for 3.5 miles, contouring under the peak of Taylor Mountain, before it begins a series of very long, shallow switchbacks to the 8,400-foot level above a stand of trees. The switchbacks were built for mining trucks, so the road base is wide and the grade shallow. As you work your way down, you'll see several 4WD roads coming up from the Idaho side and the remains of open pit mining to the southeast. Two miles of switchbacks crisscross the physical Divide as it bends southwest. Make sure that you take the switchbacks down and do not continue west on the upper branch of the road.

At a 4WD road intersection (mile 20.2), the trail enters trees on a closed road that was partially choked with deadfall when we were there. There is another agricultural/sheep sign at the road intersection. The road that is the route of the CDT is not shown on the topo or the Forest Service map, but it certainly looks like a road when you're hiking it. Its "road" character quickly disintegrates into "trode" status and then a trail. The trail rounds a series of low, red rock cliffs on what used to be a road cut, and then climbs to an open, grassy ridge, staying on the Divide.

Rock cairns mark the trail as it traverses a long ridge just below the crest of the Divide. In clear weather, you can see the peaks of Wyoming's Grand Tetons to the southeast. An experienced eye will discern traces of a 4WD track that appears and disappears. We spotted and walked around a rusting coyote trap, which had been set directly on the route of the CDT. Apparently not all the coyotes have been trapped, because we heard them howling at night. Other animal sightings in this section included moose, deer, and elk.

There's a V-shaped dip in the trail where it crosses a spring that feeds the West Fork of Sheridan Creek, and then climbs 200 feet again to the Divide. The rest of this section, from the monster switchbacks to the intersection with East Dry Creek Road 327 (mile 25.2 for this segment), is gently downhill to 7,800 feet. The grassy meadows here are often grazed by sheep, and you'll see more U.S. Sheep Experiment Station signs and will eventually come to clearly discernible two-tracks as you descend.

From the last, easily visible survey marker on the Montana/Idaho border (an iron pipe with an inscribed cap), hikers must make their own way on the Divide, going gently downhill, but staying on the Divide until they intercept a 4WD road. This road

SUPPLIES, SERVICES, AND ACCOMMODATIONS

MACKS INN, ID, is on US-20 in Idaho's Island Park area, south of the intersection with Road 053, and north of the intersection with Road 030.

Distance from Trail: 17 miles

Zip Code: 83429

Bank:	None, but Island Park, 6 miles south on US-20, has a branch of the Bank of Eastern Idaho, next to the Saddle-Up Saloon on Sawtell Road	208-558-0226
Bus:	Greyhound stops at Ponds Lodge in Island Park, a "flagstop." Flag the bus down and it will stop for pickups and departures. Service to West Yellowstone, Idaho Falls, Salt Lake City. Call Greyhound and they'll tell you the stop does not exist. Tell them it is 27 miles southwest of West Yellowstone and they'll find it on their schedule.	800-231-2222
Camping:	Flat Rock Campground (across the highway from Macks Inn)	
Dining:	Macks Inn Dinner Theater	208-558-7871
	Hungry Bear Market, 2.5 miles north of Macks Inn on US-20	208-558-0100
Gear:	Limited gear at Stage Stop Texaco	208-558-7751
	(the town of West Yellowstone has more complete gear shops)	
Groceries:	Hungry Bear Market	208-558-0100
	Robin's Roost Grocery & Chevron Gas Station	208-558-7440
	Elk Creek Station, junction of US-20 and Kilgore Road	208-558-7571
Information:	Macks Inn Resort	208-558-7272
	Elk Creek Station	208-558-7571
Laundry:	Macks Inn Shower House & Laundry, Big Spring Road	
Lodging:	Macks Inn Resort, US-20, Macks Inn, ID 83429 ($44–$115)	208-558-7272
Medical:	None; Clinic at West Yellowstone	406-646-7668
Post Office:	U.S. Post Office, Big Springs Road, Macks Inn, ID 83429	208-558-7070
Showers:	Macks Inn Shower House & Laundry, Big Springs Road	

is normally closed to motorized traffic, and is used only once or twice a year by shepherds, so do not expect it to look well-traveled. At an Agricultural Research sign, the two-track disappears as it goes uphill in a grassy meadow, but reappears only 20 feet farther on. It leads to an intersection with a better 4WD track (East Dry Creek Road 327), the left-hand fork of which leads to a locked gate. If you come to the locked gate, you've gone too far. Turn around and go back less than 0.25 mile to the intersection and look for the rougher track leading uphill, on the Divide.

Where East Dry Creek Road 327 crosses the CDT, hikers continue up a grassy knoll on a two-track that is rocky and rutted in spots. The meadows were full of wildflowers when we were on the trail in July. There is a faded, wooden CD sign on a post 0.7 mile up the two-track. One mile up the two-track there is a Montana/Idaho border marker, and at 1.3 miles there is another wooden CD sign on a tree. The two-track becomes more of a single-track trail here and turns westerly. At 1.9 miles from the 327-road intersection, there is a sign that says "Agricultural Research Service ... Danger, Guarding Dogs." There is also a newer, wooden CD sign on a tree, so walk on—into the teeth of the dangerous dogs. A footbridge is provided for crossing Odell Creek, a good water source, but filter the water in deference to the sheep. The CDT intersects Trail 822 here, a pack trail that crosses the Divide and leads into both Montana and Idaho.

After crossing Odell Creek, the trail disappears in a meadow, but reappears periodically on dryer ground. Look for a CD sign where the trail continues. Cross another tributary of Odell Creek at 2.5 miles from East Dry Creek Road (mile 27.7 for this segment). The crossing is marked with a CD sign above the creek.

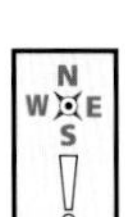

The trail becomes difficult to follow here. Look for sawed-out logs and indistinct tread for a few hundred yards, then find your way to the saddle (7,700 feet) at the head of a grassy meadow. The meadow is filled with springs and streams. Cross to the left (south) side where the ground is somewhat dryer and continue a gentle climb for about a mile. On a pine tree halfway to the saddle, there is one CD sign, adorned with a set of small elk antlers, but it is hard to see. Closer to the saddle, faint tread reappears and there are two faded CD signs on trees.

Where the trail crosses the saddle, it is filled with deadfall, but you can find the path by looking for previously sawed-out logs. Both tread and trail markings improve dramatically where the downhill section toward Aldous Lake begins. From the saddle, it is 1.3 miles to the Aldous Lake Trailhead (7,100 feet, mile 30.1 for this segment).

DETOUR

If the bridge over Hell Roaring Creek is washed out, and/or the new bridge is not completed, walk 2.1 miles west of Red Rock Pass on the Red Rock Pass Road (one mile past the "Nemesis Mountain" sign) and turn left (south) on Road 1811 (Corral Creek Road). There is a gate here and the BLM has purchased an easement through private land. Be sure to close the rancher's gate. Keep left at a fork in the road (0.3 mile from the turn), and follow the road as it swings east, coming to a dead end (0.5 mile from the turn) in a grove of aspen trees at the base of Nemesis Mountain Trail. The trail is signed. It leads steeply uphill and due south via some switchbacks, and is well-blazed. It intersects the CDT near the Lillian Lake sign, about 0.65 mile from the grove of aspen trees.

OTHER EXCURSIONS

RED ROCK LAKES NATIONAL WILDLIFE REFUGE

DIFFICULTY: Moderate

DISTANCE: About 4.5 miles

THE RED ROCK LAKES NATIONAL WILDLIFE REFUGE in Montana's Centennial Valley offers views of endangered trumpeter swans and hundreds of other birds. Go west from Red Rock Pass about 13 miles to Upper Red Rock Lake Campground. You can continue on the Red Rock Road through the Centennial Valley to Interstate 15, with good views of the Centennial Mountains most of the way.

A good, short hike is the loop off the CDT that goes to Lillian Lake. The loop trail gives hikers a better look at Hell Roaring Canyon.

Segment 3
1:100,000 MAP:
HEBGEN LAKE
5/8
SCALE: 5/8 INCH = 1 MILE
1 CM = 1 KM
Continental Divide
Continental Divide Trail
(current segment)
Continental Divide Trail
(previous and next segments)
River or stream
Lake or pond
Marsh or swamp
Primary highway
Secondary highway
Light duty road
Unimproved road
Trail
Quarry or open mine pit
Water Tank
Springs
RED ROCK VALLEY
RED ROCK LAKES NATIONAL WIL
RED ROCK LAKES WILDE
Lower Red Rock Lake
Upp Red Roc
Lookout Tower
Landing Strip
WILDERNESS BOUNDARY
RRL NWR
Lakeview
REFUGE AND WILDERNESS BOUNDARY
REFUGE BOUNDARY
RRLNWR
RRLW
REFUGE
Sheep Mountain
Baldy Mountain
Slide Mountain
EASTERN CENTENNIAL
U S SHEEP EXPERIMENT STATION
CONTINENTAL DIVIDE
MONTANA
IDAHO
Hancock Lake
Aldous Lake
TARGH

MADISON CO
BEAVERHEAD CO
Antelope Basin
Conklin Lake
Hidden Lake
Elk Lake
Deer Mountain
Elk Mountain
Saddle Mountain
Lone Tree Pass
RRLW
REFUGE
REFUGE BOUNDARY
BOUNDARY
Widgeon Pond
Culver Springs
Alaska Basin
Squaw Pass
Red Rock Pass
BEAVERHEAD NATIONAL FOREST
Nemesis Mountain
Red Rock Mountain
U S SHEEP EXPERIMENT STATION
Taylor Mountain
MOUNTAINS
BEAVERHEAD CO
CONTINENTAL DIVIDE
Mount Jefferson
Lillian Lake
Canyon
Reas Peak
CLARK CO
FREMONT CO
NATIONAL FOREST

Segment 4
Aldous Lake Trailhead to Interstate 15: Centennial Mountains

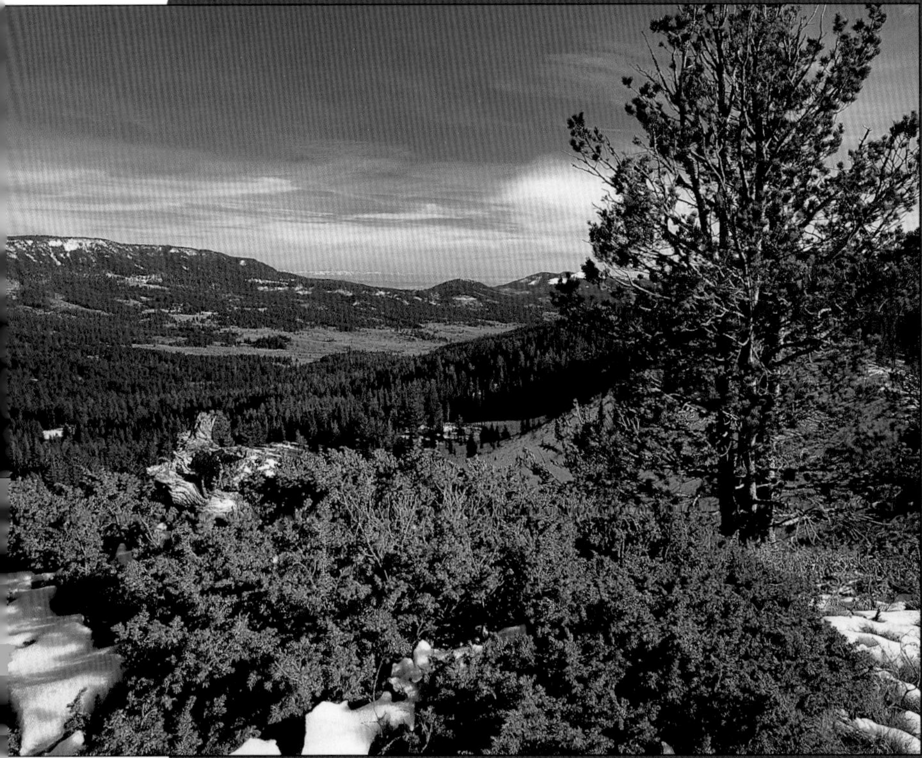

View from the trail in the Centennial Mountains about 15 miles east of Monida Pass

30.7 miles
Difficulty: Moderate

Segment 4 **Total Elevation Gain:** 4,540 feet
From Wyoming 99.6 miles
To Canada 881.1 miles

CONTINENTAL DIVIDE TRAIL ALLIANCE

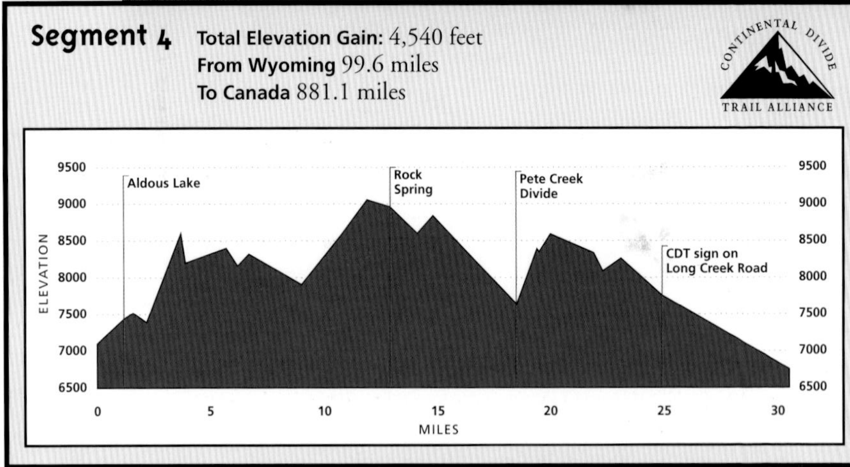

TRAIL OVERVIEW Review the precautions and safety guidelines for hiking and camping in bear country. We saw signs of black bear near Salamander Lake when we hiked the trail in July.

Also be aware of avalanche danger in the spring. The trail ascends via a set of switchbacks on a steep northern slope at mile 10.8. Avalanche danger diminishes by July. Depending on weather conditions, the trail is usually impassable in early June.

My 12-year-old nephew came along on this trek and helped us put up CDT signs. The Forest Service had marked the route through a meadow with carsonite posts, but no signs, so we put the signs up. Cow elk were calling to their calves in the background while we signed an area west of Rock Spring—an experience my nephew won't soon forget. Support crew quote: "If they want to call it a trail, then you ought to be able to find it."

Right. There are several opportunities to get lost in this segment. We took most of them. Topographical maps are a must for this segment.

Water sources are relatively frequent. Rock Spring at mile 12.9 is a good stopping point for both water and camping.

MOUNTAIN BIKE NOTES: Deadfall will require some stop-and-lift action. There is one boulder field that is too steep to ride from west to east, but could be ridden downhill. A section of switchbacks above Jones Creek on the north side of the Divide is too steep to ride from east to west. Choose your poison.

LAND ADMINISTRATORS (SEE APPENDIX A)

Targhee National Forest, Dubois Ranger District

MAPS

USGS QUADRANGLES: Slide Mountain, Winslow Creek, Big Table Mountain, Corral Creek, Monida; Antelope Valley recommended for access

USFS: Targhee National Forest, Dubois; Dubois Travel Map recommended for access

BEGINNING ACCESS POINT

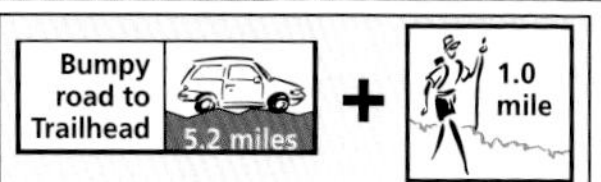

ALDOUS LAKE TRAILHEAD: (See Segment 3.) Hikers who want to leave the trail or resupply from Aldous Lake should arrange for a ride from the parking lot 1 mile south of the lake. The trailhead is too far off the beaten track to serve well for hitchhiking.

ENDING ACCESS POINT

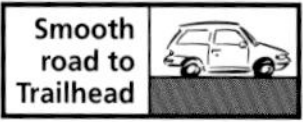

MODOC UNDERPASS, INTERSTATE 15: Exit Interstate 15, 6 miles south of Monida Pass at exit 190. Drive north on a paved but rough frontage road to Humphrey. There are no services at Humphrey. It is 3.6 miles from the exit to the Modoc Access (an underpass) on the Continental Divide Trail.

SUPPLIES, SERVICES, AND ACCOMMODATIONS

KILGORE, ID: The Kilgore Store in Kilgore, ID, is 11.5 miles from the Aldous Lake Trailhead. There is no post office, gas station, or lodging in Kilgore, but the store will accept resupply packages to hold for hiker pickup. Kilgore Store, Kilgore Route, Dubois, ID 83423, 208-778-5334. Groceries and camping gear, plus items of historical interest.

INTERSTATE 15: There are no towns or services at the ending point on Interstate 15. Monida is 3.7 miles north of the trail on I-15, but has only a pay phone and no other services. Spencer is 12 miles south on I-15, a tiny burg with limited services. Lima is 20 miles north on I-15 and has most services (see Segment 5).

TRAIL DESCRIPTION This segment begins at the Aldous Lake Trailhead on the Idaho side of the Centennial Mountains. Access to the trailhead is well-signed and the 1.2-mile trail to the lake is like a freeway compared to the rest of the CDT. The trail follows Ching Creek as it climbs to the lake. There are no campsites near the lake, but good sites are abundant on the trail to the west.

Round the southern edge of the lake and continue west on good tread. The Ching Creek Trail crosses the creek on a bridge at mile 1.6. You'll leave the human crowds behind after the creek crossing. The trail descends to contour around high terrain, then turns northwesterly to climb steadily, gaining 1,210 feet in 4 miles.

Rough terrain around Slide Mountain and Baldy Mountain forces a southerly detour. From Aldous Lake westward, the trail remains below the Divide for about 7 miles.

At mile 3.0, the trail leaves the trees and crosses open areas in a long traverse across a rocky slope. Views of the distant Grand Tetons are a highlight of the traverse across the dry hillside. There is water near the headwaters of Kay Creek.

At mile 3.9, descend via a few switchbacks to a long, narrow meadow. Visible tread disappears in the meadow, but the route is marked with tall poles that have a CD symbol carved into the pole itself. A tiny stream that is a tributary of Trail Creek runs through the southern edge of the meadow.

Climb through the meadow, following CD symbols and posts. Tread and signs improve as the trail nears Salamander Lake. The route is marked with CDT symbols, and bog bridges cross most of the marshy areas. Salamander Lake looks more like a pond, but we did see fish jumping. The trail rounds the southern edge of the lake and turns briefly south to meet a trail intersection that is poorly signed.

An old blaze has fallen apart on a tree near the Lake Creek Trail sign at the intersection south of Salamander Lake. Because there is no blaze and no visible tread for the first 30 feet, it is easy to miss the CDT trail entirely. Walk west from the sign to find a footbridge and CDT sign. The Lake Creek Trail sign also says "Divide Trail." A pack trail continues south here on the Idaho side. The CDT continues west and northwest. Once you find the footbridge, the tread improves and is easy to follow uphill to a meadow below the Divide.

SOUTHBOUND HIKERS: Finding the section of trail between the Divide and Salamander Lake is even more difficult for southbound hikers. Where the trail leaves the Divide, there is no trail intersection, no visible tread, and no nearby markings for the CDT. On the crest of the Divide, southbound hikers will have recently passed a sign that says "Tipton Winslow Trail 1814." Begin watching carefully on your right (south) for a CDT symbol. If you come to another sign that also says "Tipton Winslow Trail" (next to a tall Montana/Idaho boundary marker), you have gone too far. The cut-off to Salamander Lake is between the two signs. Go back along the trail, looking carefully for the turn, which is marked with a single wooden CD symbol on a tree. I asked a ranger if there was a policy against marking turns and intersections *at the turn,* and a directive to place CDT signs 100 feet off the trail—he assured me that no such policies exist, but I have my doubts. The CD symbol that southbound hikers are looking for is about 50 yards from the trail and partially obscured. At least the sign is attached to a live tree. Most of the other CD signs in this section are on dead trees. I predict that most of these will soon be blown down or pushed over by drifting snow.

Both southbound and northbound hikers will be scratching their heads in the 0.4 mile between the Lake Creek Trail (south of the Divide) and the Tipton Winslow Trail (on the crest). The CD signs are not on regulation posts. Hike from CD sign to CD sign. The signs are weathered to obliteration, and the dead tree substitutes for posts make it difficult to spot them from a distance. As near as I can tell, the CDT traverses an open area in section 7 on the Winslow Creek quadrangle to intersect the Lake Creek Trail.

SOUTHBOUND HIKERS: Once you have found this difficult turn and negotiated the meadows to intercept the pack trail, continue southeasterly toward the treeline, watching for a large, antique blaze where the trail enters trees. Good tread begins where the trail enters trees. A few yards farther on, when you don't need it, there is a wooden CD sign on a tree as confirmation that you're now on the right track. Descend to the footbridge over the outlet stream from Salamander Lake.

When northbound hikers come to a brown-and-white sign that says "Salamander Lake; Divide Trail," do not continue on the obvious pack trail. Look uphill, toward the Divide (north) for a wooden CD sign that is almost, but not quite, impossible to see. Hike from one CD symbol to the next until you reach the crest. Breathe a sigh of relief and continue west, on visible tread, with the world laid out at your feet, having hiked 6.7 miles from Aldous Lake without getting lost.

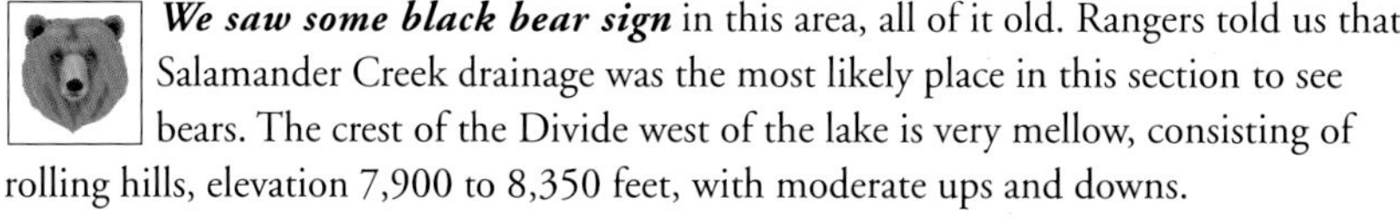

We saw some black bear sign in this area, all of it old. Rangers told us that Salamander Creek drainage was the most likely place in this section to see bears. The crest of the Divide west of the lake is very mellow, consisting of rolling hills, elevation 7,900 to 8,350 feet, with moderate ups and downs.

Follow an old boundary fence (a line of poles with no wire) west along the Divide. Above the Lake Creek drainage, you will pass the "Tipton/Winslow" trail signs, which are new. Tipton/Winslow is on the Montana side and the new trail seems to join the CDT here.

At mile 8.4 (2.2 miles west of Salamander Lake), the CDT intersects Jones Creek Trail 1835. The Jones Creek trail leads into Montana, so don't be misled into following it. The Divide turns south and descends slightly to a saddle above an abandoned coal mine.

SOUTHBOUND HIKERS: Your turn east is not marked. Southbound hikers need to turn east where the tread disappears in a meadow and a CD symbol and a blaze are just visible on a distant, dead tree.

Beyond the defunct coal mine and the various pack trail intersections, northbound hikers climb about 700 feet over 1.8 miles of trail, enough to get you warmed up for the trials ahead. At mile 10.8 a set of steep switchbacks climbs 400 feet in 0.3 mile. Whew! This is where mountain bikers wish they were riding the other way. These north-facing switchbacks hold snow well into July. Support Crew quote: "These switchbacks will be character-building for mountain bikers."

At the top of the climb, several trails meet at a signed intersection. The CD symbols have been weather-sanded but are still readable. The trail turns west again and traverses below the crest of the Divide. Climb about 30 feet to the ridgeline for excellent views of the Centennial Valley and the distant peaks of the Lee Metcalf Wilderness in Montana.

At Rock Spring (mile 12.9) a watering trough is signed with the spring's name, and the CDT is identified with a wooden symbol on a tree. Rock Spring barely runs enough water for filtering. The CDT intersects an old pack trail here that is marked with ancient blazes. The spring is below the Divide, on the Idaho side. As the CDT continues west, the trail stays below the crest for 2 miles, shortcutting the higher terrain to the north.

West of Rock Spring, the CDT enters a broad, shallow basin, the concave face of Big Table Mountain. The route is signed with brown carsonite posts marked with a single white arrow, and with carsonite posts that have no markings. This is where we signed the trail with brown-on-white CD symbols the Dubois rangers had given us. There is no tread in the meadow, so the posts are necessary.

Cross the headwaters of East Camas Creek (mile 14.1) near a spring at the meadow's low point. This is a good water source. West of the spring, the carsonite posts are signed with CDT symbols. Follow them up slope to the Divide and an intersection with Table Mountain Pack Trail.

SOUTHBOUND HIKERS: You'll have a difficult time knowing when to leave the pack trail unless you spot the line of thin, brown posts leading out across the meadow. Naturally, the divergence from the pack trail is not signed. Where you leave the pack trail there is no visible tread. Watch the mileage and terrain on the topo so that you know when to turn east into the Big Table Mountain meadow. Where the trail goes through ribbons of forest, the carsonite posts end and there are no blazes on the trees. Stay on the same contour line from your last carsonite post and you will encounter another one once you are through the trees.

Visible tread reappears at the intersection with the pack trail. Northbound hikers make a right-hand turn to follow the pack trail northwest. This section of trail is mostly through forested areas, with a few breaks that offer long-distance views of the Beaverhead and Tendoy mountain ranges. The trail switchbacks down a boulder field at mile 16.3 and continues its descent to Pete Creek Divide. The black, glassy rocks in and near the trail are obsidian, magma that cooled so fast it didn't have time to crystallize. This volcanic glass is essentially frozen liquid. Native Americans used it to make tools, making use of the conchoidal fractures to create sharp edges.

The "Divide" in Pete Creek Divide refers to the terrain that separates "Peet Creek" on the Montana side from "Pete Creek" on the Idaho side, but it is also a saddle on the Continental Divide. A blue and white CDT sign and various Forest Service signs, including one for Table Mountain Trail, festoon the saddle.

Water is available in Pete Creek, about a hundred yards south of the Divide. This is a good spot to camp. Pete Creek Divide is accessible from the Montana side via the Price Peet Road, a 2WD gravel road that comes up from the Centennial Valley.

Enter the trees west of Pete Creek Divide on visible but not well-traveled tread, where a wooden CD symbol marks the route. Follow a fenceline, blazed trees, and occasional signs to a ridge overlooking Little Table Mountain, another uplift with a dished face. Deadfall in the trail and a steep ascent will create difficulties for mountain bikers. To mark a turn in the trail near an iron ID/MT border marker, there are newer CD signs. Northbound hikers turn south and steeply uphill.

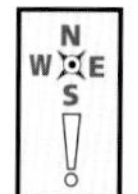

On the west edge of Little Table Mountain, newer CD signs and new blazes lead hikers to what used to be a gate in what used to be a fence. Make a sharp left, a U-turn, at the gate and parallel the fenceline again, going back the way you just came. We couldn't believe the trail or the signs, but that is the way it is. You could carry on a quiet conversation with hikers approaching the gate you just passed through. Although the fence is no longer a fence and the gate is a ghost of its former self, like actors in an absurdist comedy, CDT trekkers must proceed to the gate before they cross the fenceline.

Follow wooden CD symbols and the posts of a past fence to curve around the southern edge of Little Table Mountain. The fenceline is on the Divide and is a lovely, scenic walk once you have accepted your fate in the comedy with no audience.

At mile 21.9 (3.4 miles west of Pete Creek Divide), the path along the fence meets a 4WD road. Descend with the fence and the road to a saddle above the West Fork of Camas Creek. From the saddle, a well-used 4WD road is visible as it switchbacks uphill. This is Long Creek Road 020 and it will take you all the way to Interstate 15.

The road parallels Long Creek and crosses its tributaries several times. Filter drinking water before you descend into cow country. The Long Creek Valley is heavily grazed. Water can also be filtered from Berry Creek near the Modoc Access underpass on I-15.

Interstate 15, the ending point for this segment, is reached at mile 30.7.

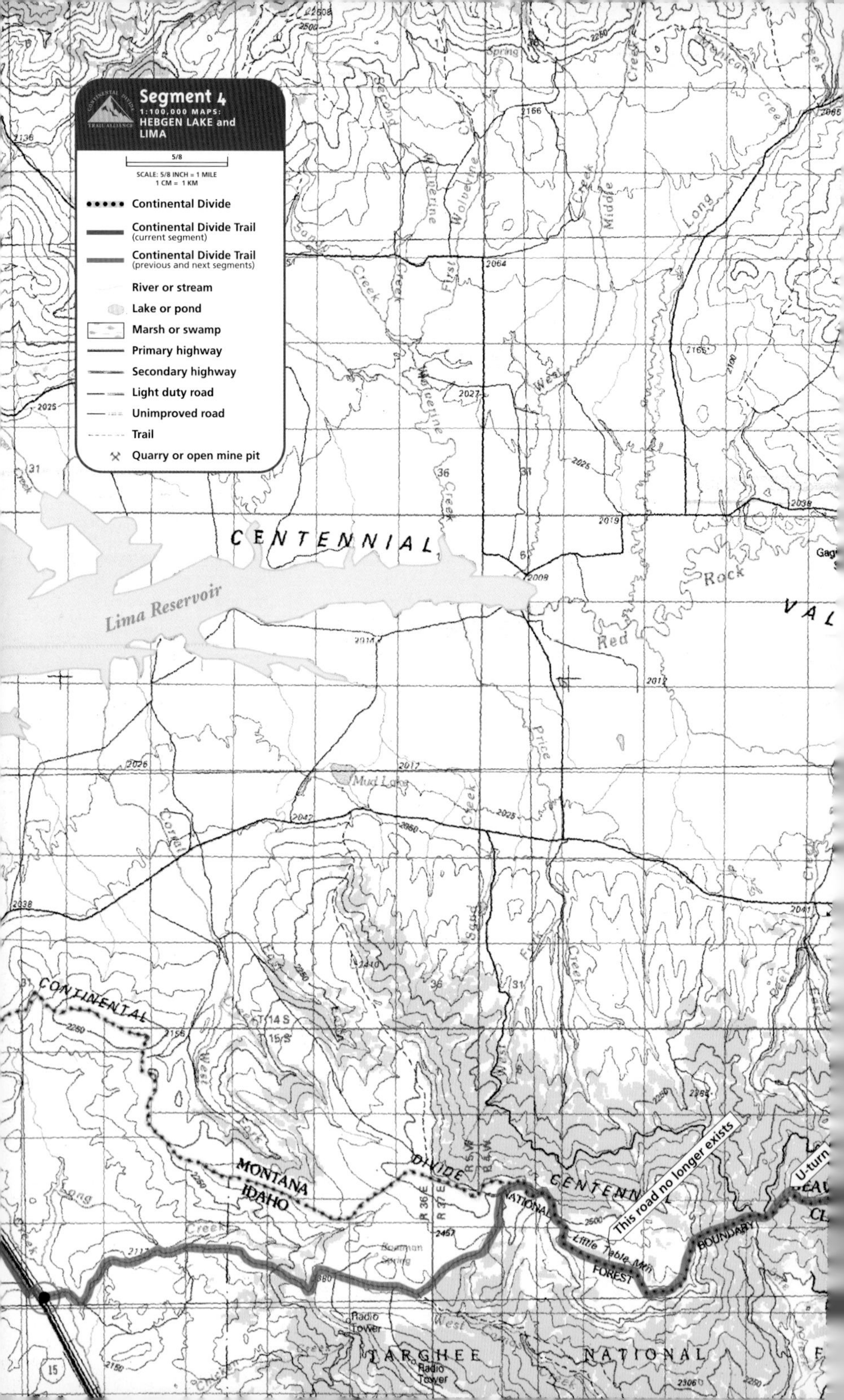

Segment 4
1:100,000 MAPS:
HEBGEN LAKE and
LIMA
5/8
SCALE: 5/8 INCH = 1 MILE
1 CM = 1 KM
Continental Divide
Continental Divide Trail
(current segment)
Continental Divide Trail
(previous and next segments)
River or stream
Lake or pond
Marsh or swamp
Primary highway
Secondary highway
Light duty road
Unimproved road
Trail
Quarry or open mine pit
CENTENNIAL
Lima Reservoir
VAL
Rock
Red
Mud Lake
Price
Creek
Long
Middle
Wolverine
First
CONTINENTAL
MONTANA
IDAHO
DIVIDE
CENTENNIAL
This road no longer exists
U-turn
Little Table Mtn
NATIONAL
FOREST
BOUNDARY
Radio Tower
TARGHEE
NATIONAL
Bowman Spring
T 14 S
15 S
R 36 E
R 37 E
15

USGS: LIMA
USGS: HEBGEN LAKE
CENTENNIAL
Lower Red Rock Lake
Antelope Peak
Lonsy Springs
Landing Strip
Water Tank
Coyote Spring
Bruhdage Creek
Rock
River
Murphy Creek
Winslow
Jones
Tipton Creek
Bear Creek
Curry Creek
Humphry
Baldy Mountain
Slide Mountain
EASTERN
CONTINENTAL
WILDERNESS
BOUNDARY
REFUGE AND WILDERNESS BO
BEAVERHEAD CO
CLARK CO
Salamander Lake
NATIONAL FOREST BDY
Coon Creek
Cottonwood
Burnt Canyon
East Camas Creek
Hancock Lake
Alden Lake
Little Creek
Table Mountain
Trail under construction, route is approximate
4WD
PACK

Segment 5

Interstate 15 to Bannack (Medicine Lodge) Pass: Beaverhead Mountains of the Bitterroot Range

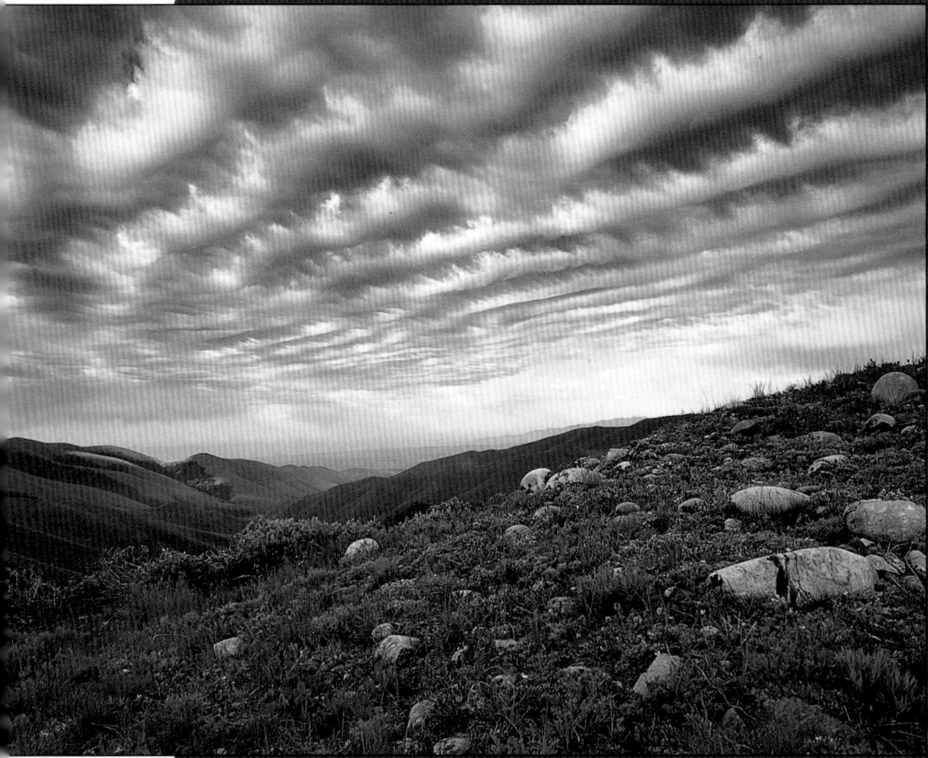

Eagles and hawks frequent the area around this ridge in the Beaverhead Mountains, about 10 miles west of Monida Pass.

42.0 miles
Difficulty: Moderate

Segment 5 **Total Elevation Gain:** 5,951 feet
From Wyoming 130.3 miles
To Canada 850.4 miles

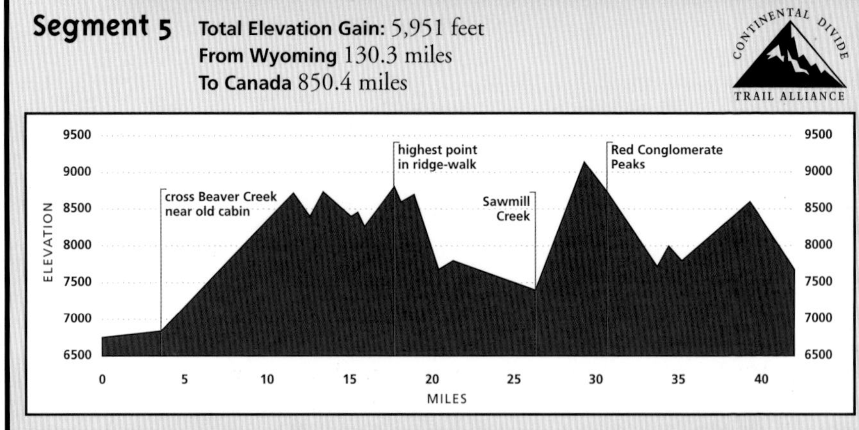

TRAIL OVERVIEW In this segment, the Continental Divide Trail enters the Beaverhead Mountains of the Bitterroot Range. From Monida Pass in the south to Chief Joseph Pass in the north, the CDT follows the Beaverhead Mountains, first southwest, then west, and finally, north. The name "Beaver's Head" appeared in Lewis and Clark's journals in 1805, when their guide, Sacajawea, identified a rock formation on what is today the Beaverhead River.

The Continental Divide Trail climbs from Interstate 15, south of Monida Pass, to the crest of the Divide in the southern Beaverheads. Lightning and dehydration are the biggest dangers on a 12-mile ridge-walk that follows the Montana/Idaho border.

Rough terrain forces the trail from the Divide at mile 19, and hikers enjoy the meadows and ample water sources below "The Thumb," Knob Mountain, and the Red Conglomerate Peaks. Route-finding is a challenge in the grassy meadows. Hikers should not attempt this segment without topographical maps. The trail appears accurately on the Beaverhead Forest Service map, but not on the topos. Hikers must combine both maps to find the trail on the ground.

We saw black bear sign, but no bears, in the Little Sheep Creek basin. Hikers should review the bear avoidance techniques in "Safety Concerns."

This segment ends at Bannack Pass, named for the Indians who used the passes across the Continental Divide to access buffalo hunting grounds in what is now Montana. On some maps, this pass is named "Medicine Lodge Pass" in reference to Native American sweat houses that used to exist along the creek on the Idaho side of the pass. The similarly named "Bannock Pass" (more than 50 miles to the north) is also crossed by the CDT. Major map-induced confusion can result if hikers fail to distinguish between Bannack and Bannock.

Water can be filtered from Berry Creek near the Modoc Access underpass on I-15; where the road crosses Beaver Creek at mile 3.6; and also at Horse Creek where the trail leaves the road and climbs to the Divide. Once you are on the crest of the Divide, water becomes a serious problem, with about 12 miles of dry ridge to walk before Shineberger Creek. Water is plentiful for the remainder of the journey.

MOUNTAIN BIKE NOTES: This segment of the trail is open to mountain bikes. The first 7 miles are easy. Tortuous trail prevails for most of the middle section. An intersection with a 4WD track improves biking conditions 5 miles east of Bannack Pass. Frankly, I wouldn't ride the middle section, but I have seen a few riders who could manage it. You will end up carrying your bike quite a bit.

LAND ADMINISTRATORS (SEE APPENDIX A)

Targhee National Forest, Dubois Ranger District
Beaverhead/Deerlodge National Forest, Dillon Ranger District

MAPS

USGS QUADRANGLES: Monida, Paul Reservoir, Tepee Draw, Snowline, Lima Peaks, Edie Creek, Fritz Peak, Gallagher Gulch, Deadman Lake

USFS: Targhee National Forest, Dubois; Beaverhead National Forest

BEGINNING ACCESS POINT

Smooth road to Trailhead

EXIT 190, INTERSTATE 15: The CDT does not cross I-15 at Monida Pass. Contrary to past descriptions of the trail, this segment begins 3.7 miles south of Monida Pass. Exit I-15, 6 miles south of Monida Pass, near Humphrey, and proceed north from there to intercept the CDNST. On the Idaho side of the Continental Divide, take exit 190 and go north on a paved but rough frontage road to Humphrey. Humphrey has seen better days, and now offers no services whatsoever. It is 3.6 miles from exit 190 to the Modoc Access (an underpass) on the Continental Divide Trail.

ENDING ACCESS POINT

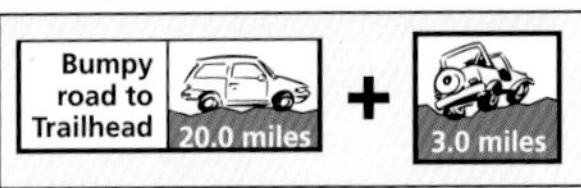

BANNACK PASS: Exit I-15 at either Lima or Dell, Montana. Take Forest Service Road 257, the Big Sheep Creek Road, to the intersection with Forest Service Road 951. Road 951 goes to Bannack Pass. This road is impassable when wet and 4WD is recommended for the last 3 miles.

TRAIL DESCRIPTION This segment begins where the Continental Divide Trail crosses Interstate 15 at an underpass signed as "Modoc Access." A gravel frontage road (005, West Modoc) parallels the interstate for 2.4 miles, leading CDT hikers northwest. Although this is road-walking, it is relatively pleasant because there is almost no traffic, and there are excellent long-distance views of the peaks of the Divide to the southwest. We were here several times and saw antelope grazing in the foothills every time. Grasses and sagebrush dominate this relatively dry area.

At mile 2.4, follow the road as it turns left (southwest). The quality of this road diminishes as it gets farther from the freeway, but it is still suitable for 2WD vehicles in good weather. Shortly after the southwest turn, the road crosses Beaver Creek near a picturesque old cabin. At mile 5.5, another postcard-pretty cabin and barn sit in a grassy meadow on Modoc Creek, south of the road. Hikers will have been climbing steadily, but gently, since leaving the interstate. The pretty cabin is at 7,000 feet elevation.

The first CD sign is on the north side of the road at mile 6.6. This sign is off the road just enough to be misleading. Do not leave the road yet. Signs at mile 7 note the entrance to the Targhee National Forest. Cross a cattle guard here and continue south on the road for about 0.5 mile to Horse Creek.

Make sure you get water at Horse Creek. It is a long, dry walk on the crest of the Divide to the next water source at Shineberger Creek, 12 miles to the west.

Horse Creek is signed—stop at the sign and look west/northwest, toward the Divide, to see a CD symbol on a post. The CD sign is hard to find because it tends to blend in with a fence that also runs along the Divide. A very rough, dim two-track leads steeply up to the Divide. Follow the two-track for 0.3 mile to the fenceline, then turn southwesterly on the crest of the Divide.

The treeless spine of the Divide was so windy when we hiked it that we had a difficult time making any forward progress. The winds also added to the dehydration factor. CDT signs are few and far between, but there is a border fence to follow.

Hikers follow the border fence for many miles in open country, along a ridge decorated with rocks, grass, and sagebrush. Posts with wooden CD placards are placed about every half-mile along the route. The rolling nature of the Divide and the distance between posts prevents hikers from seeing from one post to the next in many places. Binoculars are a good idea for this section. We tried to escape the wind by hiking on the lee side of the Divide, but got lured onto a spur ridge. Stay high enough that you can see the fence line and/or the CD posts.

At about 10 miles, there is a CD post in a rock cairn and a "closed to motorized vehicles except for snowmobiles in winter months" sign. This sign is near a high point of 8,601 feet in elevation. Hikers will have climbed 1,300 feet since leaving the road at Horse Creek and almost 2,000 feet since leaving the interstate. Most of the land below you on the Montana side is private land owned by various cattle companies, including the Snowline Cattle Company. The Snowline USGS topo map is named after the Snowline Ranch.

Occasional survey markers of the iron-pipe variety delineate the Idaho/Montana border, and some of them have longitude/latitude information on their caps. Look for one of these markers at mile 11.6, where the Divide turns northwest (a right turn for Northbound hikers). The frequency of these survey markers is reflected on the topographical map, which gives precise elevation readouts along the Divide, though the map is incorrect where it shows an elevation of 8,141 feet; it should be 8,741 feet.

From a distance, this ridge-walk looks deceptively easy, but a quick look at the elevation chart will give you a true picture. There a lot of ups and downs and some of them are steep, with no switchbacks to help you out. Where the ridge is wider, it's easier to hike your own, self-invented switchbacks up the steep parts.

You can obtain water along the ridge at mile 15.1 (7.5 miles west of Horse Creek). Leave the trail on the 8,400 contour line and hike downhill to a spring that feeds a tributary of Middle Creek at 8,120 feet. This is on the Montana side of the Divide, and the spring is marked on the topographical map. Buildings that are part of the Middle Creek Cow Camp can be seen in the valley below, and this is one of the few spots where pine trees come up almost to the Divide.

Hikers reach the highest point in the ridge-walk at mile 17.7 (about 10 miles west of Horse Creek), above the Left Fork of Middle Creek on the Idaho side (same name, different creek). From this point, it is only 1.2 miles to the spot where the trail leaves the Divide to descend to Shineberger Creek. Watch closely for a line of three posts (no signs, just the posts) placed close together. These posts mark the departure from the Divide. There is no visible tread here. Northbound hikers have been hiking generally west on the Divide, but turn north here.

The trail comes down off the Divide and follows a low, rolling, spur ridge that is heavily grazed by cattle. Descend to Shineberger Creek, cross to the west side of the creek and look for the trail. The trail tread is not very clear where it departs the creek drainage and heads uphill, still going generally north and climbing parallel to the creek. At the top of a short climb, there is a CD sign, wooden and faded.

Follow a fenceline again as it twists and turns above and west of Shineberger Creek. The trail looks like a cow path. When you come to another CD symbol on a

SUPPLIES, SERVICES, AND ACCOMMODATIONS

LIMA, MT, is north of the trailhead, on Interstate 15. There are no towns near the beginning access point. Lima is small, but has most services. Monida is 3.7 miles north of the trail on I-15, but has only a pay phone and no other services. Spencer is only 12 miles south on I-15, but is tiny with limited services.

Distance from Trail: 20 miles

Zip Code: 59739

Bank:	None	
Bus:	Greyhound Bus Lines, Butte, MT	406-723-3287
Camping:	See Sportsman Inn	
Dining:	Jan's Cafe and Cabins, 108 Bailey	406-276-3484
Gear:	Ralph's Exxon, hunting/fishing, maps, P.O. Box AC	406-276-3431
	Big Sky Sports & Services, 27 S. Harrison Street	406-276-3637
Groceries:	Mountain View Mercantile, 12 N. Harrison Street	406-276-3281
Information:	See Ralph's Exxon	
Laundry:	See Sportsman Inn	
Lodging:	Sportsman Inn, P.O. Box 93	406-276-3535
	Jan's Cabins, 108 Bailey	406-276-3484
Medical:	None	
Outfitters:	Lakeview Guest Ranch & Guide, Monida HC	406-276-3300
	Big Sky Sports & Services, 27 S. Harrison Street	406-276-3637
Post Office:	U.S. Post Office, P.O. Box 9998, Lima, MT 59739-9998	406-276-3515
Showers:	See Sportsman Inn, $5	

post, you stop following the fence above the creek, and as the directional arrow on the CD sign indicates, go through the gate and head west. There is no visible tread and no tree blazes are within sight. Hike straight across the small meadow and look for a blazed tree on the other side.

This turn from north to west is near a "TH" marker on the Forest Service map, indicating a trailhead where the Shineberger Creek road ends. However, CDT trekkers never see a trailhead or the road, because the trail turns west before the point shown on the map.

As it heads west toward Little Beaver Creek and beyond, the trail alternately appears and disappears. Tread can be seen in stands of aspen trees and conifers, but disappears in every grassy meadow. Most of the time, hikers continue across meadows in a more-or-less straight line to find the trail again where it enters trees—but in some cases, the route does turn in a meadow. Where you are supposed to turn, but there are no markers of any kind, you must search the far perimeter of the meadow for clues such as visible tread, blazed trees, or rare CD signs on posts. Beware of mistaking elk-antler rubbings for blazes. A man-made blaze should resemble a lowercase "i."

A topographical map is essential here. Conundrums such as CD posts with two directional arrows that give conflicting information will have you scratching your head. The topo map, combined with the Forest Service map, will show you generally where you need to go. Consider the CD posts to be only assurances that you are still on the correct route. Don't trust the directional arrows.

Ford Little Beaver Creek at mile 22.8. There is good camping in grassy areas near the creek. A CD post and sign on the west bank points northwest, but the trail is to the southwest. Climb the rise on the west bank, where a faint two-track can be seen, and look southwest to see the next CD post. That post southwest of the creek crossing is equally confusing in terms of directional arrows, but head west from the post, keeping the Lima Peaks off your right shoulder, and you'll be on the right track. It is helpful to stay near the 7,600 contour line on the topo map.

As you approach Sawmill Creek, the trail intersects a 4WD road. A CD post/sign directs hikers onto the road. This road does not appear on the FS map. East of Sawmill Creek, on a rise near a tributary stream, there is an excellent camping spot with a view to the south of "The Thumb." Coyotes serenaded us with a long melody of howls when we camped there.

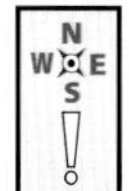

At the Sawmill Creek crossing, mile 26.3, the branded directional arrows on a CD post conflict with the arrows on the CD signs attached to the post. The combination of signs and post-arrows indicates four different directions for the Continental Divide Trail, which must set some kind of record for misdirection on a single post. Southbound hikers turn east at this puzzle. Northbound hikers turn left (southwest). Cross a tributary stream and then cross Sawmill Creek.

The CDT joins a better trail on the west side of Sawmill Creek. Look for a suite of signs: "Closed to Motorized Vehicles, Medicine Lodge Pass 14 miles, Buffalo Spring 9 miles." And, lo, a blue and white CD sign that points in the right direction. This trailhead appears on the Forest Service map.

From Sawmill Creek, the CDT climbs steadily for about 3 miles to reach a high saddle at elevation 9,145 feet (mile 29.3 for this segment). On the way up to the saddle, there are two more CD signs on posts. From the saddle, the trail descends to a long ridge below the Red Conglomerate Peaks. Trail tread is visible, especially in the trees. Take advantage of one stream crossing west of the saddle. The trail intersects some old mining roads (not on the maps) near this saddle, and there are dilapidated cabins and other signs of abandoned mines.

The Red Conglomerate Peaks are identified by a sign at mile 30.7, where the trail is, briefly, back on the physical Divide. At this sign, visible tread disappears and it becomes difficult to tell where to go next. Look downhill, in the meadow below the sign, for a single tree that is blazed. There are three CD posts in the meadow, but they are so far away that you can only see them with binoculars. Leave the Divide and hike down into the meadow.

A rock cairn and a blazed tree mark where the trail crosses a gully in the meadow northwest of the Red Conglomerate Peaks. When we were there, the entire meadow had been pulverized by cattle, and potential water sources churned into mud holes. The enormous, bare pile of rocks to the north is Garfield Mountain, a 10,961-foot peak that dominates the northern horizon along the CDT for 5 miles beginning at the saddle east of the Red Conglomerates.

There is better camping and cleaner water 2 miles farther, at mile 32.7, where the trail enters a stand of spruce trees and crosses a tributary of Little Sheep Creek. The CDT intercepts a 4WD track in the trees southwest of Garfield Mountain. Ignore other jeep tracks that enter from the north and follow the jeep track that continues west.

Cross another tributary of Little Sheep Creek at mile 33.7 and climb a short hill to a clearing. In the clearing, there is a classic "They went that-a-way" CD sign, with directional arrows pointing in conflicting directions, none of which are correct. Even though this sign points the wrong way, hikers can just see the next CD posts if they look east/west. Hike to the next post.

Bear scat, prints, and claw marks were numerous from mile 33 to Buffalo Spring. In this area, there are black bears, not grizzlies. As one might expect, there are also lots of elk in this forested and amply-watered area south of Little Sheep Creek. The CDT looks like a game trail here—no human sign, but mass quantities of animal sign. The trail is blazed, but not signed.

The trail climbs steeply to the ridge above Buffalo Spring. A cattle trough is fed by the springs here, and CD signs mark the trail. CD posts that are well within sight of each other mark the route where it heads west, parallel to, but not on, a jeep track.

At 1.7 miles (mile 38.3 for this segment) west of Buffalo Spring, the trail rejoins both the jeep track and the Divide. About 3 miles west of Buffalo Spring, the road passes a large quarry whose white calcium carbonate stones are impressively austere, but beautiful. There are several 4WD tracks that intersect the main road. Ignore the side routes, staying on the well-used mining road as it switchbacks down a steep section near the quarry. This is Road 8265 on the Forest Service map, and is suitable only for 4WD vehicles.

The CDT diverges briefly from Road 8265 to contour around steep places, but it always comes back to the road. The posts marking these divergences are easier for Northbound hikers to see. Bannack Pass is reached at mile 42 (5.4 miles west of Buffalo Spring). The pass is signed as "Bannack," the Montana/Idaho border, and the Continental Divide Trail. We crossed this pass on June 23, with rain obscuring the valleys and light snow coating our gear.

Spring flowers on the Divide in the Beaverhead Mountains of the Bitterroot Range

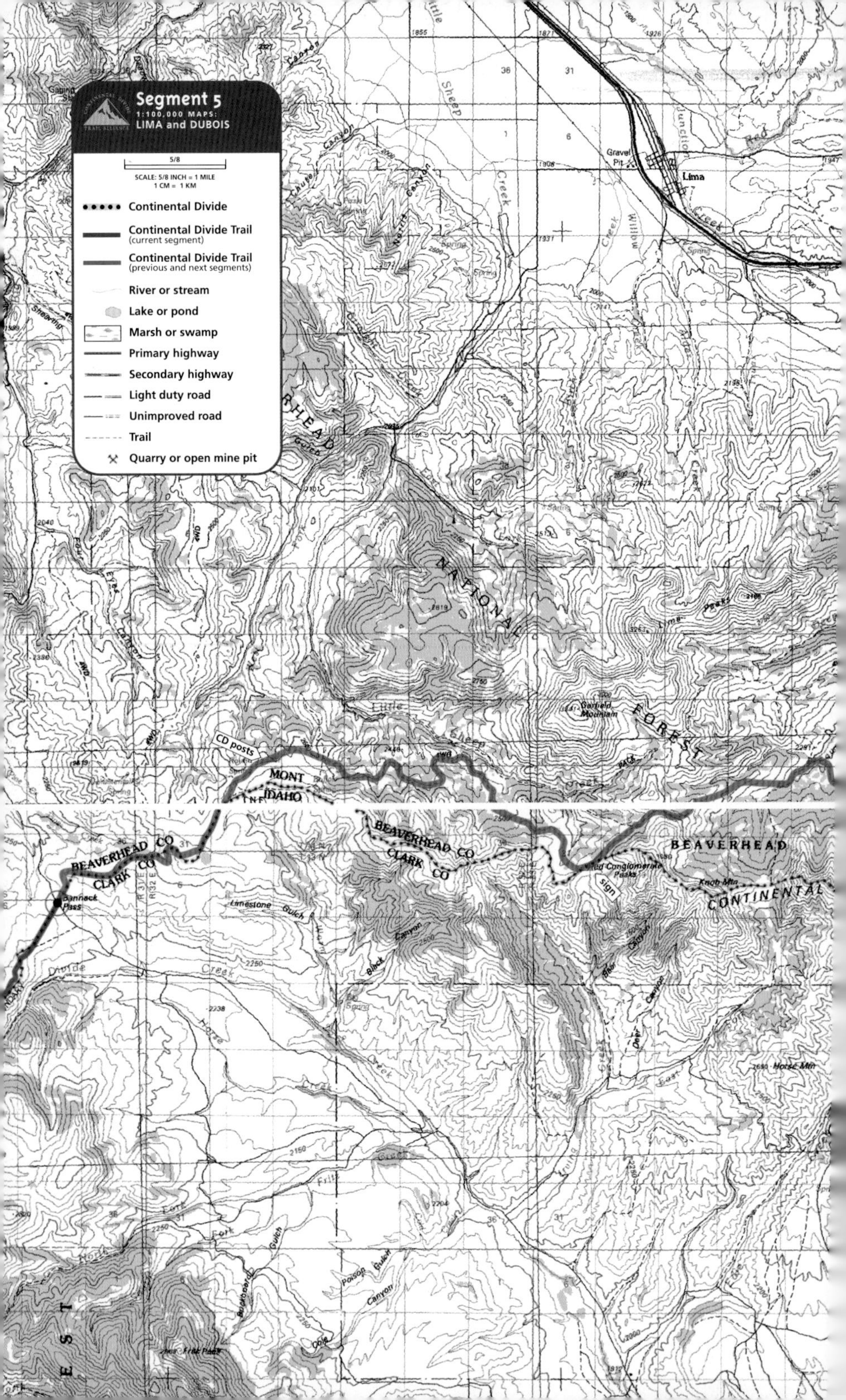

Segment 5
1:100,000 MAPS:
LIMA and DUBOIS
SCALE: 5/8 INCH = 1 MILE
1 CM = 1 KM
Continental Divide
Continental Divide Trail
(current segment)
Continental Divide Trail
(previous and next segments)
River or stream
Lake or pond
Marsh or swamp
Primary highway
Secondary highway
Light duty road
Unimproved road
Trail
Quarry or open mine pit
Lima
Gravel Pit
CD posts
MONT
IDAHO
BEAVERHEAD CO
CLARK CO
Bannack Pass
sign
Knob Mtn
CONTINENTAL
Garfield Mountain
NATIONAL
FOREST
Horse Mtn
Limestone Gulch
Black Canyon
Poison Gulch

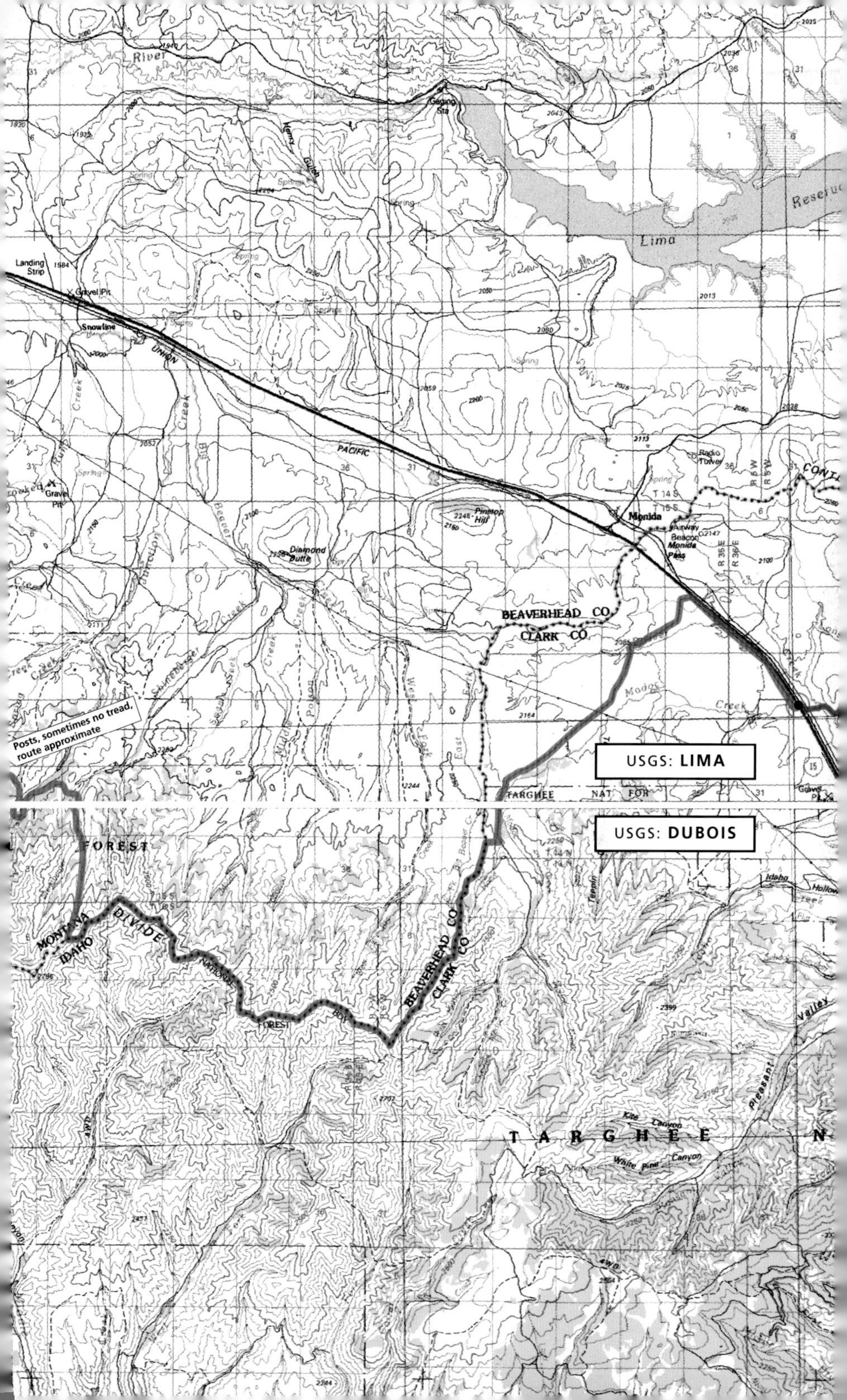

USGS: LIMA
USGS: DUBOIS
Posts, sometimes no tread, route approximate
Lima
Monida
Monida Pass
Snowline
Landing Strip
Gravel Pit
Diamond Butte
Pinetop Hill
Radio Tower
Airway Beacon
UNION
PACIFIC
BEAVERHEAD CO
CLARK CO
MONTANA
IDAHO
DIVIDE
NATIONAL
FOREST
TARGHEE NAT FOR
T A R G H E E
Kite Canyon
White Pine Canyon
Pleasant Valley

Segment 6

Bannack (Medicine Lodge) Pass to Morrison Lake: Beaverhead Mountains of the Bitterroot Range

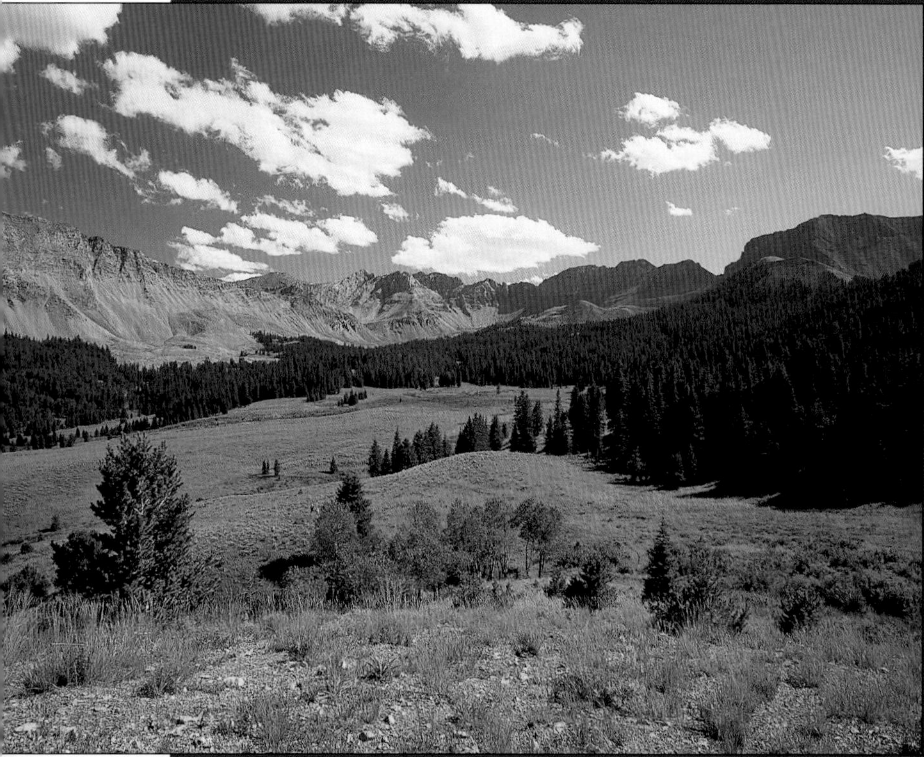

The CDT shortcuts these high peaks in the Beaverhead Mountains, crossing Nicholia Creek in the lower meadows.

32.8 miles
Difficulty: Strenuous

Segment 6 **Total Elevation Gain:** 5,179 feet
From Wyoming 172.3 miles
To Canada 808.4 miles

CONTINENTAL DIVIDE TRAIL ALLIANCE

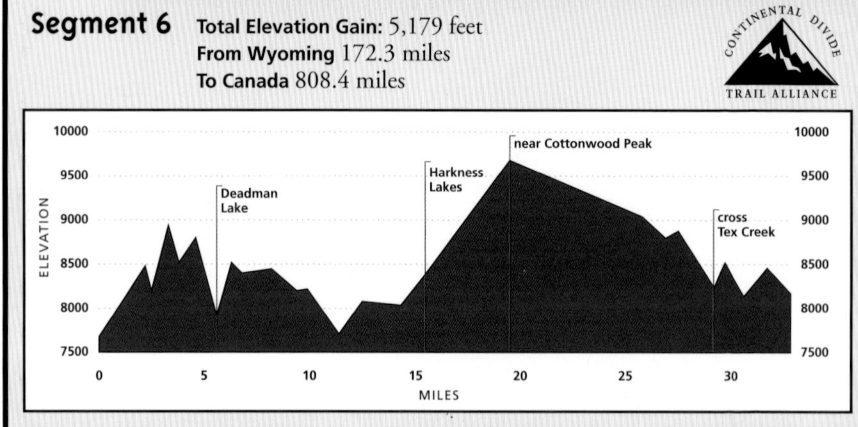

TRAIL OVERVIEW In this segment, the Continental Divide Trail ends its westward trek and follows the northward bend of the Beaverhead Mountains on the Montana/Idaho border. About 15 miles of this segment cross lower terrain below the Divide where 10,000- and 11,000-foot peaks force the trail down to 8,000 feet on the Montana side. The trail dips below the Divide at Deadman Lake and returns to the crest north of Cottonwood Peak.

This segment earns its strenuous rating with a steep, 1,642-foot climb from the head of Rock Creek to the Divide near the head of Meadow Creek. The saddle at the head of Meadow Creek is like a window on a world of mountains. Over the shoulders of the ubiquitous Lemhi Range, Idaho's Lost River Range can be seen, including the highest peak in Idaho, Borah Peak, whose 12,655-foot summit is more than 45 miles away as the crow flies (or in this case, as the eagles fly). The Montana side of the window is filled with the southern Beaverhead, Centennial, and Tendoy Mountains.

In contrast, the traverse across lower terrain has hikers fording more than half-a-dozen creeks, all of them full of trout. A different view of the Switzerland-like peaks of the Divide is offered from the creek basins. Near the head of Henderson Gulch, and above Nicholia Creek, there are spectacular views to the south and to the northwest. Scott Peak, the highest peak in the southern Beaverheads, rises 11,394 feet and its neighbor, Italian Peak, is 10,996 feet of snow-capped beauty. Cottonwood Peak and Eighteenmile Peak, also responsible for the detour off the Divide, are 11,024 and 11,141 feet, respectively.

This trek is more pleasant in June than later in the season when hikers are likely to encounter extensive cattle grazing. Mosquitoes and flies are also more plentiful as the season progresses. Cold nights reduce the insects in late August. Our wildlife sightings included two silver foxes, many deer and antelope, large herds of elk, coyotes, eagles, hawks, and schools of trout.

Don't confuse the beginning point of this section, Bannack Pass, with the similarly named Bannock Pass to the north. There is no water for the first 5.6 miles, but after that, water is plentiful in frequent stream crossings.

MOUNTAIN BIKE NOTES: Mountain bikers will have a relatively easy time from Bannack Pass to the saddle above Deadman Lake. The trail to Deadman Lake is ridable but steep. A combination of new trail tread, grassy two-tracks, and 4WD roads requires some technical riding from Deadman Lake to Rock Creek. Bikes will have to be carried across stream fords. The trail from the head of Rock Creek to the Divide above Meadow Creek is not ridable. If you could somehow get there, it would be possible to ride along the Divide north to Coyote Creek. From Coyote Creek to Morrison Lake, the trail is relatively easy to ride, with only three difficult creek crossings.

LAND ADMINISTRATORS **(SEE APPENDIX A)**

Targhee National Forest, Dubois Ranger District
Beaverhead/Deerlodge National Forest, Dillon Ranger District

MAPS

USGS QUADRANGLES: Deadman Lake, Eighteen Mile Peak, Cottonwood Creek, Morrison Lake

USFS: Beaverhead National Forest

BEGINNING ACCESS POINT

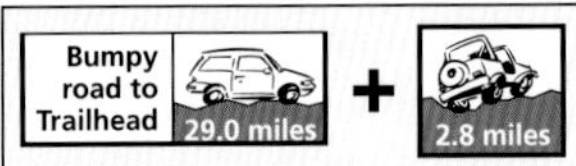

BANNACK PASS (also known as Medicine Lodge Pass) in the Southern Beaverhead Mountains: Exit from Interstate 15 at Lima or Dell, Montana. Take Big Sheep Creek Road (257) to Road 951, then go southeast on 951 to the pass. Road 951 is 2WD in good weather, but rough—4WD is recommended. There is good camping on BLM land near Deadman Creek.

ENDING ACCESS POINT

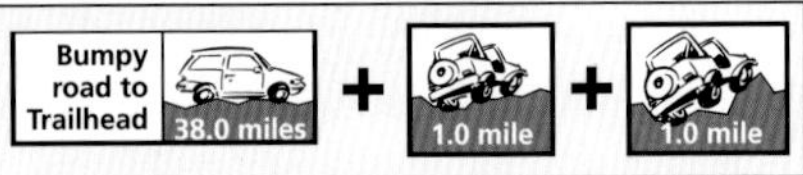

MORRISON LAKE, on the eastern side of the Continental Divide in the Beaverhead Mountains: A rough 4WD road (3920) leads from the lake to an intersection with gravel road 257, Big Sheep Creek Road. Morrison Lake is 40 miles from Lima, MT on I-15.

SUPPLIES, SERVICES, AND ACCOMMODATIONS

LIMA, MT, on Interstate 15 offers most services. (See Segment 5.) There are no supplies or services near the trailhead.

Distance from Trail: 31.8 miles from Bannack Pass

TRAIL DESCRIPTION

There are no water sources and no camping spots at Bannack Pass. Deadman Lake at mile 5.6 is the first water source. The Continental Divide Trail heads southwest from Bannack Pass on a rough 4WD track that parallels a fenceline. At mile 0.8, open a gate in the cattle fence to continue. Be sure to close the rancher's gate, though it is hard to close. At 1.1 miles, hikers see their first CD signs, two wooden placards on posts. At 2.2 miles, on a higher knoll, the trail leaves the fenceline.

From the knoll at mile 2.2, look back to the east for a novel view of the Red Conglomerate Peaks. The peaks look more intimidating from a distance, which is a good opportunity to exercise your bragging rights.

Continue on a 4WD two-track to a saddle at mile 2.5. Look for a post with a wooden CD symbol in the saddle. This is where the trail leaves the Divide. Northbound hikers make a 90° turn at the post, heading to Deadman Lake.

It is 5.8 miles from Bannack Pass to Deadman Lake. For both northbound and southbound hikers, the descent and climb to Deadman Lake is long and steep. We joked that the lake probably got its name from hikers who arrived at the lake but couldn't climb back out again. The small lake makes a good camping spot.

Several 4WD roads and pack trails meet at or near the lake. Northbound hikers cross the outlet stream and climb northwesterly, up the steep bank. A rough,

4WD track crosses several seeps and streams on its way to the ridge above the lake. The 4WD track becomes a road above the lake. Northbound hikers bear left at all jeep-track intersections until you come to new tread and a CD sign.

The CDT diverges from the road and heads directly west at mile 6.8. New tread, new CD signs on posts, and rock cairns lead across a hillside covered with sagebrush and grass. On the Forest Service and topo maps, this area is called "Henderson Gulch." Another stream crossing and a short climb bring the trail to the ridge above Nicholia Creek. The trail turns southwest, descending gradually along a sagebrush-covered hill to the Nicholia Creek basin.

The Continental Divide Trail goes toward, but not to, Scott Peak and Italian Peak, the two highest summits to the south. The trail crosses Nicholia Creek about 4.5 miles northwest of Scott Peak, cutting off a southern loop in the Continental Divide. The creek basin is full of springs and marshes, and the deep green color of the grasses, willows, and shrubs contrasts sharply with the sagebrush on the surrounding hills. There were so many trout swimming in the creek that we stopped to watch them.

After crossing to the west side of Nicholia Creek at mile 9.5, the CDT makes a U-turn and follows a pack trail northwesterly. Signs on the pack trail say, "Medicine Lodge Pass 9 miles, Deadman Lake 4 miles" (it is actually 9.5 miles to Bannack/Medicine Lodge Pass). Signs on this trail also confirm that you are on 91, the Nicholia Creek/Deadman Lake Trail.

At mile 11.4 from Bannack Pass, hikers reach the trailhead for 91 and an intersection with Road 657. From the trailhead and parking spot on Road 657, the CDT follows 657 for 0.6 mile to another signed intersection, "Deadman Lake 7 miles, Medicine Lodge Pass 12 miles, Harkness Lakes 3.5 miles, Morrison Lake 18.5 miles, Tendoy Creek Trail 148, Bear Creek."

CDT trekkers turn southwest to follow Tendoy Creek Trail 148, crossing the creek at mile 12.5, where a CD placard on a post marks the route. Shortly after crossing Tendoy Creek, the trail crosses 4WD Road 3928, which is not signed on the ground, but is numbered on the Beaverhead FS map. A rock cairn shows the continuation of the CDT.

Bear Creek, at mile 14.3, offers yet another opportunity for fishermen to try their luck. From Deadman Lake to Morrison Lake, there are more fishing streams in close proximity than anywhere else along the Montana/Idaho Divide.

On the north side of Bear Creek, at the top of the hill, there is a CD sign on a post at mile 14.5. At this post, turn west to hike toward Harkness Lakes. The trail continues to look like a rough 4WD road. One mile of fairly level walking brings hikers to Harkness Lakes at mile 15.5. The "lakes" look like a smattering of ponds thrown onto the landscape.

From Harkness Lakes on Cottonwood Creek, the trail trends northwesterly toward the head of Rock Creek. A short series of switchbacks climbs the steeper terrain above Rock Creek as the trail makes its way toward the Divide. To the southwest, 11,024-foot Cottonwood Peak forces the trail to ascend up the steep ravine that holds the headwaters of Rock Creek.

Watch carefully for the route of the CDT where the trail crosses Rock Creek. A trail on the left (west) has more visible tread, but the CDT climbs steeply via switchbacks on the northwest bank at mile 17.3. When we hiked the trail, the switchbacks had not been cut, but were marked with ribbons and stakes. Two elk calves were bedded down near one of the stakes, unaware of the contrast between the fluorescent orange-painted stake and their soft brown coats.

From the narrow ravine above Rock Creek, the trail continues to climb, trending northwest to get around the bulk of Cottonwood Peak. On a ridge that separates Rock Creek from Meadow Creek, the trail is supposed to descend to a tributary of Meadow Creek, but we could not find the trail or any markers. We could see a trail cut high on the slope of the U-shaped cliffs at the head of the tributary of Meadow Creek, so we took that higher route, crossing some snowfields and talus to reach the Divide. The high route was easy to follow and quite scenic, but lingering snowdrifts could make it difficult to negotiate. Also, a descent to the tributary of Meadow Creek would provide both water and a campsite. Hopefully, the ridge between Rock Creek and Meadow Creek will be more clearly signed for future hikers.

The correct route of the CDT climbs along the south bank of the middle fork of Meadow Creek to reach the Divide at elevation 9,680 feet, just north of Cottonwood Peak. Once on the Divide, the trail turns north and descends to a saddle. The saddle is signed with all sorts of information, including the directions and distances to Morrison Lake, Harkness Lake, and Nicholia Creek. This saddle is where the "window" to the world of mountains on both sides of the Divide is so impressive. We were almost blown off our feet by the venturi effect of the wind as it funneled through the low spot.

N W E S !

From the saddle, continue to follow the Divide toward Coyote Creek. The first two rock cairns marking the way are easy to see. After that, route-finding is problematic because the cairns are too far apart and hard to distinguish in the rocky terrain. Using the topographical map, cross peak 9625 and peak 9328, but stay west of peak 9743. It is easier for southbound hikers to see the route. Northbound hikers could use binoculars for spotting the cairns.

Cut tread appears again where the trail contours around a rocky slope south of, and above, the Coyote Creek drainage. Near Coyote Creek, CD signs on posts, rock cairns, blazed trees, and visible tread make for an easy-to-find trail again. The trail descends from the Divide on the Montana side to cross the creek at mile 25.8. Coyote Creek was a good source of water when we were there, but it can be dry in the fall. Signs here identify Coyote Creek and give the distance to Morrison Lake as 7 miles.

A grassy two-track leads north from the ridge above Coyote Creek toward the Tex Creek Basin. Depart the road 0.3 mile north of the Coyote Creek Basin, where a left (northwesterly) turn is marked with a CD symbol on a post. The grassy track leads to a stand of conifers on a ridge above Tex Creek. The trail is signed and blazed where it enters the trees, and is closed to motorized vehicles. Descend to Tex Creek and cross the creek at mile 28. The trail through the Tex Creek Basin is both mellow and beautiful.

The clear-running stream waters grassy meadows below a crescent of sheer cliffs. This is actually a better place to camp than Morrison Lake.

The non-motorized section near Tex Creek is about 1.5 miles long. A CD post in a rock cairn marks the beginning of a motorized track on the north bank of the creek. Follow this track to another crossing of Tex Creek and up a short but steep hill above Simpson Creek.

The trail drops into a gully to cross Simpson Creek at mile 30.6, following the 4WD road that leads north to Morrison Lake. Other 4WD roads and dim two-tracks intersect the trail, but frequent, wooden CD placards on posts show the correct route.

Near Morrison Lake, mile 32.8, there is a faded, wooden CD sign just east of the lake, on the rise crossed by a 4WD jeep track. Baldy Mountain is the massive peak to the west that holds Morrison Lake in its outstretched rocky arms. At 10,773 feet (3,284 meters), its size overwhelms the small alpine lake. Hikers continuing north from Morrison Lake should refill water bottles here.

Sunrays fill a meadow below The Thumb, in the Beaverhead Mountains of the Bitterroot Range near Sawmill Creek.

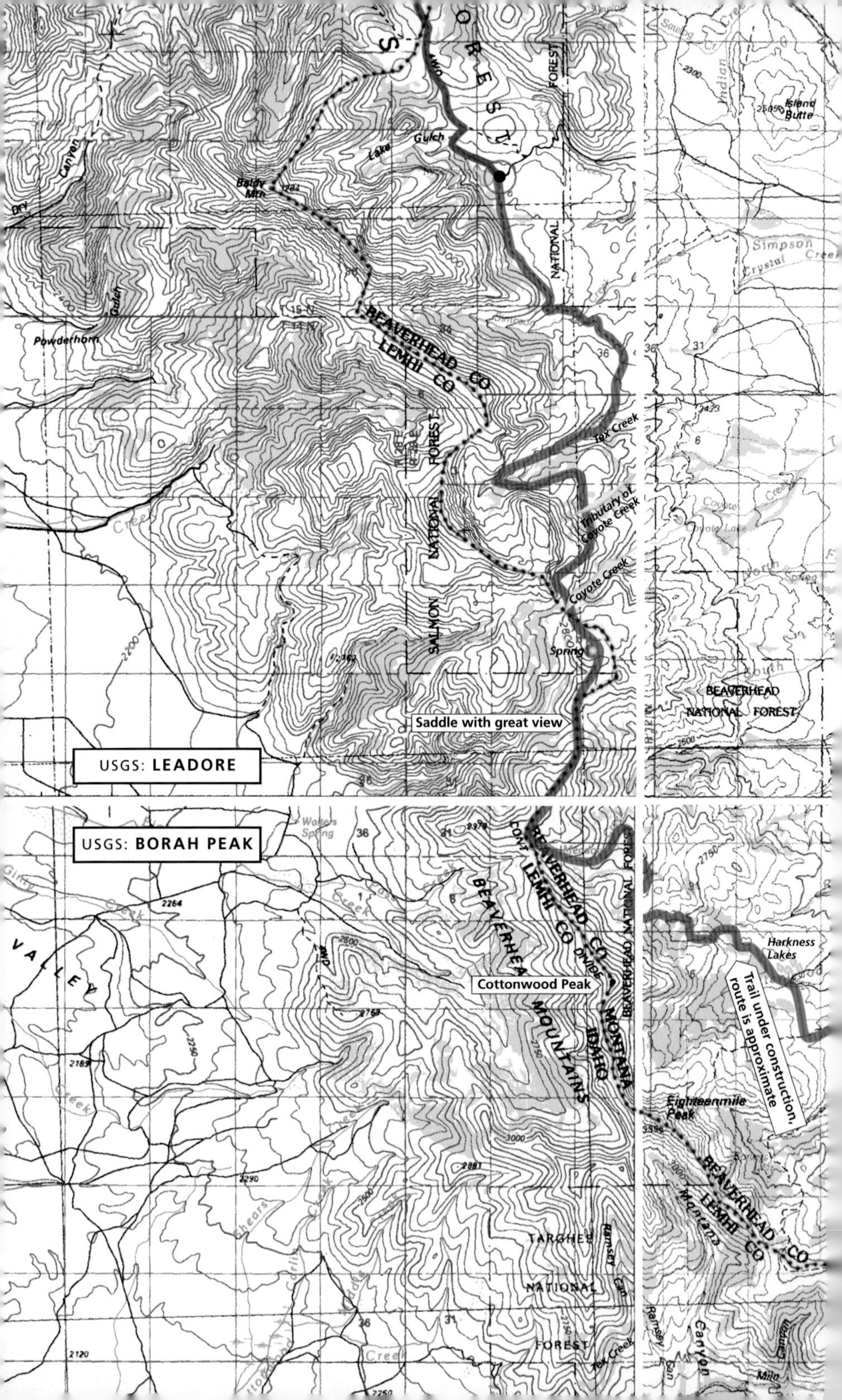

USGS: LEADORE
USGS: BORAH PEAK
Saddle with great view
Cottonwood Peak
Trail under construction, route is approximate
Baldy Mtn
Lake Gulch
Powderhorn
Tex Creek
Tributary of Coyote Creek
Coyote Creek
Spring
BEAVERHEAD CO
LEMHI CO
SALMON NATIONAL FOREST
BEAVERHEAD NATIONAL FOREST
BEAVERHEAD MOUNTAINS
MONTANA
IDAHO
Eighteenmile Peak
Harkness Lakes
Island Butte
Simpson Creek
Crystal Creek
TARGHEE NATIONAL FOREST
Ramsey Canyon
Tex Creek

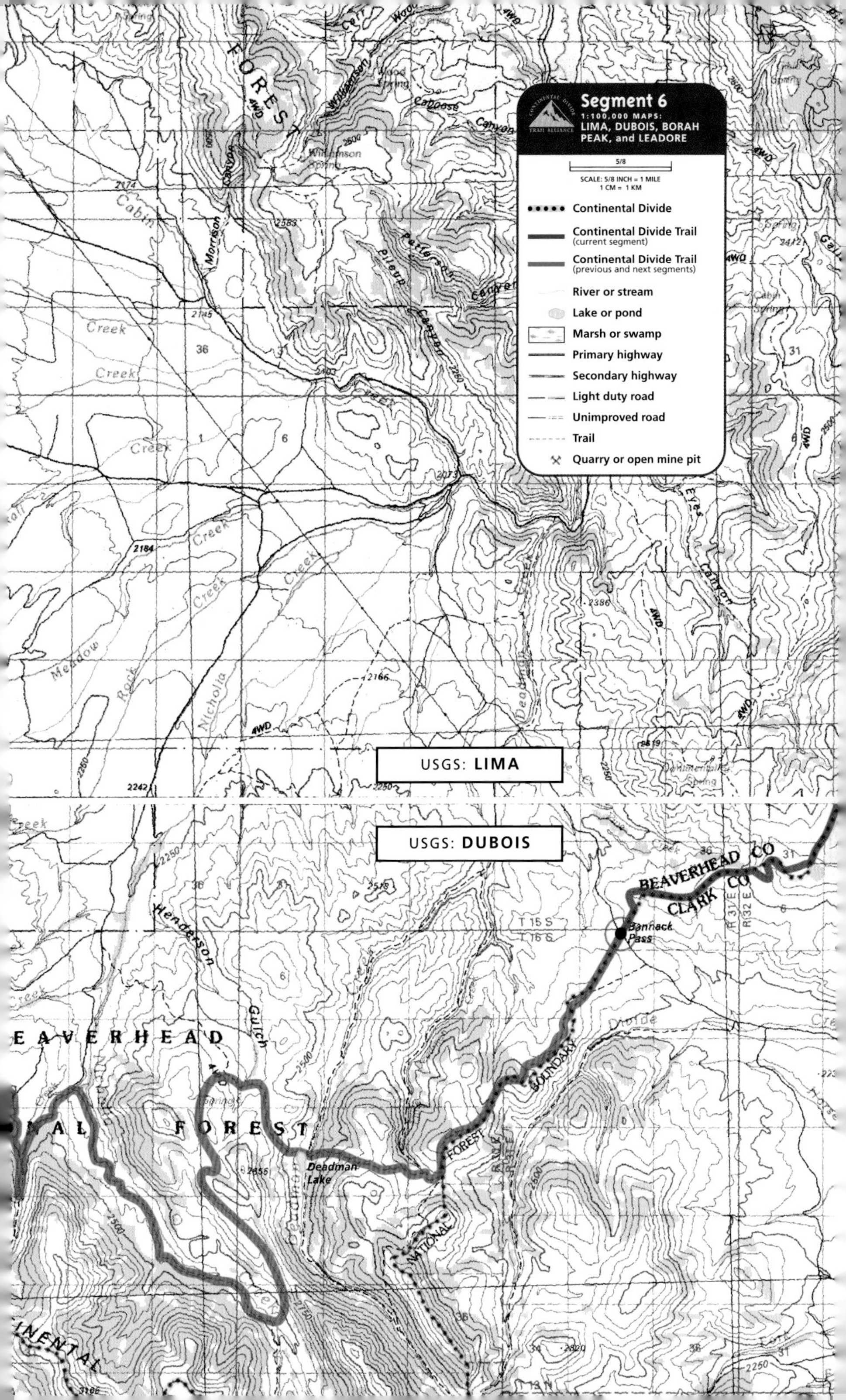

Segment 6
1:100,000 MAPS:
LIMA, DUBOIS, BORAH PEAK, and LEADORE
CONTINENTAL DIVIDE TRAIL ALLIANCE
5/8
SCALE: 5/8 INCH = 1 MILE
1 CM = 1 KM
Continental Divide
Continental Divide Trail
(current segment)
Continental Divide Trail
(previous and next segments)
River or stream
Lake or pond
Marsh or swamp
Primary highway
Secondary highway
Light duty road
Unimproved road
Trail
Quarry or open mine pit
USGS: LIMA
USGS: DUBOIS
FOREST
Williamson
Caboose
Canyon
Williamson Spring
Cabin
Morrison
Canyon
Peterson
Pileup
Canyon
Creek
Meadow
Rock
Nicholia
Deadman
Eyes
Canyon
Henderson
Gulch
BEAVERHEAD CO
CLARK CO
Bannack Pass
T 15 S
T 16 S
BEAVERHEAD
NAL FOREST
Deadman Lake
BOUNDARY
FOREST
NATIONAL
INENTAL
Divide
4WD

Segment 7

Morrison Lake to Bannock Pass: Beaverhead Mtns.

On a windswept ridge of the Continental Divide north of Morrison Lake, a midday storm builds in late August.

22.8 miles

Difficulty: Moderate

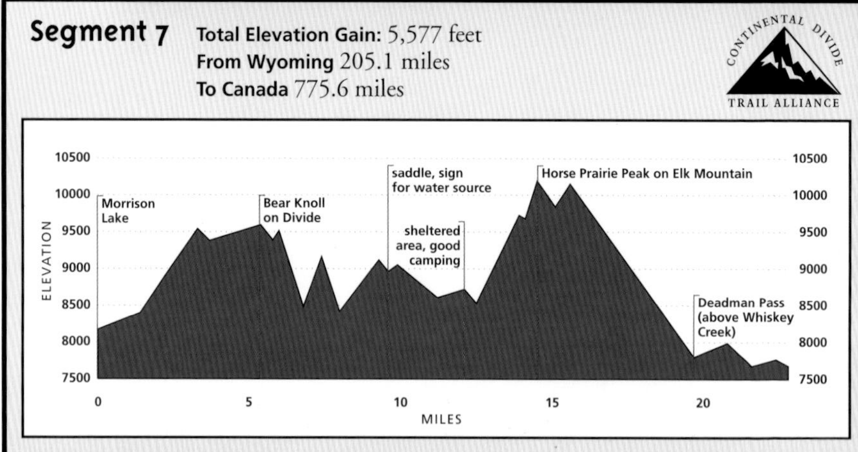

TRAIL OVERVIEW It is a symptom of the drier climate in the southern Beaverhead Mountains that Morrison Lake is a major landmark. The locals refer to all other terrain features in relation to this tiny alpine lake. You are either north, south, or east of Morrison Lake. The imposing cliffs of the Continental Divide cut off travel to the west.

Less snowfall and less rain make for an earlier start to the hiking season. This segment can be hiked in June, when the Centennial and Henrys Lake Mountains to the south and east are still snowed in. Avalanche danger is also less here, thanks to the rolling, open nature of the Divide. The only exception is about 3 miles of trail near Elk Mountain, and Morrison Lake itself.

The highest point on the Idaho/Montana Continental Divide Trail is Horse Prairie Peak on Elk Mountain, elevation 10,194 feet. When we hiked this segment, the Forest Service was constructing a reroute of the CDT to skirt Elk Mountain. I was glad the new trail was incomplete because I enjoyed the views from Horse Prairie Peak and the company of a band of mountain goats that had adopted the CDT as their own personal trail. Still, I can see the logic behind the reroute because the climb is steeper than regulation grade and puts hikers in more danger as far as lightning is concerned. It is not a good idea to climb Elk Mountain in threatening weather.

Elk Mountain is aptly named. About 400 elk graze in this area, with the largest concentrations to the south. There are also deer, fox, wolves, and black bears. Bear sightings are rare, but fishermen at Morrison Lake reported seeing one black bear when we were there in June. The Forest Service rangers suggested hanging food, but the main concern was mice, not bears.

Sagebrush steppe dominates the land east of the lake, but hikers pass through an astonishing variety of trees north of the lake, including ponderosa pine (rare at this altitude), whitebark pine, spruce, lodgepole pine, and limber pine. Beautiful stands of whitebark pine dominate the subalpine zone along the ridge of the Divide. Their twisted and wind-polished stumps are compelling even in death. The southern flank of Elk Mountain harbors one of the best alpine flower gardens I've seen.

Bannock Pass, at the end of this segment, was on the route of a sorrowing and wounded band of Nez Perce in August 1877, when they crossed the pass after the Battle of Big Hole. The Indians descended to the Idaho side of the Divide and hiked southeast through the Lemhi Valley toward Yellowstone National Park. The tribe assured settlers along the Lemhi Range that they would not be molested, but a later skirmish in the National Park ended in death for several tourists.

Although this segment has the highest average elevation along the Idaho/Montana CDT, the snow-capped peaks of the Lemhis give one the false impression of hiking in low country, surrounded by higher terrain. With 23 peaks that top 10,000 feet, Idaho's Lemhi Range dominates the western horizon for most of this segment.

Water is scarce from mile 1.4 to mile 9.6, and again from mile 12.5 to Bannock Pass at mile 22.8. Look for the water alert icons in the trail description to plan your camping spots.

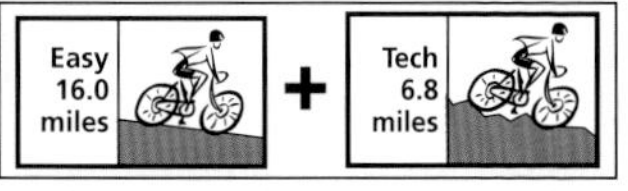

MOUNTAIN BIKE NOTES: This segment is open to mountain bikes. The trail follows rough 4WD roads and two-tracks for many miles. About 7 miles of foot and horse path is encountered near Elk Mountain, but there are very few places where bikes would have to be carried.

LAND ADMINISTRATORS (SEE APPENDIX A)

Salmon National Forest, Leadore Ranger District

MAPS

USGS QUADRANGLES: Morrison Lake, Tepee Mountain, Medicine Lodge Peak, Deadman Pass, Bannock Pass

USFS: Beaverhead National Forest

BEGINNING ACCESS POINT

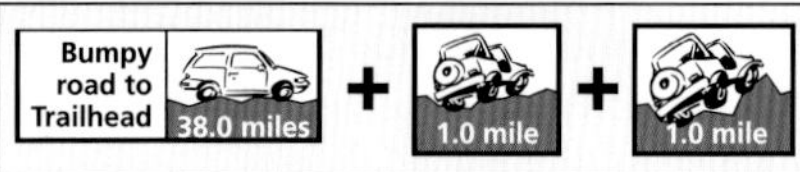

MORRISON LAKE IN THE SOUTHERN BEAVERHEAD MOUNTAINS: Exit from Interstate 15 at Lima or Dell, Montana. Take Big Sheep Creek Road (257) to Indian Spring Creek and turn west on Road 3920 to Morrison Lake. The first mile of Road 3920 is 2WD in good weather. There is good camping on BLM land where the road crosses the creek. A rough 4WD road, with quality varying from hair-raising to normal, depending on the weather, continues to the lake.

ENDING ACCESS POINT

Bumpy road to Trailhead

BANNOCK PASS: Bannock Pass can be reached from both the Idaho and Montana sides of the Continental Divide. The best route is from Leadore on the Idaho side, where Road 29 climbs northeast for 13.5 miles to reach the pass. Where 29 leaves Hwy. 28, it is paved for a short distance, then gravel/dirt to the pass.

SUPPLIES, SERVICES, AND ACCOMMODATIONS

LIMA, MT, on Interstate 15 offers most services. (See Segment 5.) There are no towns near the beginning of this segment.

Distance from Trail: 40.0 miles from Bannack Pass

TRAIL DESCRIPTION

Hikers should fill water bottles at Morrison Lake as it is 9.6 miles to the next reliable water source. From Morrison Lake north, the Continental Divide Trail is well-marked with wooden, branded CD symbols mounted on posts. Some of these are weather-faded, but it is easy to walk from post to post, following a 4WD jeep track in the open country. At a Y-shaped intersection at mile 0.5, northbound hikers keep right (east). At mile 0.9 there is a CD post where another jeep track comes in. The directional CD arrows are too faded to read—look further north for the next post, which is just barely within sight.

The jeep track that the CDT follows climbs and descends to cross two gullies. The second gully, at mile 1.4, is marshy where springs feed the headwaters of Indian Springs Creek. In wet years, this is a good water source.

From Indian Springs Creek, the trail climbs to the rolling, open ridge of the Divide. For about 10 miles, the trail is no longer marked, but there is no need for markers as there is just one ridge to follow and the two-track stays right on top of it. The only markers are survey markers for the Montana/Idaho border, which look like capped iron pipes, most of them surrounded by rock cairns.

The trail climbs to one bare knoll after another, gaining and losing from 100 to 600 feet in elevation repeatedly. Most of the ridge is higher than 8,500 feet—above the timberline. The open grasslands offer unobstructed views for mile after mile—the best views outside of Glacier National Park that the Montana/Idaho Continental Divide has to offer. The Tendoy Mountains parallel the trail to the east, and the Lemhi Range to the west. The long curve of the Divide to the south can be seen for more than a hundred miles in clear weather.

At 6.4 miles north of Morrison Lake, the two-track enters a stand of whitebark pine and trends downhill. Snow lingers here into June and can be used as a water source. A high camp here will give you spectacular sunrise and sunset vistas.

A reliable water source is reached at 9.6 miles. Forest Service signs in a saddle on the ridge say, "Water not tested. Boil for ten minutes." A water trough is visible east of the trail.

10.7 miles north of Morrison Lake, the trail follows the Divide as it turns northwest and downhill near Tepee Mountain. The jeep track is dim in the grass here, but reappears in the saddle below. One CD post with a faded, wooden sign confirms the route at mile 11.2.

There is another water source at mile 12.5. Look for a fenced-off spring in the trees east of the trail. A cat cut and a sheltered area near here provide a good camping spot. At the cat cut, the 4WD track ends and a foot/horse path skirts Tepee Mountain. Reservoir Creek is about 400 yards below the trail.

The trail is blazed where it enters trees west of Tepee Mountain, and remnants of an old jeep track can be seen. Steep terrain near the head of Reservoir Creek forces the trail to switchback as it climbs close to, but not on, the Divide.

At about mile 13.5, hikers have a choice of the new route that is cut below the Divide, or the old route that stays on the crest. The old trail climbs steeply, gaining more than a thousand feet to top an unnamed knoll at mile 13.9. Visible tread ends here and rock cairns mark the route from the knoll to Elk Mountain. The trail descends again to a saddle south of Elk Mountain, and a thick carpet of alpine wildflowers covered the ground when we were there. Mountain goats grazed nearby and their paths intercepted the CDT at the top of Horse Prairie Peak, mile 14.5 and 10,194 feet, the highest elevation on the Montana/Idaho CDT.

From Elk Mountain, a series of switchbacks descends to a low point on the Divide above Dad Creek Lake. This "low point" only seems low in relation to the peak —which is 9,842 feet. At this saddle, the new trail begins a 0.5-mile contour below the Divide on the Idaho side (southwest). Once again, hikers can choose to walk the crest, but be wary of turning north at peak 10,153 where a long spur ridge leads temptingly away from the Divide.

A gradual descent on the Divide leads to a jeep track at mile 17.9. This two-track is followed for about 5 miles to Bannock Pass. The track parallels a fenceline most of the way. A spring at the head of Deadhorse Canyon is shown on the topo, but it is usually dry.

Deadman Pass at mile 19.7 is about one hundred feet above the headwaters of Whiskey Spring Creek, a short climb down for hikers who need water. There are two stories behind the name "Deadman Pass." The most often repeated tale is that Alexander

Cruikshank, a scout for the army during the Nez Perce war of 1877, found a dead man on the pass in the 1880s, but no one could identify the body. The second tale involves a prospector who died when he fell from his horse. Whiskey Spring Creek was a stopover for freight wagons hauling whiskey from Red Rock, Montana, to Salmon, Idaho. There ought to be a connection there somewhere.

An abandoned railroad tunnel can be seen emerging from the hillside at mile 21.6. The Gilmore & Pittsburgh Railroad ran trains through the tunnel from 1910 to 1939, serving the mining industry. Logging and ranching predominate today. Cattle graze most of the Divide near Bannock Pass, and small logging operations are active on private land west of the pass.

Bannock Pass, elevation 7,681, is reached at mile 22.8. Water and good camping can be found at Canyon Creek about 1 mile southwest of the pass.

Sunset on ridge, Beaverhead Mountains, south of Bannock Pass

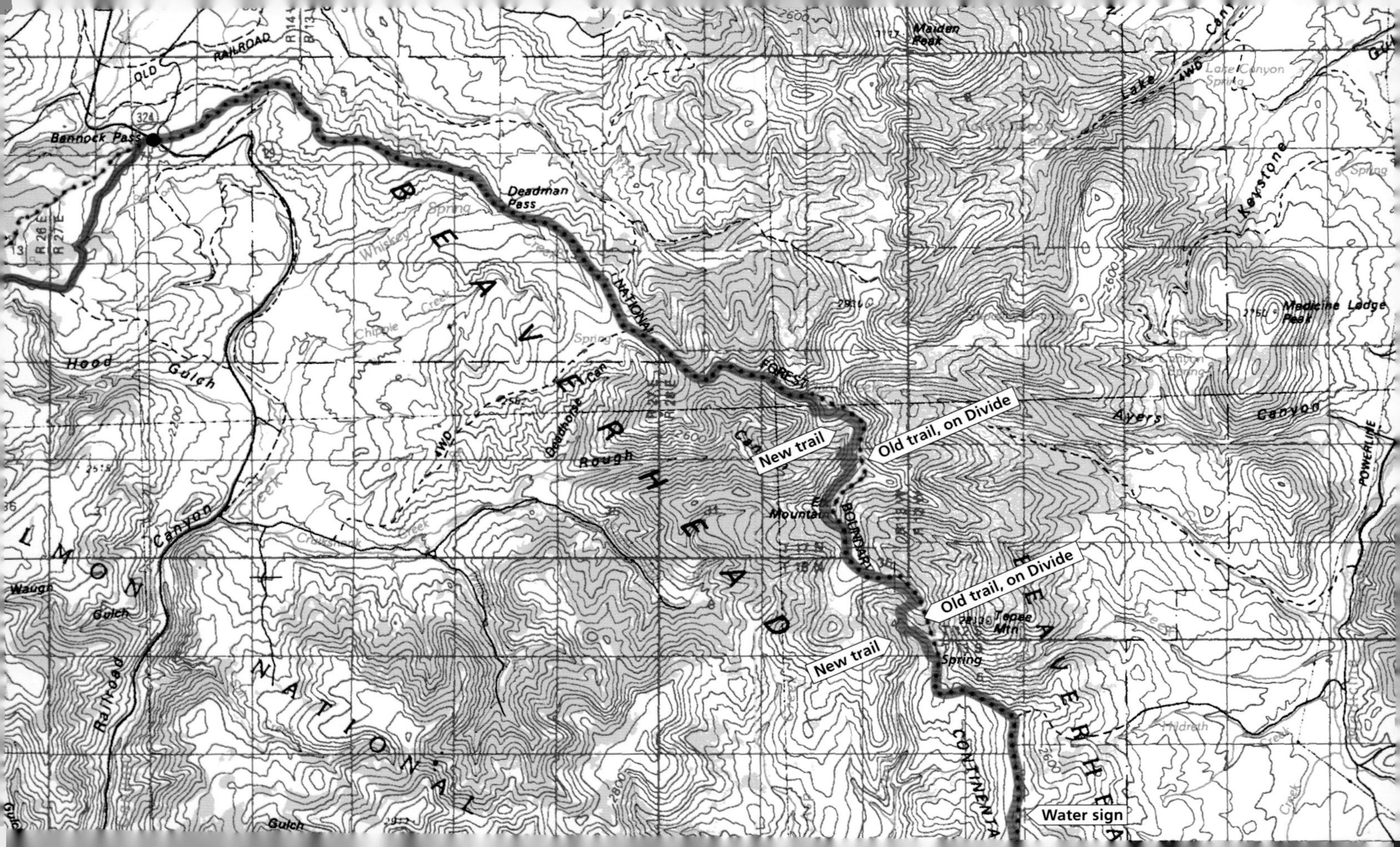

Bannock Pass
Deadman Pass
Maiden Peak
Medicine Lodge Peak
Keystone
Ayers
Canyon
POWERLINE
Rough
Elk Mountain
Tepee Mtn
Spring
Hood
Gulch
Canyon
Railroad
OLD
RAILROAD
BEAVERHEAD
NATIONAL
FOREST
BOUNDARY
CONTINENTA
New trail
Old trail, on Divide
New trail
Old trail, on Divide
Water sign

Segment 7
1:100,000 MAP:
LEADORE
5/8
SCALE: 5/8 INCH = 1 MILE
1 CM = 1 KM
Continental Divide
Continental Divide Trail
(current segment)
Continental Divide Trail
(previous and next segments)
River or stream
Lake or pond
Marsh or swamp
Primary highway
Secondary highway
Light duty road
Unimproved road
Trail
Quarry or open mine pit
NATIONAL FOREST
MOUNTAINS
DIVIDE
Springs
Lake Gulch
Baldy Mtn
Canyon
Dry
Gulch
BOUNDARY
Fork
Rocky
Canyon
FOREST
NATIONAL
Hawley
Eighteenmile
Bull
LEMHI
EY
2554
2537
2000
2600
3000
2400
1880
1882
1955
31
36

Segment 8

Bannock Pass to Lemhi Pass: Beaverhead Mtns.

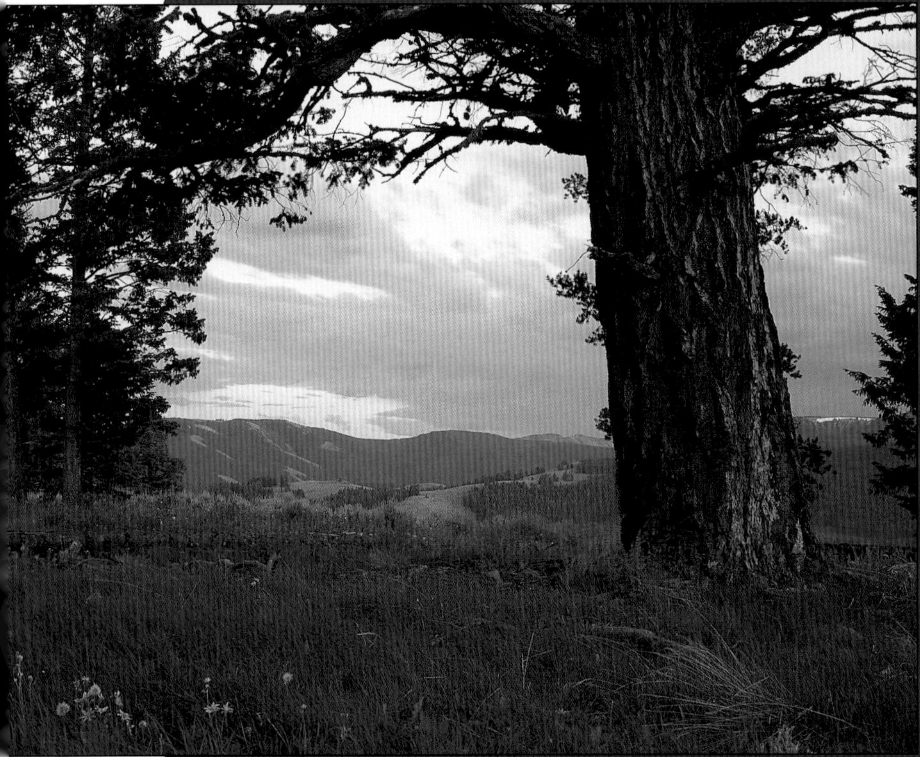

Sunset as seen from the Divide just south of Lemhi Pass, where Lewis and Clark twice crossed the Rocky Mountains

27.6 miles

Difficulty: Moderate

Segment 8 **Total Elevation Gain:** 4,027 feet
From Wyoming 227.9 miles
To Canada 752.8 miles

CONTINENTAL DIVIDE TRAIL ALLIANCE

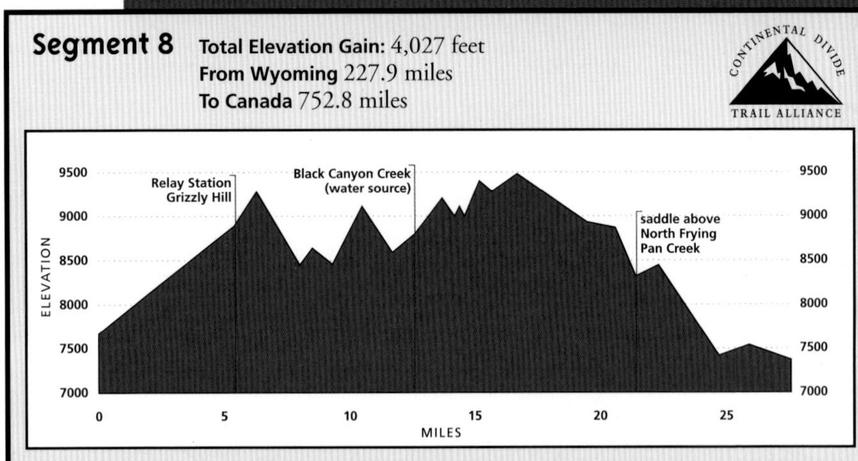

TRAIL OVERVIEW Bannock Pass was part of a traditional Native American travel route heavily used to access buffalo hunting grounds in Montana and salmon fishing streams in Idaho. In the 1800s, prospectors and wagon freighters traveled frequently over the pass on their way to Bannock, Montana.

Lemhi Pass is named after Limhi, a character in the Book of Mormon. Mormon settlers came to the Lemhi Valley in the 1850s. Lewis and Clark crossed the Continental Divide many times during their 1805–1806 expedition, but Lemhi Pass is the only spot that Lewis crossed three times and Clark crossed once. The Lewis & Clark National Backcountry Byway and Adventure Road crosses the pass today.

Sagebrush, grass, and pine trees share the slopes along the Divide in this segment. Lower annual precipitation accounts for the predominance of sagebrush steppe ecosystems. It is possible to hike this drier section of the CDT in early June if you don't mind a few leftover snowdrifts. The passes often remain accessible into November.

There is a lot of road-walking in this segment, but the roads receive very little traffic. The proposed route of the CDT is directly on the Divide, but the section from Bannock Pass to a relay station at mile 5.4 is not yet complete, so the trail drops below the Divide to follow a road. There is a 2.6-mile section where cross-country travel is required. A compass and topographical maps are needed for navigation through this forested area.

Water is scarce in this segment. Wagon Box Spring at mile 2.2, the headwaters of Black Canyon Creek at mile 12.6, a developed spring at Yearian Creek (mile 19.5), and the Sacajawea Memorial Spring at Lemhi Pass, mile 27.6, are the only reliable water sources.

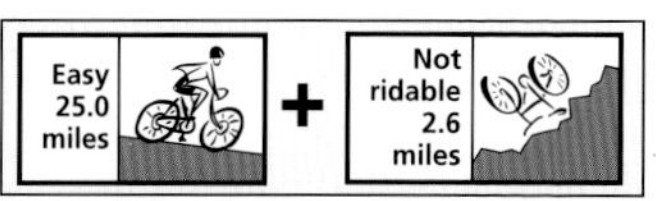

MOUNTAIN BIKE NOTES: This segment is open to mountain bikes. There is a section where trail has not yet been constructed from mile 5.4 to mile 8.0.

LAND ADMINISTRATORS **(SEE APPENDIX A)**

Bureau of Land Management, Lemhi Resource Area

MAPS

USGS QUADRANGLES: Bannock Pass, Goat Mountain, Lemhi Pass

USFS: Beaverhead National Forest (South West)

BEGINNING ACCESS POINT

BANNOCK PASS: This segment begins 13.5 miles from the town of Leadore, ID on Hwy. 28 to Bannock Pass via Road 29.

ENDING ACCESS POINT

LEMHI PASS: Tendoy is on Idaho State Highway 28. It is 13 miles from Tendoy to Lemhi Pass on the Lewis & Clark National Backcountry Byway.

TRAIL DESCRIPTION The Continental Divide trends southwest from Bannock Pass. New tread planned for the crest of the Divide was not complete when we hiked the trail, so we used the interim route.

Leave the Divide on the Idaho (south) side to follow Road 12, a 2WD gravel road, to a relay station at mile 5.4. The road climbs steadily from the pass at 7,681 feet, to the relay station at 8,890 feet on Grizzly Hill.

Road 12 crosses the headwaters of Canyon Spring Creek and passes Wagon Box Spring — both are potential water sources. Ignore all other road intersections until the relay station is in sight. There are no CDT signs at this turn, but the relay station is unmistakable.

Find a jeep road behind the station (north side) and follow it into the forest. An old log fence parallels the road. Hike this road for a short distance until the fence line begins to diverge from the road, then follow the fenceline northwesterly.

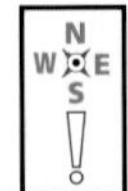

For about 0.5 mile, stay with the fenceline, which is close to the Divide. Where the fence diverges dramatically from the Divide, take a compass reading of 330° and continue on a faint track through the trees. Keep to your heading of 330° for 0.4 mile. You should arrive at an open spot, a knoll where the Divide turns northeast. One large rock cairn marks the spot. At the cairn, make a northeasterly turn to a heading of about 62°, which you will hold for 0.5 mile, then turn to a heading of 340°. Steeper terrain will prevent you from erring too far west, but gentle terrain will lure you to the east. Aim for a saddle above Little Eightmile Creek. When you reach the saddle, you can see another fenceline that leads uphill, and across a meadow to a 4WD road. The 2.6 miles of navigation is in trees except for the knoll with the rock cairn. Goat Mountain can be glimpsed from the open area.

Climb from the saddle above Little Eightmile Creek to an intersection of FR 3900 and an unidentified two-track (mile 8.5). The two-track does not appear on the Forest Service map, but it is directly on the Divide and leads to the shoulder of Goat Mountain. East of Goat Mountain, the track passes through a whitebark pine graveyard, an old blow-down where vicious winds leveled all the trees. Their twisted trunks line the route of the CDT, with their bare limbs eerily pointing skyward. The two-track becomes a single-track at mile 12.2.

Skirt the mountain on the northeast side, following the path through one boggy area where it crosses the headwaters of Black Canyon Creek, a water source that hikers must not pass up. There were no CDT signs when we were there, but the tread was visible and the route was occasionally blazed and marked with blue metal diamonds. The footpath portion is only 0.8 mile long, and emerges from the trees at mile 13, slightly below a saddle on the Divide.

Veer left (northwest) and uphill to the saddle. A dead tree in the middle of the meadow is marked with a blue metal diamond symbol. From the meadow, hikers can also see a two-track 0.2 mile ahead. When you reach the saddle on the shoulder of Goat Mountain, the trail is blazed again. The two-track is also signed with metal BLM/Department of Interior symbols.

Continental Divide Trail Alliance "Hundred Milers" put up some posts with chain-sawed "CD" emblems between Goat Mountain and Lemhi Pass.

The two-track intercepts a well-defined 4WD road 0.7 mile from where the footpath exits the trees north of Goat Mountain. From this intersection to Lemhi Pass, the route is open to motorized vehicles but is seldom used. Stay on the main jeep track

SUPPLIES, SERVICES, AND ACCOMMODATIONS

LEADORE, ID, is in the Lemhi Valley, west of the Beaverhead Mountains.

Zip Code: 83464

Bank:	None	
Bus:	None	
Camping:	Rodeo Grounds, north of town	
Dining:	Silver Dollar Cafe, Main Street	208-768-2311
	McRea's Double E Cafe & Bar, Main Street	208-768-2300
	Silver Dollar Bar, Railroad Avenue	208-768-2363
Gear:	None	
Groceries:	J & T Grocery, Hwy. 28	208-768-2313
Information:	See Groceries	
Laundry:	None	
Lodging:	Leadore Inn, P.O. Box 68	208-768-2237
Medical:	None	
Post Office:	U.S. Post Office, Hwy. 28, Leadore, ID 83464	
Showers:	None	

all the way to Lemhi Pass, though you will pass some spur roads that lead temptingly uphill. The CDT and the road follow the Divide as it trends northwest, then north, then northeast. Views are quite good through scattered trees.

Volunteers developed a spring and access trail (0.25 mile) at the headwaters of the north fork of Yearian Creek, mile 19.5 for this segment.

The elevation along the crest remains high, rolling from 8,300 to 9,400 feet as hikers descend to saddles and climb to knolls on the Divide. The Sacajewea Memorial Camp below the pass is well-signed and the spring is easily accessible.

Lemhi Pass (7,339 feet) is reached at mile 27.6 (14.6 miles from Goat Mountain). There are nine signs at Lemhi Pass, so you'll definitely know where you are. From here it is 13 miles to Tendoy on the Idaho side. The pass is marked as the Montana/Idaho border. There are quotes from the *Lewis & Clark Journals* that reveal their dismay on seeing the view of the Lemhi Mountains: "I discovered immense ranges of high mountains still to the west of us, with their tops partially covered with snow." What they expected to see was an end to mountain ranges and the beginning of a good waterway to the Columbia River, but the view from Lemhi Pass put an abrupt end to that misconception.

When Lewis and Clark passed this way, they also followed a "road," a well-traveled Indian road that was wide enough in places for two to ride abreast.

At Sacajawea Memorial Camp, water, pit toilets, picnic tables, and fire pits provide a good campsite. Another quote from Lewis's journal: "At the distance of four miles further, the road took us to the most distant fountain of the waters of the mighty Missouri, in search of which we have spent so many toilsome days and restless nights. Thus far I had accomplished one of those great objects on which my mind has been unalterably fixed for many years. Judge then of the pleasure I felt in allaying my thirst with this pure and ice-cold water. Here I halted a few minutes and rested myself."

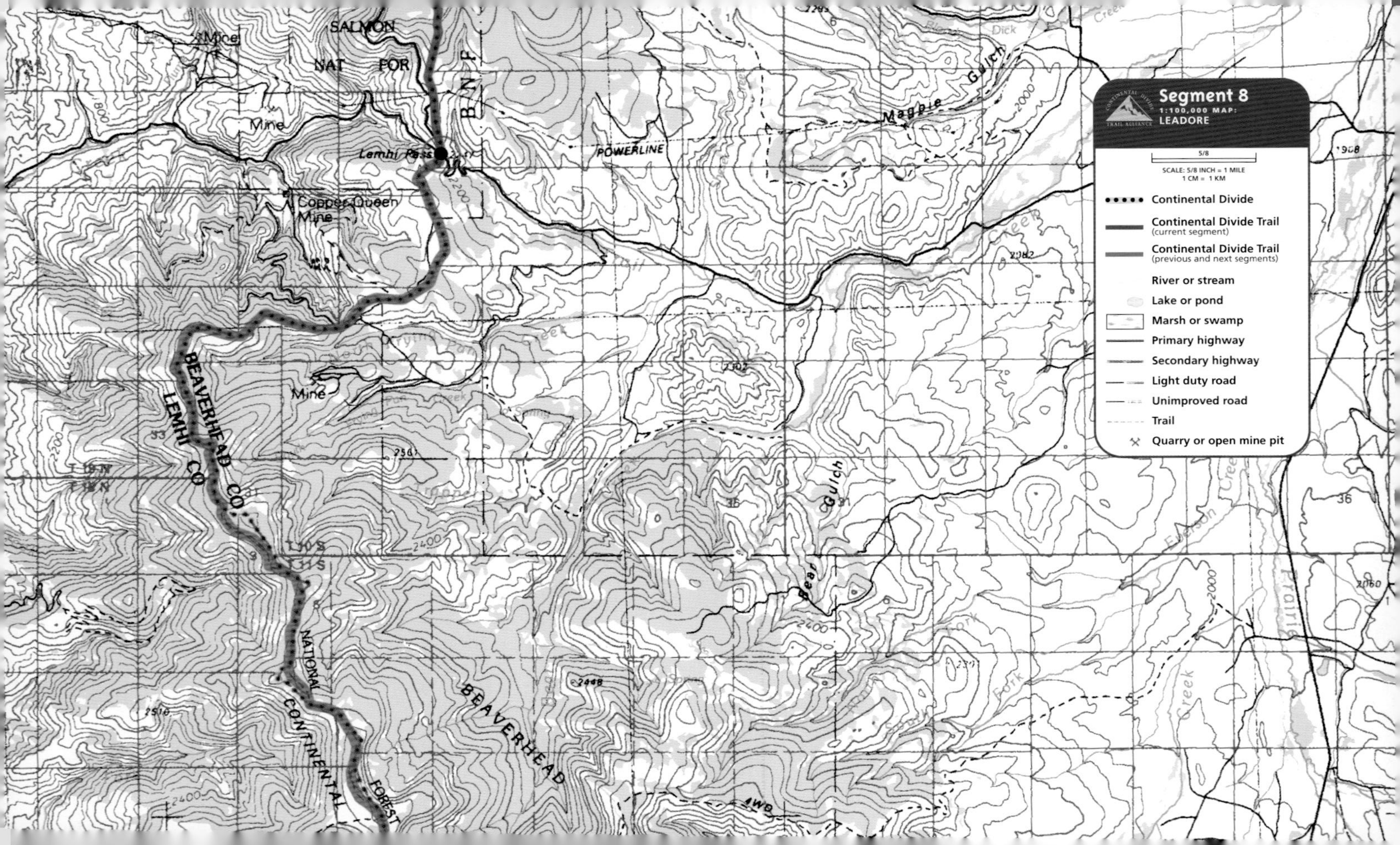

Segment 8
1:100,000 MAP:
LEADORE
CONTINENTAL DIVIDE TRAIL ALLIANCE
5/8
SCALE: 5/8 INCH = 1 MILE
1 CM = 1 KM
Continental Divide
Continental Divide Trail
(current segment)
Continental Divide Trail
(previous and next segments)
River or stream
Lake or pond
Marsh or swamp
Primary highway
Secondary highway
Light duty road
Unimproved road
Trail
Quarry or open mine pit
SALMON
NAT
FOR
B N F
Lemhi Pass
Copper Queen
Mine
Mine
Mine
POWERLINE
Magpie
Gulch
Dick
BEAVERHEAD
CO
LEMHI
CO
NATIONAL
CONTINENTAL
FOREST
BEAVERHEAD
Gulch
Bear
Prairie
4WD
2200
2400
2000
1800
2302
2561
2448
2510
2082
1908
2060
36

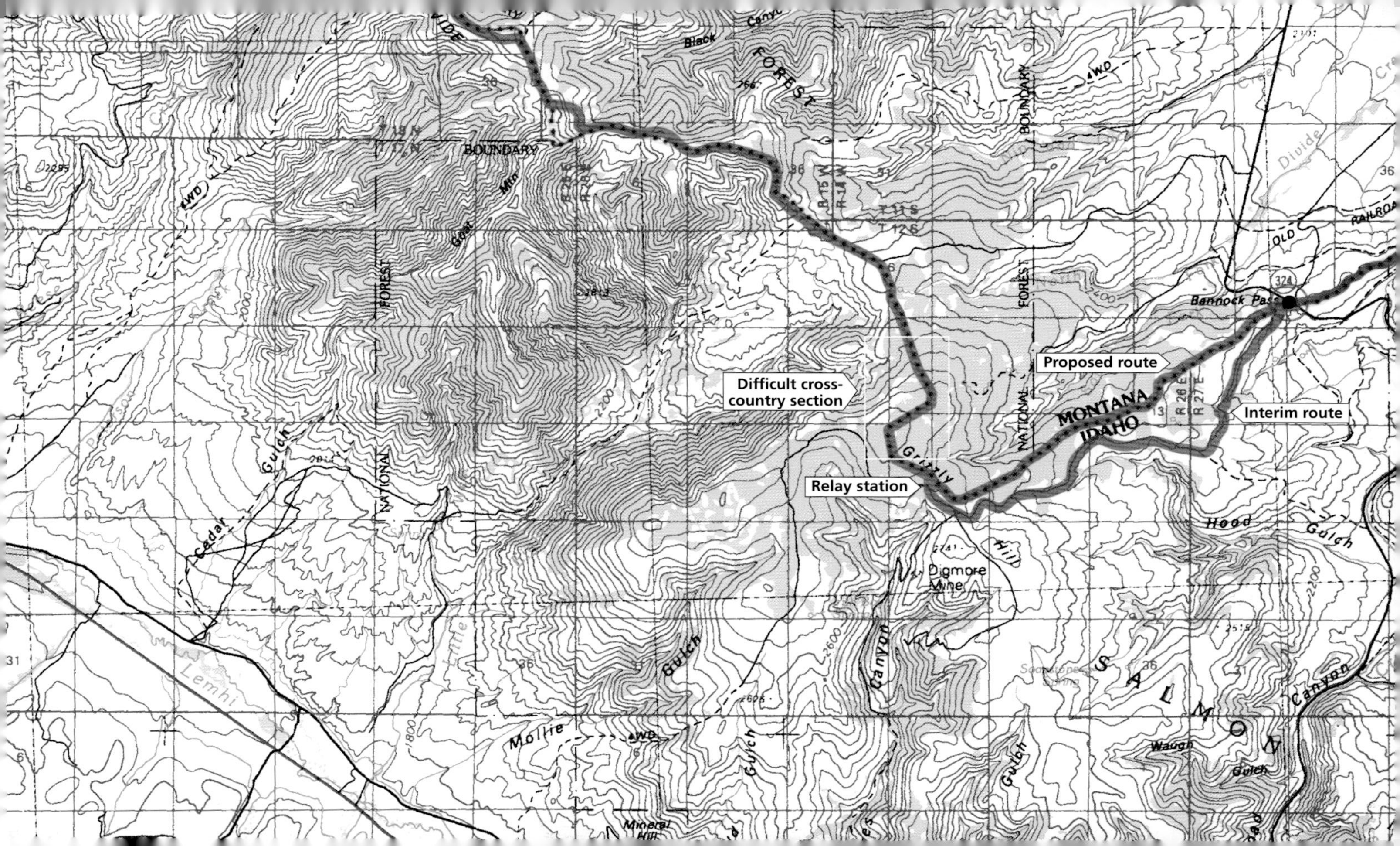

Proposed route
Interim route
Difficult cross-country section
Relay station
Bannock Pass
324
MONTANA
IDAHO
Grizzly
Digmore Mine
Hood Gulch
SALMON
Black Canyon
FOREST
BOUNDARY
NATIONAL
Goat Mtn
Cedar Gulch
Mollie Gulch
Waugh Gulch
Lemhi
OLD RAILROAD
4WD

Segment 9
Lemhi Pass to Goldstone Pass: Beaverhead Mtns.

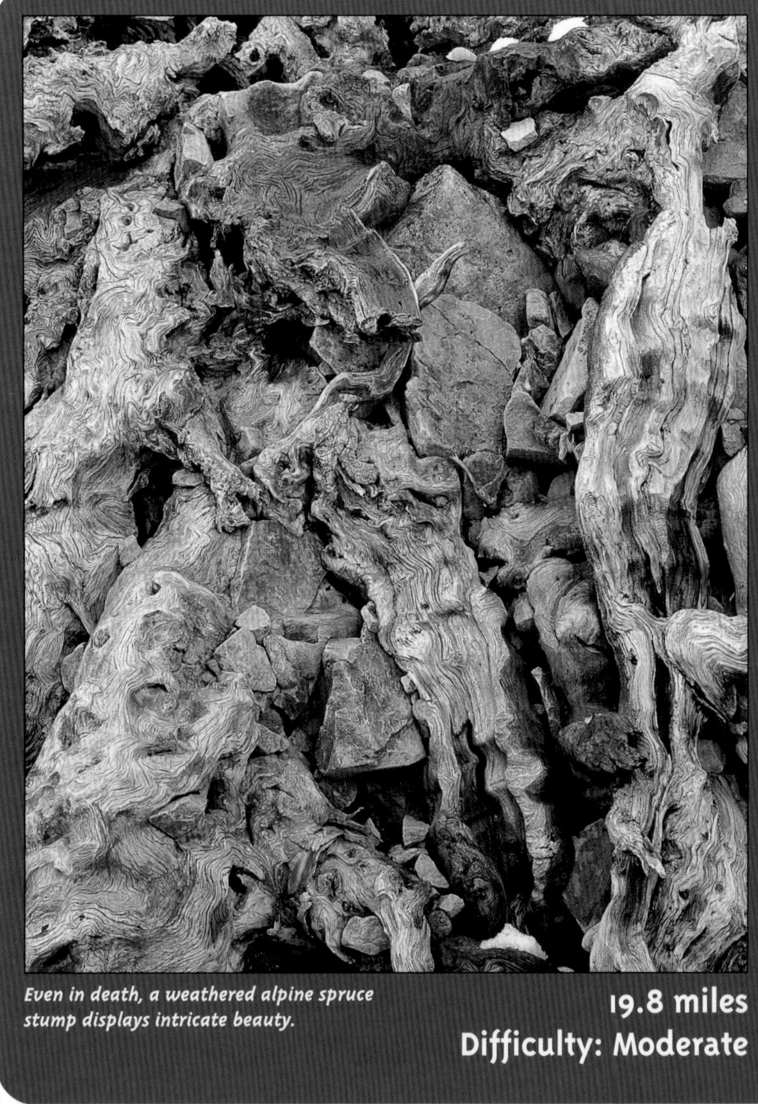

Even in death, a weathered alpine spruce stump displays intricate beauty.

19.8 miles
Difficulty: Moderate

TRAIL OVERVIEW This segment begins at historic Lemhi Pass (see Trail Overview for Segment 8) and ends at Goldstone Pass, with the trail on the crest of the Divide for almost the entire route. For the first 10 miles, the trend of the trail is due north, but the trail would be very hard to find if crews had not blazed the trees.

With the exception of good views from the rocky ridges near Goldstone Mountain, this segment is in trees, mostly lodgepole pines. There is very little in the way of understory plants where the lodgepoles are thick and sunlight reaches the forest floor only fitfully. When we were there, wisps of fog caught stray bands of sunlight to create a sort of glimmering gloom that is peculiar to lodgepole forests. The lack of clear tread through the trees adds to the adventure.

Water is scarce in this segment. Sacajawea Memorial Spring provides water near Lemhi Pass. Other water sources are close to but not on the trail. See the Trail Description for details.

MOUNTAIN BIKE NOTES: This segment is open to mountain bikes, but some sections are rocky and steep, requiring technical riding skill. There are several places where mountain bikers can intersect the CDT from the Warm Springs Road. These are noted in the Trail Description.

LAND ADMINISTRATORS (SEE APPENDIX A)

Salmon National Forest, Leadore Ranger District

MAPS

USGS QUADRANGLES: Lemhi Pass, Kitty Creek, Goldstone Mountain, Goldstone Pass

USFS: Beaverhead National Forest (South West)

BEGINNING ACCESS POINT

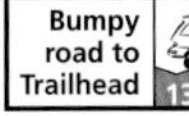

LEMHI PASS: It is 13 miles from Tendoy, ID, to Lemhi Pass on the Lewis & Clark National Backcountry Byway. Tendoy is on Idaho State Highway 28.

ENDING ACCESS POINT

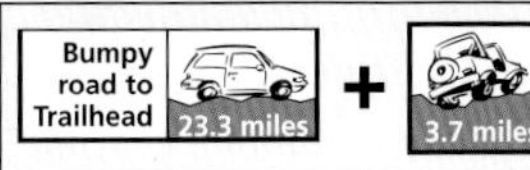

GOLDSTONE PASS (See Segment 10.)

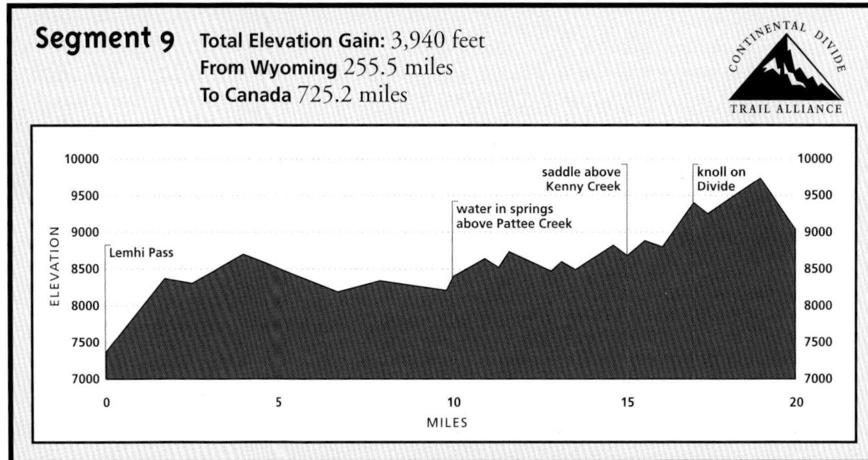

SUPPLIES, SERVICES, AND ACCOMMODATIONS

TENDOY, ID, is on Hwy. 28, and is basically a one-store town. The post office is in the same building as the store.

Distance from Trail: 13 miles

Zip Code: 83468

The Tendoy Store, Hwy. 28, 208-756-2263, groceries, limited camping gear, gas, post office.

Post Office: U.S. Post Office, Hwy. 28, Tendoy Store, Tendoy, ID 83468 208-756-2263

TRAIL DESCRIPTION

Water and good camping exist at Sacajawea Memorial Spring near Lemhi Pass. Going north from Lemhi Pass, follow the fenceline on the crest of the Divide where a very faint two-track appears and disappears. At 0.5 mile north of the pass, intersect a well-defined two-track and a cattle guard, but continue to follow the fenceline uphill, under the power lines. Enter a stand of trees at 0.9 mile.

Continue to follow the fenceline on the Divide. A wooden CD sign on a tree shows where the trail enters a stand of pines. At 1.1 miles, the trail follows a faint two-track and tree blazes. The trail stays on the Divide, though the "crest" flattens and becomes more obscure. The faint two-track becomes a narrow footpath at 1.7 miles. Watch carefully for tree blazes.

If you neglected to get water at Sacajawea Memorial Spring, you'll have another opportunity 2.5 miles north of Lemhi Pass. Hike cross-country (downhill on the Idaho side) to Horseshoe Bend Creek. The creek is about 0.25 mile off the trail and may also be reached by hiking along Warm Springs Road instead of on the crest of the Divide.

Where the trail crosses open areas, the route is marked with stone cairns, with blazes resuming whenever the path enters a stand of trees. Watch for a combination of old and new blazes.

An intersection at 4.9 miles is signed as "Flume Creek, CD, Pattee Creek." If you are hiking or mountain biking the Warm Springs Road instead of the crest of the Divide, you'll come to a "Flume Creek" sign 5.3 miles from Lemhi Pass. A large CDT sign also announces "This portion of the trail travels through the Beaverhead Mountains of the Bitterroot Range. You can hike along the flat-topped and tree-covered crest by following the dot-over-slash blazes on the trees to the east." Quite odd to find such a good sign off the trail and so few signs on the trail. For mountain bikers, however, this is a good thing. Bikers can stay on the road until they come to this sign and then continue on the official route of the CDT, avoiding the rougher sections of the trail on the crest. (There is another opportunity for mountain bikers riding on Warm Springs Road to intercept the CDT at mile 13, at the "Kitty Springs Spur Road," which leads easterly to the trail.)

At 5.1 miles, the trail intersects several two-tracks. These two-tracks lead down to the Warm Springs Road. The CDT crosses, but does not follow, the two-tracks. The trail is so close to the road here that you can see it through the trees on the Idaho side.

On the Divide above the Kitty Creek and Eunice Creek drainages, it's very easy to get lost. A ranger we spoke to said that he once spent three or four hours "wandering around in Montana" looking for the CDT. The Divide is flat and broad, covered with evenly spaced trees, and crisscrossed with game trails so that hikers can't tell where the correct route is without following the blazes. The blazes are critical. If you don't see one in front of you, don't continue. Go back to the last known blaze and scout from there. There are also five stone cairns in this section, two of them built around pipe border markers, but these cairns cannot be seen through the trees.

Near a rock outcropping, the trail makes a U-turn. Watch for blazes to find the turn. You'll come to a "Warm Springs Rd" sign at mile 8.6. This would be an opportunity for north-to-south hikers to leave the trail and take to the road if bad weather precluded navigating in the trees.

At this point, hikers enter a labyrinth of roads and tracks that is difficult to decipher:

- 9.1 miles: The trail intercepts a two-track in a previously logged area.
- 9.9 miles: There is another intersection with a two-track; the CDT continues straight ahead.
- 10 miles: There is a four-way intersection of two-tracks; the CDT continues straight ahead, almost due north. The only difference between the CDT and all these two-tracks is that the CDT is blazed.

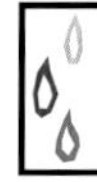

Water can be obtained in springs at the head of Pattee Creek, 0.3 mile west of the trail.

- 11.1 miles: Another intersection, with what looks like a 4WD road but is marked with snowmobile trail symbols. The CDT crosses this trail and does not follow it.

You get the idea. After noting that intersection, I gave up. The CDT north from this point to the long ridge near Goldstone Mountain crosses more than 20 4WD roads, snowmobile trails, two-tracks, and paths. Sometimes the trail follows one of these for a short distance; often it crosses them. I stopped counting at 20 intersections, interceptions, and divergences. Your only hope is to follow the blazes. If you're on a track and the blazes stop, you missed a divergence. Hats off to the crew that blazed a trail through this mess.

At 16.3 miles, the trail finally breaks out of the trees and climbs onto a rocky ridge where the views into Montana are quite good. Ten miles is a long way to hike with no water, and there will be no water at Goldstone Pass either, so take advantage of any snowdrifts left on this high ridge.

The ridge-walk above the eastern cliffs continues for 3.5 miles to Goldstone Pass. Tread appears and disappears, but is there when you need it. A constructed trail leads across talus rock a mile south of Goldstone Pass. This section is more suited to mountain goats, and mountain bikers may not feel comfortable riding above the considerable drop-off.

Goldstone Pass is reached at mile 19.2, elevation 9,040 feet. The pass is not identified on the ground. A post with its sign missing marks the apex of Road 7327, which crosses the Montana/Idaho border at the pass. Northbound CDT hikers cross the 4WD road and continue directly uphill.

The closest water is at Cowbone Lake, 1.4 miles north on the CDT; or in "Goldstone Lake" (more of a pond really) 0.6 mile east on Road 7327.

CONTINENTAL DIVIDE TRAIL ALLIANCE
Segment 9
1:100,000 MAPS:
LEADORE and SALMON
5/8
SCALE: 5/8 INCH = 1 MILE
1 CM = 1 KM
Continental Divide
Continental Divide Trail
(current segment)
Continental Divide Trail
(previous and next segments)
River or stream
Lake or pond
Marsh or swamp
Primary highway
Secondary highway
Light duty road
Unimproved road
Trail
Quarry or open mine pit
SALMON
MOUNTAINS
FOREST
CONTINENTAL
DIVIDE
NATIONAL
HOLE
Canyon
Blind
Skinner
Meadows
Black
Mountain
Lookout
Selway
Mountain
Goldstone
Pass
Goldstone
Mountain
BEAVERHEAD CO
LEMHI CO
Landing
Strip
Hughes
Gulch
T 22 N
T 21 N
T 20 N
T 7 S
T 8 S
T 9 S
R 24 E
R 25 E
R 16 W
R 15 W
2890
2750
2981
2409
2500
2470
2801
2712
2547
2786
2805
3020
2207
1750
2250
2527
2640
2324
2448
2766
2551
2154
1905

USGS: SALMON
USGS: LEADORE
FOREST
BOUNDARY
Water
Pyramid Hill
Hamilton Gl
Big Hollow
Powerline
SALMON
NAT FOR
B N F
Lemhi Pass
POWERLINE
Copper Queen Mine
Mine
Mine
Mine
BEAVERHEAD CO
LEMHI CO
INDIAN
RESERVATION
BOUNDARY
Tendoy
Lemhi
Gaging Station
Big Dry Gulch
Gulch
T 20 N
T 19 N
2500
2250
2032
1750
1450
2200

Segment 10

Goldstone Pass to Miner Lakes Trailhead: Beaverhead Mountains of the Bitterroot Range

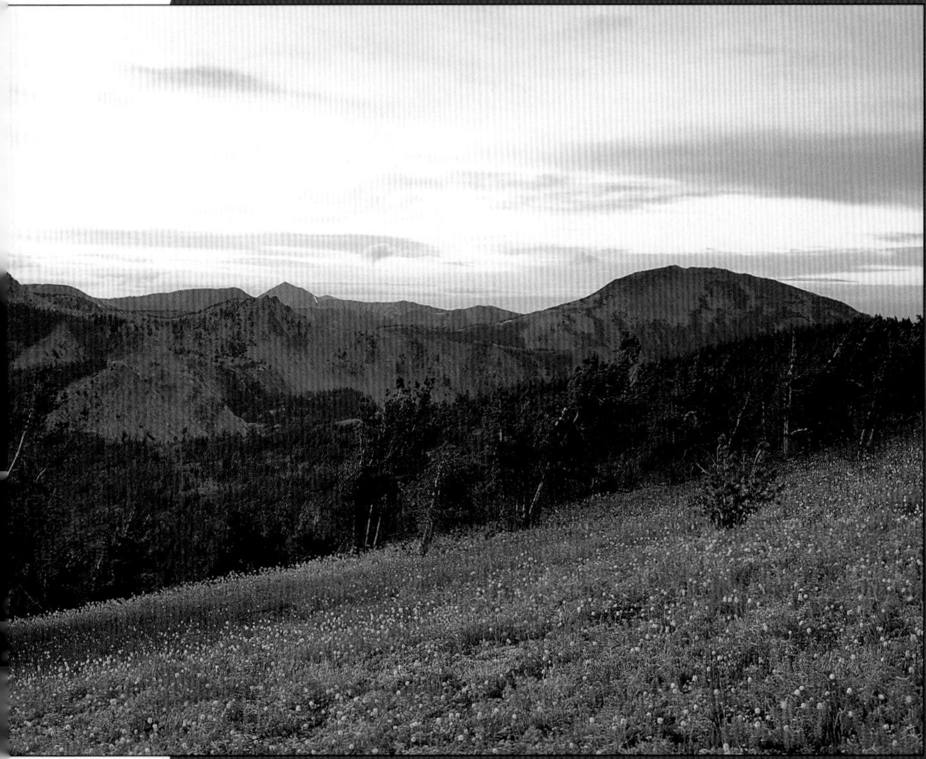

Looking north from the ridge above Jahnke Lake with lupine in the foreground and the pyramidal shape of Homer Young's Peak in the background

26.6 miles

Difficulty: Moderate

Segment 10 **Total Elevation Gain:** 2,667 feet
From Wyoming 275.3 miles
To Canada 705.4 miles

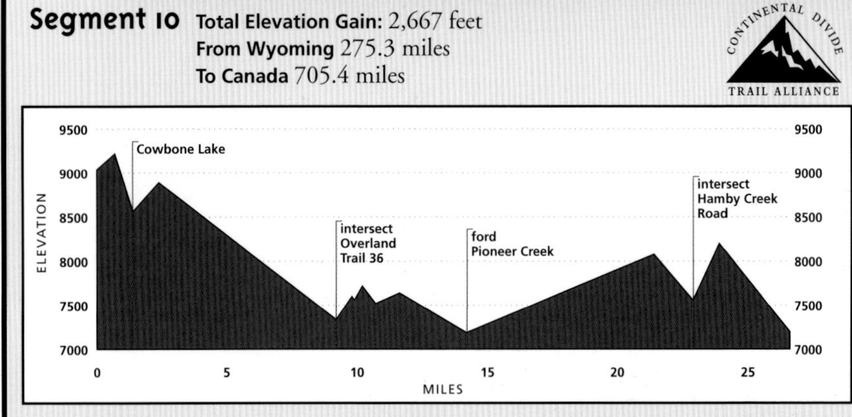

TRAIL OVERVIEW In August, my brother, Leland, and I went back for the third time to hike the Continental Divide Trail going north from Goldstone Pass in the Beaverhead Mountains. Snow and avalanche danger had stopped us before, with as much as 20 feet of snow still lingering on the east-facing slopes as late as July 5.

Part of the trail was not signed; other portions were well-marked. Proposed trail routes were either impossible bushwhacks through thick forest and boggy meadows, or breathtaking alpine excursions that ended in cliffs so steep even the mountain goats didn't attempt the descent.

For now (proposed routes aside), the trail zigzags up and down several creek drainages, almost taking the hiker down into the Big Hole Valley before climbing toward the Divide again and again. The good thing about this is that the creeks are beautiful: seldom grazed by cattle, full of fish, and graced with wildflowers. The bad thing is that trekkers put in a lot more miles than would be necessary if they stayed up closer to the Divide.

This segment of the CDT is the land of posts with no signs. These mute testaments to past signing efforts are often your only guide to the trail. To make matters worse, if you get off the correct route, you may encounter falsely reassuring CDT signs. On the crest of the Divide west of Cowbone Lake, there is a weathered CD sign that looks like it was erected by prehistoric man. This sign is on the route that the Forest Service proposed in 1989, but is not on the current route. If you stay on the crest, you can make your way happily northward for a few miles, but then serious trouble begins. No trail is cut to get you down again on the Montana side, and tempting ridges leading northwest will only take you into never-never land in Idaho where endless cliffs block every descent.

The 1989 proposal shows the CDT descending the north face of cliffs above Pioneer Creek, a feat that is possible very late in the season (August), if you like doing some Class IV climbing with your backpack on. Current proposals include a trek from Cowbone Lake to Jahnke Lake. Private property around the Jahnke mine and insufficient trail construction funds have temporarily halted this plan. The interim route descends along Darkhorse Creek (see the trail description). From Cowbone Lake, it is possible to bushwhack to Jahnke Lake, but you'll still have to descend via the Jahnke Creek Road to the foothills. Directions for the bushwhack are given in the trail description.

There is no water at Goldstone Pass, but water is plentiful in numerous stream crossings from Cowbone Lake north to Miner Lakes.

MOUNTAIN BIKE NOTES: This segment is open to mountain bikes. The sections that follow 4WD roads are easy but rocky, and the rest is difficult technical riding. The trail from Berry Creek to Miner Lakes is not a section I would recommend for mountain bikes. It's not impossible, just tortuous.

LAND ADMINISTRATORS **(SEE APPENDIX A)**

Beaverhead/Deerlodge National Forest, Wisdom Ranger District

MAPS

USGS QUADRANGLES: Goldstone Pass, Selway Mountain, Jackson, Miner Lake. Note that the Miner Lake quadrangle does not show the Berry Creek Road correctly in the southeast corner of the map.

USFS: Beaverhead National Forest. On the Forest Service map, the route of the CDT appears and disappears because the trail was incomplete when the map was issued. From south to north, look for Road 7330, Road 181, Overland Trail 36, Road 7325, and Trail 203.

BEGINNING ACCESS POINT

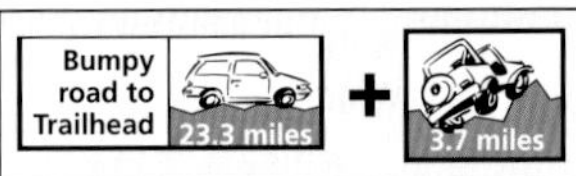

GOLDSTONE PASS: From Highway 278 (Lewis and Clark National Scenic Byway), it is 11 miles to the Van Houten Campground in the Big Hole Valley. Forest Service Road 181 (signed as "Skinner Meadows/Van Houten Campgrounds") continues past the campground and provides access to the 4WD road leading to Goldstone Pass. Road 181 is a gravel 2WD road; road 7327 to Goldstone Pass is suitable only for short-wheel-base, high-clearance 4WD vehicles and experienced drivers. The road is washed out and cannot be accessed on the Idaho side.

ENDING ACCESS POINT

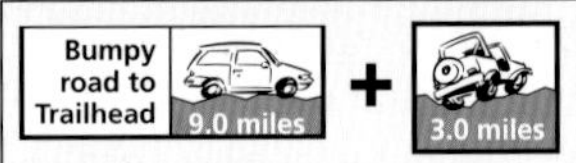

MINER LAKES TRAILHEAD: From the town of Jackson on Hwy. 278, go west on Miner Lake Road 182 for 9 miles to the Lower Miner Lakes Campground. In good weather the road is 2WD to the campground. A 4WD is recommended for the last 3 miles to the trailhead.

TRAIL DESCRIPTION

Goldstone Pass is not identified on the ground. A post with its sign missing marks the apex of Road 7327, which crosses the Montana/Idaho border at the pass. Northbound CDT hikers cross the 4WD road and continue directly uphill.

S **SOUTHBOUND HIKERS:** You could easily miss the spot where the CDT diverges from a 4WD track north of the pass to intercept a footpath that is marked with a small cairn and one blaze (on your left as you walk south). If you miss the turn, you can intersect the road on the Idaho side and then climb a short distance to the pass and the continuation of the CDT.

There are two rock cairns and two blazes where the trail crosses Goldstone Pass. Northbound hikers follow a 4WD track for 0.2 mile to an intersection with a footpath. At the intersection, there is another post with its sign missing, and a hiker registration box with no paper in it. At the sign-in box, turn left (northwest) on a footpath through scrubby whitebark pine and subalpine fir. Take the foot trail instead of continuing on the 4WD track, which ends abruptly at a nice view over the Big Hole Valley.

Where the footpath exits the trees, look for rock cairns that mark the trail close to the actual Divide. A barely discernible 4WD track leads to a ridge overlooking

SUPPLIES, SERVICES, AND ACCOMMODATIONS

JACKSON, MT, is a small town, but has most of the services you will need.

Distance from Trail: 27 miles from Goldstone Pass, 12 miles from Miner Lakes Trailhead.

Zip Code: 59736

Bank:	None	
Bus:	None	
Camping:	RV and Tenting, Jackson Hot Springs Lodge, Main Street, $7.50 tents, $20 RVs, $5 to use hot springs and pool	406-834-3151
Dining:	Jackson Hot Springs Lodge & Restaurant, Main Street	406-834-3151
	Roses Cantina, Main Street	406-834-3100
Gear:	Jackson Mercantile, Main Street	406-834-3107
Groceries:	Jackson Mercantile, Main Street	406-834-3107
Information:	Jackson Hot Springs Lodge, Main Street	406-834-3151
Laundry:	None	
Lodging:	Jackson Hot Springs Lodge, Main Street, $59.95, includes use of hot springs	406-834-3151
Medical:	None	
Outfitters:	Lapham Outfitters, Max Lapham	406-834-3134
	Horn Outfitters, Ken Murdoch, Box 793, Jackson	406-834-3146
	(Advance notice required for special-use permits. Call ahead to arrange for delivery of resupplies at trailheads in the Big Hole Valley area of the Beaverhead Mountains.)	
Post Office:	U.S. Post Office, One Jardine Street, Jackson, MT 59736	406-834-3107
Showers:	See Camping	

Cowbone Lake. At 0.5 mile north of the sign-in box, the trail appears to end. Do not be misled into following the ridge of the Divide as it climbs above Cowbone Lake. Follow a game trail that begins in the saddle and finds its steep way down a short cliff to a tree-covered basin that holds the lake.

It is easy for northbound hikers to miss the trail going down the cliff. The only marker is a small, ill-made cairn. If in doubt, climb the ridge until you can see Cowbone Lake, which is your next destination. Make your way down the cliff and hike 0.7 mile cross-country to the eastern edge of Cowbone Lake, rumored to be a good fishing spot. A good trail (4WD road) begins again on the northeast side of Cowbone Lake.

The 4WD road on the northeast side of Cowbone Lake leads uphill toward Darkhorse Lake, 0.6 mile from Cowbone Lake. An old cabin is sinking into the ground next to the lake.

An unsigned intersection of roads at mile 2.4 (1 mile from Cowbone Lake) should be called "Confusion Corner." Four or five old buildings are weathering nicely in the high-altitude sun, their pine boards ripening to every color from gold to red. At the road intersection it looks like hikers should take the left (west) fork and climb back up to the Divide. Do not do so, unless you are hankering for a wondrous view and are willing to climb back down the same way.

At Confusion Corner, descend on Road 7330 toward Road 181. Road 7330 is on the FS map, but not marked on the ground. The Darkhorse Creek Road is a rough 4WD track that loosely parallels the creek for 5.7 miles.

At 1.8 miles from Cowbone Lake (mile 3.2 for this segment), in a small meadow, you can see the saddle to the north that you must bushwhack over if you decide to attempt the proposed but unfinished route to Jahnke Lake. Head a bit farther down Road 7330 to access an easier route to the saddle.

Two miles from Cowbone Lake, a 4WD track leads uphill (on your left for northbound hikers) to two abandoned mining cabins and a mine. This is the beginning of the best approach to the saddle above Jahnke Lake. Walk past and above the cabins to a level spot on the tailings from the mine and begin a self-made "switchback" going west/northwest to the saddle. Once you reach the saddle, you can see a game trail to Jahnke Lake. Keep in mind that this is a proposed route. The interim, and easier, route continues to descend in an easterly direction along Darkhorse Creek.

Intersect Road 181, the Skinner Meadows Road, at mile 8.1 and turn left (north). (Southbound hikers, note that there is a post with no sign at the intersection of Road 181 and the Darkhorse Creek Road. About 100 yards from the intersection, it is signed as "Primitive Road. Not Maintained.") Hikers are on Road 181 for 1.1 miles.

At 9.2 miles, leave Road 181 and enter a footpath cutting up into the forest on your left (northwest). This is part of Overland Trail 36. Keep a sharp lookout for the indistinct track and one blaze. Trail tread becomes more obvious once you are well into the trees.

This short section of Overland Trail 36 leads to Jahnke Lake Road at mile 11.4. Two creek crossings, Blind Canyon Creek and Jahnke Creek, are good water sources. The Blind Canyon crossing is signed as "Overland Trail 36," but there are no CDT signs. Where Overland Trail 36 intersects Jahnke Road, there are two posts, one with a CD sign, and one that is missing its sign. This intersection is also signed for Jahnke Lake to the west.

Cross Jahnke Road and continue on a 4WD track, in a northerly direction, to an intersection with Pioneer Creek Trail and the continuation of Overland Trail 36. CDT hikers stay on Overland Trail 36, which is a right-hand fork for northbound hikers. This intersection boasts two wooden CDT signs.

The proposed route of the CDT turns west along Pioneer Creek to follow a rough two-track for 2.5 miles, where it then turns north through Berry Meadows to Berry Creek. It's easy to follow the track along Pioneer Creek, but where the proposed trail would lead to Berry Creek, the bushwhack is nearly impossible. We strongly recommend that hikers stay on Overland Trail 36, which is signed as the interim route of the CDT.

Overland Trail 36 intersects and follows a better-quality 4WD road at mile 13.3 (1.7 miles from the intersection on the Pioneer Creek Trail). Northbound hikers keep right on the fork that is signed with a wooden CD symbol.

Ford Pioneer Creek at mile 14.2. This is a long ford that actually stays in the creek before emerging on the opposite bank. It could be a challenge earlier in the season. In an open meadow north of the ford, there is an unsigned two-track intersection. Northbound hikers keep right, on the main track, which is still Overland Trail 36. The trail trends northeast, descending further into the foothills of the Big Hole Valley.

Intersect the Berry Creek Road (#7325) at mile 14.9. Turn west, toward the Divide, and follow the rough 4WD road up Berry Creek for 5.5 miles. A hundred yards past an old cabin (not depicted on the FS map), look for a CDT sign that is faded gray on the north side of the road. This north turn onto Trail 203 is hard to spot—use the old cabin as a reference. Very dim tread leaves the road and heads north to Hamby Creek. Another clue to look for is ancient, sawed-out logs from a fire line probably cut in the Paleozoic Era. The tread becomes somewhat clearer as you climb into the trees. Deadfall blocks the trail in several places—watch for tree blazes to stay on track.

Near Hamby Creek, the visible tread ends. Follow blazes and one rock cairn to a meadow watered by Hamby Creek. (For southbound hikers, there is a CD sign on a tree at the edge of the meadow, but no sign is visible for northbound hikers.) Cross the meadow and stream as best you can to intersect Hamby Creek Road at mile 22.9. You should emerge where the road is signed as "Hamby Creek." Careful inspection will yield two CD signs, one on the south side of the road and one on the north, both hard to see.

S **SOUTHBOUND HIKERS:** At the Hamby Creek ford, look for a blaze on the south side of the meadow. Look for cut limbs on one side of the tree if you can't see the blaze. Ford the creek and head gently uphill on the east side of that tree. The tread is barely discernible, but you can follow some ill-made blazes. The blazes are also easy to lose, especially where the trail turns. The trail trends east to contour around the south side of higher terrain. Tread becomes visible in the trees. The IFTMA (Idaho Falls Trail Machine Association) was once here and carved their club initials in two logs, and the trail has not been cleared since.

There is no visible tread where the trail goes north from Hamby Creek Road. Look for one CD sign on a tree. Once you get into the trees, tread appears. This 4-mile trail to Miner Lakes needs quite a bit of work. It is so steep in places that horsemen would not be able to ride stock over it without dismounting. Switchbacks are non-existent or far steeper than regulation grade. The trail disappears in bogs and meadows, but there are usually enough blazes to put you back on the track. On the Forest Service map, this is still Trail 203.

Ford Miner Creek at mile 26.5, a deep, swift ford that could be trouble earlier in the hiking season. Trail 203 intersects the Miner Lakes Trailhead (Trail 9 on the FS map) at mile 26.6. A big sign and a well-marked trail entrance announce "Trail 203, Hamby Creek"—this is the first time that northbound hikers see a trail number for 203.

The Miner Lakes Trailhead is 0.2 mile northeast of the Hamby Creek Trail intersection. Follow the closed road to a gate and then to the trailhead. For hikers who are not stopping here, the next best camping spot is at Rock Island Lakes 3.2 miles west on Trail 9, which is also the CDT.

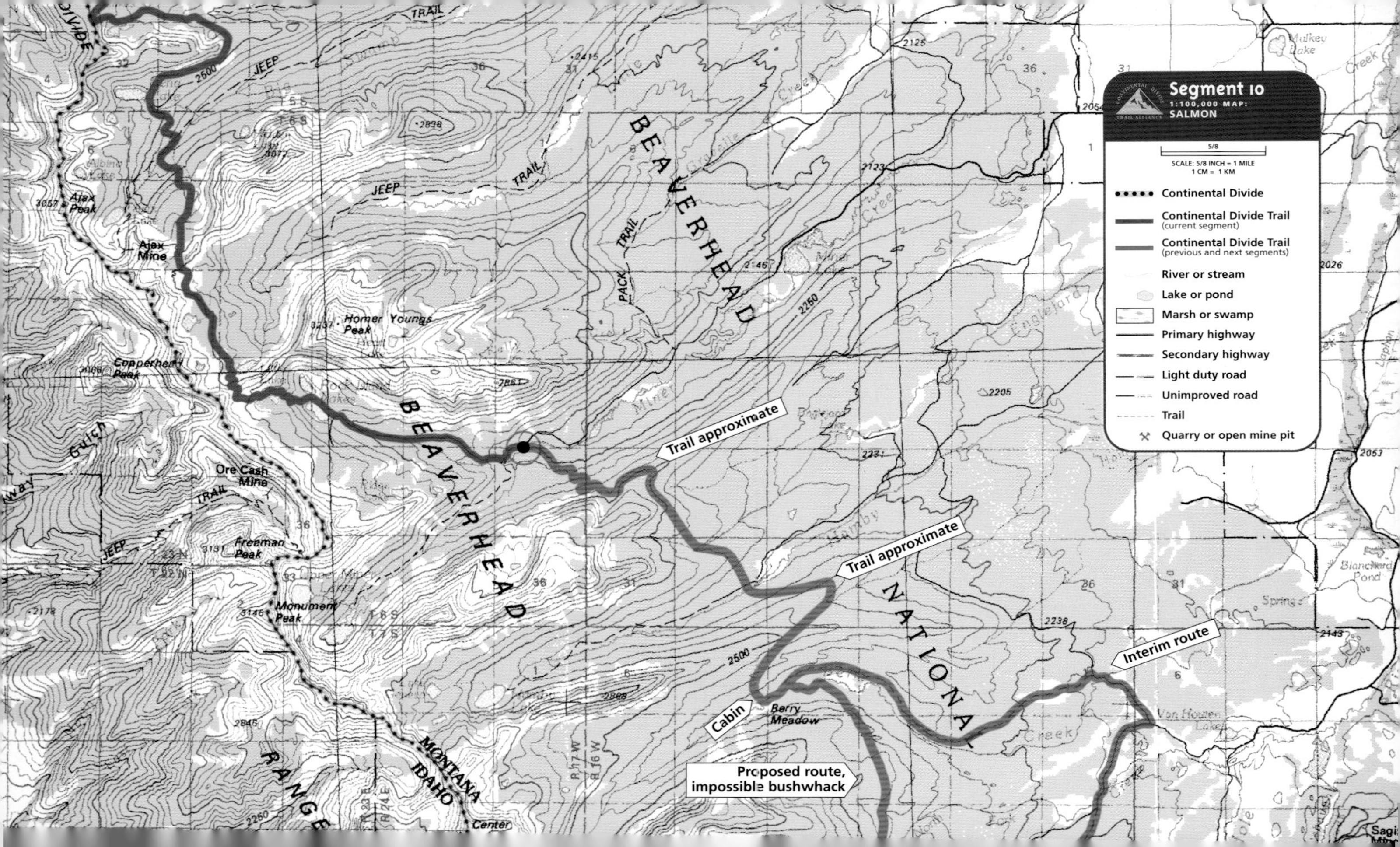
Segment 10
1:100,000 MAP: SALMON
5/8
SCALE: 5/8 INCH = 1 MILE
1 CM = 1 KM
Continental Divide
Continental Divide Trail (current segment)
Continental Divide Trail (previous and next segments)
River or stream
Lake or pond
Marsh or swamp
Primary highway
Secondary highway
Light duty road
Unimproved road
Trail
Quarry or open mine pit
Trail approximate
Trail approximate
Interim route
Cabin
Berry Meadow
Proposed route, impossible bushwhack
BEAVERHEAD
BEAVERHEAD
NATIONAL
RANGE
MONTANA
IDAHO
DIVIDE
Ajax Peak
Ajax Mine
Homer Youngs Peak
Copperhead Peak
Ore Cash Mine
Freeman Peak
Monument Peak
Gulch
JEEP
TRAIL
PACK TRAIL
Mulkey Lake
Blanchard Pond
Von Houten Lake
Creek
Center

FOREST
MOUNTAINS
SALMON
CONTINENTAL
DIVIDE
NATIONAL
Proposed route
Proposed route
Cabin
Cabin
Interim route
Goldstone Pass
Goldstone Mountain
Skinner Meadows
Black Mountain
Lookout
Selway Mountain
Brind Canyon
BEAVERHEAD CO
LEMHI CO
Baker

Segment 11

Miner Lakes Trailhead to Big Hole Pass: Beaverhead Mountains of the Bitterroot Range

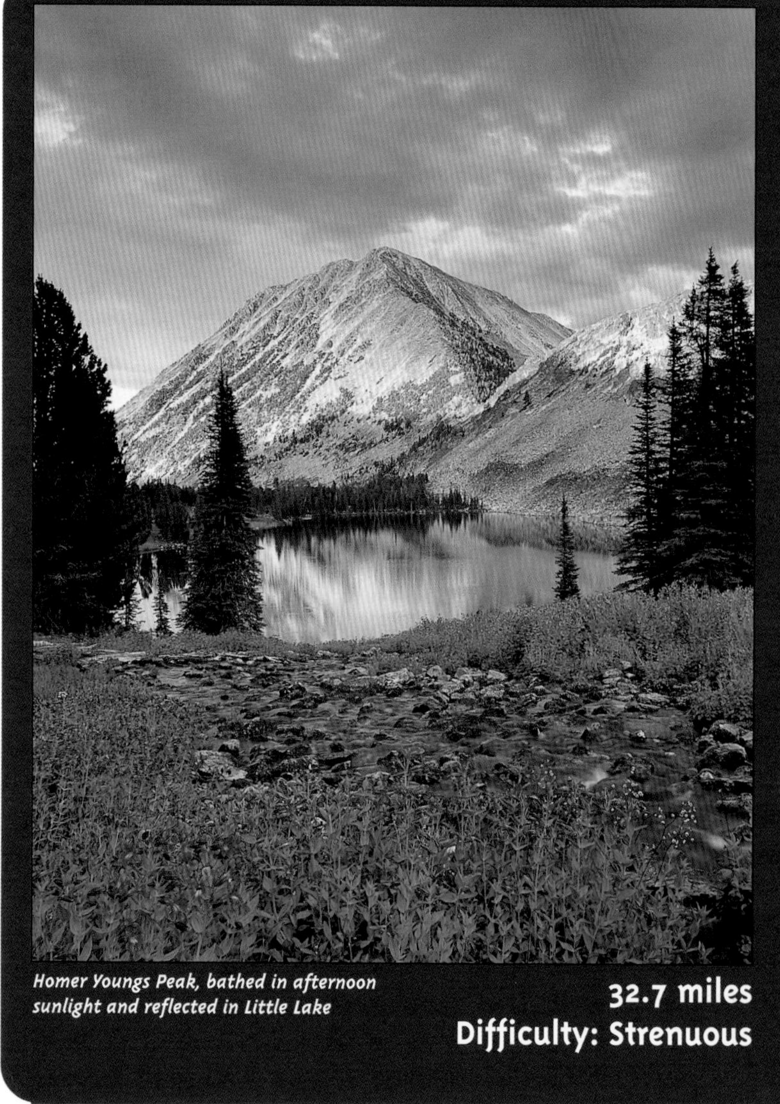

Homer Youngs Peak, bathed in afternoon sunlight and reflected in Little Lake

32.7 miles
Difficulty: Strenuous

TRAIL OVERVIEW The Beaverhead Mountains of the Bitterroot Range are certainly not as glaciated as those in Glacier National Park, but they are rugged enough to make it difficult to cut a trail along the Divide. The terrain near Little Lake in this segment is some of the most glacier-carved terrain that CDT trekkers will see outside of Glacier National Park.

There are three steep climbs in this section, with long stretches of milder terrain between each climb. Some of the steep terrain is also on north-facing slopes, making this a treacherous hike earlier in the season. Snow does not usually melt off the trail until late July. At the highest elevations, we found lingering snowdrifts in the first week of August.

You can get lost in this section before you even get to the trail. Oddly, there are lone CD signs scattered around in confusing spots far from the actual route of the CDT. If you stay on the current route of the CDT, you'll never see these signs, but if you're off the route, they can be misleading.

Water is plentiful along the entire route.

MOUNTAIN BIKE NOTES: Most of this segment is not ridable; however, mountain bikers could cycle from the trailhead to Rock Island Lakes, and there are almost endless opportunities for biking along the 4WD roads that lead toward the Divide from Highway 278 in the Big Hole Valley. All of the trail in Idaho, beginning at the saddle above Fourth of July Creek, is open to mountain bikes and is ridable if one is willing to carry the bike through short sections.

LAND ADMINISTRATORS (SEE APPENDIX A)

Beaverhead/Deerlodge National Forest, Wisdom Ranger District
Salmon National Forest, North Fork Ranger District

MAPS

USGS QUADRANGLES: Miner Lake, Homer Youngs Peak, Jumbo Mountain, Shewag Lake, Big Hole Pass

USFS: Beaverhead National Forest

BEGINNING ACCESS POINT

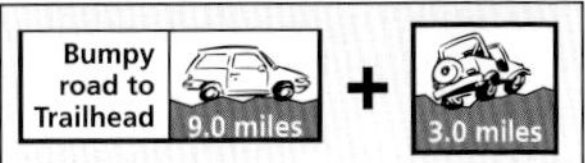

MINER LAKES TRAILHEAD: The small town of Jackson is on Highway 278, 18 miles south of Wisdom, in the Big Hole Valley. From Jackson,

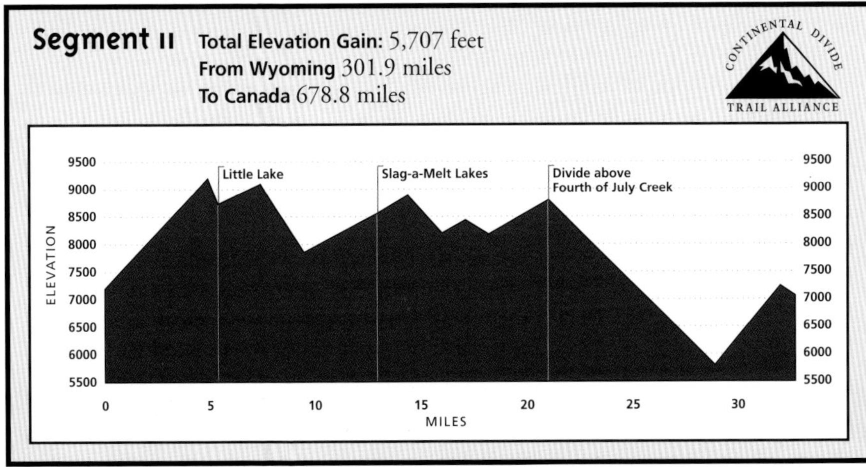

go west on Miner Lake Road 182 for nine miles to the Lower Miner Lakes Campground. In good weather the road is 2WD to the campground. 4WD is recommended for the last three miles to the trailhead.

ENDING ACCESS POINT

BIG HOLE PASS: Gibbonsville, ID, on US-93, is 8.5 miles from Big Hole Pass. From US-93, drive eastward through Gibbonsville, up the Dahlonega Creek Road (079) to Big Hole Pass. The road is 2WD in good weather. Along the access road up to Big Hole Pass are many beautiful ponderosa pines, with their characteristic reddish trunks and well-spaced, park-like setting. Big Hole Pass is also accessible from the Montana side via FS Road 943 from Highway 43.

SUPPLIES, SERVICES, AND ACCOMMODATIONS

JACKSON, MT, is a small town, but has most of the services you will need. (See Segment 10.)
Distance from Trail: 12 miles

TRAIL DESCRIPTION

This segment begins at the Miner Lakes Trailhead in Montana's Big Hole Valley. About 500 yards up the trail is an intersection with Hamby Creek Trail 203 and the Miner Lakes Trail (Trail 9 on the FS map). There is a large sign and a well-marked trail entrance for southbound hikers. There are also wooden CD signs on trees adjacent to this trail intersection.

The Miner Lakes Trail, a long-since-closed road, is good all the way to Rock Island Lakes. Not surprisingly, we saw a few horsemen and some day hikers on this section. Trail 9 becomes less of a road and more of a trail as you approach Rock Island Lakes. Multiple stream crossings offer plenty of opportunities to filter drinking water.

At a trail intersection with the Upper Miner Lake Trail (mile 1.2), CDT hikers continue on Rock Island Lake Trail 54. There is also a wooden CD sign at this intersection. It is 2 miles from the Upper Miner Lake Trail intersection to Rock Island Lake (mile 3.2 for this segment). We saw a 12-inch trout in the shallows near the trail, and that's no fish story. There is good camping on the south shore of the lake, which is accessed via a spur trail from the CDT.

Northwest of the first and largest of the Rock Island Lakes, the trail begins a climb to a saddle that crosses a ridge just below the Divide. The climb is steep, with a few short, very steep switchbacks. As the trail nears the saddle, it is marked with rock cairns and the tread is barely discernible.

The silver lining is that this sharp climb diminishes the traffic to Little Lake. Solitude and quiet are assured. The trail tops out above Little Lake at an elevation of 9,200 feet, giving hikers a mountain goat's view of the surrounding alpine terrain. A shallow tarn above Rock Island Lakes is visible as one climbs to the saddle.

Little Lake is 2.2 miles from the lower end of Rock Island Lake at mile 5.4 for this segment. This area is a pristine paradise that suggests glaciers had only an artistic intent when they scooped a cirque for the lake and created a headwall above an emerald-green sward where mountain goats graze.

A pretty inlet, replete with multiple waterfalls, courses into Little Lake. The inlet is not on the topos, but it apparently runs all year and is some of the best-tasting water I've pumped through my filter. Lewis's monkeyflowers line the banks of the inlet in such profusion that the band of shocking pink color can be seen from the saddle above the lake. Homer Youngs Peak sits at the foot of the lake, a perfect pyramid of a peak that looks at its own reflection in Little Lake's waters throughout the afternoon and evening. My brother, Leland, was in photographer heaven.

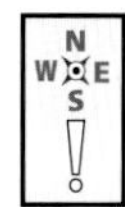

The trail is marked with stone cairns as it continues northward from Little Lake, and then the trail disappears in meadows and braided streams of snowmelt. We could guess where a trail ought to be, so we followed a bench below the Divide until we intercepted a marked trail. In the meadow, there is one metal sign on a tree that says "Little Lake Creek Trail," which refers to a trail that descends along the creek to intercept jeep track 180. CDT trekkers continue north/northwest at this sign, staying high on the bench below the Divide.

The trail that is intercepted after about 0.25 mile of cross-country travel was marked with orange paint by Joe Phillips in 1953. He signed his name and the date on a house-sized boulder below the Divide. (I guess Joe did not have access to the aesthetics committee of the CDNST.) We followed Joe's orange blazes and crossed more spectacular alpine zones, the views so good that I kept stumbling as I looked over my shoulder instead of at the trail.

One mile north of Little Lake, the trail descends slightly to cross a stream where an old cabin is slowly disintegrating on the mossy banks. Two miles north of Little Lake (mile 7.4 for this segment), the trail crosses a saddle on a spur ridge before it descends to Little Joe Lake. Little Joe Lake is not named on the topo, but that's what the locals call it. Joe Phillips must have made quite an impression in his day. According to local sources, Joe was a trail crew foreman who worked out of a ranger station in Jackson (now closed). A retired military man from Wisconsin, he came to Montana to work on the trails every summer, and was known for his exceptional endurance.

Trees obscure views of the 10,000-plus-foot peaks east of Little Joe Lake, and of Ajax Peak on the Divide to the west. Water is abundant as the trail loosely parallels a nameless feeder stream to Little Joe Lake. Below Little Joe Lake, many switchbacks, some of them steep, take the trail across 2.1 miles of forested terrain to an intersection with the jeep track along Big Swamp Creek, elevation 7,856 feet, mile 9.5 for this segment.

Ajax Lake can be reached by detouring about 1 mile west, and uphill toward the Divide. Follow the jeep trail, which dead-ends at a mine beyond the lake. Ajax Lake sits in a glacial cirque below Ajax Peak and would be more scenic were it not for a burned area on the shore. Waterfalls in the outlet stream are quite pretty, making this a worthwhile detour.

Follow the jeep track northeast along Big Swamp Creek for a hundred yards before turning north into the trees. Newly cut tread and new signs mark the trail that contours below Lena Lake. The new signs say "CDNST"—initials that puzzled even seasoned CDT hikers that we met on the trail. Apparently, the "Continental Divide National Scenic Trail" nomenclature is not yet well-known.

A short, feeder trail leads to Lena Lake from the CDT (at mile 10.4). North of Lena Lake, the trail swings eastward to round an 8,740-foot knob. The trees thin here and islands of sagebrush are a welcome change from the viewless terrain at Lena Lake. Southbound hikers will see the intimidating, glaciated peaks of the Beaverheads they will soon be climbing, and northbound hikers can pause to look back and be equally impressed by the terrain they have covered.

1.4 miles from the Lena Lake trail intersection, the CDT crosses above a small pond at 8,400 feet elevation, then bends northwest and descends for 0.5 mile to intercept the four-wheeler track on Slag-a-Melt Creek, Trail 186. At mile 12.3, northbound hikers turn left (west) to climb 0.7 mile to the first of two Slag-a-Melt Lakes.

SOUTHBOUND HIKERS: When descending from the lakes, take care to keep right and ascend the new tread. There is no CD sign on the new footpath for southbound hikers, and the one CDNST sign at the intersection misleads descending hikers, as it seems to indicate that one should stay on the four-wheeler route. Look for a "non-motorized" sign on the footpath that is uphill to the right (southeast).

Note that this section of the trail from Big Swamp Creek to the intersection with Trail 186 does not appear on the topo or on the Forest Service map.

At the first, and smallest, of the Slag-a-Melt Lakes, a sign cautions against grazing horses near the lake, but there is no CD sign. However, only one path leads up from here, so there is little chance for confusion. The four-wheeler track continues past the lake, leading around its southern edge to the second lake. Look for a footpath departing from the track to the right (northwesterly) near the spot where the second lake is just visible. A sign at the intersection says "Closed to Motorized Vehicles," and a few feet farther there is a faded wooden CD sign on a tree.

There are visible tread, some blazes, and a few rock cairns marking the way to the saddle above Slag-a-Melt Lakes. The route is somewhat counter-intuitive, switchbacking up to a bench far south of where it actually crosses the Divide. The saddle where it does cross the Divide is at 8,890 feet, above the first of the Slag-a-Melt Lakes. The path makes up for its 1.4-mile meandering route by providing impressive views, including long-distance panoramas of the Big Hole Valley, and bird's-eye views of the Slag-a-Melt Lakes. From the saddle itself, the higher peaks of the Anaconda Range are visible.

Newly built switchbacks bring the trail down from the saddle into a bowl of trees hemmed in on the east by Squaw Mountain and on the west by the Divide. Tributaries of Big Lake Creek make for boggy spots in the trail, but also offer welcome water sources. The coniferous forest is thick and there are some old growth Douglas-fir trees on the northern slopes. This portion of the trail melts out late due to heavy snowfall and northern exposure. Snow lingers until the last week of July.

The trail dips to a low of 8,200 feet west of Squaw Mountain before climbing again to the Divide. On the crest there is no water, so bring some up with you if you want to camp on top where the views are better.

It is 3.1 miles from the saddle above Slag-a-Melt Lakes, through the bowl of trees, and back up to the Divide. On the crest, the Carmen Creek Trail comes up from the Idaho side to meet the CDT at mile 17.1 for this segment. The Carmen Creek Trail is visible tread, but marked only with a "C" carved into a tree. CDT hikers continue north at this intersection, walking the almost-level crest of the Divide for about 0.5 mile before descending on the Montana side. The route is marked with stone cairns.

After a short cruise on the crest of the Divide, the trail switchbacks down on the Montana side to a small pond where several signs mark the "CDNST 9" and an intersection with a trail coming up from Twin Lakes, signed as "Big Lake Creek Trail/ Twin Lake Road 183." Hikers who want to exit the CDT and meet friends or support crews at Twin Lakes Campground would descend here. North-to-south hikers will also find signs directing them to Slag-a-Melt Lakes.

From the pond the trail climbs gently, staying on the Montana side just below the cliffs that mark the Divide. There is a good camping spot at mile 19 for this segment, on the eastern shore of an unnamed lake—but it is likely to be snowed in until late July. We saw many elk in this remote area. "Spring" flowers were blooming in the first week of August and snow lingered in shaded, north-facing nooks and crannies.

Follow the visible tread northward from the unnamed lake (6 miles north of Slag-a-Melt Lakes), cruising along below the Divide for 2 miles to a saddle above Idaho's Fourth of July Creek, where you'll see a weathered CD sign.

From the saddle above Fourth of July Creek, the trail leaves the Divide and continues northerly on the Idaho (western) side. It follows a narrow spur ridge that has a top-of-the-world feel and features long views and high-quality trail construction, including rock retaining walls. The trail crosses many talus slopes from which hikers have a clear view of Idaho's Lemhi Range.

The Fourth of July Creek Trail comes up from the Idaho side at mile 24, elevation 7,520 feet. This intersection is not signed. CD hikers will continue on the blazed trail straight ahead.

From the intersection with Fourth of July Creek, the CDT goes gently downhill to the South Fork of Sheep Creek. It parallels the creek for 1 mile in a straightforward manner, with the exception of one S-shaped curve that has hikers briefly doubling back to the south. The trail crosses Sheep Creek 2.5 miles from the Fourth of July intersection (mile 26.5 for this segment).

The CDT continues to parallel the South Fork of Sheep Creek, crossing the creek many times before reaching the lowest elevation (5,800 feet) for this portion of the trail. At mile 28.9, a pack trail enters from the North Fork of Sheep Creek in Bradley Gulch. There are very few open spots in this section as hikers make their way through dense forest, with rock slides on steeper terrain offering the only views.

Bradley Gulch is a narrow defile through which the CDT climbs, following an old jeep trail that is now open only to two-wheeled ATV traffic. One-fourth mile south of the Divide, the CDT bypasses an old footpath on the right (west) and climbs directly and steeply to the Divide. At 7,140 feet and mile 30.9 (6.9 miles from the intersection with Fourth of July Creek), the trail crosses the Divide, leaving the jeep track near a locked gate. The gate is signed with motor vehicle travel restriction notices, and there are two CD signs north of the gate.

At the locked gate, northbound hikers leave the ATV trail and follow a newly constructed footpath on the Montana side of Morgan Mountain. The footpath winds around a bit as it closely follows the 7,200 contour line for 1.9 miles to an intersection with Road 078 to Big Hole Pass. Note that the topo map shows "Big Hole Pass" twice on the jeep road, first at elevation 7,243 feet, and then at elevation 7,060 feet.

It is easy walking for 0.9 mile on Road 078, going north to Big Hole Pass and the intersection of Roads 079 to Gibbonsville, Idaho, and 624 to Wisdom, Montana.

S **SOUTHBOUND HIKERS:** 0.9 mile south of Big Hole Pass, the CDT leaves the 4WD road. This intersection is quite hard to find because the wooden CD sign is 20 feet back in the trees. There is one blaze below the sign and the blaze is easier to spot. No visible tread shows where the trail leaves the road, and deadfall and grass obscure the beginning of the path. To ensure that you don't walk past the intersection, estimate your mileage by hiking time and begin looking for the path south of where a two-track leaves the road on the left (east) side. The two-track is a short loop of road that is a scenic detour. The footpath diverges from Road 078 south of this two-track.

There is no water at Big Hole Pass, but a short hike off the Divide on the Montana side leads to water in Pioneer Creek. On the Idaho side, it is about 3.5 miles to water in Thompson Gulch.

OTHER EXCURSIONS

BANNACK, the site of Montana's first major gold rush, is an interesting ghost town about 30 miles south of Jackson. Take Highway 278 to Road 5. Look for the "Bannack State Park" signs. Bannack was Montana's territorial capital in 1864. A walking tour gives visitors an understanding of the cultural and historical background of this boomtown gone bust.

BIG HOLE BATTLEFIELD is 12 highway miles west of Wisdom, Montana. This is the site of the 1877 battle between the U.S. Army and the Nez Perce Indians. The walking trails explore the campsites, battle zones, and the ridge where the Indians captured the army's howitzer.

THE BIG HOLE RIVER is internationally famous for its recreational fishing. Other states stock their rivers with hatchery trout, but Montana's fish and game department manages most of the rivers for wild trout. A Montana fishing license is required. The town of Wise River on Highway 43 is a good place to inquire about fishing and campgrounds.

Big Swamp Creek, an outlet stream, leads from Ajax Lake above Montana's Big Hole Valley.

Segment 11
1:100,000 MAPS:
SALMON and WISDOM
CONTINENTAL DIVIDE TRAIL ALLIANCE
5/8
SCALE: 5/8 INCH = 1 MILE
1 CM = 1 KM
Continental Divide
Continental Divide Trail
(current segment)
Continental Divide Trail
(previous and next segments)
River or stream
Lake or pond
Marsh or swamp
Primary highway
Secondary highway
Light duty road
Unimproved road
Trail
Quarry or open mine pit
USGS: WISDOM
USGS: SALMON
Gibbonsville
Big Hole Pass
LEMHI CO
BEAVERHEAD CO
Morgan Mountain
Gulch
Eagle Mountain
Eagle Mtn
PACK TRAIL
Stein Gulch
TRAIL
Stein Mtn Lookout
N Mountain
NAT FOR BDY
BOUNDARY
Sheep Mtn
FOREST
NATIONAL
Pyramid Peak
CONTINENTAL
PACK
TRAIL
Jumbo Mountain
JEEP
TRAIL
Gulch

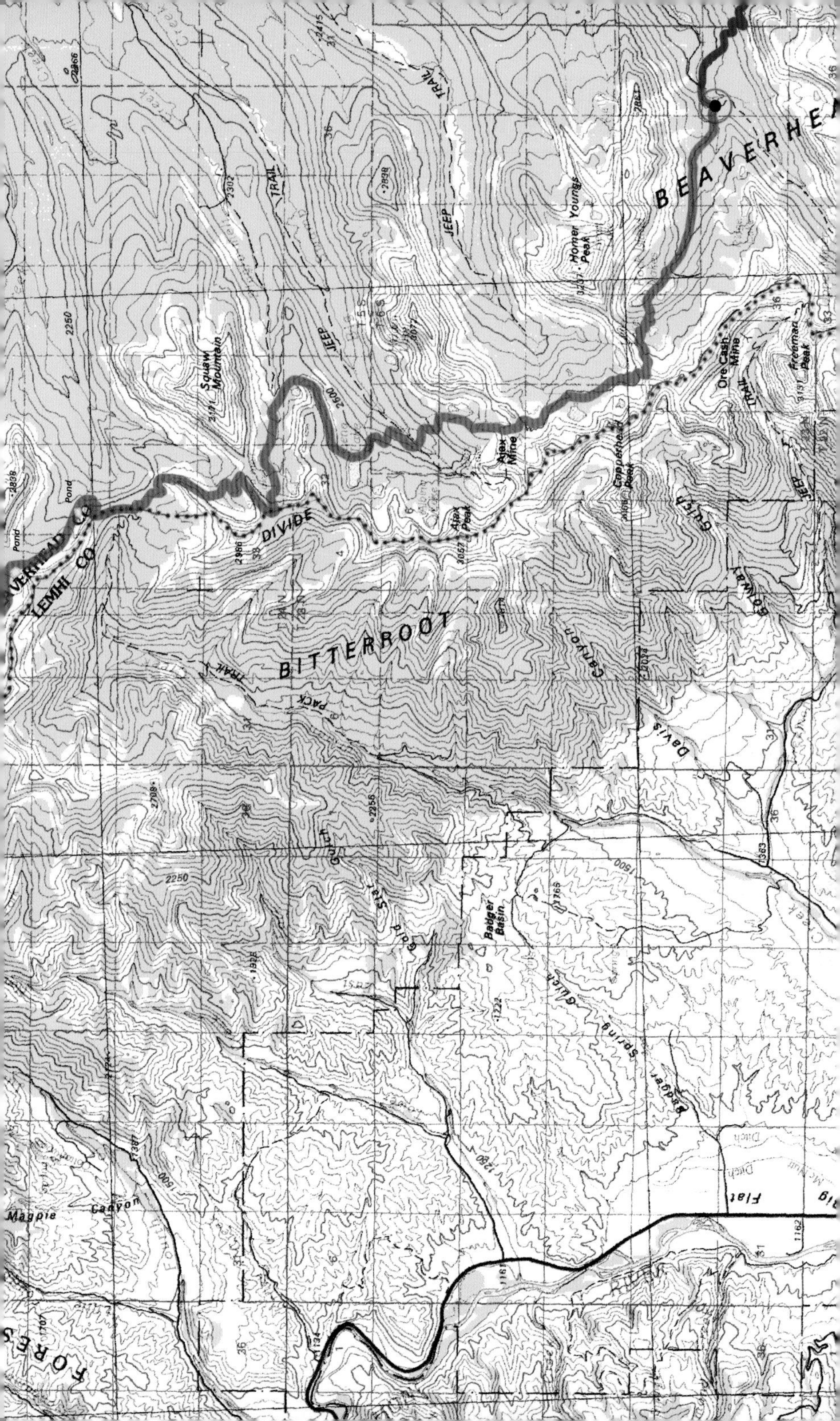
BEAVERHE
BITTERROOT
DIVIDE
LEMHI CO
Squaw Mountain
Homer Youngs Peak
Ajax Mine
Ajax Peak
Copperhead Peak
Ore Cash Mine
Freeman Peak
Gulch
Canyon
Davis
Badger Basin
Spring Gulch
Gold Flat Gulch
Badger
Magpie Canyon
PACK TRAIL
TRAIL
JEEP
Pond
Ditch
Flat
FORES

Segment 12
Big Hole Pass to Chief Joseph Pass: Beaverhead Mtns.

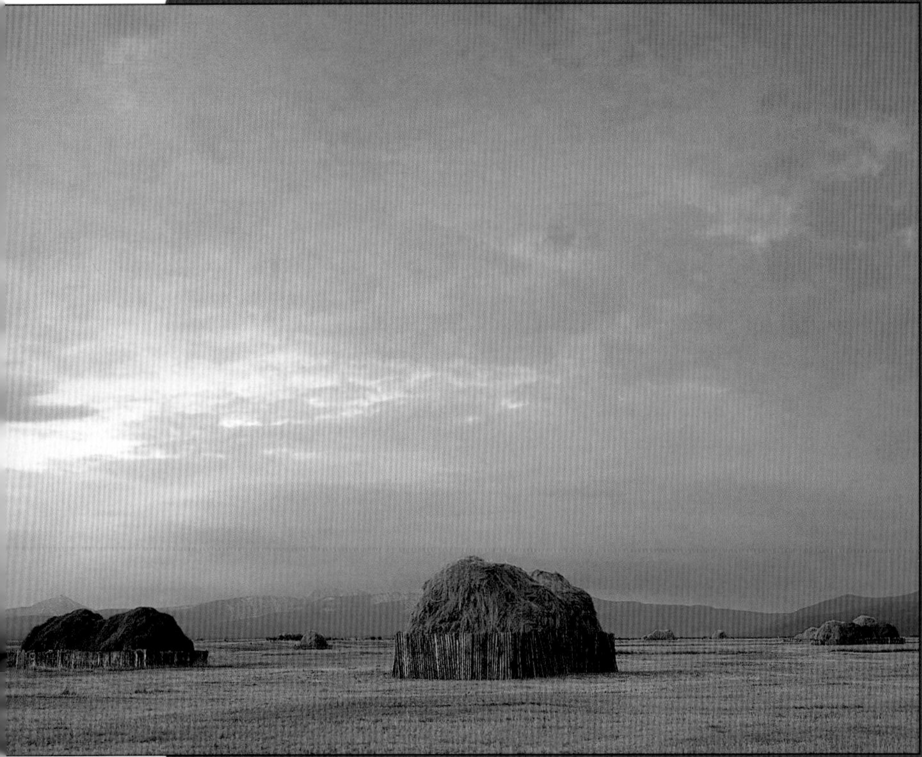

Continental Divide trekkers hike above and along Montana's Big Hole Valley, the "land of 10,000 haystacks" and home to some of the state's richest ranchlands.

16.8 miles
Difficulty: Moderate

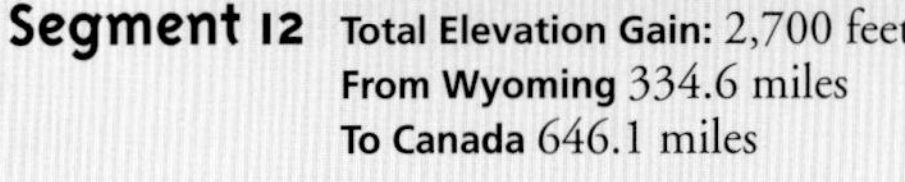

Segment 12 **Total Elevation Gain:** 2,700 feet
From Wyoming 334.6 miles
To Canada 646.1 miles

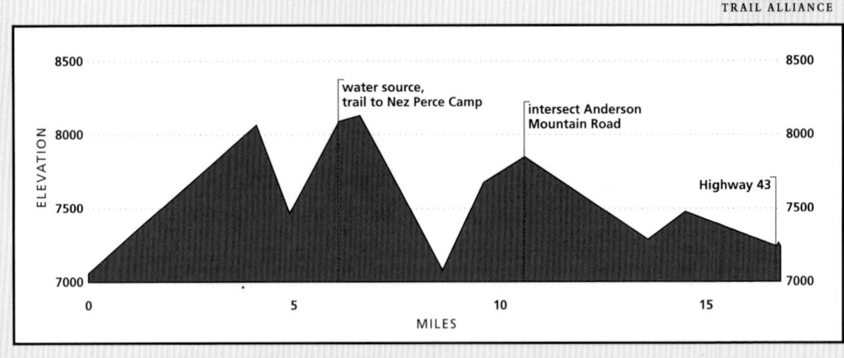

TRAIL OVERVIEW Along much of this segment, hikers could put one foot in Idaho and one in Montana as they walk the crest of the Continental Divide in the Beaverhead Mountains of the Bitterroot Range. The ridge is narrow, with frequent views into the Big Hole Basin and over the steeper terrain of Idaho's Salmon River. Despite its short length, this segment is moderately strenuous as it follows the Divide's ups and downs, climbing 600 to 1,000 feet.

The Idaho/Montana Continental Divide National Scenic Trail was dedicated at Chief Joseph Pass, the northern terminus of this segment, on June 21, 1989. The pass is named for the Nez Perce chief who, in 1877, led more than a thousand of his people on a winding journey from Oregon's Wallowa Valley to within 45 miles of the Canadian border before being defeated by the U.S. Army. Chief Joseph died in 1904 on a reservation in Washington. He said: "The earth is the mother of all people, and all people should have equal rights upon it. You might as well expect the rivers to run backward as that any man who was born free should be contented penned up and denied liberty to go where he pleases."

Water is extremely scarce in this segment, with only one water source at a spring 0.3 mile west of the trail (see Trail Description). There is no water at Big Hole Pass, but a short hike off the Divide on the Montana side leads to water in Pioneer Creek. On the Idaho side, it is about 3.5 miles to water in Thompson Gulch. There is no water at Chief Joseph Pass and it is 5.3 miles on the CDT north of the pass to a tributary of Trail Creek.

MOUNTAIN BIKE NOTES: This segment is open to mountain bikes and, with the exception of some steep climbs, is technically easy.

LAND ADMINISTRATORS (SEE APPENDIX A)

Salmon National Forest, North Fork Ranger District

MAPS

USGS QUADRANGLES: Big Hole Pass, Gibbonsville, Lost Trail Pass

USFS: Beaverhead National Forest

BEGINNING ACCESS POINT

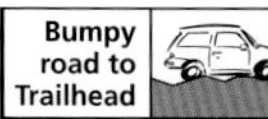

BIG HOLE PASS: Gibbonsville, Idaho, on US-93, is 8.5 miles from Big Hole Pass. Follow Dahlonega Creek Road 079, which is 2WD in good weather, east to the pass. From the Montana side of the Divide, it is 27 miles from the town of Wisdom on Highway 43, via Forest Service Roads 934 (Gibbonsville Road) and 624.

ENDING ACCESS POINT

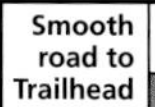

CHIEF JOSEPH PASS on Montana Highway 43

SUPPLIES, SERVICES, AND ACCOMMODATIONS

WISDOM, MT

Distance from Trail: 27 miles from Big Hole Pass and 25 miles from Chief Joseph Pass

Zip Code: 59761

Bank:	None	
Bus:	None	
Camping:	American Legion Campground, Hwy. 43	
	May Creek Forest Service Campground, Hwy. 43, 15 miles east of Chief Joseph Pass	
Dining:	Big Hole Crossing, 101 Main Street	406-689-3800
	Fetty's Bar & Cafe, Hwy. 43	406-689-3260
Gear:	Conover's Trading Post, Hwy. 43	406-689-3271
Groceries:	Wisdom Market, Main Street & Hwy. 43	406-689-3271
Information:	Fetty's Bar & Cafe (see Dining)	
Laundry:	Conover's Laundromat, behind Conover's Apartments	
Lodging:	Sandman Motel, P.O. Box 82, Hwy. 43, $32–$35	406-689-3218
	Nez Perce Motel, Hwy. 43, 406-689-3254	
Medical:	Call 911 in Wisdom to page paramedics	
Post Office:	U.S. Post Office, Hwy. 43, Wisdom, MT 59761	406-689-3224
Showers:	See Sandman Motel, $3.50	
Special Notes:	Gibbonsville, ID, on US-93, has a post office, Zip 83463.	208-865-2262

Salmon, a larger, full-service town, is 34 miles south of Gibbonsville on US-93.

TRAIL DESCRIPTION The trail begins as a 4WD track, but very quickly becomes an ATV trail and then a footpath. For most of the route, it looks like a trode that makes its way through coniferous forest and across occasional open spots. It is impossible to get lost in this segment. There's only one ridge and visible tread all the way.

A CD sign on a tree marks the beginning of the trail as you start north from the pass. Although there is no water for the first 6 miles, snowbanks can be found at the higher elevations into late June. The initial part of the trail is not blazed, but at mile 3.0 occasional blazes appear and the trail is then blazed for about 5 miles. Round iron pipes, topped with survey information, mark the Montana/Idaho border along the ridge. At mile 4.9 the trail turns with the Divide to trend northwest.

The most important landmark is a sign at mile 6.1 that says "water." The water sign is at a trail intersection with the Nez Perce Ridge Trail, which leads to the Three Mile Ridge Trail and the Nez Perce Camp. At the signs, leave the Divide and hike 0.3 mile to the Nez Perce Camp, an outfitters camp on a knoll on the Idaho side.

To find the water source, walk through the middle of the outfitters camp, look for a broken sign that used to say "3 mile trail," and listen for water below the trail. The outfitters have hooked up a hose at the spring. Nez Perce Camp is a mess, with rotting hunks of foam, plastic utensils, and other debris scattered about, but hikers cannot afford to walk past this water source.

From the spring, return to the Divide along the same spur trail and continue northwest. About 2 miles past the water sign, the Divide bends to the west and descends sharply to a saddle above Threemile Creek. The trail climbs 600 feet to join the Anderson Mountain Road and turns north again at mile 10.6. Hikers walk on the 4WD road for about 6 miles, all the way to Chief Joseph Pass.

Montana Highway 43 is reached at mile 16.7. The entrance to the CDT is marked with a blue and white CD sign south of the highway. Hikers turn right (east) on the highway and walk 0.15 mile to Chief Joseph Pass, crossing the Divide one more time.

The Forest Service map shows the CDNST crossing the Divide at Lost Trail Pass, but that is not correct. From Chief Joseph Pass, the trail follows a snowmobile trail directly north to intercept a 4WD road to Gibbons Pass.

There are pit toilets, ski trail maps, CDT signs, and a large parking lot for skiers and snowmobilers at Chief Joseph Pass. Unfortunately, there is no water. One mile north of the pass, hikers can access water by turning right (east) on another snowmobile trail, and descending 0.3 mile to a tributary of Joseph Creek, where there is also a spot level enough for a campsite. The trail is shown on the topo as a 4WD road. It is 5.3 miles to water in a tributary of Trail Creek on the road to Gibbons Pass.

OTHER EXCURSIONS

See Segment 11.

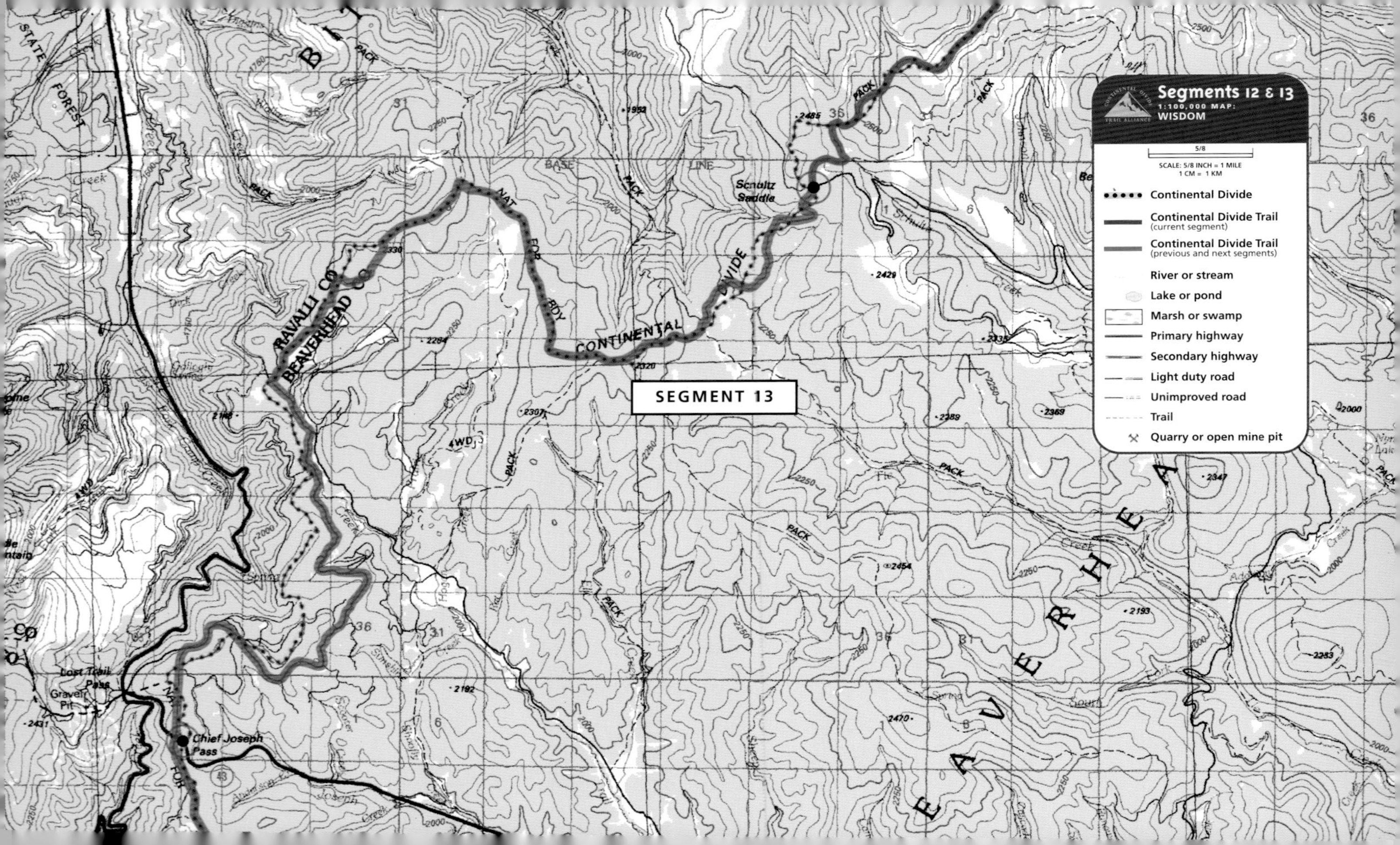

Segments 12 & 13
1:100,000 MAP:
WISDOM
CONTINENTAL DIVIDE TRAIL ALLIANCE
5/8
SCALE: 5/8 INCH = 1 MILE
1 CM = 1 KM
Continental Divide
Continental Divide Trail
(current segment)
Continental Divide Trail
(previous and next segments)
River or stream
Lake or pond
Marsh or swamp
Primary highway
Secondary highway
Light duty road
Unimproved road
Trail
Quarry or open mine pit
SEGMENT 13
Schultz Saddle
CONTINENTAL DIVIDE
NAT FOR BDY
RAVALLI CO
BEAVERHEAD CO
Lost Trail Pass
Gravel Pit
Chief Joseph Pass
STATE FOREST
BASE LINE
PACK
4WD

SEGMENT 12
Water source
MONTANA
IDAHO
Big Hole Pass
BEAVERHEAD CO
LEMHI CO
DIVIDE
MOUNTAINS
SALMON NATIONAL FOREST
Nickel Bar Gulch
Wenger Gulch
Gibbonsville
Anderson Mountain
Morgan Mountain
Historical Monument
PACK
4WD

Segment 13
Chief Joseph Pass to Schultz Saddle: Anaconda Range

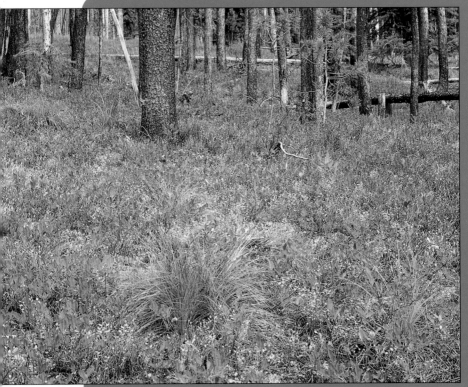

Oval and thinleaf huckleberry and other shrubs turn brilliant red when cool autumn weather descends upon the Continental Divide near Gibbons Pass.

18.7 miles
Difficulty: Easy

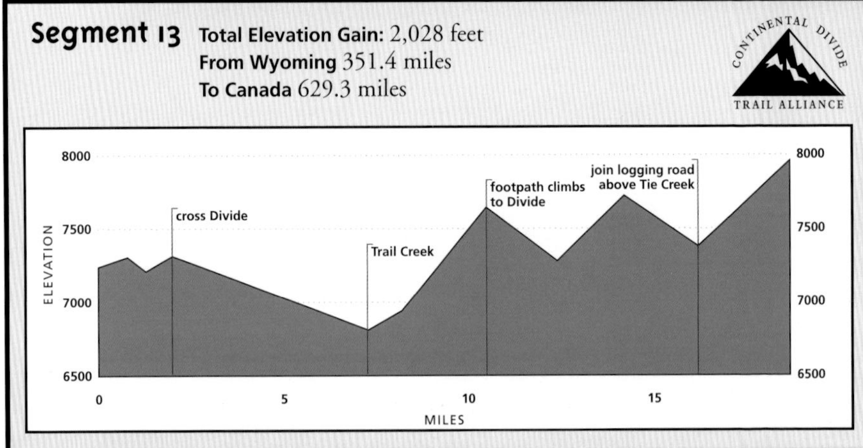

TRAIL OVERVIEW

Continental Divide Trail hikers leave the Idaho/Montana border in this segment and turn northeasterly into Montana. Chief Joseph Pass is near the northern limits of the Beaverhead Mountains of the Bitterroot Range and Schultz Saddle is at the southern end of the Anaconda Range. The Bitterroot Range continues its march along the Montana/Idaho border, but it now becomes a backdrop for the Divide.

This approach brings hikers to within 7 miles of the Anaconda-Pintler Wilderness. It is an easy walk along roads and footpaths through rolling, tree-covered hills. The Forest Service has plans to cut a trail through the trees above the road to Gibbons Pass, but that trail was incomplete when we hiked the CDT. The Divide is a wide tabletop north of Chief Joseph Pass, making it very easy to get lost in the trees because no "crest" is discernible. Surrounding topographical landmarks are not visible through the dense forest. Our advice is to stay on the road unless the new trail has been cut and signed.

At Gibbons Pass, the CDT continues on a 4WD road and then diverges onto a footpath. The footpath joins a logging road again southwest of Schultz Saddle. Some new tread and newer, wooden CD signs have been added to this section of trail, but there are also some older, faded signs near Schultz Saddle. When in doubt, follow new signs and fresh blazes.

The CDT crosses the Nez Perce National Historic Trail (406) and the Lewis and Clark Trail near Gibbons Pass. (See "History of Montana and Idaho's Continental Divide" on page 38.)

Water is accessible at mile 5.3 in a tributary of Trail Creek, and again where the road to Gibbons Pass meets the main channel of Trail Creek. There are no reliable water sources from Gibbons Pass to Schultz Saddle. Some stream tributaries, such as upper Trail Creek and Tie Creek, may provide water earlier in the season. Hikers should carry the topographical maps for this section to see where water can be accessed by descending from the Divide. Continue on the CDT northeast from Schultz Saddle to reach water in Schultz Creek, about 1 mile from the saddle.

MOUNTAIN BIKE NOTES: This segment is open to mountain bikes and is an easy ride.

LAND ADMINISTRATORS (SEE APPENDIX A)

Bitterroot National Forest, Sula Ranger District

MAPS

USGS QUADRANGLES: Lost Trail Pass, Sula, Schultz Saddle (Big Hole Battlefield recommended for access to Schultz Saddle)

USFS: Beaverhead National Forest or Bitterroot National Forest

BEGINNING ACCESS POINT

CHIEF JOSEPH PASS on Highway 43

ENDING ACCESS POINT

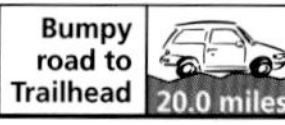

SCHULTZ SADDLE: Schultz Saddle can be accessed via Road 1203 from Highway 43. The signed gravel road is near Placer Creek east of Chief Joseph Pass. A maze of 4WD roads that are unsigned makes navigation difficult once you leave the highway. Road 1203 intersects Road 1137, which leads to the saddle. The Big Hole Battlefield quadrangle is recommended for route-finding. In wet weather, 4WD is also recommended. There are both parking and camping spots on the saddle, but water is a mile away in Schultz Creek.

SUPPLIES, SERVICES, AND ACCOMMODATIONS

WISDOM, MT, is on Highway 43. (See Segment 12.)

Distance from trail: 25 miles

Special Note: Lewis and Clark named the three tributaries of the Jefferson River "Wisdom, Philosophy, and Philanthropy," in honor of President Jefferson's virtues. But down-to-earth fur traders later renamed the rivers as the simpler "Big Hole, Beaverhead, and Ruby." Only the town of Wisdom, Montana, retains the name.

TRAIL DESCRIPTION

A large sign at Chief Joseph Pass commemorates the dedication of the Montana/Idaho CDNST in 1989. A blue and white CDT sign is affixed to the same post, but from there it is difficult to tell where to begin the trek north. It should be improved by the time this guide is published.

From the parking lot at the pass, choose the road/snowmobile trail that goes straight north and follow it as it bends northwest to intersect Road 1260 to Gibbons Pass. The trail crosses the imperceptible Divide at mile 0.8, elevation 7,308 feet. Road 1260 was not signed when we hiked the trail, but its higher quality makes it an obvious choice. Several 4WD spur roads and snowmobile trails intersect the Gibbons Pass road, but hikers stay on the main route for 8 miles. Gibbons Pass is well-signed, so you'll know when you get there.

S **SOUTHBOUND HIKERS:** Where southbound hikers should leave the Gibbons Pass road and continue on a lesser-used track toward Chief Joseph Pass, there is a CD post, but when we were there the sign was missing—look for the green post. If you plan to travel by auto to a resupply point on US-93 (Idaho), stay on Road 1260 to Lost Trail Pass.

The Gibbons Pass road crosses a tributary of Trail Creek at mile 5.3, and reaches the main channel of the creek at mile 7.3. Refill water bottles at Trail Creek as there is no other reliable water source in this segment.

At Gibbons Pass (mile 8.2), a four-way intersection is signed for everything under the sun, except the Continental Divide Trail. Northbound hikers turn right on a 4WD road that runs along the crest of the Divide. The narrow road becomes boggy at the least hint of wet weather. Dense lodgepole pines line both sides of the grassy two-track. After you've hiked 0.4 mile on this track, there is a reassuring wooden CD symbol on a tree.

The two-track closely follows the actual Divide for about 2 miles. Where the footpath diverges from the two-track, look for another CD symbol marking the route. The footpath was constructed by a group of international volunteers in 1990. It closely follows the physical Divide for 6 miles. Southeast of Schultz Saddle, in a saddle above Tie Creek, the path joins a logging road at an intersection signed with CDT symbols. The logging road climbs to reach Schultz Saddle at mile 18.7, elevation 7,960.

OTHER EXCURSIONS

See Segment 11.

SEE PAGE 148 FOR SEGMENT 13 MAP.

Segment 14

Schultz Saddle to Johnson Lake: Anaconda-Pintler Wilderness

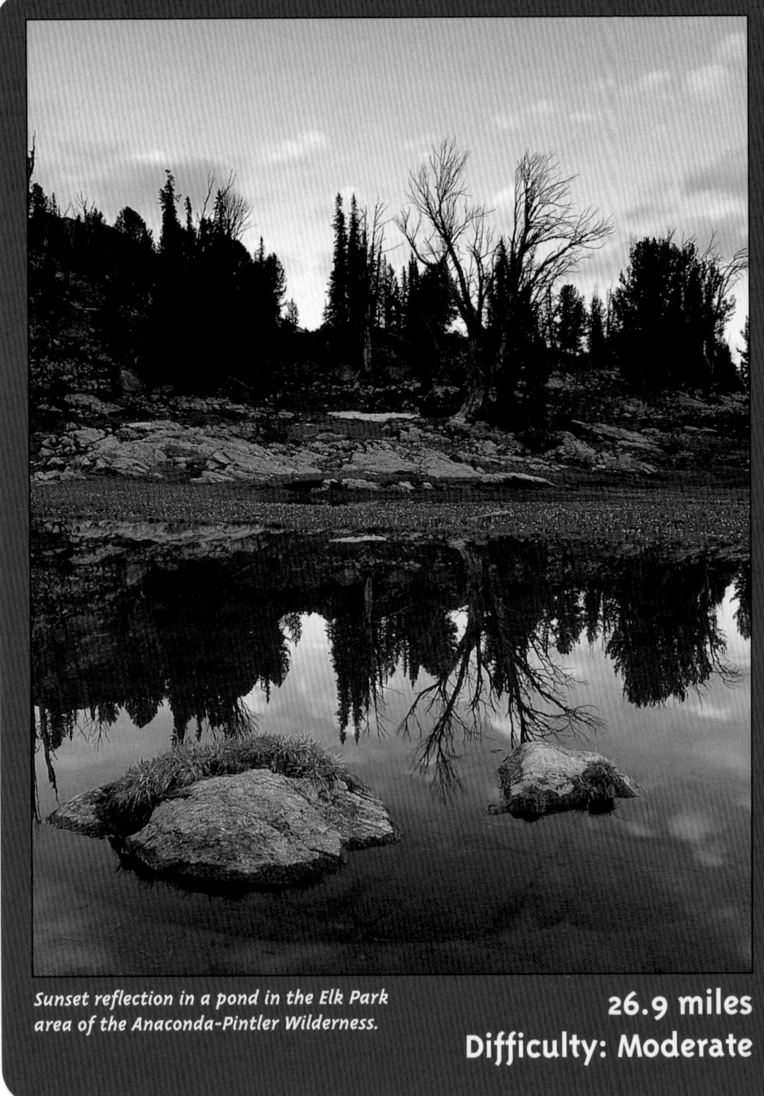

Sunset reflection in a pond in the Elk Park area of the Anaconda-Pintler Wilderness.

26.9 miles
Difficulty: Moderate

TRAIL OVERVIEW As with most wilderness areas, access is limited. To begin our trek through the Anaconda-Pintler, we chose Schultz Saddle for our starting point and exited from Johnson Lake via trails to the Middle Fork Trailhead. Schultz Saddle is on an unsigned, hard-to-find gravel road but it has the distinct advantage of intersecting the Continental Divide Trail directly. If you decide to use the Schultz Saddle access point, make sure that you have the Big Hole Battlefield topographical map for access navigation.

Once you enter the wilderness, it's easy to stay on track thanks to well-signed trails. With few exceptions, route-finding is easy.

Review the bear avoidance techniques in "Safety Concerns." We saw one black bear near Hope Lake, and signs of others. We spotted a herd of elk on the climb up to Pintler Pass. The pass itself was only just clear of snow—higher elevations may not melt out until late July.

Johnson Lake was jumping with fish—a good place for a backpacker to supplement his/her diet. From Johnson Lake, we left the CDT and hiked 5 miles to a trailhead to meet our support crew and resupply. From July 1 onward, that 5 miles is heavily traveled by horses and mules, so expect to share the trail, stepping off on the downhill side to let the horses pass. Support crew quote: "Don't step in the exhaust."

MOUNTAIN BIKE NOTES: Most of this segment is in the Anaconda-Pintler Wilderness, where mountain bikes are prohibited.

LAND ADMINISTRATORS (SEE APPENDIX A)

Beaverhead/Deerlodge National Forest, Philipsburg Ranger District
Beaverhead/Deerlodge National Forest, Wise River Ranger District

MAPS

USGS QUADRANGLES: Schultz Saddle, Bender Point, Mussigbrod Lake, Kelly Lake, Warren Peak

USFS: Anaconda-Pintler Wilderness (Beaverhead/Deerlodge and Bitterroot National Forests); Beaverhead/Deerlodge National Forest

BEGINNING ACCESS POINT

SCHULTZ SADDLE: See Segment 13.

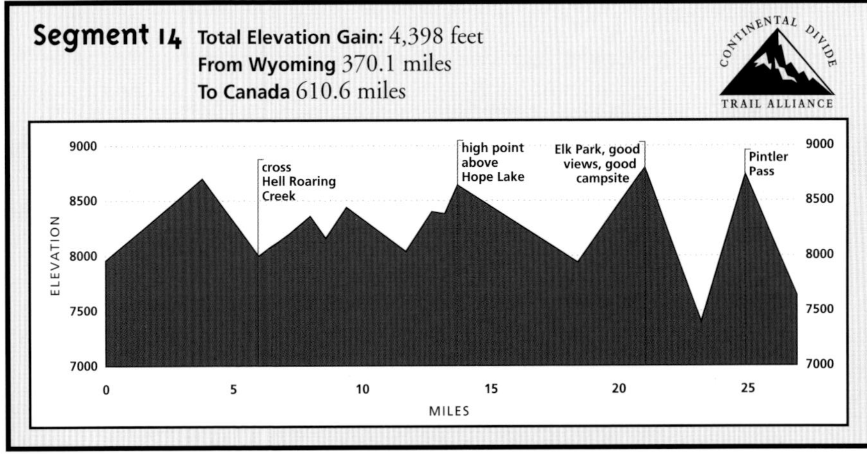

ENDING ACCESS POINT

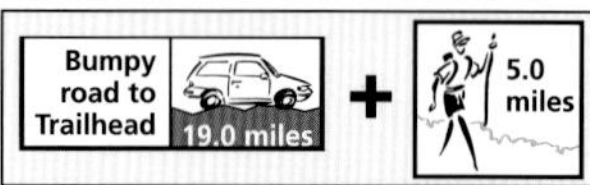

MIDDLE FORK TRAILHEAD, ANACONDA-PINTLER WILDERNESS: From Montana Highway 38, take Road 5106 to Moose Lake. Continue south, past Moose Lake, to TRHD 9, the Middle Fork TRHD. Hike 5 miles to Johnson Lake.

SUPPLIES, SERVICES, AND ACCOMMODATIONS

WISDOM, MT, is on Highway 43. (See Segment 12.)

Distance from Trail: 30 miles

TRAIL DESCRIPTION The Anaconda-Pintler Wilderness is named for the Anaconda Mountain Range and for Charles Pintler, a Big Hole Valley settler of the late 1800s. The 159,086-acre wilderness was designated in 1964. Please remember the special rules that pertain to wilderness travel:

WILDERNESS ALERT

1. No groups over 15, and no more than 35 head of stock.
2. No motorized vehicles of any kind.
3. Observe "Leave No Trace" guidelines.
4. Shortcutting of switchbacks is prohibited.
5. Cutting or damaging trees is prohibited.
6. All attractants must be made unavailable to bears.
7. Observe posted camping closures.
8. Additional regulations apply to stockmen, and licenses are required for hunting and fishing. Contact the Forest Service for details.
9. Permits are not required for backpackers, but trailhead registration is requested.
10. Fire permits may be required during periods of extreme fire danger.

As the CDT heads northeast from Schultz Saddle, it dips below the Divide on the south side and then climbs to the crest again. You'll see wooden CD symbols at the beginning of the trail and at most intersections. A combination of visible tread, blazes, and stone cairns marks the way to the border of the Anaconda-Pintler Wilderness, but the tread disappears often as you near the wilderness border. Easy walking and small changes in elevation characterize the first 2 miles of the trail.

The CDT intersects Trail 110 at 0.8 mile near a crossing of Schultz Creek. Northbound hikers keep left (north). Leave the thickly forested area and climb to good views over an outcropping of rock at mile 2.8.

An intersection with Meadow Creek Bridge Trail 462 is signed at 3.8 miles, and the continuation of the CDT on the crest of the Divide is also signed. Hikers have gained a thousand feet of elevation at this intersection. The trail remains at about 8,700 feet for 1.5 miles, and then descends below the crest at mile 4.9.

Above the Hell Roaring Creek drainage, views into the Big Hole Valley open up again as the trail crosses a ridge that is sparsely forested. The trail becomes difficult to follow where it skirts the edge of the Anaconda-Pintler Wilderness. There is no visible tread and trail markers are sparse. Despite a few small rock cairns, the trail is easy to miss as it turns to the southeast (right) and descends. To make matters worse, there are some misleading game trails and deadfall in the seldom used trail. Worse yet, the Bitterroot and Beaverhead FS maps do not correctly depict this section of trail. Only the Anaconda-Pintler Wilderness map (also a Forest Service map) shows the correct route.

The intersection of CDT 9 and Bender Cabin Trail at 5.3 miles is well-signed. From this point on, the trail improves markedly. Switchback down on the good trail to a marshy area with multiple, small, stream crossings and wet meadows.

Hell Roaring Trail 379 intersects the CDT at 5.7 miles. Early explorers seem to have been fond of the name "Hell Roaring," as it appears in the Centennial Mountains, again here, and in other mountain ranges farther north. After crossing the third tributary of Hell Roaring Creek, there is a good camping spot on a level bench at mile 6.

Cross the wilderness boundary at mile 6.8. A few feet beyond the boundary signs, the intersection of Johnson Peak Trail 435 is also well-signed, and the continuation of CDT 9 is clear. Surprise Lake, at 7.2 miles, does come as a surprise. North of Surprise Lake, the trail climbs to the Divide and commences a long ridge-walk through mostly forested terrain. A few breaks in the trees offer views of Mussigbrod Lake and the shoulders of the hills bordering the Big Hole Valley.

Buck Creek Trail 198 intersects the CDT at 11.7 miles, 4.5 miles east of Surprise Lake. Just past the Buck Creek intersection, a trail leads to Mussigbrod Lake. Traffic increases from this point on, as popular fishing destinations are numerous.

We had some problems finding filterable water in this section because the trail stays above most of the creek drainages. Watch for a small tributary of Plimpton Creek a hundred yards or so below the trail at mile 12.7, southwest of Hope Lake.

Hope Lake Trail 424 intersects the CDT at 13.2 miles. Hope Lake is closed to stock and is a pleasant, scenic detour if you have the time—though it is a steep climb down the north side of the Divide to the lake.

At the intersection to Trail 371 (unsigned when we were there), climb a few feet to the top of the ridge for a spectacular view of Hope Lake. Water was a problem here again. Too much water falling from the sky, but not enough stream crossings.

The trail follows the physical Divide closely, not descending until it reaches the intersection with the Mystic Lake trail at mile 16.6. Mystic Lake is not on the CDT, but is close enough to make a reasonable campsite. For CDT hikers, the trail takes a 90° turn here, heading due north before swinging to a northeasterly direction and descending below the Divide.

At 17.4 miles (0.8 mile from the Mystic Lake intersection), the CDT crosses a tributary of Park Creek on a footbridge. This water crossing is not shown on the map. Bog bridges, footbridges, and wider tread become the norm in this well-used section of the wilderness.

Hikers make their way through dense forest for a couple of miles, climb back to the Divide through trees, and are then rewarded with excellent views (assuming that it's not raining again) from a rocky ridge just south of the intersection with Bitterroot River Trail 313.

North of this intersection, the CDT continues to cross open, rocky areas that are sparsely populated with stunted trees as the trail climbs to 8,800 feet in the "Elk Park" area (mile 21). Don't miss the opportunity to climb two hundred feet above the trail for magnificent views of West Pintler Peak, dozens of other unnamed peaks, and a sea of trees marching to the horizon on all sides. A high camp can be made here, using snowmelt for water.

At mile 22, the trail descends from Elk Park and intersects Trail 368 to Pintler Meadows. A sign here says that it is 5 miles to Johnson Lake, the CDT hiker's next destination. As the CDT continues to descend through thick spruce and pine forest, it crosses tributaries of Pintler Creek several times.

At mile 23.2, the trail crosses the main channel of Pintler Creek on a good bridge and enters the hiker's version of a freeway interchange, with multiple signs for other trails and horse camps, and mileage notations for many destinations. Of all these signs, the one you're looking for is northwest of the open, trampled area, where a CD symbol is posted on a tree. This is a greater-than-90° turn for northbound hikers. Also look for "Pintler Pass" and "Johnson Lake" signs, both being on the route of CDT.

From a low point of 7,400 feet at Pintler Creek, the CDT climbs to 8,738 to cross Pintler Pass, an elevation gain of over 1,300 feet in 3.1 miles. About halfway up the climb to Pintler Pass, there is an unmarked intersection with the trail to Oreamnos Lake, a very scenic side trip if you have the time. The route of the CDT turns right (east) here to continue to Pintler Pass.

Johnson Lake is visible from the top of Pintler Pass, as is the trail where it switchbacks down. On July 20, we still had many snowfields to negotiate wherever the trail crossed north-facing slopes.

N W E S !

There is a confusing trail intersection just before you reach Johnson Lake. An unmarked intersection leaves CDT hikers guessing. Choose the right fork of the trail, the one with a blaze. The left fork of the trail leads to one of the prettiest spots we saw in the wilderness, with ponds and waterfalls arranged in artistic splendor below rocky cliffs—but this area is not for you. The sign says "This tract is occupied under permit from the Forest Service, United States Department of Agriculture, which authorizes exclusive possession of the property by the permittee."

Johnson Lake itself is a very popular destination for both hikers and horsemen. Here, for the first time, you will encounter rules and regulations about where to camp, where grazing is permitted, and so forth. Nevertheless, the lake (mile 26.9) makes a pleasant camp if you're not seeking solitude. All of the northern and western lake shore is closed to camping, so hikers should seek tent sites near, but not on, the southeastern shore.

Four wilderness trails meet at Johnson Lake, with the CDT comically signed as if one had to walk on water across the lake to continue. Actually, the CDT turns sharply east/northeast here to climb over Rainbow Pass (not named on the map, but named on the ground) to Rainbow Lake.

If you elect to hike out to the Middle Fork Trailhead from Johnson Lake, you will add 5 miles each way to your journey, but there are two beautiful waterfalls on the route that are worth seeing. Signs at the trailhead do not inform hikers about the CDT, nor do they clearly show that Trail 29 is an access trail to the CDT.

Sunset reflections, Elk Park, Anaconda-Pintler Wilderness

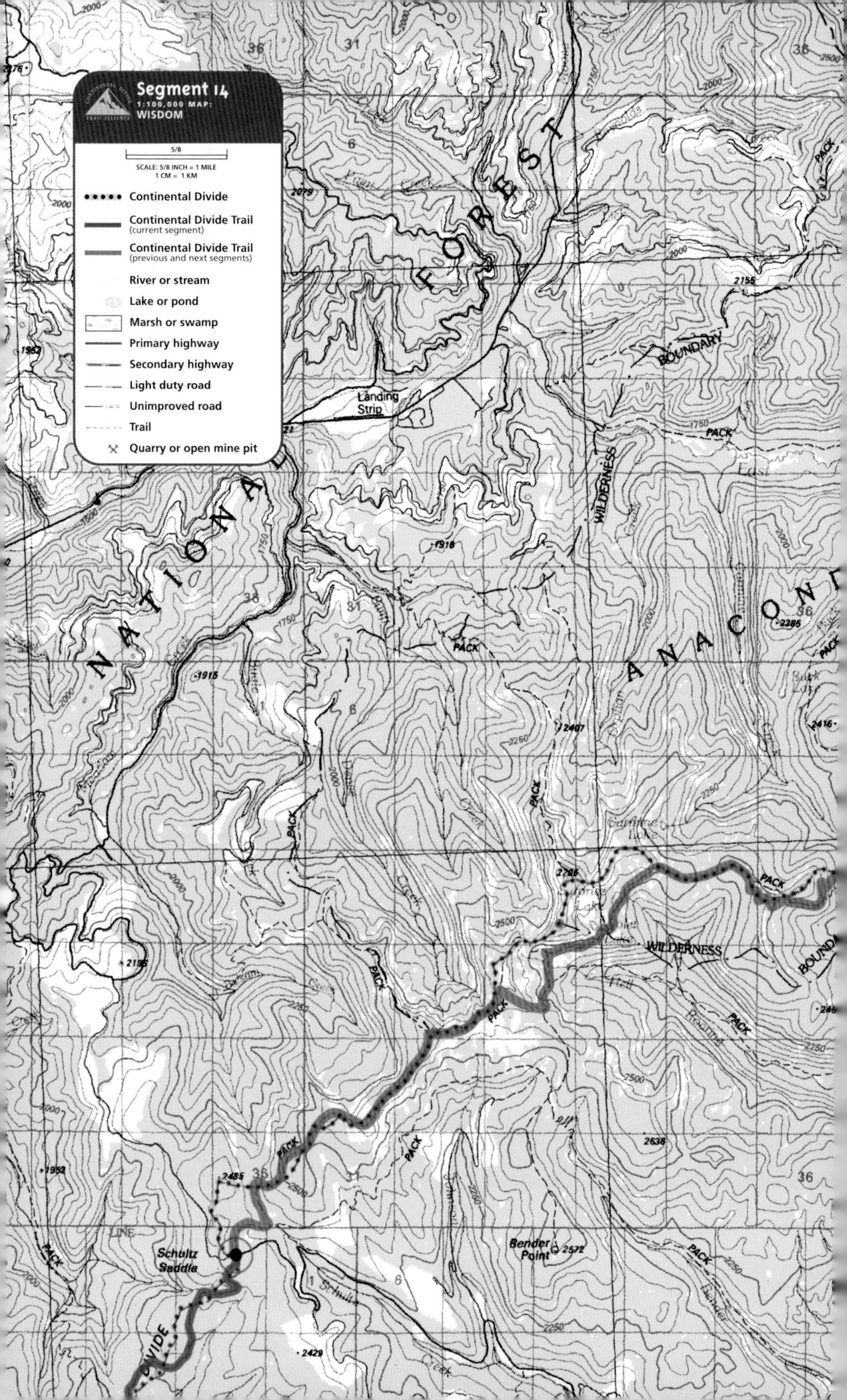

Segment 14
1:100,000 MAP:
WISDOM
CONTINENTAL DIVIDE TRAIL ALLIANCE
5/8
SCALE: 5/8 INCH = 1 MILE
1 CM = 1 KM
Continental Divide
Continental Divide Trail
(current segment)
Continental Divide Trail
(previous and next segments)
River or stream
Lake or pond
Marsh or swamp
Primary highway
Secondary highway
Light duty road
Unimproved road
Trail
Quarry or open mine pit
FOREST
NATIONAL
ANACOND
WILDERNESS
BOUNDARY
Landing
Strip
PACK
Schultz
Saddle
Bender
Point
DIVIDE
LINE

PINTLER RANGE
ANACONDA
NATIONAL
FORE
WILDERN
GRANITE CO
RAVALLI CO
BEAVERHEAD CO
DEER LODGE CO
Bitterroot Pass
West Pintler Peak
East Pintler Peak
Clifford Point
DIVIDE
NAT
FOR
BDY
PACK
Mudd
NATIONAL FOREST
4WD

Segment 15
Johnson Lake to Lower Seymour Lake: Anaconda-Pintler Wilderness

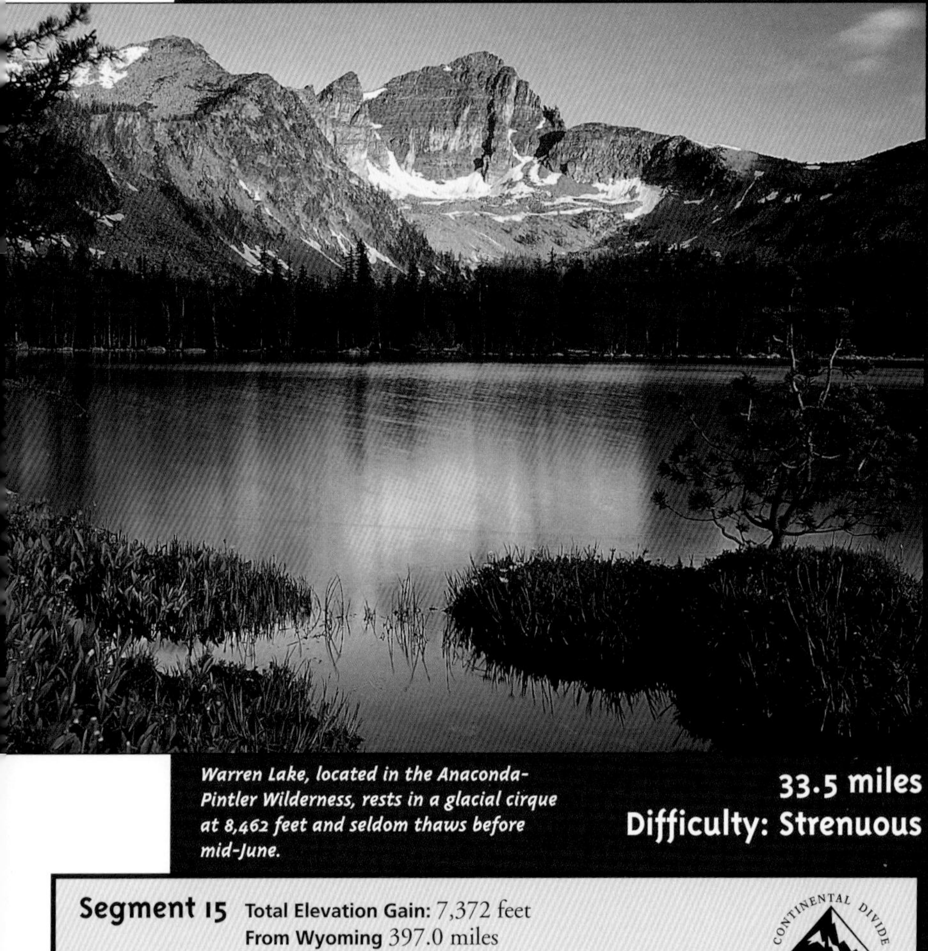

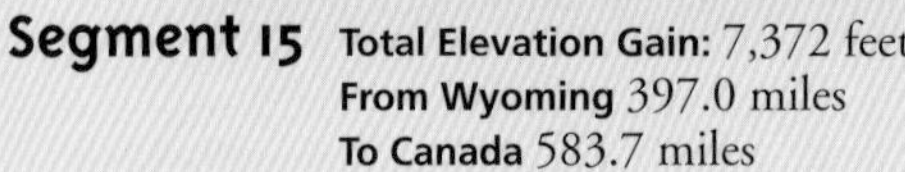

Warren Lake, located in the Anaconda-Pintler Wilderness, rests in a glacial cirque at 8,462 feet and seldom thaws before mid-June.

33.5 miles
Difficulty: Strenuous

Segment 15 **Total Elevation Gain:** 7,372 feet
From Wyoming 397.0 miles
To Canada 583.7 miles

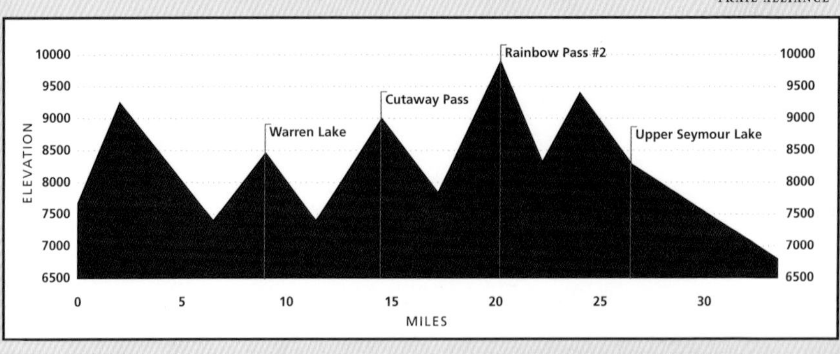

TRAIL OVERVIEW The northeastern half of the Anaconda-Pintler Wilderness is both more scenic and drier. Hikers are constantly climbing up and down in this section, but the view from each successive pass is well worth the effort. All those ups and downs are easier to take thanks to excellent trail work. The directional signs are good for the most part— a few exceptions are noted in the trail description.

Larch trees grace the north-facing slopes of the descent from Cutaway Pass and Rainbow Mountain. These deciduous trees have needles, but the needles turn yellow and gold, falling in September. The graceful, feathery profile of larch trees is very appealing, and the delicate shade beneath larch groves is conducive to wildflowers and grasses. Hikers pass through another stand of larches below Goat Flat, making the Anaconda-Pintler Wilderness the premier location along the Montana/Idaho Continental Divide for enjoying these rare, subalpine trees.

Wildlife is abundant in the wilderness. We camped in Queener Basin and there were so many deer in the area that they ran into my tent during the night, knocking into tie-downs and pulling up stakes. I heard the drumbeat of hooves all around me, so I just covered my head with my arms and hoped for the best. Luckily, no harm was done. I was surprised that they came right through camp. Perhaps they don't see a lot of human traffic.

We also saw quite a bit of black bear sign near Queener Basin, so be sure to review the bear avoidance tips before hiking this section.

Water is plentiful throughout the hike, but plan ahead and fill water bottles before ascending each pass.

MOUNTAIN BIKE NOTES: This segment is in the Anaconda-Pintler Wilderness, where mountain bikes are prohibited.

LAND ADMINISTRATORS (SEE APPENDIX A)

Beaverhead/Deerlodge National Forest, Philipsburg Ranger District
Beaverhead/Deerlodge National Forest, Wise River Ranger District

MAPS

USGS QUADRANGLES: Warren Peak, Carpp Ridge, Storm Lake, Mount Evans, Lower Seymour Lake

USFS: Anaconda-Pintler Wilderness (Beaverhead/Deerlodge and Bitterroot National Forests); Beaverhead/Deerlodge National Forest (Deerlodge Forest Area Visitor/Travel Map, West Half)

BEGINNING ACCESS POINT

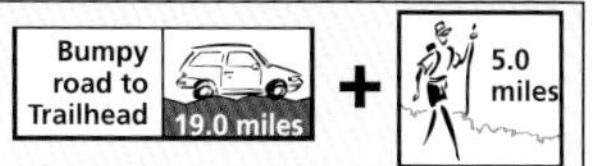

MIDDLE FORK TRAILHEAD, ANACONDA-PINTLER WILDERNESS: From Montana Highway 38, take Road 5106 to Moose Lake. Continue south, past Moose Lake, to TRHD 9, the Middle Fork TRHD. Hike 5 miles to Johnson Lake.

ENDING ACCESS POINT

SEYMOUR CREEK TRAILHEAD 10: As you drive southbound on County Road 274, there is no sign (just an empty and broken post) to mark the entrance to Forest Service Road 934, which leads to the Lower Seymour Lake Campground and Trailhead. Northbound drivers will see a sign that says 'Boy Scout Camp/Anaconda-Pintler Wilderness."

SUPPLIES, SERVICES, AND ACCOMMODATIONS

WISE RIVER, MT, on Highway 43, is a small town with limited services.

Distance from Trail: 23 miles

Zip Code: 59762

Bank:	None	
Bus:	None	
Camping:	H Bar J Campgrounds, Hwy. 43	406-832-3226
Dining:	Wise River Club, Hwy. 43	406-832-3258
Gear:	Gnose Mercantile, Hwy. 43	406-832-3271
Groceries:	Gnose Mercantile, Hwy. 43	406-832-3271
Information:	Gnose Mercantile, Hwy. 43	406-832-3271
Laundry:	None	
Lodging:	Wise River Club, Hwy. 43	406-832-3258
	Sundance Lodge, 4000 Lamarche Creek Road	406-689-3612
Medical:	None	
Outfitters:	Complete Fly Fisher, P.O. Box 127	406-832-3176
Post Office:	U.S. Post Office, Hwy. 43, Wise River, MT 59762	406-832-3280
Showers:	None	
Special Notes:	Anaconda has full services and is 29 miles to the north.	

TRAIL DESCRIPTION

WILDERNESS ALERT

As mentioned in the previous segment (Segment 14), special rules pertain to hiking and camping in the Anaconda-Pintler Wilderness. Be sure to keep them in mind.

The CDT climbs north/northeast from Johnson Lake toward Rainbow Pass (one of two passes so named in the Anaconda-Pintler Wilderness). There are several stream crossings in this switchbacking climb, and numerous, picturesque waterfalls.

Near the pass, the trees thin and views open to the west, including a good look at Johnson Lake from another perspective and, in the far distance, the peaks of the Bitterroot Mountains.

Close to where the trail tops-out on Rainbow Pass, a broken sign confirms that you're on Trail 9 and also notes that Johnson Lake is 2 miles distant.

Cross Rainbow Pass at 9,250 feet, a change of more than 1,500 feet from Johnson Lake's 7,680-foot elevation. This pass is named on the ground, but not on the maps. The scenic prospect from the pass is exceptional, including close-up views of half-a-dozen glaciated peaks that top 9,500 feet.

Rainbow Lake (mile 3) is a dark blue jewel, seen clearly at first from the switchbacking trail and then periodically through the trees. Miniature waterfalls and rivulets feed narrow bands of wildflowers in the rocks above the lake. Other hikers we met at the lake (mile 3) said that the fishing was good.

The roller-coaster trail loses a lot of elevation again as it descends along the West Fork of Fishtrap Creek. At mile 6.5, the CDT intersects Trail 130 (7,400 feet). Cutaway Pass is the next climb in store for CD hikers and Trail 9 is signed here as "Warren Lake/Cutaway Pass." The turn to Warren Lake is a sharp left (north) for northbound hikers and it would be easy to walk past it, so watch carefully for the signs.

There is no lack of water on the trail to Warren Lake. Stream crossings are frequent, with some muddy sections. The trail parallels a lesser tributary of Fishtrap Creek for about 2 miles and then climbs, via a set of tight switchbacks, to the lake, reached at mile 9. The lake sits in a glacial cirque at 8,462 feet and is both higher and shallower than Rainbow Lake. Snow lingers on its shores well into July.

The CDT is well-signed as Trail 9 where it departs Warren Lake and continues northeasterly to Cutaway Pass. By now, hikers should be used to the up/down scenario in the Anaconda-Pintler, so it is no surprise when the trail descends steeply from Warren Lake to cross the West Fork of LaMarche Creek at 7,400 feet.

The descent from Warren Lake is steep, but it offers good views of the LaMarche Creek valley through scattered trees. At 2.4 miles from Warren Lake (mile 11.4 for this segment), the CDT intersects Trail 126, an interesting route that leads southeast to Sundance Lodge, a potential stopping point for those who don't wish to hike the whole wilderness.

The CDT is not signed as such at LaMarche Creek. Remember that your destination is Cutaway Pass and follow the signs for the pass. According to the Forest Service, it is 5 miles from Warren Lake to Cutaway Pass, but it's closer to 5.5 miles. You top the pass at elevation 9,000 feet, mile 14.5.

Signs at Cutaway Pass say "Highline Trail 111" and "Carpp Creek Trailhead 3." The Continental Divide is not mentioned. The climb to Cutaway Pass is rocky but open, providing breathtaking views all around.

If you start at Johnson Lake, cross Rainbow Pass, climb to Warren Lake, and then make Cutaway Pass in a single day, you will have survived 3,732 feet of elevation gain (just gain, not loss). Of course, you can't camp on waterless and narrow Cutaway Pass, so another descent is required to find good camping near Rock Creek, or farther on in Queener Basin.

Less than 1 mile down the north side of Cutaway Pass, the trail crosses the first of several tributaries of Rock Creek, so water is plentiful here. So, apparently, are black bears. We came across bear sign, including a recent kill.

The intersection with the Queener Basin trail, mile 17.2, was not well-marked when we were there. A CDT sign pointed correctly back to Cutaway Pass, but incorrectly down East Fork Trail 38, instead of up Queener Basin. CDT hikers coming from south to north should make a right-hand (southeast) turn here, beginning a gradual climb to Queener Basin.

There are some hunters' camps in Queener Basin and signs of low-level horse use. Trail crews have done an excellent job of putting in long bog bridges to take the trail over delicate riparian areas. The trail crosses one major and two minor tributaries of Rock Creek, so there is plenty of water until you begin the climb up to Rainbow Pass (yes, another "Rainbow Pass") on the shoulder of Rainbow Mountain. The climb takes hikers out of the trees, across talus and boulder fields on a gradual U-shaped traverse above the Rock Creek drainage. The trees are few, and one can see Cutaway Pass and Cutaway Mountain to the west. This trail is officially open to stock, but I would be wary of taking stock over the extremely narrow and sometimes eroded trail.

The trail crosses Rainbow Pass at mile 20.2. The 9,900-foot pass is the highest elevation reached along the CDT in the Anaconda-Pintler Wilderness. A short, half-mile climb will take you to the top of 10,250-foot Rainbow Mountain if you want an unimpeded 360° view.

Yeoman trail work has been done to cut switchbacks down the rocky, northern face of Rainbow Pass; still it was just passable in late July due to lingering snowdrifts. Below the rock cliff, the trail enters a grove of larches and one of those scenes that poets would call "sylvan." The perfect trail, with the perfect backdrop, just like everyone imagines the Continental Divide Trail to be, but what it so often is not. As the trail levels out at 8,400 feet, it crosses three tributaries of Page Creek, skirts Flower Lake (which cannot be seen from the trail), and rounds Page Lake, which looks more like a stagnant pond.

About 2 miles below Rainbow Pass, west of Page Lake, there is a signed trail intersection that is not on the map. Signs here guide hikers to Page Lake/ Continental Divide, to Queener Basin, and to East Fork Trailhead 2. Another trail intersection, not signed, appears at mile 23.2 (3 miles from Rainbow Pass). The conclusion is that there are two paths leading to the Page Creek Trail, not one as shown on the map. Both trail intersections will offer an opportunity to hike northwest down the Page Creek Drainage to the East Fork Trailhead. Part of the trail intersection east of Page Lake is nearly choked with deadfall, so the confusion may be due to a reroute. The CDT continues east to Goat Flat.

The climb to Goat Flat is quite steep. Where the trail crosses a saddle below Goat Flat, there is one weather-beaten CD sign. From here, the trail briefly swings north on the 8,840 contour line before bending southeast to climb to Goat Flat. More larch trees line the trail for about a mile. Five or six elk were browsing within sight of the trail when we hiked through.

Visible tread disappears in the grass above the timberline on Goat Flat. Trail markers were lying on the ground, so we wandered around a bit until we spotted a stone cairn that led to the ridge top (9,400 feet).

On the crest of the Divide, where the trail begins its descent to Upper Seymour Lake, a sign warns "Trail not recommended for stock." The trail down to the lake is an example of expert trail building on a nearly vertical cliff. With no transition, the character of the trail goes from no-tread to visible-tread-with-a-vengeance.

Upper Seymour Lake is easily accessible from the east. As a result, it is well used by horsemen, families, and day hikers. The lake lies in a deep cirque, at mile 26.5 for this segment, elevation 8,280 feet. The setting is postcard perfection, with Kurt Peak, Queener Mountain, and the cliffs of Goat Flat surrounding the water. Their sheer rock walls fade from red to steely gray in the sunrise. When we revisited this lake in September, the hills were alive with the sound of elk bugling.

Unofficial trails around the lake make it hard to find Trail 131, where the route of the CDT continues southeasterly to the Seymour Creek Trailhead. Make your way to the outlet stream and you'll end up on the right path. From Upper Seymour Lake to Lower Seymour Lake, the trail is a persistent downhill track through forest. A border sign marks the point where hikers leave the wilderness. The trailhead is reached at mile 33.5 for this segment (7 miles from Upper Seymour Lake).

SOUTHBOUND HIKERS: You will experience a 2,600-foot climb in elevation from the trailhead to the Divide on Goat Flat. Enjoy.

OTHER EXCURSIONS

HIKE TO UPPER SEYMOUR LAKE and establish a base camp for several dayhikes. Climb to Goat Flat for access to more challenging climbs, including Mount Tiny and Little Rainbow Mountain. Trail 41 is the only obvious official trail on Goat Flat, and it leads northerly to Storm Lake, a scenic excursion into rough and glaciated terrain. Difficulty: Strenuous.

Segment 15
1:100,000 MAPS:
WISDOM and
PHILIPSBURG
5/8
SCALE: 5/8 INCH = 1 MILE
1 CM = 1 KM
Continental Divide
Continental Divide Trail
(current segment)
Continental Divide Trail
(previous and next segments)
River or stream
Lake or pond
Marsh or swamp
Primary highway
Secondary highway
Light duty road
Unimproved road
Trail
Quarry or open mine pit
Carpp Ridge
Carpp Mine
Cutaway Mountain
ANACONA-PINTLER
Cutaway Pass
Beaverhead Mountain
Porter Ridge
Maloney Basin
Warren Peak
GRANITE CO
DEER LODGE CO
FOREST
WILDERNESS
Long Peak
Needle Peak
West Goat Peak
East Goat Peak
Saddle Mtn
Nipple Peak
East Pintler Peak
Pintler Peak
DEER LODGE CO
BEAVERHEAD CO
BEAVERHEAD CO
RANGE
McDougal Gulch
Gulch
BOUNDARY
CONTINENTAL
DEER

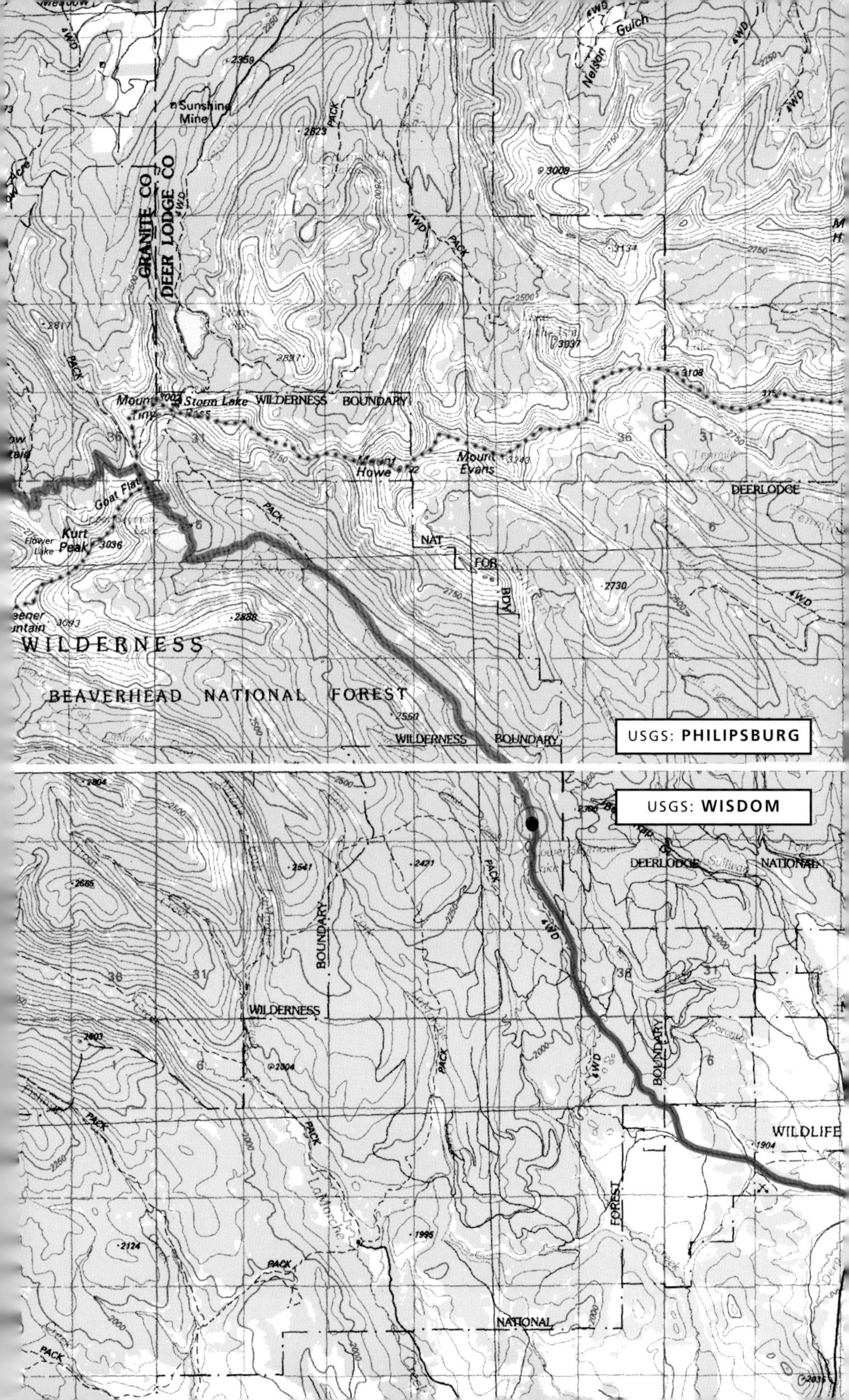

USGS: PHILIPSBURG
USGS: WISDOM
WILDERNESS
BEAVERHEAD NATIONAL FOREST
GRANITE CO
DEER LODGE CO
Sunshine Mine
Storm Lake WILDERNESS BOUNDARY
Mount Howe
Mount Evans
Goat Flat
Kurt Peak
Flower Lake
Nelson Gulch
DEERLODGE
NAT FOR BDY
WILDERNESS BOUNDARY
DEERLODGE NATIONAL
BOUNDARY
WILDERNESS
WILDLIFE
FOREST
NATIONAL

Segment 16

Lower Seymour Lake to I-15/Deer Lodge Pass: Fleecer Mountain Range

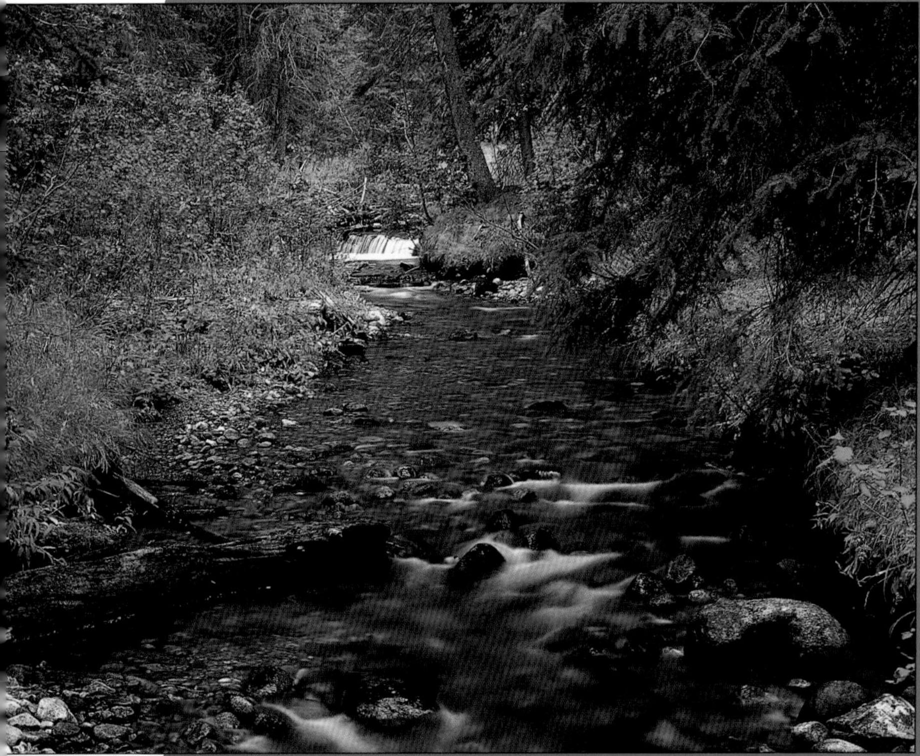

The CDT parallels Seymour Creek as it finds its way through shrubs and conifers in the area east of the Anaconda-Pintler Wilderness.

45.2 miles
Difficulty: Easy

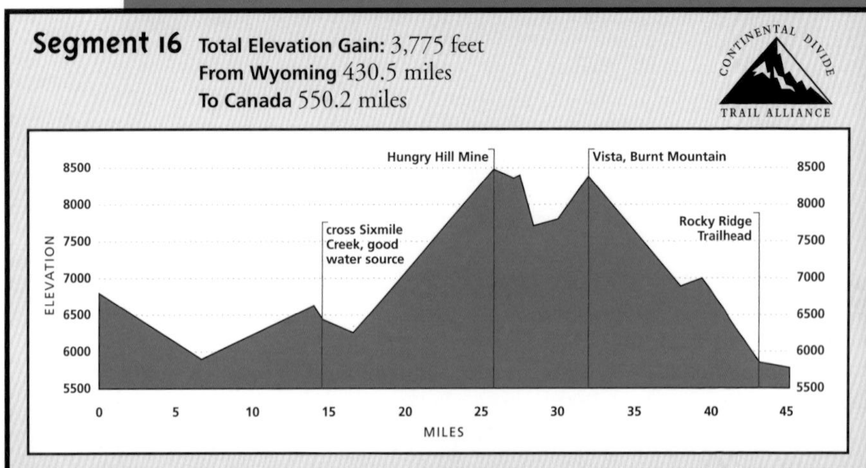

TRAIL OVERVIEW Northbound hikers leave the high peaks of the Anaconda-Pintler Wilderness and begin a long detour around Butte, Montana, following roads, 4WD trails, and trodes (used to be a road, now a trail). That said, the walking is more pleasant than one might expect. There is very little traffic on the roaded sections and the 4WD trail over Burnt Mountain feels like a footpath unless you're there on a weekend or holiday.

For the most part, the trail traverses rolling, tree-covered hills interspersed with islands of sagebrush. The trail is not well-signed until you reach the Hungry Hill Mine. From the mine to Divide Creek Road, near the eastern end of this segment, the signing is quite good. Hikers should carry the Forest Service map as an aid to negotiating all the dirt roads.

History buffs will enjoy the repeated encounters with the ghosts of Montana's mining past. The Mule Ranch in the Mount Haggin Wildlife Management Area is particularly interesting. In addition to this state-administered land, hikers also cross private and national forest lands. Respect private property by staying on the road and by closing all cattle-control gates.

Water is plentiful at the trailhead and adequate for the remainder of the segment. Don't pass up Sixmile Creek as a water source. Water, however, is too plentiful in June. Veritable lakes of snowmelt fill the trail, requiring a lot of slogging through mud.

MOUNTAIN BIKE NOTES: This segment is on roads and ATV trails. There are some steep ups and downs, but no real technical challenges until you come to the newly built trail around Burnt Mountain.

LAND ADMINISTRATORS (SEE APPENDIX A)

Beaverhead/Deerlodge National Forest, Wise River Ranger District
State of Montana Department of Fish, Wildlife, and Parks
Beaverhead/Deerlodge National Forest, Butte Ranger District

MAPS

USGS QUADRANGLES: Lower Seymour Lake, Lincoln Gulch, Dickie Peak, Burnt Mountain, Buxton, Tucker Creek

USFS: Beaverhead/Deerlodge National Forest (Deerlodge Forest Area, Forest Visitor/Travel Map, West Half and East Half)

BEGINNING ACCESS POINT

SEYMOUR CREEK TRAILHEAD 10: As you drive southbound on Montana Highway 274, there is no sign to mark the entrance to Forest Service Road 934, which leads to the Lower Seymour Lake Campground and Trailhead. Northbound drivers will see a sign that says "Boy Scout Camp/Anaconda-Pintler Wilderness." Highway 274 intersects Highway 43 to the south, and Highway 1 to the north. The closest towns are Wise River and Anaconda.

ENDING ACCESS POINT

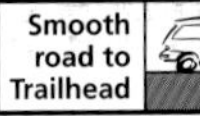

INTERSTATE 15, DEER LODGE PASS: From I-15, take the "Feely" exit 111. Divide Creek Road is a gravel road, suitable for 2WD. Deer Lodge Pass is 7 miles north of the hamlet of Divide and 16 miles southwest of Butte.

SUPPLIES, SERVICES, AND ACCOMMODATIONS

WISE RIVER, MT, is on Hwy. 43. (See Segment 15.)

Special Notes: The tiny hamlet of Divide does have a post office: U.S. Post Office, Hwy. 43, Divide, MT 59727, 406-267-3386. Anaconda, to the north, is a full-service town.

TRAIL DESCRIPTION

At Seymour Creek Trailhead 10 on the eastern edge of the Anaconda-Pintler Wilderness, northbound hikers have two route choices: Continue southeast on FR 934, or take a right-hand fork that is a four-wheeler-path, neither of which is signed. The path through the trees leads to Lower Seymour Lake Campground. Hike around the western edge of the campground (next to the creek) to find a continuation of the trail, which looks like a trode. The value of going this way is that the trode leads to Lower Seymour Lake itself and to an excellent, grassy tent site. The bad part is that the trode appears to end in a field of boulders just past the good camping spot. Be brave and walk through the boulders and a slightly boggy area along the remnants of the trode to intersect FR 934. FR 934 is paved near the trailhead and gravel for most of its length.

S **SOUTHBOUND HIKERS:** Stay on the road all the way to the trailhead because your chances of finding the boulder-strewn route to Lower Seymour Lake are practically nil.

There are multiple side roads, most of them 4WD, off the Seymour Creek Road. The side roads are not part of the CDT route, so hikers can ignore them. At 3.8 miles from the trailhead, northbound hikers leave the Beaverhead National Forest and continue road-walking through private land.

At mile 4.4, there is an intersection with the Boy Scout Camp road. An open meadow offers unobstructed views of the intimidating Anaconda Range to the west, an opportunity for southbound hikers to pause and question their sanity.

A Mount Haggin Wildlife Management sign and 4WD road at mile 5.2 could cause some confusion for northbound hikers. The CDT does traverse the Mount Haggin area, but this is not the correct access route—continue on FR 934 toward Hwy. 274.

At 6.5 miles, within sight of Hwy. 274, the proposed route of the CDT looks to be blocked by a locked gate, a "No Trespassing" sign, and a log-decorated entrance to private land. The Forest Service map shows the CDT leaving 934 here, a left (northerly) turn on the road that leads to Home Ranch (identified on both topo and Forest Service maps). Climbing over a locked gate and ignoring a "No Trespassing" sign is more than I'm comfortable with, so we continued 0.2 mile to the highway and walked north to the next entrance to the Mount Haggin area.

Hike 1.4 miles north on the highway shoulder, and turn left again (northwest) at the "Wildlife Observation" sign. At the "Mount Haggin Management Area" sign, keep right and open a barbed wire gate (remember to close it) at the top of the hill. The locals call this "Seven-mile Ridge Road." It roughly parallels Hwy. 274 as it trends northeast in the foothills below the Anaconda Range. Grassland, scattered trees, and grazing cattle form a pastoral foreground to the impassable peaks on the western horizon.

There is a tricky junction of gravel and 4WD roads 5 miles from the barbed wire gate (mile 13.3 for this segment). A road comes in from the west, followed by another "Y" intersection 0.3 mile farther on. The CDT continues northeast on the well-traveled gravel road. Note that there are more 4WD road intersections than are shown on the Forest Service map, and no CDT signs mark the route.

Sixmile Creek is crossed at 6.3 miles from the barbed wire gate (mile 14.6 for this segment)—a good source of water. The road trends downhill from the creek and approaches Hwy. 274 again. Continue toward the highway, though you will encounter more tempting 4WD roads leading north to the Divide. The CDT leaves the gravel road within sight of Hwy. 274 at mile 16.1 (7.8 miles from the barbed wire gate).

No sign, no visible tread, and no road (though one is shown on the topographical map) exist where CDT hikers make their way 0.5 mile down a grassy hill to the historical "Mule Ranch" site. Just pick a good cross-country route and aim for the parking lot east of the Mule Ranch. You'll see vague remnants of a wagon road. Near the parking lot, an "Authorized Personnel Only" sign is disconcerting because it apparently indicates that hikers have broken the law by crossing the grassy hill above the ranch. I spoke to land administrators and they assured me that foot—not motorized—traffic is allowed. Still, don't be surprised if you draw questioning looks from tourists in the parking lot. Southbound hikers will be especially intimidated by the signs because they encounter them from the front. The State Fish and Wildlife Department does not have a budget for signing the CDT, so this situation is unlikely to change.

From the Mule Ranch parking lot, hike east, cross Hwy. 274, and continue on a 4WD road up Little American Creek. Excellent camping sites abound, all with a view of the Anaconda Range. American Creek (mile 16.7) is a good water source.

The big game list for the Mount Haggin area does include black bears, so in spite of the fact that you seem to be surrounded by civilization, continue to hang your food out of reach when you camp.

There are other 4WD tracks intersecting the main road along Little American Creek; stay on the main road until you come to a "Y"-shaped intersection. At this Y, bear right (southeast). A locked gate 2.5 miles from the Mule Ranch (mile 19.1) makes you wonder if you're on the right trail. You are. This is just another case of Montana's Fish and Wildlife Department attempting to limit motorized travel. The gate is not signed and a lodgepole fence abuts both sides of it. You will have to climb over the gate or the fence to continue on the closed road.

The FS map does not show the road going as far as it actually does, but the topo gives an accurate representation. The closed section is about 3.8 miles long. There are many offshoots from this closed road—you need the topo to decipher the correct route. The road emerges in an open, rocky area west of the Hungry Hill Mine. No CDT sign and no tread can be seen, but if you walk uphill about 20 feet, a CD post comes into view. Follow infrequent CD posts along a two-track to the Hungry Hill Mine, mile 25.8.

SOUTHBOUND HIKERS: Look for a Mt. Haggin Wildlife Preserve boundary sign, and non-motorized signs to find the continuation of the CDT where it enters the Mount Haggin area.

Near the Hungry Hill mine area, CD symbols have been ripped off the posts. Northbound hikers (west-to-east here) will see only one blue and white CD sign. The knoll above the mine is actually the high point for this segment; its 8,734 feet tops the Burnt Mountain Vista of 8,383 feet.

From the mine, the trail descends to Larkspur Spring at mile 27.1. The spring is about 50 feet below the trail; an easier water source is Jerry Creek at mile 28.4 (2.6 miles east of the Hungry Hill Mine). Before you get to Jerry Creek, there is a 4WD road/snowmobile trail intersection. Northbound hikers keep left (northeast). The creek crossing is 0.9 mile from this intersection. The FS map shows the route going around a knoll to the east, which seems unnecessary.

Cross Jerry Creek and climb to the Divide on a 4WD road. An unsigned intersection 0.4 mile east of the creek could be confusing for hikers coming the other way (walking east to west). New trail work was being done when we were there and no signs had been put up. "Jerry Creek" was spray painted on a log as a temporary directional sign. This intersection does not appear on any of the maps. It would be a left (southwest) turn for southbound hikers. Northbound hikers will not have a problem here.

The CDT climbs to a four-way intersection signed as "Ditch Saddle" at mile 30. This intersection and "Ditch Saddle" do not appear on any of the maps. On the topo, it is on the Divide above Flume Creek. Northbound hikers can take Fleecer Trail 94 straight ahead to Burnt Mountain, or take the left fork here to access a stream crossing within 0.3 mile. A CD sign is partially hidden east of the intersection. Both forks of the trail end up in the same place, but one offers a good water source. The official route is blazed, with the blazes painted orange.

From Ditch Saddle, it is two miles to the "Vista" trail on Burnt Mountain. The Vista is a 0.2-mile spur trail. The trail around Burnt Mountain is a new four-wheeler route — quite rocky and steep for mountain bikers. You'll reach the intersection with Rocky Ridge Trail in about 7 miles. There are three minor intersections along the way, but all are well-signed. Stay on Burnt Mountain Trail 125.

North of Sunday Gulch Road, the Burnt Mountain Trail makes a 90° turn to the south (right-hand turn for northbound hikers). It crosses a tributary of Hanson Gulch Creek, and then crosses Sunday Gulch Road at mile 38.9. Watch for the Rocky Ridge Trail sign and continue south/southeast on Rocky Ridge Trail to the trailhead on Divide Creek Road. Trail signs give the distance as 5 miles, but it is actually 4.3 miles from the Sunday Gulch Road intersection to the trailhead. There are no CDT signs at the trailhead, which is a parking lot for ATVers. Water is available in nearby Divide Creek.

From the Rocky Ridge Trailhead at mile 43.2 for this segment, it is two miles east to Interstate 15. The Beaverdam Campground is 4 miles west on Divide Creek Road, a possible meeting point for friends or resupply crew.

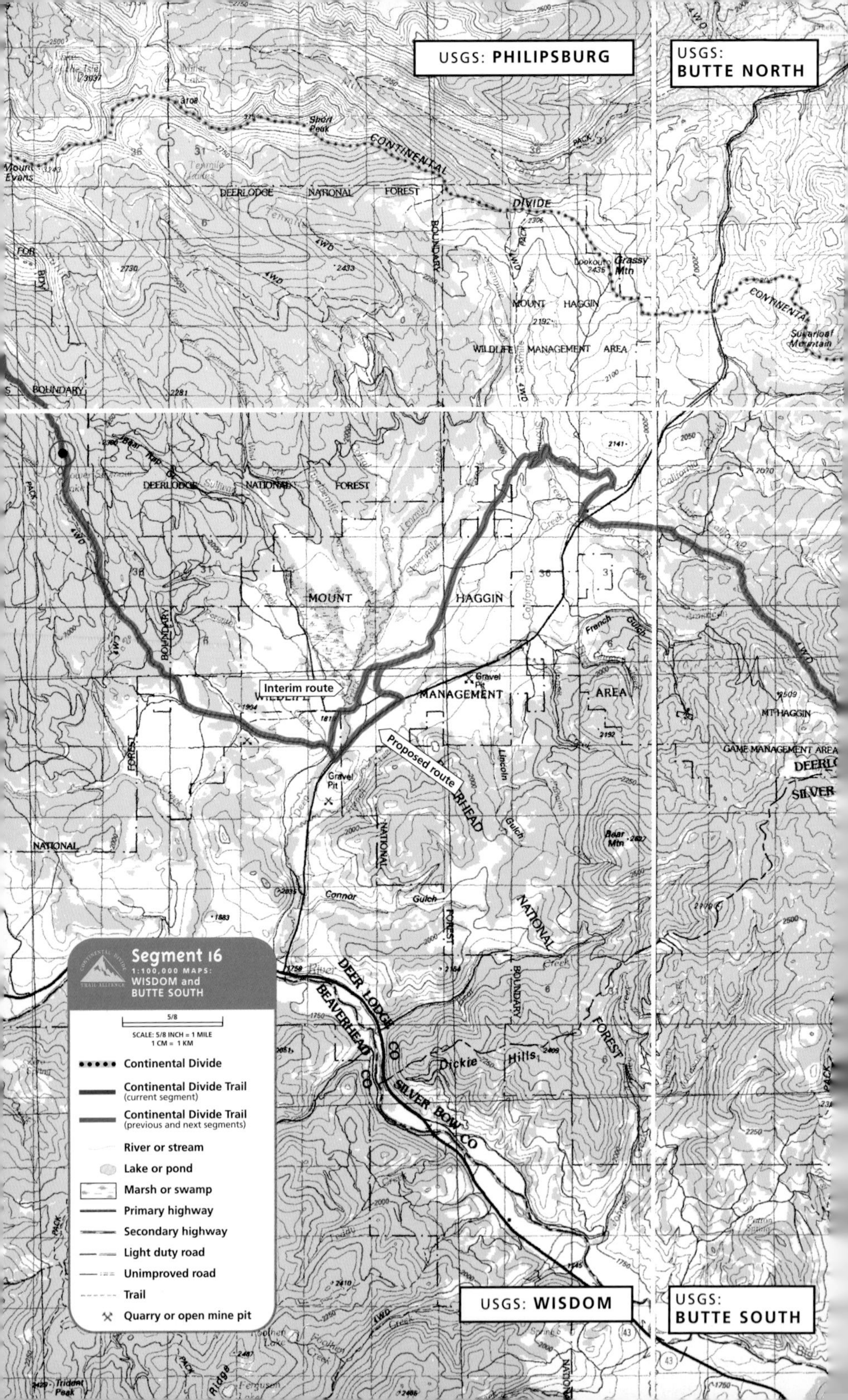

USGS: PHILIPSBURG
USGS: BUTTE NORTH
USGS: WISDOM
USGS: BUTTE SOUTH
Segment 16
1:100,000 MAPS:
WISDOM and
BUTTE SOUTH
CONTINENTAL DIVIDE TRAIL ALLIANCE
5/8
SCALE: 5/8 INCH = 1 MILE
1 CM = 1 KM
Continental Divide
Continental Divide Trail
(current segment)
Continental Divide Trail
(previous and next segments)
River or stream
Lake or pond
Marsh or swamp
Primary highway
Secondary highway
Light duty road
Unimproved road
Trail
Quarry or open mine pit
Interim route
Proposed route
CONTINENTAL DIVIDE
DEERLODGE NATIONAL FOREST BOUNDARY
MOUNT HAGGIN WILDLIFE MANAGEMENT AREA
MT HAGGIN GAME MANAGEMENT AREA
Short Peak
Mount Evans
Tenmile Lakes
Grassy Mtn
Lookout
Sugarloaf Mountain
Gravel Pit
Bear Mtn
French Gulch
Lincoln Gulch
Connor Gulch
Dickie Hills
DEER LODGE CO
BEAVERHEAD CO
SILVER BOW CO
Trident Peak

Crackerville
DNF
DEER LODGE CO
SILVER BOW CO
Fairmont
Gregson
Hot Springs
Finlen
Beacon
HAGGIN STATE
MANAGEMENT AREA
DNF
German Gulch
Miles Crossing
Dawson
Ramsay
Silver Bow
FLEECER MOUNTAIN STATE
WILDLIFE MANAGEMENT AREA
HAGGIN GAME MANAGEMENT AREA
Silver Bow
Beals Hill
German
Gulch
Lone
Tree
Gulch
DEERLODGE
Powder
Gulch
Sunday
Gulch
Selway Meadows
CONTINENTAL
DIVIDE
4WD
Buxton
NATIONAL
Hanson
Gulch
Fleecer
Ridge
CONTINENTAL
Pink
Gulch
BEAVERHEAD
FOREST
4WD
DIVIDE
Feele
Hill
NATIONAL
Burnt
Dam
Ridge
FOREST
Fleecer
Ridge
Swede
Woodin
Mitchell Park

Segment 17
I-15/Deer Lodge Pass to Homestake Pass: Highland Mtns.

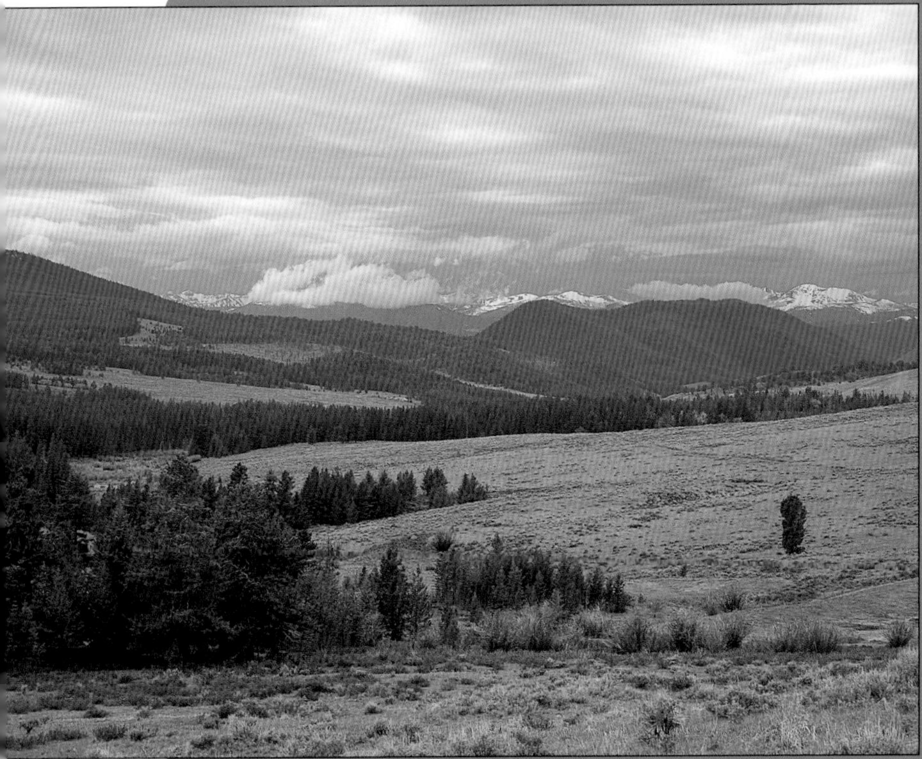

Near Mount Humbug in the Highland Mountains, where the CDT follows 4WD roads in the Deerlodge National Forest

39.3 miles
Difficulty: Easy

Segment 17 **Total Elevation Gain:** 4,072 feet
From Wyoming 475.7 miles
To Canada 505.0 miles

CONTINENTAL DIVIDE TRAIL ALLIANCE

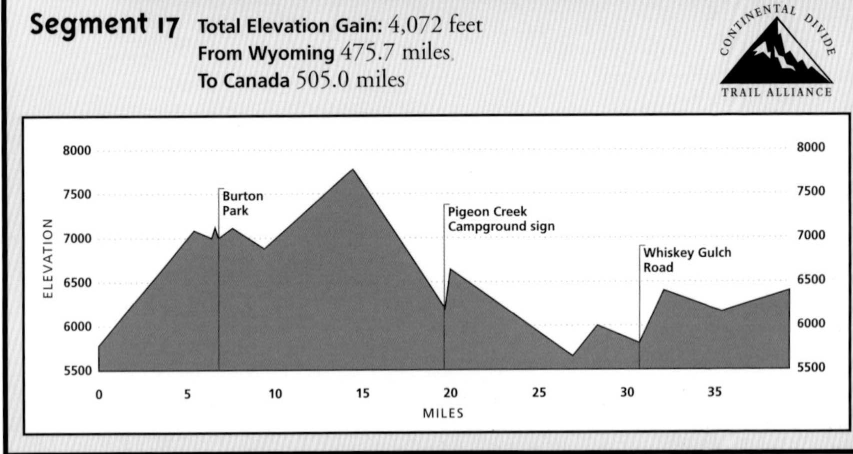

TRAIL OVERVIEW Our support crew called this section "Circling Butte," an accurate description. Northbound hikers find themselves hiking southeast and east to make a detour around Butte, Montana.

Lower elevations make for easy walking, mostly on dirt roads that can be accessed by 2WD vehicles. Aspen trees and cottonwoods mix with conifers along the stream banks, and the forest is often interrupted by large islands of sagebrush. This segment can be hiked at the end of May if you don't mind crossing a few snowfields; most of the trail is open by the first week of June.

This area is highly trafficked and you'll encounter many motorized vehicles as well as various groups of people and wilderness survivalist clubs. It's not uncommon to encounter people who are armed, even outside of hunting season. We strongly suggest that you never hike alone in this area and remain alert.

Apart from all this, the road-walking is pleasing in a mellow, almost rural, way. Cows graze, trout swim, and a wide variety of birds, including red-tailed hawks, cruise above the sagebrush steppe and grasslands. Hikers with a historical bent will enjoy all the 1880s-vintage mines, cabins, and rusting evidence of past ambitions.

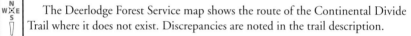

The Deerlodge Forest Service map shows the route of the Continental Divide Trail where it does not exist. Discrepancies are noted in the trail description.

Water is plentiful along most of the route. Short dry sections of about 4 miles are noted in the trail description.

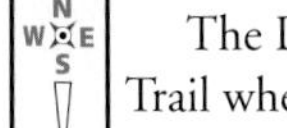

MOUNTAIN BIKE NOTES: All of the trail is open to mountain bikes and the riding is easy. There is a 1,306-foot gain in elevation from Interstate 15 to Burton Park on Highland Road, 5.4 miles on a gravel road.

LAND ADMINISTRATORS (SEE APPENDIX A)

Beaverhead/Deerlodge National Forest, Butte Ranger District
Beaverhead/Deerlodge National Forest, Jefferson Ranger District

MAPS

USGS QUADRANGLES: Tucker Creek, Mount Humbug, Pipestone Pass, Grace, Delmoe Lake, Homestake

USFS: Beaverhead/Deerlodge National Forest, East Half

BEGINNING ACCESS POINT

INTERSTATE 15, DEER LODGE PASS

ENDING ACCESS POINT

INTERSTATE 90, HOMESTAKE PASS

SUPPLIES, SERVICES, AND ACCOMMODATIONS

See **BUTTE, MT,** in Segment 19. Butte is north of Deer Lodge Pass on I-15.

Distance from Trail: 15 miles

TRAIL DESCRIPTION Exit Interstate 15 at Deer Lodge Pass, exit 111. Deer Lodge Pass is identified by name on highway maps, but not on the Forest Service or topographical maps. Turn south on the frontage road that parallels the west side of the freeway.

At 1.1 miles on the frontage road, turn east to go under the freeway. There is ample water in Divide Creek. There are no CDT signs here; look for a sign that says "Private Property Next 3.8 miles." Cross a cattle guard east of the freeway and continue east/southeast on a gravel road. The road is identified on the maps as 84, Highland Road, but is not signed on the ground. For the next 11.2 miles, hikers road-walk on this 2WD road.

The next sign that hikers see is "Garrison Ranch, Crossing Private Property, Stay on the Road." Don't turn on the rancher's road, but continue on the Highland Road.

At mile 4.9 hikers leave private property and enter the Deerlodge National Forest. From the road, one can see Mount Humbug and the Humbug Spires Wilderness Study Area to the south. The Deerlodge National Forest is heavily used by 4WD and four-wheeler traffic, so there is a maze of road intersections, some of them not shown on the maps. Northbound hikers stay on Highland Road, ignoring all the intersections until you come to Camp Creek Road 8520.

Burton Park, a large, open meadow watered by the North Fork of Moose Creek, is reached at mile 6.8. The park is identified on the ground as "Burton Pasture." Road 84 turns directly south to skirt the edge of Burton Park.

At mile 9.4, where Highland Road intersects Moose Creek Road, both roads are signed. Camping sites are nearly unlimited. Lesser-used 4WD roads give hikers an easy way to get off the main road, and frequent stream crossings provide water. Near Moose Creek, there are unobstructed views across sagebrush flats to the peaks of the Highland Mountains that form the Continental Divide to the east. Red Mountain, at 10,070 feet, is the highest visible peak. Past the Moose Creek intersection, Highland Road goes more directly east, curving around some interesting rock formations.

Leave Highland Road and turn south (right) on Camp Creek Road at mile 12.3. Highland Road continues north at this intersection, so it is tempting to follow it. Camp Creek Road is signed, so watch for the sign. Hike south for 1 mile to a three-way intersection. Turn left (east) on Fish Creek Road 668.

Fish Creek Road 668 soon bends to the north and then east again. It climbs to cross a saddle north of Red Mountain at 7,780 feet, mile 14.5 for this segment. In the saddle, there is another intersection of multiple 4WD roads. The road leading south is a nice side trip to the top of Red Mountain.

North of the four-way intersection there is a large amount of abandoned mining equipment. Not a good choice for a campsite. You can find this intersection on the topographical map by looking for the thickest concentration of "prospects" and "mine shafts."

Don't be misled by the Deerlodge Forest Service map, which shows the CDT diverging from Fish Creek Road, going over Coyote Hill, and then proceeding cross-country along the Divide. This is the proposed CDT route, but it hasn't even been surveyed and staked due to controversy about both the route and the nature of the trail. Construction is likely to be delayed for several years. Cross-country travel without a trail is not advised because dense lodgepole forest makes navigation difficult.

The interim route of the CDT stays on Fish Creek Road 668. This road is numbered on the FS map, but infrequently signed on the ground. At one point, it is identified as both "Lime Kiln Road" and "Fish Creek Road."

Fish Creek Road is rougher and 4WD is recommended for support or resupply crews. Unsigned intersections with logging roads complicate route-finding. Use both the FS map and the topo to stay on the right track. The route you want passes south of Mountain View Gulch, near Pigeon Creek Ridge.

Fish Creek Road and Lime Kiln Road part company at mile 16.5. Hikers pass an old cabin, then descend to cross Tanner Creek. Northbound hikers keep right (southeast) on Fish Creek Road. When we were there, a bridge on Fish Creek Road had washed out and the road was closed to motor vehicles near Mountain View Gulch. Camping is limited due to private property along the creek.

At a sign for the Pigeon Creek Campground, turn left (north), staying on Road 668. Both the FS map and the topo do not show a road intersection here, but there certainly is one on the ground. The campground road climbs through a scenic combination of trees and boulders, massed in strangely sculptural combinations. The Pigeon Creek Campground at mile 20 makes a good campsite. Spur roads intersect Road 668 as it goes through the Pigeon Creek Campground, but if you keep to the main road, you'll come to a highway which is identified on the topo as US-10 and on highway maps as Montana State Highway 2.

The Forest Service map shows the CDT crossing Pipestone Pass and following the Divide to Homestake Pass. This is incorrect. The proposed route has not yet been constructed. When hikers reach Hwy. 2 on the route described above, turn east (not west) on the highway and hike 2.4 miles to Rader Creek Road 240. The intersection is identified on the topo as "Nineteen Mile" and on the ground as Rader Creek/Toll Mountain. At this intersection, Pipestone Creek is a good water source. The next reliable water is 3.8 miles north where the road crosses Rader Creek.

From Hwy. 2, turn north on Rader Creek Road 240. The road is bumpy, but 2WD in good weather. Re-enter the Deerlodge National Forest 1.4 miles from the turn onto Road 240. Stay on the main road. Private property is often marked with orange or red paint on fence posts—don't enter lands behind orange/red markers.

At mile 30.7 (3.8 miles north of Hwy. 2), there is an intersection with Whiskey Gulch Road. Northbound hikers should keep left at this sign. The road climbs about 500 feet from this intersection and enters a public firewood cutting area. Here you may likely encounter a wilderness version of graffiti, which many hikers will no doubt find offensive. You might want to avoid camping overnight in this area south of Homestake Pass.

At mile 35.4 there is another unsigned intersection where the road crosses Moose Creek. Stay on the well-traveled road. The right fork leads to private property. From Moose Creek, the road climbs to a bluff overlooking Interstate 90 and turns west.

Parallel I-90 for 2 miles and turn north to cross the freeway at Homestake Pass, mile 39.9, ending this segment. The intersection of Rader Creek Road 240 and I-90 is signed. A short, paved spur off the freeway leads to an overpass where hikers can cross to Homestake Lake, 0.25 mile distant. There is a campground, picnic area, water source, and pit toilets at Homestake Lake.

Segment 17
1:100,000 MAP:
BUTTE SOUTH
CONTINENTAL DIVIDE TRAIL ALLIANCE
5/8
SCALE: 5/8 INCH = 1 MILE
1 CM = 1 KM
Continental Divide
Continental Divide Trail
(current segment)
Continental Divide Trail
(previous and next segments)
River or stream
Lake or pond
Marsh or swamp
Primary highway
Secondary highway
Light duty road
Unimproved road
Trail
Quarry or open mine pit
Gulch
Sunday
Gulch
Buxton
1706
Smith
Creek
Gulch
Sand
Hanson
Gulch
Gulch
Pink
DIVIDE
1988
Grove
Gulch
Creek
Basin
1911
2000
1940
Feeley
Hill
36
31
East
Fork
Creek
Gulch
CONTINENTAL
Climax
Swede
Creek
1750
Curly
Gulch
2000
Bear
Creek
DIVIDE
2292
China
1747
Fly
Creek
2250
2138
North
Fork
Creek
DEERLO
Mt
Humbug
2250
36
31
Fork
2087
2086
Moose
HUMBUG SPIRES
PRIMITIVE AREA
2250
Divide
1742
15

Cem
Cem
County Airport
375
Goldflint Mtn
DEERLODGE
Legget Hill
Pipestone Rock
NATIONAL
FOREST
Highview
Homestake Pass
Substa
Beacon
Nine Mile
THOMPSON
PARK
Proposed route
SILVER BOW CO
JEFFERSON CO
Interim route
Toll Mtn
Nineteen Mile
Quarry
NATIONAL
FOREST
Coyote Hill
BASE
LINE
Red Mtn
East Peak
White

Segment 18
Homestake Pass to Interstate 15 at Elk Park

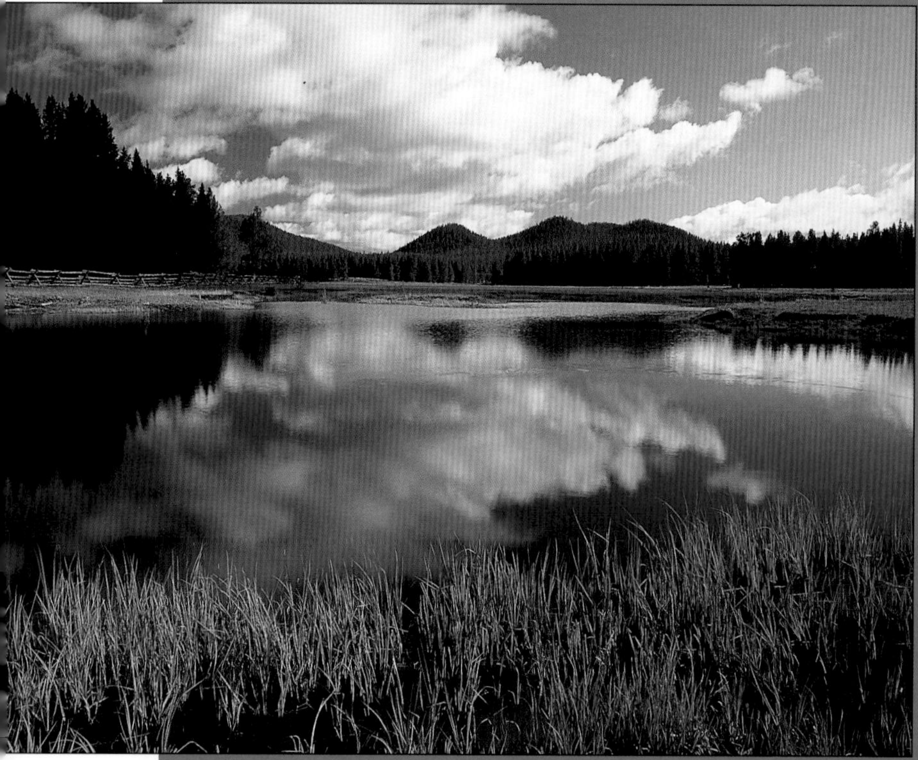

Halfway Park in the Deerlodge National Forest, north of Delmoe Lake

27.7 miles
Difficulty: Easy

Segment 18 **Total Elevation Gain:** 2,949 feet
From Wyoming 515.0 miles
To Canada 465.7 miles

CONTINENTAL DIVIDE TRAIL ALLIANCE

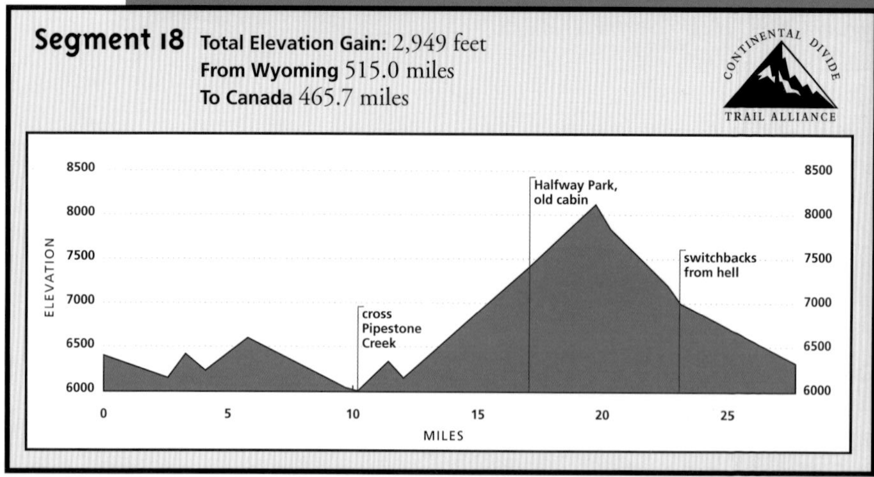

TRAIL OVERVIEW Road-walking in lower terrain continues in this segment, as hikers round Delmoe Lake east of Butte, Montana. Expect to share the roads and trails with four-wheelers and motorcycles. A complicated nest of trails makes it luck more than navigation when it comes to finding Halfway Park. When we were there, we met some ATVers who were lost—and they were locals.

When we hiked this section, there were no CDT signs; in fact, there were no signs at all past Delmoe Lake. Rangers and volunteer organizations are planning to sign the CDT. The prettiest scenery in this segment is at Halfway Park. Catch-and-release fishing is allowed for cutthroat trout. A newly constructed trail from Halfway Park in the south to Nez Perce Creek in the north is a respite from the motorized section. The trail reaches its highest point for this segment near Whitetail Peak, at 8,120 feet. Snow melts out of the lower elevations by early June, but there is about a mile of snowdrifts near the peak that will linger until mid-June or later.

The old route of the CDT used to be further east, following pack trails to Upper Whitetail Park near the reservoir. Although this is no longer the official route, it is still possible to hike that longer trail. The pack trails and four-wheeler trails to the reservoir are well-used and can easily mislead you into taking a wrong turn.

This entire segment is east of the Continental Divide. The Highland Mountains are to the south, the Elkhorn Mountains to the north, the Bull Mountains to the east, the Tobacco Root Mountains to the southeast, and the Boulder Mountains to the northwest.

In the middle of all the named mountain ranges is an uplift of igneous rocks that have been dated at 75 million years old and identified as part of the Boulder batholith (see the section entitled “Geology”). These mountains show little to no evidence of glaciation. The result is tree-covered terrain with a dearth of cliffs or other dramatic changes in elevation.

Water is plentiful in frequent stream crossings, and sometimes too plentiful in boggy areas.

MOUNTAIN BIKE NOTES: The entire trail is open to mountain bikes and is relatively easy to ride except for the area south of Nez Perce Creek (see trail description). It is far easier to ride the switchbacks south to north.

LAND ADMINISTRATORS (SEE APPENDIX A)

Beaverhead/Deerlodge National Forest, Butte Ranger District

MAPS

USGS QUADRANGLES: Delmoe Lake, Homestake, Whitetail Peak, Elk Park Pass

USFS: Beaverhead/Deerlodge National Forest, Deerlodge Forest Area, East Half

BEGINNING ACCESS POINT

HOMESTAKE PASS ON INTERSTATE 90

ENDING ACCESS POINT

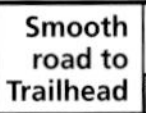

ELK PARK ON INTERSTATE 15, TRASK INTERCHANGE

SUPPLIES, SERVICES, AND ACCOMMODATIONS

BUTTE, MT, is at the intersection of Interstates 90 and 15. (See Segment 19 for details.)

Distance from Trail: 6 miles

TRAIL DESCRIPTION

Take exit 233 from I-90 at Homestake Pass and go east on Delmoe Lake Road 222. A signed intersection with Homestake Trailhead indicates a spur road to Homestake Lake Campground at mile 0.3. The campground has tent sites, water, pit toilets, and picnic areas.

Cross the Burlington Northern Railroad tracks and continue east on Delmoe Lake Road. The gravel road is 2WD and heavily traveled. Delmoe Lake Road turns north at mile 2.1.

There are numerous side roads entering Road 222, but hikers stay on the main road for more than 12 miles. At mile 10.7 from Homestake Pass, Road 9371 leads west to the Delmoe Lake Campground. The CDT continues straight ahead on Road 222 and crosses Big Pipestone Creek at mile 11.2.

In case the trail signs are missing, count the roads that enter from the left (west), beginning your count at milepost 10, which you will see after passing the entrance to the Delmoe Lake Campground. Ignore the first two roads and take the third one, Road 8695 on the FS map, at mile 12 for this segment (2.3 miles past the campground entrance road). When we were there, Road 8695 had no identifying signs of any kind.

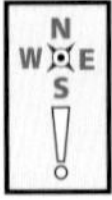

The Forest Service map is deceptively simple—it doesn't show even a fourth of the trails and 4WD tracks east and northeast of Delmoe Lake. The topo is no better. Herewith begins a guide through the maze:

- Let's assume you found Road 8695 and turned north toward Halfway Park. We'll use the intersection of 8695 with Delmoe Lake Road 222 as our zero mileage point.
- 0.1 mile, Y-shaped intersection; keep left
- 0.8 mile, Y-shaped intersection; keep right
- 1.5 miles, keep left at an intersection that looks like the road splits to go around an island of trees.

- Cross a cattleguard and go downhill to an intersection at 2.2 miles that is signed "Delmoe Lake Trail" to the left (west); stay straight ahead, do not take the left.
- 2.9 miles, Y-shaped intersection. Near the left fork is a barbed wire fence, near the right fork is a corral; keep right. This intersection is critical—if you mistakenly turn left, you enter a confusing maze of roads, tracks, and trails. The bones of lost CDT hikers are strewn along the trails (just kidding).
- 4.5 miles. Come upon a gray metal gate that used to have two signs on it, which were missing when we were there. Consistency is a virtue. When you come to this gate, you have gone too far. Turn around and go back to an intersection that you passed without even seeing it. (Don't worry, it's only 0.2 mile.) Look on the north side of the road for a dim track that goes north and parallels the west side of Halfway Park. This trail should be signed as "Nez Perce Trail 101," but you guessed it—no sign.
- 4.3 miles. We've backed up 0.2 mile from the metal gate at Halfway Park, and are now at last on the CDT and heading north. A sign on this trail says it is not recommended for four-wheeler traffic.
- 5.0 miles. Pass an old cabin and a view of Halfway Park. This portion of the trail appears on the topo as a pack trail and on the FS map as the CDT.
- 5.1 miles. Pass a brown gate and step onto new trail construction. You're sailin' now!

If you added all the miles up, you'd find the cabin to be 17 miles from Homestake Pass. Continue to climb toward the high country east of Whitetail Peak. The newly improved tread follows the route of an old pack trail.

At mile 18.6, the new tread diverges from the pack trail, a left (west) turn for northbound hikers, crossing a feeder stream of Halfway Park in the process. At mile 19.7, the trail crosses its highest point for this segment, 8,120 feet. It's all downhill from here.

Cross a tributary of Nez Perce Creek at mile 20.3, and intersect an old jeep track at mile 22. Look carefully for the new tread to take a 90° turn to the left (west) at the intersection with the old jeep track. The intersection was not signed when we were there.

North of the intersection with the jeep track, the trail begins to switchback down steeper terrain, reaching a set of bog bridges at mile 22.6. Follow the bog bridges over another tributary of Nez Perce Creek and continue downhill to a set of switchbacks. We dubbed this portion "Switchback Hell," as the entire mountainside is terraced with long, shallow switchbacks.

Cross the main channel of Nez Perce Creek on a bridge and intersect Road 78154 near Bakers Meadows at mile 25.1. (Southbound hikers look for a sign that says "Whitetail Park" near the creek crossing.) Follow the road west through a mixture of private property and National Forest land to I-15. The Trask Interchange on I-15 is reached at mile 27.7.

Although this freeway intersection is identified as "Trask Interchange" on the topo, it is identified as exit 138/Sheepshead Mountain Recreation Area/Elk Park on the ground. Bison Creek, east of the freeway, is a good water source, but it runs through private property. A nice camp can be made on a knoll 1.2 miles east of the freeway, near the "Entering Public Lands" sign. It is 7 miles to good camping on the west side of the freeway.

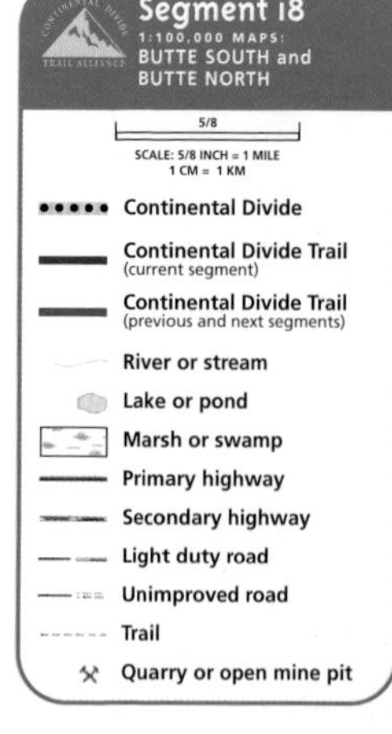

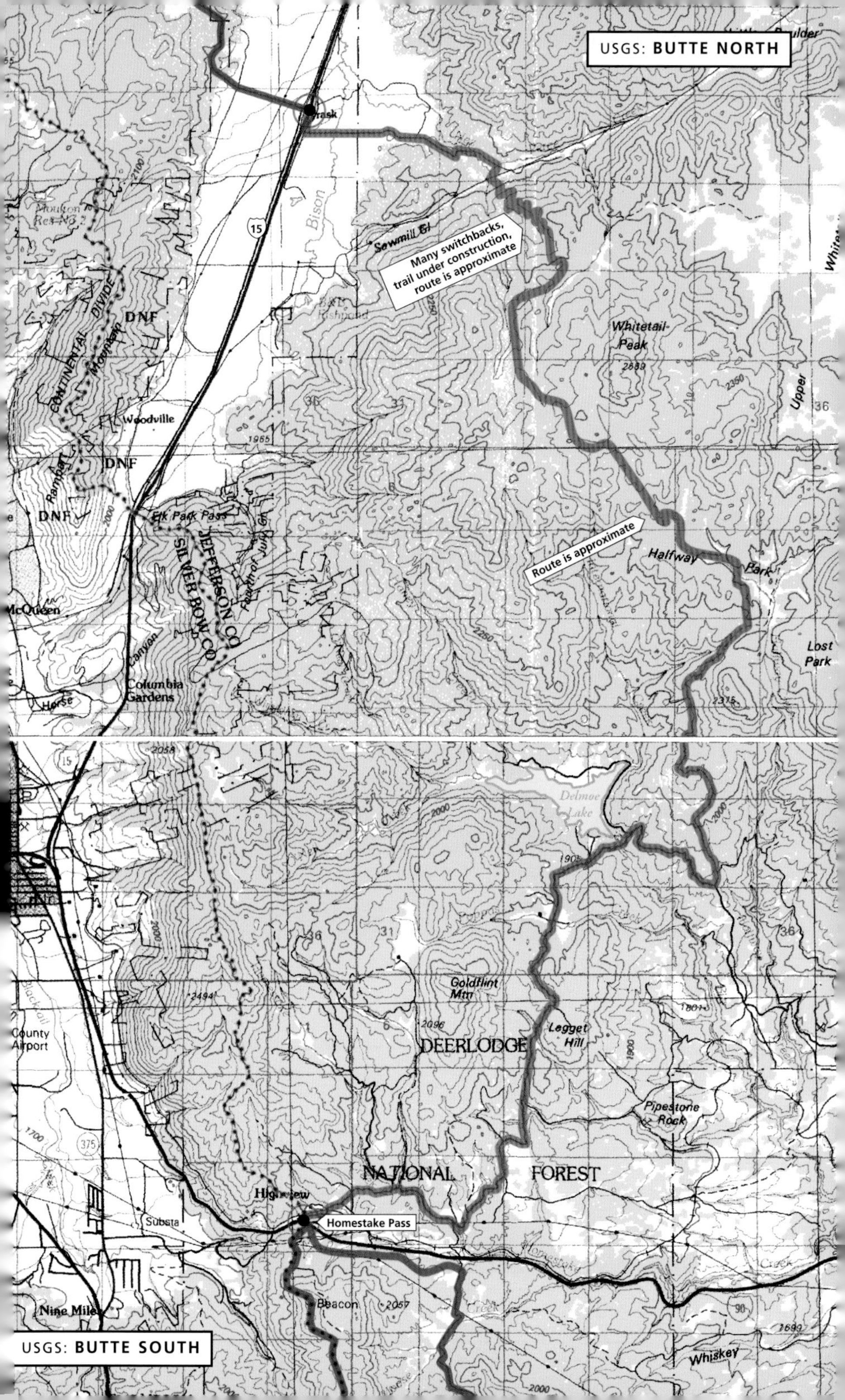
USGS: BUTTE NORTH
Many switchbacks, trail under construction, route is approximate
Route is approximate
Homestake Pass
USGS: BUTTE SOUTH
Trask
Sawmill Gl
Whitetail Peak
Halfway Park
Lost Park
CONTINENTAL DIVIDE
DNF
Woodville
Elk Park Pass
JEFFERSON CO
SILVER BOW CO
McQueen
Columbia Gardens
Delmoe Lake
Goldflint Mtn
Legget Hill
DEERLODGE
NATIONAL FOREST
Pipestone Rock
Highview
Substa
County Airport
Nine Mile
Beacon
Whiskey

Segment 19
Interstate 15 to MacDonald Pass: Boulder Mtns.

Cumulus clouds build over the meadows near Champion Pass, where the CDT makes its way through these gentle hills—home of ranchers and miners, past and present.

65.5 miles
Difficulty: Moderate

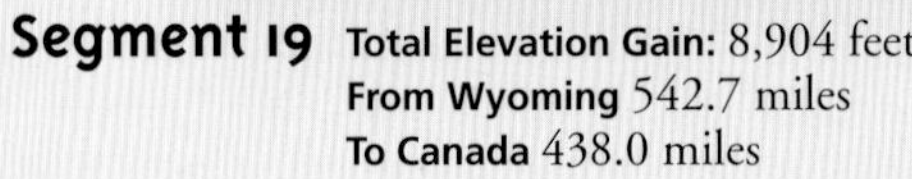

Segment 19 **Total Elevation Gain:** 8,904 feet
From Wyoming 542.7 miles
To Canada 438.0 miles

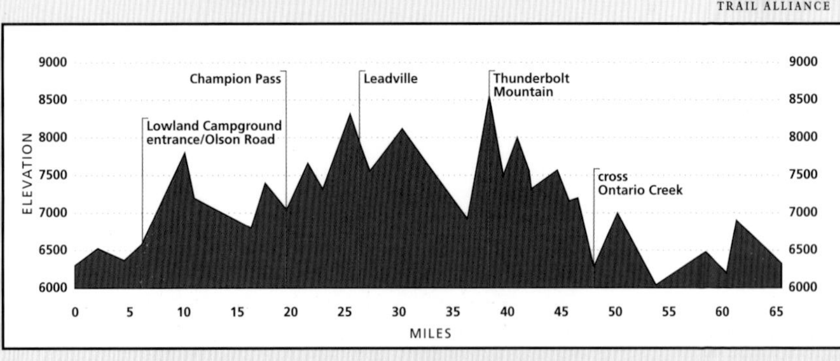

TRAIL OVERVIEW North of Butte, Montana, the Continental Divide Trail crosses Interstate 15 for the third time as it wends its way from Yellowstone National Park to Canada. For through-hikers, it is always a little strange to come down out of the mountains and hike across the freeway. One gets used to a speed of about 2.5 miles per hour (sometimes less), and suddenly there's a whole world of people rushing along at 75 miles per hour.

Civilization, past and present, crops up over and over in this segment of the trail. Logging, mining, cattle ranching, and recreational use, both as ghosts of the past and in their present incarnations, have left an imprint on the land. From Lowland Campground north, the route of the CDT follows logging roads, some in use, some defunct. Near Champion Pass, the sides of the trail are pocked with so many prospect holes from previous mining activities that the land resembles an old bombing range, now grown over with vegetation. Further north, there's the ghost town of Leadville, sled-dog racing trails south of MacDonald Pass, and one high peak, Thunderbolt Mountain, that overlooks it all.

Much unexpected beauty is to be found and experienced here. It's surprising how strongly nature regenerates itself from the abuses of the past: Log cabins meld back into the earth, and ghost towns contain a silence deeper than where man has never been. The gentle landscape is furred green with second- and third-growth forests. My brother's photographs from this section of trail remind me of the Appalachian Mountains, mist-filled and tree-covered—some little town or road never far away.

Sometimes it is more confusing to be surrounded by roads than to have no trail at all. Make sure you have the Deerlodge and Helena Forest Service maps, as well as the topographical maps, for this section. You'll need all the clues you can get to follow the route of the CDT, although since we were there, road intersections have been signed with wooden CD symbols and a new section of trail from Leadville to Cottonwood Lake is complete. One more warning about maps: The Deerlodge map shows the proposed route of the CDT, and not the route as it currently exists. Where they differ, follow the trail description in this guide, not the map.

Don't let the relatively civilized nature of this segment fool you—there are still bears, thunderstorms to treat with due respect, and the threat of hypothermia, courtesy of June snowstorms. We saw black bears but no grizzlies. Refresh your bear avoidance skills by reading the "Safety Concerns" section of this book.

Water is not a problem here, thanks to frequent stream crossings. Check your water supply before you climb Thunderbolt Mountain, but you seldom have to hike more than 5 miles between water sources.

MOUNTAIN BIKE NOTES: Experienced mountain bikers will find the roaded sections of the trail easy, the footpath sections difficult, but possible, and the trail over Thunderbolt Mountain impassable.

LAND ADMINISTRATORS

(SEE APPENDIX A) Beaverhead/Deerlodge National Forest, Butte Ranger District
Beaverhead/Deerlodge National Forest, Jefferson Ranger District
Helena National Forest, Helena Ranger District

MAPS

USGS QUADRANGLES: Elk Park Pass, Sheepshead Mountain, Lockhart Meadows, Sugarloaf Mountain, Thunderbolt Creek, Bison Mountain, Three Brothers, MacDonald Pass

USFS: Deerlodge Forest Area, Helena National Forest

BEGINNING ACCESS POINT

INTERSTATE 15, ELK PARK/SHEEPSHEAD MOUNTAIN RECREATION AREA EXIT 138: From Butte, Montana, go north on I-15 about 9 miles to exit 138. From the exit, the Continental Divide Trail goes west on Forest Service Road 442, which is signed for both the Sheepshead Mountain Recreation Area and for Lowland Campground. The gravel and dirt road is suitable for 2WD vehicles, but may be downgraded to 4WD due to mud and ruts in wet weather. The Deerlodge Forest Service map correctly depicts the CDT here.

ENDING ACCESS POINT

MACDONALD PASS: MacDonald Pass is on US-12, west of Helena, Montana. The city of Helena is 14.5 miles to the east. The small town of Elliston is 7 miles west of MacDonald Pass, also on US-12. There is a campground at the pass.

TRAIL DESCRIPTION

Take exit 138 from I-15, north of Butte, Montana. This exit is signed as "Elk Park" and "Sheepshead Mountain Recreation Area." Bison Creek runs through a meadow east of the overpass. Walk under the freeway and proceed westward on a gravel/dirt road toward Lowland Campground. A sign here says "Lowland Campground 7 mi."

The gravel road to Lowland Campground is suitable for 2WD vehicles except in wet weather. At 2.1 miles, hikers enter the Deerlodge National Forest and the Boulder Mountains.

At 2.7 miles there is a T-shaped intersection, with a road coming in from the left. The route of the CDT continues straight ahead on the main road. Mile 4.5 brings you to the "Lowland Campground/Hail Columbia" sign. The campground is to the left (west) and Sheepshead Recreation Area is to the right (north). The route of the CDT proceeds west, toward Lowland Campground, crossing tributaries of Lowland Creek twice.

A T-shaped intersection at 6.1 miles marks the Lowland Campground entrance and the turn north onto Olson Gulch Road. New CD signs should be up. Olson Gulch Road climbs through a lodgepole forest, with occasional clearings created by previous logging efforts. There are limited views of the Elkhorn Mountains to the east/northeast.

SUPPLIES, SERVICES, AND ACCOMMODATIONS

BUTTE, MT, is at the intersection of Interstates 90 and 15.

Distance from Trail: 9 miles

Zip Code: 59701-3219

Bank:	First National Bank of Montana, 1940 Dewey Blvd.	406-496-6111
	Norwest Bank, 3650 Harrison Avenue	406-496-7000
Bus:	Greyhound Bus Lines, 101 E. Front Street	406-723-3287
Camping:	LaRue MountainView, 5103 S. Warren Avenue	406-494-3211
	KOA Kampgrounds, 1601 Kaw Avenue	406-782-0663
Dining:	Cafe Ippity Bop, 302 E. Broadway	406-782-2329
	Colombian Garden Espresso, 1285 Harrison Avenue	406-782-8828
	Deville's Uptown Bakery & Bagels, 205 S. Arizona Street	406-723-8900
Gear:	Outdoorsman, 2700 Harrison Avenue	406-494-7700
	Pipestone Mountaineering, 829 S. Montana Street	406-782-4994
Groceries:	Albertsons, 1301 Harrison Avenue	406-723-7944
	Buttrey Food & Drug, 3745 Harrison Avenue	406-494-8880
Information:	Butte/Silver Bow Chamber of Commerce, 1000 George Street. Take exit 126, Montana Street to George Street	406-723-3177 800-735-6814
Laundry:	Park Street Laundromat, 209 W. Park Street	406-723-9814
	Suds & Fun Laundromat, 2711 Harrison Avenue	406-494-3744
Lodging:	Best Western Inn, 2900 Harrison Ave., $55–$75	406-494-3500
	Budget Motel, 920 S. Montana Street, $31.20	406-723-4346
	Holiday Inn, 1 Holiday Way, $62	406-494-6999
Medical:	St. James Community Hospital, 400 S. Clark Street	406-723-2500
	Rocky Mountain Clinic, 1101 S. Montana Street	406-782-9132
Post Office:	U.S. Post Office, 701 Dewey Blvd., Butte, MT 59701	406-494-2107
Showers:	See "Camping" above	

Special Notes: Butte is also known as the "Mile High City" because of its location virtually on the Continental Divide. The Berkeley Pit, a huge open-pit copper mine, dominates the landscape. This pit mine grew so outlandishly that it consumed portions of the town of Butte until it was shut down in 1983. The large, lighted statue that overlooks Butte from the Divide is called "Our Lady of the Rockies." Proposed rerouting of the CDT will eventually take hikers around the feet of the 90-foot lady who appears to be blessing the Berkeley Pit. The World Museum of Mining and the 1899 Mining Camp at West Park Street give visitors a look at Butte's history.

There are numerous, rough 4WD jeep tracks leading off of Olson Gulch Road; ignore them all until you come to a four-way intersection at mile 7.3. Olson Gulch Road descends briefly just before the intersection where the CDT turns west (left), and uphill on a much rougher track. This looks like a four-way intersection, but the route north is blocked by a gate. All four dirt roads meet in a previously logged area, now full of pint-sized lodgepole pines.

The road becomes more of a "trode" (trail/road), as it climbs uphill from the four-way intersection. The track is rutted and steep. At mile 8.1, there is an apparent Y-shaped intersection, but it is just a split that soon rejoins the main track. The left-hand (west) fork leads out to a view over Brown's Gulch.

The Forest Service map doesn't show it, but the track you are on crosses the Divide twice in quick succession, and then joins Road 8620. At mile 11, the trail reaches a four-way crossing that can be confusing because it is tempting to continue north. But this is where the CDT turns west to follow Road 8620 toward Four Corners. There were no signs when we were there. Road 8620 is shown as 2WD on the topographical map, but is so rough that it should be categorized as 4WD. Water is plentiful, as the road parallels a tributary of the Boulder River.

Beware: the FS map also shows the CD marching westward along the Divide south of the intersection with Road 8620. The map shows a proposed route that hasn't even been flagged yet, so don't attempt to follow the Divide where it turns west. If the trail has not been completed and marked, stay on the road. Rangers assured me they are working hard to sign the road intersections with CD symbols.

To add to the confusion, there are multitudes of minor intersections in this area, some of them not on either the FS or topo maps. Watch your mileage/hiking time in order to make the correct turns. We hiked about 10 miles out of our way before we figured out the correct path.

After you've made the turn west on Road 8620 at the four-way intersection, hike westerly for 3 miles, passing intersections with roads 8621 and South Fork. This South Fork Road is part of the proposed, future route of the CD and is shown that way on the FS map, but for now, you do not turn south. Continue past this intersection, following what is now Road 8444 north (right). The road crosses and then parallels the South Fork of the Boulder River.

The route of the CDT is on Road 8444 for only 0.8 mile before it again turns west, this time on Road 8638 (though it is not signed as such at the intersection). Northbound hikers bear left (west) to Four Corners on a well-maintained gravel, 2WD road.

The Four Corners intersection (mile 16.3) is not very reassuring, as it also is not well-signed. There is no "Four Corners" sign, but Road 8638 is noted at the crossing of the Continental Divide, and its counterpart that continues west to the Deerlodge Valley is signed as Road 8634. You can find Road 8634 on the FS map and use that as a landmark.

The route of the CDT north from Four Corners was labeled only as "Closed to Motorized Vehicles" when we were there. Cross the cattleguard and look for the closure sign. This "trode" leads northwesterly toward Champion Pass. Shortly after making the turn, the trail crosses Cottonwood Creek. There are 3 miles of trode before an intersection with a jeep track 0.8 mile south of Champion Pass (mile 18.9 for this segment).

Northbound hikers turn right (northeasterly) on the jeep track leading to Champion Pass. (Southbound hikers look for a sign that says "Restricted to Administrative

Use Only" and for a blue/white CD sign.) As is common in this area, there are several dilapidated cabins and many old logging roads near main east/west routes that cross the Divide. Champion Pass is no exception. Prospect holes from previous mining activities dot the landscape. Unless otherwise noted, ignore the side roads, including some signed as "Private Property."

At Champion Pass (mile 19.6, elevation 7,045 feet, signed as "Champion Pass"), the CDT crosses the road and continues north. Champion Pass is 15 miles from US-91, and 28 miles from Boulder. The road, 82, is 2WD in good weather and could easily be used as an exit or access point. At the pass there is a post that used to have CD signs on it, but the signs were gone when we were there. (Someone had written "CD" on the post itself with a marking pen.)

North of Champion Pass, the trail follows a dirt road that switchbacks up Blizzard Hill. On the way, it passes one snowmobile trail that appears to lead directly north, but the route of the CDT stays on the road. At mile 20.5 the small, square building that used to serve a radio tower on Blizzard Hill is visible. More snowmobile trail signs (orange diamond-shaped symbols on tall poles) dot the ridge north of Blizzard Hill.

Road 1516 continues north from Blizzard Hill, crossing under a large, metal-supported power line at mile 22.7. Briefly follow the power line, then turn north to emerge onto a grassy ridge of the Divide. Cold Spring is at mile 23. Look east of the trail for a fenced-in area, a storage barrel, and a watering trough.

From the crest of the Divide, there are views westward to the Bitterroot Range, the Deerlodge Valley, Interstate 90, and the city of Deer Lodge. The name "Deer Lodge" comes from the Deer Lodge Mound, a 40-foot-high geothermal formation. The mound's shape, with steam issuing from the top, resembled a large medicine lodge, and minerals in the water attracted large numbers of deer, so Indians in the area referred to the landmark as the Deer Lodge. The formation was a major landmark for trappers and early travelers in the area. The Deerlodge National Forest (with Deerlodge spelled as one word) was proclaimed by President Theodore Roosevelt in 1908.

1.2 miles past Cold Spring (mile 24.2 for this segment), there are two CD signs, one with a trail registration box. Signs here also say it is 8 miles to Cottonwood Lake, and 1.5 miles to Leadville. Both distances are inaccurate. It is 2.3 miles to Leadville, and 10.6 miles to Cottonwood Lake.

North of these signs, in the area labeled "Long Park" on the topo, the 4WD road gets a lot rougher, eventually becoming a jeep track that can be negotiated only by the highest clearance vehicles. Three springs provide running water in Long Park.

There are presently over 500 active mining claims on the Deerlodge National Forest. The CDT goes right through many of the inactive claims, including Leadville, a ghost town of tumble-down log buildings and rusting machinery. The trail then descends for 0.8 mile on a jeep track.

Watch for new tread and new CD signs north of the jeep track (Trail 227, the Rock Creek Trail, on the Forest Service map). Newly constructed foot/horse Trail 147 leaves the jeep track and takes hikers northward on a relatively gentle 600-foot climb through dense forest. There is one open spot above the Rock Creek drainage. This section of trail between Leadville and Cottonwood Lake tops out at 8,120 feet, which doesn't sound all that high, but the configuration of the landscape contributes to high snowfall amounts, and to very late melt-out dates.

Hikers who would like to get through this area earlier in the season should consider an alternate route, hiking east on the road from Champion Pass to Whitehouse Campground, then north to intercept the CDT at Cottonwood Lake. A proposed rerouting of the CDT would avoid the steep climb up Thunderbolt Mountain by heading east from a knoll, elevation 7,625 feet, north of Cottonwood Lake (see Trail 65). This reroute was scheduled for completion in 1999, and will greatly facilitate early-season hiking.

The new Trail 147 appears on the FS map, but not on the topographical map. It is 7 miles from the Rock Creek Trail to an intersection with Trail 65 north of Cottonwood Lake. Trail 65 leads 1 mile south to the lake, which is the best camping spot for many miles (mile 34.8 for this segment). The north end of the lake is very marshy and the lake itself is shallow, but it still boasts a small population of brook trout.

From Cottonwood Lake, continue south on Trail 65 to an intersection, at mile 36.3, with Lookout Connection Trail 119 to Thunderbolt Mountain. On your maps you'll see that this is a long, V-shaped detour, south from the lake and then northeasterly again toward the mountaintop. Until the shortcut around Thunderbolt Mountain is constructed, there is no other way to go.

The two-mile climb up Thunderbolt is lung-bustingly steep, with 40 percent grades in some spots. (Most Forest Service trails are less than 20 percent grade, with many in the 10 percent to 12 percent range.) This is the only section that is not suitable for mountain bikes. The trail tops out at about 8,550 feet and then begins an equally steep descent down the north side of the mountain. The virtue of such a difficult trail is that it offers panoramic views of the Boulder Mountains and the winding course of the Continental Divide. The trail contours around the eastern side of the mountain, but a spur trail leads to the 8,632-foot summit, where there used to be a lookout. After all that climbing, it would be a shame not to see the sights from the summit. This trail will remain in the Forest Service's trail system even after alternate routes are constructed.

From Thunderbolt Mountain, descend along the crest of the Divide on Trail 330. The trail is blazed, and stays high enough to be dry for about 3 miles. About 1.6 miles north of Thunderbolt, the Divide and the trail swing east for a 0.7-mile climb to 8,000 feet. There is one wooden CD sign near the next turn to the north.

SOUTHBOUND HIKERS: Be alert for this turn because there is a faint trail, perhaps a game trail, that continues downhill instead of making the turn west. The turn itself is not marked; you have to make the turn before you see the sign.

The trail turns north again 2.3 miles north of Thunderbolt Mountain. The trail contours just below the Divide on the west side, reaching the National Forest Service

Boundary about 1.1 miles after you make the turn north (mile 42 for this segment). Hikers enter the Helena National Forest here. Signs at the border clearly indicate "Continental Divide Trail 337" (the number changes when you cross the boundary) and distances are given to the Bison Mountain TRHD as 3 miles, and Joe Bowers TRHD as 4 miles.

A marshy area nearly inundates the trail above tributaries of Basin Creek, near the Helena boundary sign. Just 0.2 mile north of all the boundary signs, multiple trail intersections and signs fill a small, open meadow (mile 42.2). The Joe Bowers Trailhead and Blackfoot Connection Trail 98 lead east from here; Thunderbolt Mtn. and Bison Mtn. distances and directions are noted on the signs. The four-mile distance given for Thunderbolt Mountain to the south is correct.

The CDT begins to look more like a "trode" again as it approaches Bison Mountain from the south, with its previous incarnation as a jeep track or four-wheeler trail showing up in places. At mile 44.6 (6.3 miles north of Thunderbolt Mountain), there is a CD sign on a post in the middle of the trode, perhaps as a deterrent to motorized use.

The trail rounds the western side of Bison Mountain and there are some views through scattered trees to its rocky summit. At mile 45.7 there is a well-signed intersection with the Monarch Creek Trail. Look for this intersection in a logged area. Continental Divide Trail 337 is shown to be continuing both north and south. Near the Monarch Creek area, the CDT passes through the penultimate expression of "dog-hair" lodgepole pine forest. Young trees about 14 feet high grow so thickly that you couldn't squeeze a skinny backpacker between them. Trail crews have cut a wide trail through the lodgepoles.

Northbound hikers come to a Y-shaped intersection at mile 46.5, showing road 1801-A2 and the CDT. As you can tell from this trail description, there are a lot more roads, trodes, trails, and snowmobile tracks on the ground than one sees on the topographical map. Make sure that you switch to the Helena Forest Service map at this point because it shows more of the intersections than does the Deerlodge map or the topo. Even the Helena Forest Service map does not show all of the snowmobile trails/roads and their numbers. About 200 yards past the intersection described above, there is another Y-shaped intersection. Luckily, a CD post with a sign on it shows the correct route. Northbound hikers keep right (northeasterly) at the post.

Yet another intersection in this maze of roads north of Bison Mountain occurs at mile 47.5. The CD is signed and it heads uphill on a track that is not as well-used as the road. If all these intersections are confusing you, check the Helena FS map, and keep in mind that you are heading generally northeasterly to intersect 2WD roads 493, 494, and 495 near Telegraph Creek.

There are quite a few wet spots and/or tiny tributaries along this route, but the most recognizable is the major crossing of Ontario Creek at mile 48 (9.7 miles north of Thunderbolt Mountain). Two CD signs are posted above the creek, but southbound hikers may not see them until after they have crossed the creek and climbed 0.1 mile up the hill. Northbound hikers proceed downhill to the creek, where there is a log bridge for pedestrians, and it looks like four-wheelers have been fording the creek nearby. Orange diamond-shaped symbols mark this as snowmobile Trail 4104-A2. There is also a sign for Trail 325, though when, or if, we lost the 337 designation, I don't know. Trail 325 is not on the FS map. Southbound hikers will be reassured by a "Bison Mountain" sign and directional arrows.

Northbound hikers cross another, smaller tributary stream 0.9 mile past the log bridge over Ontario Creek and begin a steep, 700-foot climb up a rocky, rutted 4WD road, 495-D1, reaching an intersection with a 2WD road at mile 49.5 (elevation 6,922 feet). You are now about 11 miles north of Thunderbolt Mountain, and about 16 miles south of MacDonald Pass.

Road numbers get to be a problem here. What is signed on the ground does not always match what is on the Forest Service map, but as nearly as I could discern, northbound hikers are now on Road 494 and headed almost due north (the 494 number is not on the map, but 495 to the north and 493 to the south are on the map).

Hike north 4.3 miles to intersect a footpath at Jericho Creek. There is a lot of logging in this area, and camping opportunities are very limited. Some private property is scattered in the National Forest, including mining claims, houses, and small ranches. As a result, there are also a lot more side roads and intersections. When we were there, all of the intersections were well-signed, with the single exception of the one you're looking for, Jericho Creek.

Here are some of the details: Where you leave Road 494 and continue north on 495, the route is generally downhill on 495 toward Telegraph Creek. There are occasional CD signs on posts as you go north toward Jericho Creek. Some of the posts are naked, their signs stolen or weather-cracked.

Three miles north on your road-walk, you come to a junction of Road 495 and 1859. Continue on 495, where there is a wooden CD sign. For northbound hikers, this is a right-hand turn (east), still downhill. Cross Telegraph Creek near this intersection.

At 3.6 miles in the road-walk, cross Telegraph Creek again on a wooden bridge just before a T-shaped intersection with Road 527. There are two wooden CD signs here. Road 495, the route of the CDT, continues north here, so this is a left-hand turn for northbound hikers. Southbound hikers watch for the "Ontario Mine" sign, as well as Road 495 marking a right turn. There is no camping allowed on private property near this intersection.

At last, at mile 4.3 of your road walk, the CDT leaves 495 and heads uphill (easterly) on 495-B1 (at Jericho Creek, but the creek is not signed on the ground). There is a wooden CD sign here, but it is only visible to northbound hikers. A small camping spot, suitable for one tent, is north of the creek, near the road intersection. Jericho Creek is small, but runs all year. Because this intersection is so poorly signed, remember to watch for the first right-hand (east) turn north of the intersection with 1859. Jericho Mountain is the landmark to look for on the topographical map.

The CD trail is a mild uphill, none of it really steep, from Jericho Creek to MacDonald Pass. Briefly follow a rocky 4WD track that parallels the stream, then turn north on the signed CDT, Trail 337. There are several small, stream crossings in this section of recently cut tread north of Jericho Creek. The tread is easy to follow in the trees. There are no blazes, which could create a route-finding problem in snowy conditions. Near Jericho Mountain, the track is less obvious where it leaves the trees and heads gently downhill to intercept Road 1836.

SOUTHBOUND HIKERS: Watch carefully for a CD sign marking the southerly departure from Road 1836, slightly uphill, along a grassy, mucky, rocky track that is not numbered on the FS map.

Near Jericho Mountain, we saw a big black bear running uphill over rocks and small trees as if they were a flat racetrack. The bear crossed Road 1836 and raced up the mountain. We also saw coyote sign, several elk, and one cow moose with a calf about 2 miles north of Jericho Mountain.

When we were there, a shortcut was flagged with pink ribbons that would cut off a U-shaped section of the road, taking hikers across Mike Renig Gulch—but as it wasn't finished yet and was full of deadfall, we stayed on the road. There are two crossings of small tributary streams in the U-shaped section of the road. I'm not sure where Road 1836 becomes 1856, as there was no marked intersection, but hikers will see an 1836 sign on the west half of the U-shaped turn. These roads are colored purple on the FS maps to indicate motor vehicle restrictions, usually allowing only snowmobiles in the winter months. There are also some dogsled trails in this area.

Road 1856 is wide and looks like it was once used by logging trucks. Hikers pass through some previously logged areas. Northbound hikers should watch for the road sign for 1856-G1, as that is the next turn in your northerly progress. (With some luck, southbound hikers will have joined this road system when it was a barely discernible track and then followed it to the intersection where they would have eventually found a sign confirming their location.) Two CD signs also mark the intersection with 1856-G1 (mile 60.4). Road 1856-G1 leads to Road 1864, which is also signed with CD markers. There is plenty of water near this intersection where the trail crosses a tributary that feeds Mike Renig Gulch. Just north of the gulch, there is good camping in a grassy area.

As you continue toward MacDonald Pass, the 4WD roads and snowmobile trails become harder to see, with the tracks disappearing in grassy areas. Blazes are few and far between. Where the blazes become fewer, look for faint two-tracks in the grass and follow them uphill. Below a knob, elevation 6,901 feet on the topo map, the trail begins a northwesterly climb to the Divide.

SOUTHBOUND HIKERS: There is a confusing area where the trail leaves the grassy knob because the Bear Gulch Trail, resembling a closed road, enters the meadow from the west, but is not marked. Follow the road for a short distance and then look for blazes when you have descended enough to be in the trees again.

Northbound hikers follow blazes (some of them an ancient, faded gray) to this same unmarked road. If in doubt, check your topo map and aim for the knob at 6,901 feet (mile 61.3 for this segment). From this high point, hikers can see MacDonald Pass and a radio tower.

4.2 miles south of MacDonald Pass, at the 6,901-foot knob above Minnehaha Creek and 0.5 mile from the intersection with Bear Gulch Trail, the CDT is marked with posts, some of which have faded CD signs on them. Hikers have to walk from post to post in this grassy area as there is no visible tread. For northbound hikers, the trail makes a northeasterly turn here, heading toward another treeless knob on the Divide. This section could definitely use more signs and blazes. It would be a very difficult place to navigate in fog or clouds as the posts are too far apart. Some of the posts and signs have weathered to gray and their CD symbols are worn off.

The footpath reappears whenever the trail enters the trees. From here northward to MacDonald Pass, most of the path is visible and there are occasional wooden CD signs on the trees. There are a few boggy areas to negotiate, and some spots where spring runoff transforms the trail into a streambed. This is still Trail 337 on the FS map, though it is not signed as such on the ground.

At 0.7 mile south of the pass, the trail exits the forest and climbs through a grassy area to the "Vista Point" south of MacDonald Pass. Southbound hikers should note that the trail is not marked where it leaves the Vista Point parking lot via some stone steps. But when the trail enters the forest it is signed as the CDT and is blazed.

It is 0.6 mile from the Vista Point to Highway 12. There is a campground here, just west of the trail. The campground is signed as "MacDonald Pass Recreation Area." Hikers should detour to the campground to get water, as there is no water going north from MacDonald Pass to Priest Pass. Hikers reach MacDonald Pass at mile 65.5 for this segment, elevation 6,325 feet.

MacDonald Pass is named for Alexander "Red" MacDonald, who managed the toll gate in the 1870s and 1880s. He charged a fee for all kinds of transportation, except pedestrian, and those traveling at night (through-hikers would have had no problem). In 1911, Cromwell Dixon earned a $10,000 prize when he became the first aviator in America to fly over the Continental Divide near MacDonald Pass.

At MacDonald Pass, southbound hikers will enter at the recreation area and keep left, following the "Vista Point" road. There were no CD signs when we were there.

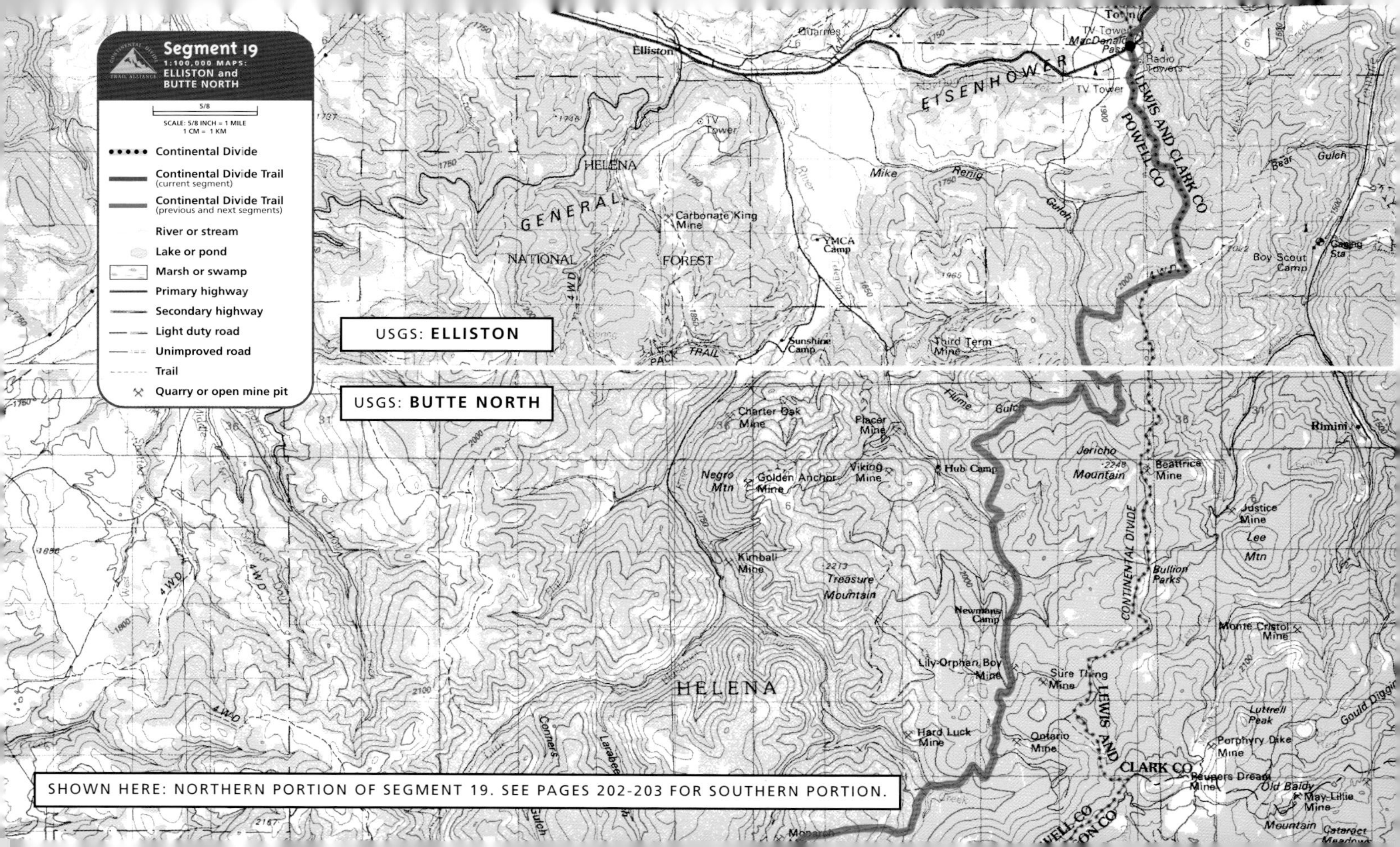
Segment 19
1:100,000 MAPS:
ELLISTON and
BUTTE NORTH
SCALE: 5/8 INCH = 1 MILE
1 CM = 1 KM
Continental Divide
Continental Divide Trail (current segment)
Continental Divide Trail (previous and next segments)
River or stream
Lake or pond
Marsh or swamp
Primary highway
Secondary highway
Light duty road
Unimproved road
Trail
Quarry or open mine pit
USGS: ELLISTON
USGS: BUTTE NORTH
SHOWN HERE: NORTHERN PORTION OF SEGMENT 19. SEE PAGES 202-203 FOR SOUTHERN PORTION.
Elliston
Quarries
MacDonald Pass
Radio Towers
TV Tower
EISENHOWER
LEWIS AND CLARK CO
POWELL CO
HELENA
GENERAL
NATIONAL
FOREST
Carbonate King Mine
YMCA Camp
Sunshine Camp
Third Term Mine
PACK TRAIL
Mike
Renig
Gulch
Bear
Boy Scout Camp
Rimini
Charter Oak Mine
Placer Mine
Flume
Hub Camp
Viking Mine
Negro Mtn
Golden Anchor Mine
Jericho Mountain
Beatrice Mine
Justice Mine
Lee Mtn
CONTINENTAL DIVIDE
Bullion Parks
Kimball Mine
Treasure Mountain
Newmans Camp
Monte Cristo Mine
Lily-Orphan Boy Mine
Sure Thing Mine
HELENA
Luttrell Peak
Hard Luck Mine
Ontario Mine
LEWIS AND CLARK CO
Porphyry Dike Mine
Old Baldy
May-Lillie Mine
Mountain
Conners
Larabee
Monarch
4WD

SHOWN HERE: SOUTHERN PORTION OF SEGMENT 19. SEE PAGE 201 FOR NORTHERN PORTION.

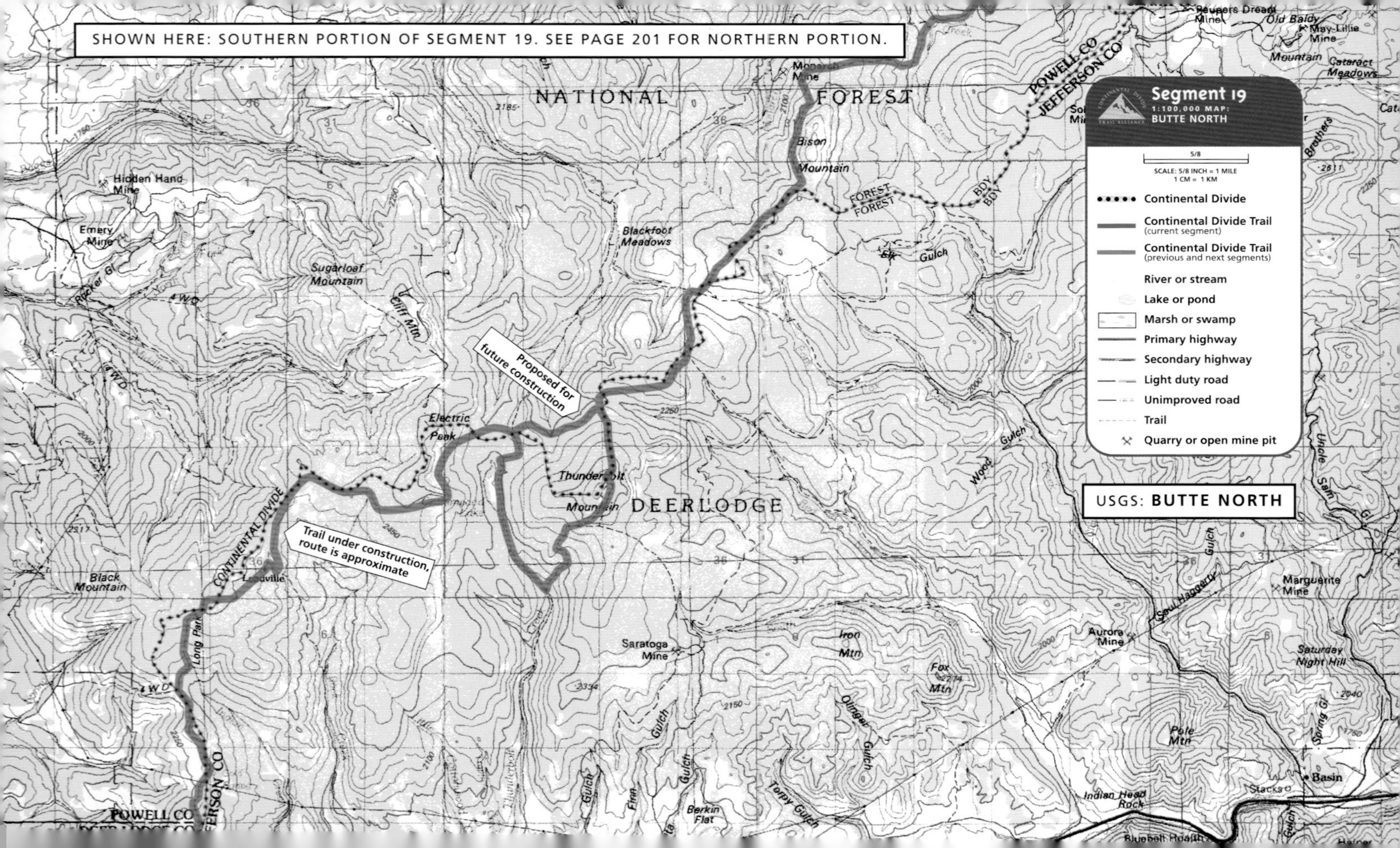

NATIONAL
FOREST
NATI
Gospel Hill
Champion Pass
Lockhart
Northey Gulch
Interim route
Proposed route
DEER LODGE CO
JEFFERSON CO
SILVER BOW CO
CONTINENTAL
DIVIDE
American Gulch
Alaska Gulch
Browns Gulch
Strozzi Gulch
Butcher Gulch
Deep Canyon
Olson Gulch
Swede Gl
Boy Scout Camp
Kit Carson Gulch
Moraine Gulch
Main Gulch
Strip Mine
Placer Gulch
South Fork
North Fork
Dry Gulch
Cluney Gulch
Buffalo Gulch
Sheepshead Mountain
DNF
Elk Park
Trask
Wilder Gulch
Shamrock Gulch
McLeod Gulch
Whiskey Gulch
Busch Gulch
Long Gulch
Bear Gulch
Sullivan Mountain
Bear Mountain
Upper Bear Gulch Meadows
Berrys Meadows
McGinley Gl
Porcupine Gl
Mt Pisgah
Moose Meadows
4 W D
Haystack Mtn
Little Boulder Park
Park

Segment 20
MacDonald Pass to Dana Spring

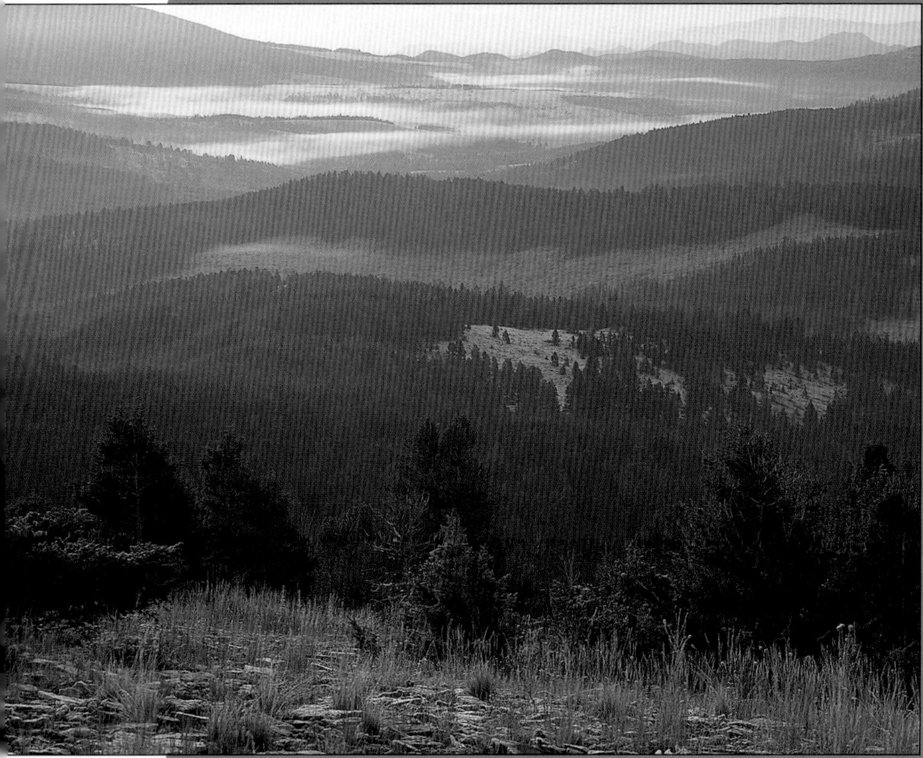

Low-lying clouds and a dusting of new snow soften the landscape southeast of Dana Spring.

24.4 miles
Difficulty: Easy

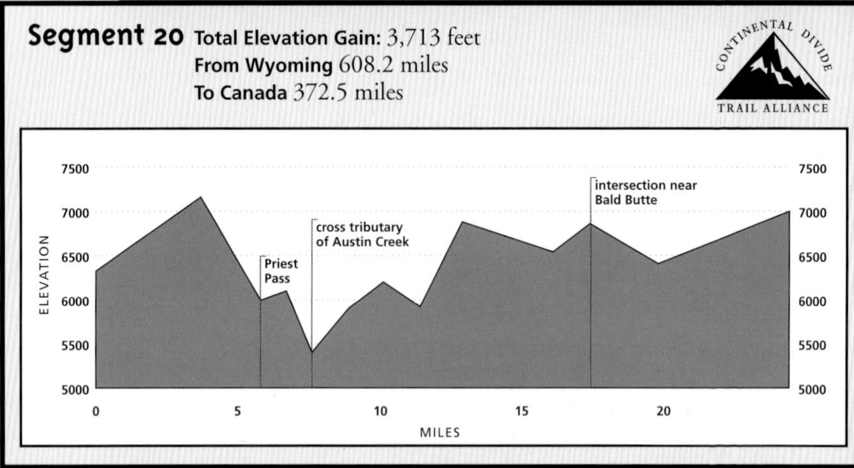

TRAIL OVERVIEW Most of this segment follows 4WD roads, but that doesn't make it easy to find. Unsigned intersections, trails that disappear in meadows, and misleading signs make for difficult navigation. A Forest Service map, along with the topographical maps, is a must.

A new route has been selected and partially constructed between Priest Pass and Mullen Pass, but expect to spend some time scouting for the trail. In the less-traveled area on top of the Mullen Tunnel, we saw quite a bit of black bear sign. We also caught a fleeting glimpse of what looked like a wolf.

There is water at the Cromwell Dixon Campground at MacDonald Pass, but there is no water on the trail for the first 7.6 miles. Water sources are infrequent, but adequate for the rest of the segment. See the trail description for water alert icons.

MOUNTAIN BIKE NOTES: The trail from Priest Pass to Mullen Pass is difficult in the middle section. You may have to carry your bike for as long as a mile.

LAND ADMINISTRATORS **(SEE APPENDIX A)**

Helena National Forest, Helena Ranger District
Bureau of Land Management, Butte District

MAPS

USGS QUADRANGLES: MacDonald Pass, Greenhorn Mountain, Esmeralda Hill
USFS: Helena National Forest (Visitor Map, West Half)

BEGINNING ACCESS POINT

MACDONALD PASS: MacDonald Pass is on Highway 12, west of Helena, Montana. The city of Helena is 14.5 miles to the east. The small town of Elliston is 7 miles west of MacDonald Pass, also on Hwy. 12. There is a campground at the pass.

ENDING ACCESS POINT

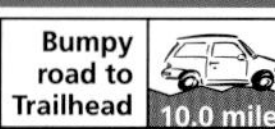

DANA SPRING: From the small town of Avon on Hwy. 12, drive 3 miles north on Highway 141, then 10 miles east on FR 136. Dana Spring is about 10 miles west of historic Marysville. Access Marysville via highways 279 and 216 (exit 200 from Interstate 15, north of Helena).

TRAIL DESCRIPTION The Continental Divide Trail crosses Hwy. 12 at MacDonald Pass. Hikers should get water at the Cromwell Dixon Campground in the MacDonald Pass Recreation Area. There is no water between MacDonald and Priest Pass.

To continue north from MacDonald Pass, walk northeasterly on Hwy. 12 for 0.7 mile to an intersection with Forest Service Road 1802. You will pass a tourist area called "Frontier Town," which has a saloon and a restaurant.

SUPPLIES, SERVICES, AND ACCOMMODATIONS

ELLISTON, MT, is on Hwy. 12. It is a small town with limited services.

Distance from Trail: 7 miles

Zip Code: 59728

Bank:	None	
Bus:	Greyhound from Helena, stops at Last Chance Saloon	
Camping:	Cromwell Dixon Campground, MacDonald Pass Recreation Area (Forest Service)	
Dining:	Stoners Last Chance Saloon, Hwy. 12	406-492-8596
	Frontier Town, 0.7 mile east of MacDonald Pass	406-449-3031
Gear:	The Elliston General Store, Hwy. 12	
Groceries:	The Elliston General Store, Hwy. 12	
Information:	See Lodging	
Laundry:	See Groceries	
Lodging:	Last Chance Motel, P.O. Box 86, Elliston, MT 59728, $28–$42	406-492-7250
Medical:	None	
Post Office:	U.S. Post Office, Hwy. 12 W., Elliston, MT 59728	406-492-6644
Showers:	See Lodging, $3/shower	

Special Note: Helena, the capital of Montana, is a city with full services. Marysville, a mixture of dilapidated mining buildings and modern residences, is 3 miles off the trail, at mile 17 for this segment. Marysville has a post office: U.S. Post Office, Main Street, Marysville, MT 59640, 406-442-5851. Directions for a detour to Marysville are given in the trail description.

FR 1802 is marked with a blue and white CDT sign. At mile three, the road enters a grassy, open area and intersects the Divide shortly after. There are several radio towers on the high point between MacDonald Pass and Priest Pass.

Completely obliterated directional arrows on a CDT post/sign leave hikers guessing at an intersection near the radio towers. The CDT leaves the 2WD road and turns onto a 4WD track at mile 3.2 for this segment. For northbound hikers this is a right (east) turn, downhill.

Watch for antique blazes on the trees where the CDT continues downhill toward Priest Pass. The aged, gray blazes, some of them almost grown shut, are hard to spot. The trail becomes less and less a road, earning "trode" status about 0.5 mile past the radio towers.

The fact that few, if any, motor vehicles use the jeep track is confirmed in the meadows, where the track disappears completely. Look for the trail to reappear where it enters trees—you may have to scout the edges of meadows to find its continuation. As the trail nears Priest Pass, some of the old blazes have been renewed and the jeep track is clearly visible.

There is one unmarked intersection about a mile south of Priest Pass. Lacking any other clues, we stayed on the better road to descend via two shallow switchbacks to the pass.

There is one CD sign at Priest Pass, but it was falling apart when we were there. There is no water at Priest Pass. The 2WD road over the pass can be followed westward to Uncle George Creek, with water first appearing beside the road about 1.5 miles from the pass. When you arrive at Priest Pass, there are no reassuring signs to tell you where you are.

Valentine Priest knew where he was when he built a road over the pass in 1879, thus stealing toll-paying traffic from MacDonald Pass. Priest suffered from tuberculosis when he arrived, but apparently was cured by the mountain air and soon went into a road-building frenzy. His road is now FR 335, the Priest Pass Road.

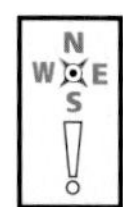

Hikers looking north from Priest Pass cannot see the first CD sign on a post that is uphill and west of the Divide. Start hiking uphill, contouring to the west (left of a 4WD track) and you'll find the route marked with CD posts and one rock cairn. The Helena Forest Service map shows the route accurately. After rounding the first hill north of Priest Pass, private property and new fences push the route of the CDT eastward, back across the Divide. There is a mixture of new trail construction, new signs, disappearing tread, and no tread in this 3-mile section. It is surprisingly hard to find your way from Priest Pass to Mullen Pass for both northbound and southbound hikers.

At 0.6 mile north of Priest Pass, the CDT follows a rough two-track, descending to pass several abandoned mines and cabins. There are no CD signs here, and intersections with other jeep tracks make it difficult to stay on the correct path. Northbound hikers keep right, continuing a long contour around higher terrain before crossing the Divide and turning north.

Both two-tracks and tread disappear where the trail crosses several marshy meadows about 1.2 miles north of Priest Pass. Look for tread to resume and for the trail to be infrequently blazed each time it exits a marsh. The last and wettest marsh is above a tributary of Austin Creek. Here the trail makes a U-turn. For northbound hikers, it is first westerly, then briefly easterly.

Austin Creek at mile 7.6 is the first water source. In its narrow drainage, bear sign was everywhere, including on the trail. A rapid descent, via a few switchbacks along newly cut tread, takes northbound hikers downhill, into the creek drainage.

The trail parallels the tributary of Austin Creek, above the Mullen Tunnel, for about 0.4 mile. Hikers follow dimly visible tread and climb over frequent deadfall. Where the trail leaves the creek and turns northwesterly, it climbs to an old railroad grade that looks like a raised dike with a visible trail on top.

SOUTHBOUND HIKERS: This can be confusing. The trail on the railroad bed is blazed to the west. The CDT looks like a game trail and is not signed or blazed. The CDT crosses the railroad bed at right angles.

"The way that can be followed is not the way." — Zen Koan

If you get lost in here, both northbound and southbound hikers should know that the route of the CDT is east of a tumble-down railroad trestle. If you come upon the trestle, you are about 0.25 mile too far west. Hike east on the railroad bed, watching carefully for what looks like a game trail descending into a creek drainage to the south, and climbing through trees to the north.

North of the Mullen Tunnel, the trail climbs through trees to an open area traversed by several cat cuts and 4WD tracks, none of which appear on the Forest Service map. Both tread and CDT signs disappear in this rocky area southeast of Mullen Pass. The cat cuts and misleading trails lead west to a new fenceline. The actual route of the CDT is east of this private property. On the Helena FS map, you can see that the CDT does not turn west until it circumvents private property in section 11, northeast of Blossburg and the Mullen Tunnel. Hopefully, this area will be better signed in the future.

There is one CD sign on a tree south of Mullen Pass, but only southbound hikers will see it. The tree is blazed on the south side. FR 1805 crosses Mullen Pass (mile 8.9) from east to west and could be used as an access route.

North of Mullen Pass, the CDT continues near a sign honoring Lt. Mullen. A post bearing a CD symbol marks a jeep track through open grasslands. At 0.8 mile north of the pass, the jeep track leads hikers to an unmarked four-way intersection, but it is fairly obvious that CDT trekkers should continue north on the road that stays closest to the Divide.

At 0.85 mile north of Mullen Pass, the route of the CDT crosses another 4WD road and enters the forest. Here the trail is blazed and there is one wooden CD sign. At 1.3 miles north of the pass, the route crosses yet another 4WD track—CDT trekkers continue to follow the blazed trail where it crosses the road. As you can tell from this trail description, there are more intersections with minor jeep tracks than are shown on the maps. Use the blazes to keep you on the right track.

SOUTHBOUND HIKERS: You face a confusing section of trail 1.5 miles north of Mullen Pass. In a meadow bordered with trees, southbound hikers leave a 4WD road at a CD sign on a post. Problems arise when you see a visible trail, NOT the route of the CDT, crossing the grassy meadow. Contrary to the straight-ahead directional arrow on the CD sign, southbound hikers must keep right (west), guided by an indistinct, ancient blaze. Stay high, near the meadow's western edge, going south in scattered trees. There is no visible tread. Once you enter the trees, newer blazes and dim tread will reassure you.

Northbound hikers have an easier time negotiating the intersection described above. Blazes and tread will lead you into the meadow, and from there you can see a post with a CD sign. Hike to the post and then to the 4WD road above it. Make a right (easterly) turn on the road. The road jogs briefly east before it turns north. Follow this road for 0.4 mile.

Depart the well-used road to proceed on a much rougher two-track that is signed. The quality of the two-track diminishes; it becomes more of a trode or trail. The route follows this trode for 0.6 mile before emerging in a meadow where it disappears completely.

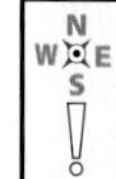

Look for a wooden CD sign on the largest tree in a meadow 2.5 miles north of Mullen Pass, mile 11.4 for this segment. Several tempting 4WD tracks lead out of this meadow. None of them are the route of the CDT. From the tall tree with a wooden CD symbol, look northerly at 340° for the next tallest tree. It also has a CD symbol on its trunk, but it is nearly impossible to see. Take a heading of 340° and hike uphill to a power line. Cross, but do not follow, a 4WD road. To locate yourself on the Forest Service map, look for a tangled intersection of six roads, including roads 622 and 1855. You are east of this intersection.

East of the power line, there is a CD symbol on a post where the trail again joins a two-track. Once northbound hikers are on this track, the route is confirmed with another CD post. Hike uphill to a line of trees. Where the track enters the trees, 3.3 miles north of Mullen Pass, there are two more wooden CD signs.

The jeep track intersects Road 622, a well-traveled road that is not signed, at mile 12.5. Northbound hikers keep right here. This road rounds the western slopes of Greenhorn Mountain. Southbound hikers have little indication that they should leave the well-traveled road and follow the jeep track under the power line.

At 4.8 miles north of Mullen Pass (mile 13.7 for this segment), near an intersection of 4WD roads, the trail crosses LaSalle Gulch, an opportunity to filter drinking water.

North of Greenhorn Mountain, the CDT enters a meadow under a power line, still following a 4WD road. Another road enters from the west, but you can ignore it. The intersection is not signed. Beyond this intersection, there are two more intersections in quick succession. Northbound hikers will stay on the ridge, still heading northerly. Signs mark the departure from the Helena National Forest. The CDT crosses BLM (Bureau of Land Management) lands near Bald Butte, southwest of Marysville.

S **SOUTHBOUND HIKERS**: The maze of intersections north of Greenhorn Mountain is no problem for northbound hikers, but is a real quandary for southbound hikers. There is one blue-and-white CD sign at a cattleguard near the Helena National Forest boundary sign. This CD sign points hikers straight ahead, but southbound hikers must make the right (southwesterly) turn on the road signed for Mullen Pass.

On the long ridge further north of Greenhorn Mountain, northbound hikers will pass more 4WD road intersections, including Dog Creek and American Gulch. Stay on Road 1853, which is signed on the ground but not on the FS map.

You can take a shortcut to Marysville here by taking the unsigned northeasterly turn at a yellow cattleguard north of the American Gulch intersection. This is Trail 622, though it is not numbered on the FS map, and is only numbered on the ground at its base on the Ottawa Gulch Road.

Two Continental Divide Trail signs mark the route at mile 17.1 for this segment, on FS 1853. These signs are posted at a Y-shaped intersection.

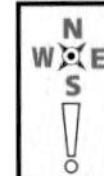

At a four-way intersection of three main roads and one minor road, there is a diamond-shaped median in the center that is not signed. For northbound hikers this is 8.5 miles north of Mullen Pass, and mile 17.4 for this segment. Here, northbound hikers turn west, heading toward Round Top Mountain. Southbound hikers turn southeasterly. On the USGS topo, you are on the north flank of Bald Butte, where the physical Divide also turns west.

At the intersection near Bald Butte, hikers who have resupplies to pick up at the Marysville Post Office have another opportunity to detour to town (3.2 miles).

At mile 18.3 for this segment, an intersection of many 4WD and 2WD roads makes up for the previous lack of signs with a veritable cornucopia of information: Lost Horse Creek, Ophir Creek, Road 136, Entering Helena National Forest, Little Prickly Pear Creek, Hope Creek, Dog Creek, Road 1855, and more. CDT hikers continue west on Road 136, toward Roundtop Mountain and Ophir Creek.

A bathtub, lawn mower, barbecue grill, and freezer (don't ask me, I just report the facts) reside in a hollow in the northwest corner of the many-signed intersection. What brought us to this camp (outfitter or hunting camp?) was a spring. Despite the bathtub, hikers can filter drinking water at the spring's source. This was one of many strange and spectacular uses of our National Forest lands that we encountered on the Continental Divide Trail.

As you go around Roundtop Mountain, stick to the route on the north side. There are some confusing intersections that could put you on the wrong track if the southern route is taken.

Lots of additional, but signed, intersections lead both south and north from Road 136. CDT trekkers pass them all by until the northerly turn to Black Mountain at mile 24.4. This area is named "Meyers Hill" on the maps. The turn is signed as "136-B1, Black Mtn 4 mi.," and as the CDT. Water is available at Dana Spring—look for the fenced area west of the intersection.

Meyers Hill, near Dana Spring, is a good place to camp with excellent views. Elk and deer often visit the spring at twilight, so pitch your camp away from the spring, but close enough to watch the animals come and go.

The small town of Avon, southwest of Dana Spring, has a cafe, general store, and post office (zip 59713). To get to Avon, take Forest Service Road 136 to Hwy. 141, about 13 miles. Dana Spring is 10 miles west of Marysville.

In the evening light, a lone tree stands sentinel over Meyers Hill near Dana Spring, located in the Helena National Forest.

Nevada Mountain
Beartrap Gulch
PACK TRAIL
Black Mountain
CONTINENTAL DIVIDE
Cottonwood Gulch
Meyers Hill
HELENA
Spring Gulch
Charity Gulch
Victory Mine
Cave Gulch
Uncle Ben Gulch
LEWIS AND CLARK CO
POWELL CO
Illinois Ridge
Blackfoot City
Strip Mine
Ward Gulch
Deadwood Gulch
McGuire Gulch
Esmeralda Hill
NATIONAL
FOREST
Nelson Gulch
Thompson Flats
American Gulch
La Salle Gulch
Greenhorn Mountain
Strawberry Mine
East Skelly
Skelly Gulch
Sawmill Gulch
Jerusha Gulch
Towsley Gulch
Penobscot Mine
Bald Butte
Empire Mine
Mt Belmont
Belmont Mine
Bald Mtn Mine
Marysville
Drumlummon Hill
Ottawa
Eldorado Gulch
China Gulch
Edward Mountain
Trinity Hill
Demijohn Gulch
Big Ox Mine
4 W.D.

Segment 20
1:100,000 MAP:
ELLISTON
5/8
SCALE: 5/8 INCH = 1 MILE
1 CM = 1 KM
Continental Divide
Continental Divide Trail (current segment)
Continental Divide Trail (previous and next segments)
River or stream
Lake or pond
Marsh or swamp
Primary highway
Secondary highway
Light duty road
Unimproved road
Trail
Quarry or open mine pit
Elliston
MacDonald Pass
Frontier Town
Priest Pass
Mullan Tunnel
Logan
Continental Divide
Lewis and Clark Co
Powell Co
Eisenhower
Helena General National Forest
Girl Scout Camp
Boy Scout Camp
YMCA Camp
Carbonate King Mine
Forest Heights
Radio Towers
TV Tower
Microwave Sta
Sawmill Gulch
Rich Spur Gulch
Bear Gulch
Quarries
Blackfoot
Gaging Sta

Segment 21
Dana Spring to Stemple Pass

The setting sun fires the sky above Black Mountain, which the CDT climbs on its way to Stemple Pass.

18.1 miles

Difficulty: Strenuous

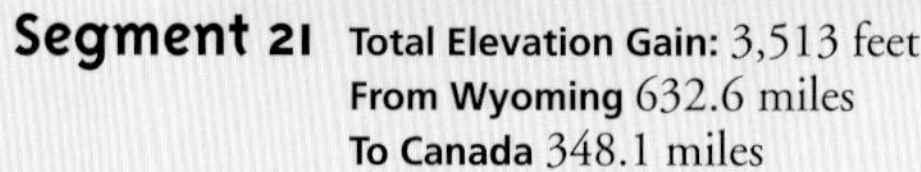

Segment 21 Total Elevation Gain: 3,513 feet
From Wyoming 632.6 miles
To Canada 348.1 miles

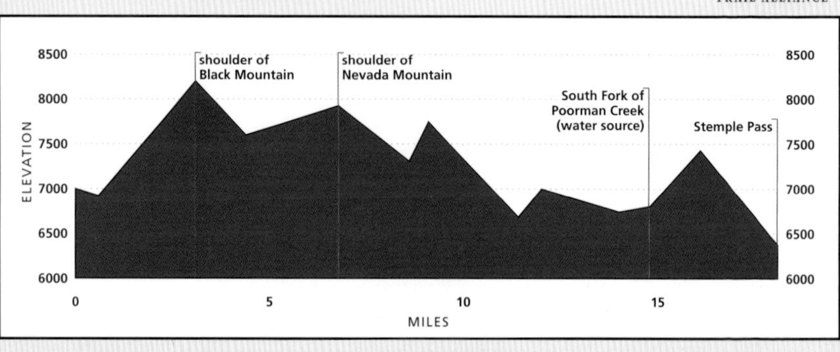

TRAIL OVERVIEW The CDT route from Dana Spring to Stemple Pass is marked with blazes, wooden CD signs, and blue/white CDT signs. The trail reaches its highest point at mile 3.1 (elevation 8,200 feet). From this perch on the eastern cliffs of Black Mountain, there are excellent views. Looking toward Marysville in the east, hikers can see the Helena Valley, and beyond that, the higher peaks of the Big Belt Mountains.

North of Nevada Mountain, the trail joins a series of 4WD roads, snowmobile trails, and ski trails that lead to Stemple Pass.

Dana Spring, on Forest Service Road 136, is an important water source. Hikers should fill water bottles there before continuing north. It is necessary to leave the trail to access other water sources in this segment.

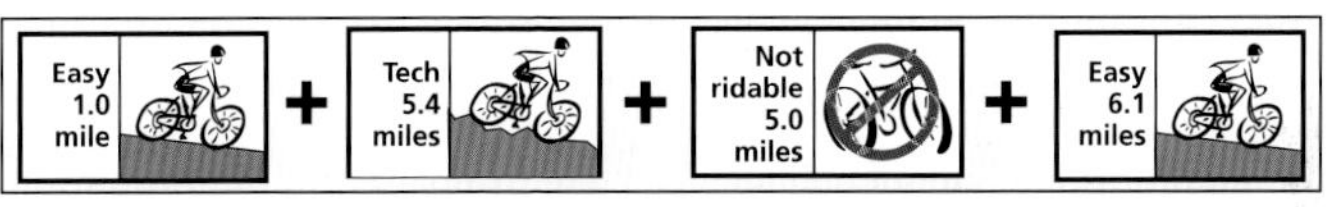

MOUNTAIN BIKE NOTES: The route is easy for the first mile, but quickly becomes a serious technical challenge as it climbs Black Mountain. There is an unridable section from mile 6.4 to mile 12 (see Trail Description). Easy riding on old jeep tracks commences at mile 12 and extends to Stemple Pass.

LAND ADMINISTRATORS (SEE APPENDIX A)

Helena National Forest, Helena Ranger District
Helena National Forest, Lincoln Ranger District

MAPS

USGS QUADRANGLES: Esmeralda Hill, Ophir Creek, Nevada Mountain, Granite Butte, Stemple Pass, Swede Gulch

USFS: Helena National Forest Visitors Map

BEGINNING ACCESS POINT

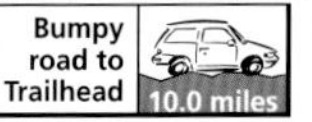

DANA SPRING: From Avon on Hwy. 12, drive 3 miles north on Hwy. 141, then 10 miles east on FR 136. Dana Spring can also be accessed from the east side via highways 279 and 216 from Interstate 15, north of Helena, exit 200.

ENDING ACCESS POINT

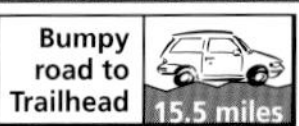

STEMPLE PASS: Stemple Pass is on Road 601, 15.5 miles southeast of Lincoln, MT; and 36.8 miles from Helena, MT.

SUPPLIES, SERVICES, AND ACCOMMODATIONS

The small town of **AVON, MT,** is 13 miles from Dana Spring (see Beginning Access Point above) and has a general store and post office (Zip 59713).

LINCOLN, MT, is on State Highway 200. (See Segment 23.)

Distance from Trail: 15.5 miles from Stemple Pass

TRAIL DESCRIPTION The trail is signed with a CD symbol where it leaves Forest Service Road 136 to follow a jeep track (Trail 337) north to Black Mountain.

Near the summit of Black Mountain, the trail splits, with the route of the CDT being the right-hand fork for northbound hikers. Strangely, the left-hand fork is also signed as the CD a few hundred yards north of the intersection. It's as if the trail crew changed their minds about building the trail to the summit, but never took the signs down. Snowdrifts linger on Black Mountain's slopes into mid-June and could be used as an additional water source for early-season hikers.

As the trail descends, the two-track becomes a foot/horse path and continues to contour around the eastern and northern slopes of the mountain. A series of switchbacks leads down to a saddle above the Three Mile Creek drainage.

Going north from the saddle above Three Mile Creek, the trail climbs again, staying close to the Divide. At mile 6.4, Trail 465, a jeep track following Mitchell Creek, enters from the west. CDT hikers should stay on the trail leading north to Nevada Mountain. Trail 337 becomes Trail 440 as it contours around the eastern side of Nevada Mountain.

The second highest elevation (7,925 feet) is reached at mile 6.8, where the trail climbs to the shoulder of Nevada Mountain. In scattered trees, hikers cruise along above the cliffs on the east side of the mountain. From Nevada Mountain northward, the trail remains near or on the Divide for about 6.5 miles. Descend to the saddle above Beartrap Gulch, losing about 600 feet of elevation. From the saddle (mile 8.6) the trail climbs again to a bare knoll on the Divide, which is not named, but is marked with the elevation of 7,748 feet on the topo.

There is a brief respite from all the ups and downs between mile 9.1 and mile 10.1 as the trail descends gradually along a ridge north of Nevada Mountain. Hikers pass through scattered stands of limber pine and emerge onto a rocky slope. A trail has been built below the Divide to cross this slope covered with loose rock.

Once past the rock slide area, the trail makes its way to the next bare knoll with only minor changes in elevation. This knoll is a good place to stop and enjoy the view of Granite Butte to the north. Looking south, hikers can see the cliffs of Black Mountain and the snakelike line of the Divide. From this knoll, hikers can also see a long, grassy saddle below them to the north. This is the saddle above Nevada Creek and the next destination.

The trail is marked with stone cairns and then with CD symbols on posts as it descends. At the last post, when you can see no more signs in front of you, turn left (west) and descend sharply to the treeline. A wooden CD sign and a blazed tree mark where the trail enters the forest. Visible tread resumes in the trees and newly cut switchbacks lead to the saddle. Hikers lose about 800 feet of elevation in 0.5 mile.

Hikers are now 11.4 miles from Dana Spring, and still no water in sight. Unless there are some lingering snowdrifts, this is a dry hike. In the saddle, there is an intersection with Trail 466, a jeep road (now closed) that comes up from the west side of the Divide, along Nevada Creek. Tall grass obscures the intersection, but it is relatively easy to find the two-track and follow it to the creek. It is a 0.3-mile descent to the headwaters of Nevada Creek.

There is one post and a wooden CD sign in the middle of the saddle above Nevada Creek. The symbol and arrows are completely worn off—a testament to the winds that funnel through this low spot. From this CD post, the trail leaves the physical Divide. Northbound hikers should angle to the right (northeast) to intercept a jeep track in the trees. Do not continue to climb along the ridge of the Divide. The jeep track you are looking for climbs more gently, in a northeasterly direction, topping out on a ridge above the north fork of Little Prickly Pear Creek.

SOUTHBOUND HIKERS: Don't be misled by a faint trail that follows the spur ridge above Little Prickly Pear Creek. The spur ridge looks like a continuation of the Divide. Stay on the jeep track, even though to southbound hikers it looks like it is diving down off the Divide.

The trail bends to the north and intersects Gould-Helmville Trail 467 at mile 12.7. For southbound hikers, this intersection is marked on the left (south) with a Continental Divide Trail 440 sign. Both trails look like 4WD jeep tracks at this intersection.

A locked gate, and various signs explaining seasonal motorized vehicle restrictions, block the jeep track at mile 13. Northbound hikers continue northwesterly on the road to an intersection with Road 485 at mile 14. Road 485 is a better-quality gravel/dirt road that is 2WD in good weather.

SOUTHBOUND HIKERS: You could be confused by the intersection of Road 485 and the unsigned jeep track that follows the Divide. Here are your clues: There is a CD post without a sign (sign ripped off) near the turn; the area shows signs of recent logging; and the unsigned track matches the Gould-Helmville Trail as shown on the topo map. This intersection is 4.1 miles south of Stemple Pass.

Northbound hikers, follow Road 485 north toward Stemple Pass. At mile 14.8 there is an opportunity to filter water near the intersection with Road 434 on the South Fork of Poorman Creek. Water is close by, about a hundred yards off the trail. Don't pass this water source, as it is your best opportunity for many miles.

Continue north on Road 485 to the intersection with Granite Butte Road 4113, half a mile north of the South Fork of Poorman Creek. Follow Road 4113 uphill (north) to the Divide.

In the past, the CDT route stayed on Road 485 to Stemple Pass, but this little jaunt uphill is well worth the climb. The remaining 2.8 miles to the pass are on the Divide and mostly in the open, with wonderful views.

Faded, wooden CD symbols on posts guide hikers along the crest of the Divide, using a grassy 4WD track as the trail. There are other two-tracks intersecting and paralleling the CDT, so watch for the posts to determine your course. A well-traveled track leads south toward the radio towers on Granite Butte.

SOUTHBOUND HIKERS: Watch carefully for a downhill (westerly) turn on Road 4113, and do not continue to the radio towers on Granite Butte.

Near the pass, the two-track descends to enter trees. At Stemple Pass, mile 18.1, a blue and white CD sign marks the entrance to the trail, which is a few feet east of Road 485. There is no water at Stemple Pass. The CDT crosses the road and continues north, through a parking lot for cross-country skiers.

Segment 21
1:100,000 MAP:
ELLISTON
5/8
SCALE: 5/8 INCH = 1 MILE
1 CM = 1 KM
Continental Divide
Continental Divide Trail
(current segment)
Continental Divide Trail
(previous and next segments)
River or stream
Lake or pond
Marsh or swamp
Primary highway
Secondary highway
Light duty road
Unimproved road
Trail
Quarry or open mine pit
Lincoln
Airport
Swede
Hollow
Gulch
Columbia
Mine
Rover
Mine
Last Chance
Mine
HELENA
NATIONAL FOREST
CONTINENTAL
Crater
2173
Mountain
Page
Gulch
Kemple
Pass
Davis
Gulch
Swansea
Mine
Silver Bell
Mine
Rochester
Gulch
NATIONAL
FOREST
Little Davis
Gulch
Cyclone
Mine
8500
8000
Granite
Butte
DIVIDE
Bear
Gulch
Mead
Gulch
Prickly
Gulch
GENERAL
ROBERT
E
LEE
Pikes
Gulch
TRAIL
PACK
Wiggins
Mine
LEWIS AND CLARK CO
POWELL CO
Gravelly Range
Lake

HELENA
NATIONAL
FOREST
LEWIS AND CLARK CO
POWELL CO
CONTINENTAL
DIVIDE
PACK
TRAIL
Meyers Hill
Black Mountain
Victory Mine
Blackfoot City
Illinois Ridge
Illinois
Gulch
Nevada Mountain
Penobscot Mine
Empire Mine
Thompson Flats
Nelson
Esmeralda Hill
Deadwood
Ward
Cottonwood
Beartrap
Cave
Placer Mines
Strip Mine
Bald Butte
Spring
Uncle Ben
Cow
American
Sixmile
Creek

Segment 22
Stemple Pass to Rogers Pass

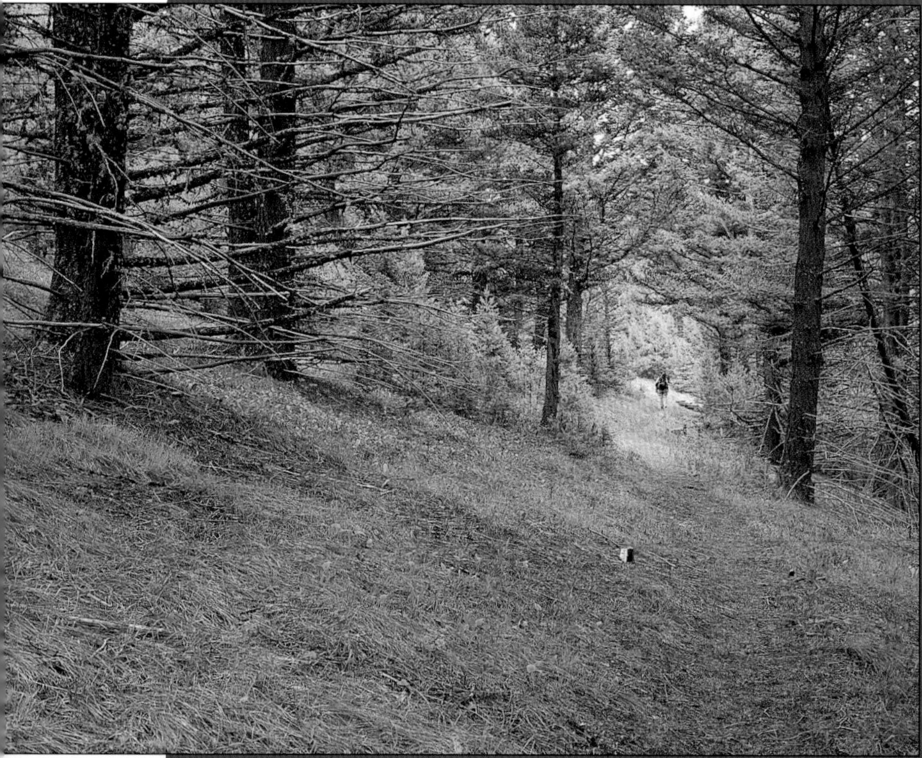

On the CDT between Stemple and Flesher passes

22.8 miles
Difficulty: Moderate

Segment 22 **Total Elevation Gain:** 4,851 feet
From Wyoming 650.7 miles
To Canada 330.0 miles

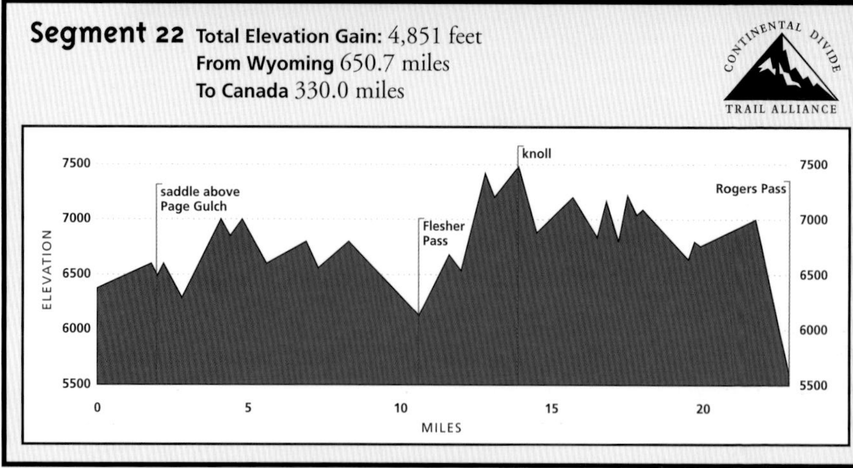

TRAIL OVERVIEW This segment crosses grizzly bear territory. Read the bear avoidance techniques in "Safety Concerns."

The CDT closely follows the actual Divide from Stemple Pass to Flesher Pass, and from Flesher to Rogers Pass. Because it stays so close to the crest, it rolls up and down like a manic roller coaster. The elevation chart for this segment tells the true story. Most of the changes are not big, but they sure add up.

Trail crews from the Helena Ranger District have recently cut new tread along much of this segment, so it is easy to follow. It is signed with CDT symbols fairly frequently, and is also blazed. Winter recreational use includes cross-country skiing. Ski trails are marked with blue, diamond-shaped metal symbols.

Another consequence of staying on the crest of the Divide is a lack of water. Hikers should bring the USGS 7.5-minute topographical maps for this segment to aid in choosing easy descents to stream tributaries.

The last third of the hike offers the best views, notably from Anaconda Hill to within a mile of Rogers Pass. Cliffs on the eastern face of the Divide overlook the South Fork of the Dearborn River and the tightly folded terrain of the Rocky Mountain Front.

MOUNTAIN BIKE NOTES: This segment is open to foot and horse traffic only.

LAND ADMINISTRATORS (SEE APPENDIX A)

Helena National Forest, Lincoln Ranger District

MAPS

USGS QUADRANGLES: Stemple Pass, Wilborn, Rogers Pass

USFS: Helena National Forest Visitors Map (West Half)

BEGINNING ACCESS POINT

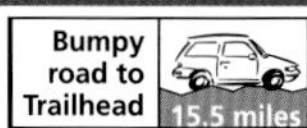

STEMPLE PASS: Stemple Pass is on Road 601, 15.5 miles southeast of Lincoln, MT; and 36.8 miles from Helena, MT.

ENDING ACCESS POINT

ROGERS PASS, on Highway 200

SUPPLIES, SERVICES, AND ACCOMMODATIONS

LINCOLN, MT, is on Highway 200. (See Segment 23.)

Distance from Trail: 15.5 miles

TRAIL DESCRIPTION At Stemple Pass, enter the pull-out/parking area and continue north on the road until you come to the first ski trail on the left (west). When we were there, it was confusing because someone had removed the CD sign for northbound hikers, so there was no way to tell which road to take at a three-way intersection. At the intersection, take the left fork. About 300 yards up the left fork, you will see a CD sign on your right. A sign that says "Continental Loop" is *not* the CDT.

There is no water at Stemple Pass, although you'll find pit toilets, picnic tables, benches, and ski trail maps. The trail is blazed and easy to follow to Flesher Pass. Near Flesher Pass, CDT signs become more frequent and the tread is easier to see. We saw a red-tailed hawk and a large owl next to the trail. Bear sign kept us alert, but we didn't see the bears themselves.

Most of the trail is through dense forest, protected from the wind. About a mile from Flesher Pass, the trail finally exits the trees and there are some welcome views. We were there on May 30 and I used snowshoes to traverse the snow that lingered at the higher elevations.

The trail descends to cross Flesher Pass at mile 10.6, elevation 6,131 feet. There is water in a tributary of Canyon Creek about 0.5 mile east of the pass, in a culvert. To continue northeast, the trail crosses Highway 279 and climbs a staircase made of wooden blocks leading steeply uphill and into the trees. The CDT is signed on both sides of the highway.

New trail construction leads to Rogers Pass. The route continues its roller-coaster character, staying close to the actual Divide. Everyone tells us that the views are magnificent from Anaconda Peak to Rogers Pass (about mile 17 to mile 21); however, we never saw them. It snowed on us every time we were there. I think Rogers Pass was living up to its reputation as the coldest spot in the continental United States. A bone-chilling minus 70° was recorded in January of 1954. We knew we were above treeline because the trail made its way through grass and scattered subalpine trees.

The trail switchbacks down to Rogers Pass through lodgepole pines and we saw white-tailed deer making their silent way through the trees on a game trail that leads to the stream. Water is available in a tributary of Pass Creek at mile 22.7. There is room both to park and to camp on the south side of Hwy. 200 near the trailhead.

Signs at the trailhead remind users that it is "closed to all motorized vehicles in order to provide a non-motorized recreational experience"—however, as you come down from Anaconda Hill and Rogers Mountain, you can hear the trucks on Hwy. 200. The highway, and the end of this segment, are reached at mile 22.8.

South of Rogers Pass, grasses bow their heads beneath a heavy coat of September frost.

USGS: DEARBORN RIVER
Segment 22
1:100,000 MAPS:
ELLISTON and
DEARBORN RIVER
5/8
SCALE: 5/8 INCH = 1 MILE
1 CM = 1 KM
Continental Divide
Continental Divide Trail
(current segment)
Continental Divide Trail
(previous and next segments)
River or stream
Lake or pond
Marsh or swamp
Primary highway
Secondary highway
Light duty road
Unimproved road
Trail
Quarry or open mine pit
Water
Trail under construction,
route is approximate
Rogers Pass
Cadotte Pass
CONTINENTAL
DIVIDE
Evergreen Cabins
Sunset Mountain
Joes Mountain
Denton Mountain
Green Mountain
Midnight Hill
Anaconda Hill
Mike Horse Mine
Water Tank
Telephone Gulch
Glen Gulch
First Gulch
Third Gulch
Surveyors Gulch
Shaue Gulch
Denton Gulch
Bear Gulch
McDonald Meadow
HELENA NATIONAL FOREST
NATIONAL FOREST BOUNDARY
NAT FOR BDY
NATIONAL FOREST BDY
WILDERNESS
HNF
4WD
200

HELENA
NATIONAL
FOREST
Trail under construction, route is approximate
Flesher Pass
CONTINENTAL
DIVIDE
TRAIL
4WD
Swede Hollow
Swede Gulch
Columbia Mine
Rover Mine
Last Chance Mine
Crater Mountain
Page Gulch
Hemple Pass
Swansea Mine
Silver Bell Mine
Rochester Gulch
Davis Gulch
Little Davis Gulch
Prickly Gulch
Cyclone Mine
Granite Butte
Bear Gulch
Pikes Gulch
Sawmill Gulch
ROBERT
E
LEE
RANGE
USGS: ELLISTON

Segment 23
Rogers Pass to Benchmark / South Fork TRHD

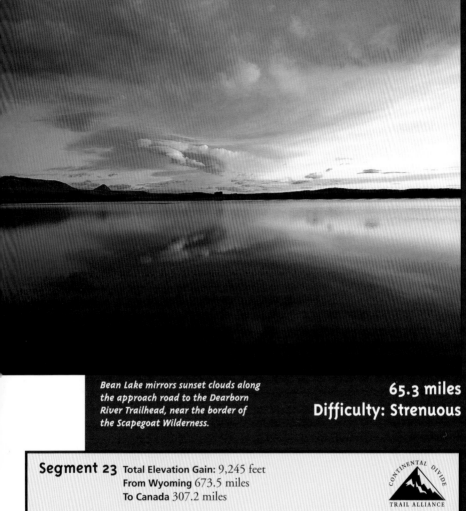

Bean Lake mirrors sunset clouds along the approach road to the Dearborn River Trailhead, near the border of the Scapegoat Wilderness.

65.3 miles
Difficulty: Strenuous

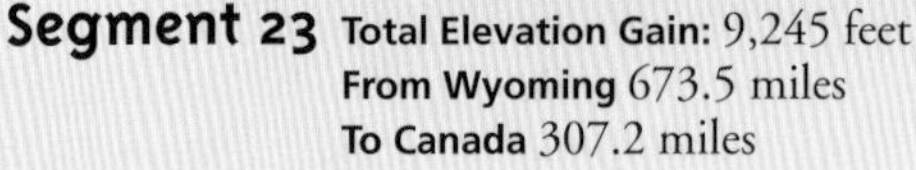

Segment 23 **Total Elevation Gain:** 9,245 feet
From Wyoming 673.5 miles
To Canada 307.2 miles

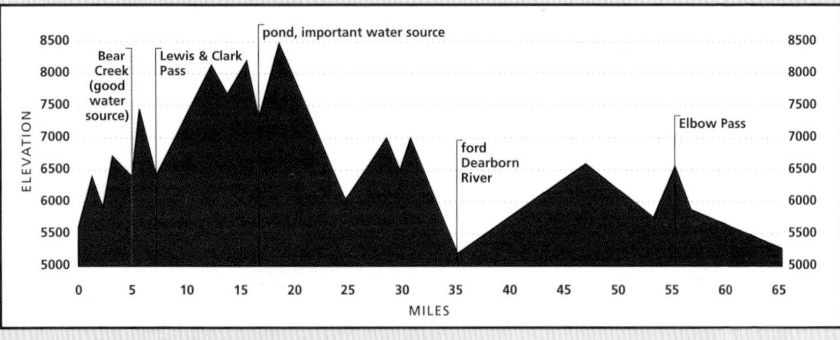

TRAIL OVERVIEW The Helena Forest Service, Lincoln District, has been working on the trail from Rogers Pass to the border of the Scapegoat Wilderness since we hiked it, so CDT trekkers may find it improved and easier to find. The trail is described here as we saw it, with some notations as to planned improvements.

Lincoln District Rangers also informed us that the Continental Divide from Rogers Pass north to Red Mountain is now a "Bear Sanitation Area," which means that grizzly bear activity has increased there so camping is prohibited on the Divide. Trekkers have to climb down from the Divide if they wish to camp before reaching Red Mountain at mile 8.8 from Rogers Pass. Hikers are required to hang their food and other bear attractants at least 10 feet up from the ground and 4 feet out from any vertical support. Read the Bear Avoidance section of "Safety Concerns."

The Scapegoat Wilderness border is reached at about mile 15. Please read the "Wilderness Alert" in Segment 14 for special regulations that pertain to backpacking in this area. The Scapegoat abuts the Bob Marshall Wilderness to the north, so hikers will be in designated wilderness for almost 140 miles as they follow the CDT northward to Glacier National Park. Locals call the entire wilderness complex "Bob Marshall Country" or simply "The Bob." The Bob is part of an important grizzly corridor that is managed to protect this most mega member of the megafauna.

When Yellowstone National Park seemed to be going up in smoke in 1988, and getting all the media attention for doing so, the Scapegoat/Bob Marshall was also devastated by extensive fires. More acres were burned in The Bob than in Yellowstone. As a result, hikers will be traversing miles and miles of burned forest. These sections are noted in the trail description.

WILDERNESS ALERT

Please remember the special rules that pertain to wilderness travel as described earlier in Segment 14. Be sure to minimize bear/human encounters: all food, garbage, livestock, pet foods, and attractants must be made unavailable to bears. During daylight and nighttime hours, all camps must be attended unless attractants are stored in a bear-resistant manner. Observe camping closures in sites such as the Chinese Wall and the Rock Creek Cabin area. Return your campsite to a natural appearance before leaving, and note that fire permits may be required during periods of extreme fire danger.

MOUNTAIN BIKE NOTES: The first 15 miles of this segment are suitable for mountain bikes, but are technically difficult in many areas. The majority of this segment lies within the Scapegoat Wilderness, where mountain bikes are prohibited.

LAND ADMINISTRATORS (SEE APPENDIX A)

Helena National Forest, Lincoln District
Lewis & Clark National Forest, Rocky Mountain Ranger District
Flathead National Forest, Spotted Bear Ranger District

MAPS

USGS QUADRANGLES: Rogers Pass, Cadotte Creek, Blowout Mountain, Caribou Peak, Heart Lake, Steamboat Mountain, Jakie Creek, Scapegoat Mountain, Wood Lake, Benchmark

USFS: Bob Marshall, Great Bear, and Scapegoat Wilderness Complex. This map is a 1:100,000 scale topographical map and is good enough that it may be substituted for USGS topos if your budget is tight.

BEGINNING ACCESS POINT

ROGERS PASS on Highway 200

ENDING ACCESS POINT

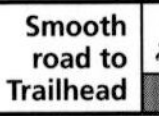

BENCHMARK/SOUTH FORK TRAILHEAD: The gravel road from Augusta, Montana, is well-traveled. Additional camping facilities are located south of the trailhead, along Road 235, including the Straight Creek, Benchmark, and Wood Lake campgrounds. Some local outfitters, including Ford Creek Guest Ranch and Benchmark Wilderness Guest Ranch, will pick up hikers and/or deliver resupplies to Benchmark for a small fee. See Supplies and Services below.

TRAIL DESCRIPTION

The CDT makes a short jog on Highway 200 before continuing north from Rogers Pass. Walk east on Hwy. 200 from the parking area at the pass, and turn north where a short flight of stairs and a CD sign lead hikers onto the trail. New tread has been cut here, leading toward Cadotte Pass. This is Trail 440 on the Forest Service map.

The trail begins switchbacking uphill immediately as it heads north from Rogers Pass. Where the trail tops out at 6,400 feet on a rocky knoll 1.3 miles north of the pass, the visible tread disappears but the route is marked with rock cairns and some survey stakes. Beyond the rocky knoll, visible tread reappears where trail has been cut to contour around a grassy hillside.

Trail tread alternately appears and disappears en route to Cadotte Pass. At mile 2.3 hikers come to a long, bare ridge crossed by a large three-pole power line. There is also a line shack, tin-roofed and tied down to rocks with cables meant to withstand the winds. The trail joins a faint two-track on this ridge. The low point (saddle) is Cadotte Pass, elevation 5,920 feet, but it is not signed. A jeep track comes up to the pass from the Cadotte Creek side, and although the area is closed to motorized vehicles, there is some evidence of motorized use on the trail.

SUPPLIES, SERVICES, AND ACCOMMODATIONS

LINCOLN, MT, is on Highway 200. It is a small town, but has most of the services you will need.

Distance from Trail: about 17 miles

Zip Code: 59639

Bank:	First Bank of Lincoln, Main Street	406-362-4248
Bus:	Missoula Greyhound, 4:30 p.m. at Rainbow Cafe for service to Great Falls; 8:30 p.m. at Rainbow Cafe for service to Missoula	
Camping:	Hooper Park, Hwy. 200	406-362-4622
	Forest Service Campground, County Road 601	
Dining:	Mom's Drive Inn, Hwy. 200	406-362-4480
	Rainbow Cafe, Hwy. 200	406-362-4543
	Lambkin's Restaurant, Hwy. 200 S.	406-362-4271
Gear:	Garland's Town & Country, 524 Main Street	406-362-4244
Groceries:	Blackfoot Market, Hwy. 200	406-362-4622
	D&D Market, Hwy. 200	
Information:	Chamber of Commerce, P.O. Box 985, in the Snowy Pines Inn,	406-362-4949
	or Susie Mason, Grizzly Hardware, Hwy. 200	406-362-4995
Laundry:	Town & Country Laundromat, Hwy. 200	
	Huckleberry RV/Trailer Court, Laundromat & Showers	
Lodging:	Blue Sky Motel, Hwy. 200, $30–$39	406-362-4450
	Leepers Motel, Hwy. 200, $35.50	406-362-4333
	Lumberjack Inn, Hwy. 200	406-362-4001
	Three Bears Motel, Hwy. 200, $32.24	406-362-4355
	Snowy Pines Inn, Hwy. 200, $40	406-362-4481
Medical:	Blackfoot Valley Medical Services, Hwy. 200	406-362-4603
Outfitters:	Ford Creek Guest Ranch, P.O. Box 329 (12 miles from Benchmark), Augusta, MT 59410	406-562-3672
	Benchmark Wilderness Guest Ranch (about 4 miles from Benchmark)	406-562-3336
	(Ford Creek Ranch and Benchmark Wilderness Ranch also offer lodging, food, and resupply delivery services.)	
Post Office:	U.S. Post Office, P.O. Box 9998, Lincoln, MT 59639	
Showers:	Huckleberry RV/Trailer Court	

North of Cadotte Pass, near an ATV barricade and a non-motorized sign, the trail leaves the Divide on the southwest side to round higher terrain, but still climbs to 6,720 feet before descending again along the ridge above Bear Creek.

We saw signs of grizzly activity above Bear Creek. For about 50 yards, the entire ridge had been rototilled, with rocks overturned and holes scraped out of the soil where a bear had been looking for insects and/or grubs to eat. The wife of a rancher who grazes cattle north of Rogers Pass said that they expect to lose one or two calves to bears every year. Don't, however, hike past Bear Creek at mile 5 without getting water. Water sources are scarce and the headwaters of Bear Creek are quite close to the trail.

The Alice Creek Basin near Green Mountain is marked as the route of the CDT on the FS maps, but this is no longer correct, as new tread has been cut that keeps the trail more closely on the physical Divide. Lewis and Clark Pass, at mile 7.2, is above the Alice Creek Basin and a 0.25-mile walk will take you to water in Alice Creek.

At Lewis and Clark Pass a sign says, "Lewis and Clark Trail. Here are faint ruts and ridges left by thousands of travois used by the Indians on their buffalo hunts. Captain Lewis followed this trail over the Continental Divide in July, 1806." Look east of this sign for another sign that says "Lewis and Clark Pass, elevation 6,000 feet." Across the dirt road from this second sign, the CDT continues north.

From Lewis and Clark Pass northward there was no cut tread and no signs when we were there. We followed a faint track right on the Divide that paralleled the posts from a long-dead fence. Even the faint track disappeared eventually and we followed the Divide and the Forest Service's ribbons and survey stakes for future trail construction. In places, trail crews had sprayed rocks with fluorescent paint, or sawed out logs in preparation for trail construction.

The route became more difficult to follow where the trail turns westerly and approaches a line of cliffs below Burned Point. We followed ribbons that had been nibbled to mere nubs by the local elk herd, and found a few blazed trees by scouting in a zigzag pattern. Eventually we just stopped, ate wild strawberries, and loudly voiced our complaints to an audience of rocks, trees, and empty sky. Feeling better, we went back to scouting for the route and soon found more ribbons where future switchbacks were planned. The route took us just below the Divide on the south side and then to the right (north side) of the cliffs.

When we hiked the trail, we only encountered one CD sign between Rogers Pass and Burned Point, a wooden one on a tree uphill from where the new route intersects the jeep track coming up from Alice Creek Basin, at mile 11. The CDT stays on the jeep track only long enough to climb to the Divide, where the lone CD sign signals a departure from the road again. The trail stays on the Divide and continues to climb steadily on a narrow ridge to 8,135 feet. As the Divide goes, so goes the trail here, rolling up and down as it heads almost due west, dipping to 7,682 feet at mile 13.8.

Views from this bare ridge are tremendous, including cliffs to the northeast that frame the Falls Creek drainage, Caribou Peak, and endless acres of the ghostly, silvered trunks of trees that burned in the 1988 fires. Keep a close eye on the weather here, as the long ridge-walk exposes hikers to lightning and high winds. Luckily, the view is even longer, so you can see the storms coming before they hit and that gives you time to scramble down into stands of small trees below the ridgeline. This area, just south of the Scapegoat Wilderness border, looks like a place where no one but trail crews ever visit, and we saw no signs of any other hikers.

Switchbacks that do not appear on the maps lead partway up Peak 8271 just north of where the Caribou Pack Trail 266 climbs to the Divide. Don't expect to see a clear trail intersection—you'd need a topo to find the Caribou Pack Trail. Indian paintbrush and fireweed have taken advantage of the increased sunlight that reaches the forest floor in the burned areas, so a colorful carpet of flowers contrasts sharply with the gray and black tree trunks.

The trail turns northwest and cruises in a scimitar shape through an alpine zone above The Middle Fork of Falls Creek, topping out at 8,200 feet at mile 15.6 (4.5 miles of ridge-walking from the intersection with the Alice Creek road). We found another sign lying on the ground where, according to our topos, the trail enters the Scapegoat Wilderness (mountain biking prohibited) and begins a descent that skirts Caribou Peak. The sign said "Continental Divide Trail 440," which was nice, since we'd been on Trail 440 for 15 miles with no reassurance.

Two sets of switchbacks, separated by long, gently downhill straightaways, take hikers below Caribou Peak to a midge-filled pond situated in a depressingly dark hole. Patches of snow linger here until late July, and the conifers are bearded with lichens and moss. Water courses on either side of this pond are shown on the maps, but are usually dry. The 1988 fires dried up some water courses and they never recovered, in part because spring runoff is faster when there are no trees and less vegetation to hold the moisture.

Don't pass up the pond as a water source, even though it doesn't look very inviting. If you got water last at Bear Creek and did not refill at Alice Creek, you will have hiked 11.7 waterless miles before reaching this pond. Steeper-than-regulation-grade switchbacks take hikers back up to the Divide from the nameless pond.

Bighorn Lake looks tempting on the map, but not so on the ground, as it would be a steep 1,000-foot drop to the lake—and think about having to climb back up again. Nevertheless, if you wish to make the side trip, there is a signed intersection north of the lake with Trail 442 (mile 18.6) that leads sharply downhill. This azure-colored lake is now surrounded on three sides by burned forest and on the fourth by steep cliffs.

From the intersection with the Bighorn Lake trail, the CDT continues northward and downhill, as the ridge of the Divide dips toward the Bighorn Creek drainage. The burned forest offers no protection from wind and a trekking pole is advised for balance on the turns. It would be a long fall if you stepped off the trail here. Tread mysteriously appears and disappears, going from a well-constructed trail to nothing several times.

At mile 20.4 (1.8 miles from the spur trail to the lake), the CDT leaves the Divide and begins the first leg of a V-shaped detour. The trail turns west, then southwest as it descends along Bighorn Creek. At the turn, the trail number changes to 441. The upper portions of the creek drainage are dry. Water is shown on the maps, but with the exception of snowmelt earlier in the season, there is no water until you reach the Lake Fork tributary at mile 23.6 (3.2 miles from the turn and 6.9 miles from the dismal pond).

Northeast of Lake Fork, trail tread disappears in grassy and marshy spots, reappearing on drier ground. South of Lake Fork, water is plentiful in multiple creek crossings.

Creek and trail names on the ground do not match the Forest Service map. Bighorn Creek on the map is signed as "Sheep Creek" on the ground, but occasionally the number 441 appears on both the map and the ground. Trail 441 intersects Trail 438 at mile 24.8, ending the southwest trek along the creek bottom and beginning a northerly trek back up to the Divide. (A branch of Trail 438 also leads south to Heart Lake and to trails leading to the Indian Meadows Trailhead, a possible exit or access point that is 5.7 miles from the CDT.) Signs on the ground also say "Landers Fork" because 438 is part of the Landers Fork Pack Trail route.

Soon after making the northerly turn on Trail 438, hikers are treated to a pretty waterfall, with several tiers, that drops from pool to pool on the west side of the trail. This is especially refreshing after so many miles of walking through burned forests.

Trail 438 is a dilapidated pack trail, gently graded, that sinuously curves into and out of every ripple in the landscape as it climbs to a 7,000-foot ridge above Landers Fork, then descends to the horse camp, in a meadow at mile 29.8 (5 miles north on 438 from the turn in the Bighorn Creek drainage). August hailstorms battered us intermittently all the way to Landers Fork. There is plenty of water in this section.

Landers Fork is an excellent campsite. It was not burned in the '88 fires and grassy meadows surround a three-way stream confluence. We saw bear sign here, so be sure to hang your food. Signs confirm the "Landers Fork" location. When we were there on August 9, we were also treated to a full-scale snowstorm and driving wind.

From Landers Fork, Trail 479 is marshy and boggy where it parallels a tributary stream as it climbs to the Divide above Blacktail Creek. When you reach the Divide at mile 30.8 (1 mile from Landers Fork), there is a confusing four-way trail intersection that is not shown on any of the maps. Remnants of the old trail descending to the Dearborn River, and of a trail that climbs eastward, confuse the picture. However, the left-hand (west) turn is a slightly better trail, with more obvious tread, and it was marked with a single stone cairn when we there. The cairn was so small that we almost missed it in the snow. We followed a trail of horse manure instead, a sure sign of a nearby trailhead.

From the saddle above Blacktail Creek, many long switchbacks lead south and southeast through the trees to the river. The switchbacks are also not shown on the maps. The trail switchbacks downhill for about 2.5 miles to reach an open meadow, where it continues southeasterly for another 1.8 miles to the Dearborn River crossing. The switchbacks add about 2 miles to your mileage if you use the topo to estimate distance. In the meadow at the bottom of the switchbacks, signs tell you what you would have paid money to know on the saddle above—that this is indeed Trail 207, the Blacktail/ Landers Fork Trail. Rangers have since assured me that they will improve the signs. Southbound hikers will have less route-finding difficulties here.

Ignore a Y-shaped intersection in the meadow on the south side of the Dearborn River—it's a horse packer's trail to their camp. Northbound hikers continue downstream at the Y intersection; southbound hikers bear left.

You are not yet done with confusing signs (or lack of them). The Forest Service map of the Bob Marshall/Scapegoat Wilderness shows the boundary of the wilderness further east than does the boundary sign on the ground. So, although your maps do not show this, you must hike past the boundary sign and out of the wilderness to ford the Dearborn River where the route of the CDT crosses to the north bank. Rangers say the map boundary is correct and they intend to move the signs on the ground and/or the depiction of the trail on the map.

Ford the Dearborn River at mile 35.2 and make a U-turn to climb above the river on the north side. The turn was not signed when we there. (Near the ford, it is possible to exit or access the CDT via the Dearborn River Trailhead, 6 miles downstream, east on Trail 206.)

On the north side of the Dearborn, hikers will pass another wilderness boundary sign and a sign for Trail 207. The sign on the ground says 207 and the map says 206. Trail 206/207 parallels the Dearborn River as it climbs gently upstream on a northwesterly path, reaching the Welcome Creek Guard Station at mile 44.2 (9 miles from the river ford). On the way, hikers pass intersections for other Scapegoat Wilderness trails. The first is Trail 218, where intersection signs also say "Dearborn River Trail 206/ Welcome Creek Cabin 6 miles/Benchmark 21 miles/Continental Divide 5 miles/ Tobacco Valley 7 miles." The "Continental Divide 5 miles" is the only worrisome note, as it leads CDT hikers to believe they should turn left (westerly) here. Don't be fooled; continue up the Dearborn on the trail to Welcome Creek. Rangers have plans to sign the CDT more clearly here.

Intersections are also passed for trails 205 and 254. (Trail 205 can be used to exit the wilderness to the east, over Elk Pass to Sky Mountain Lodge.) CDT trekkers continue straight ahead on Trail 206, up the Dearborn River. The lower reaches of the Dearborn River were not burned in the '88 fires, so this is a pleasant, though sometimes boggy, walk. Cottonwood and aspen trees mingle with conifers at the lower elevations.

Just south of Lost Cabin Creek, the trail fords the Dearborn River again and then enters a burned area. Some of the signs at Lost Cabin Creek were also burned, but are still up, alongside newer signs.

The intersection with Straight Creek Trail 212 to Welcome Pass and the Dearborn Trail 206 is well-signed (although the sign was on a dead, burned tree). Trail 206 turns left (southwest) toward the physical Divide, but the official route of the CDT turns right (northeast) toward Welcome Pass. If you want to stay on the official route, keep right; if you want to get a closer look at the Divide, you can hike a 12-13 mile loop that offers various approaches to Scapegoat Mountain and Halfmoon Park before it rejoins the CDT at Green Fork on the Straight Creek Trail.

Trail 212 takes hikers past the Welcome Creek Guard Station, which was miraculously spared during the '88 fires. Misleading horse trails to the station yard and to pastures above the station can get you off track here. The correct route is less well-traveled and crosses the river south of the station, and then crosses Welcome Creek (three fords in quick succession). Watch closely on your right (east) for the ford across the river. If you mistakenly end up at the Guard Station, keep right of the corral on a footpath that will take you back to the trail to Welcome Pass.

Shortly after the third ford near the Welcome Creek Guard Station, there is a Y-shaped intersection that is not on the map, with one branch staying on the creek and one climbing a few contour lines above it. The best option is the branch that climbs above the marshy area. Both branches come together again in a meadow below Welcome Pass, which is signed for the intersection with Jakie Creek Trail 214 and Straight Creek Trail 212. CDT trekkers continue northwesterly on Trail 212. (The Jakie Creek Trail can be used as an exit point, leading via the Petty Ford Creek Trail to the Ford Creek Resort and Guest Ranch.)

Trail 212 climbs for 1.9 miles to Straight Creek Pass, crossing Welcome Creek many times in the process. In places the trail is the creek, so water shoes or sandals are helpful. The creek banks are lined with shoulder-high fireweed that also chokes the trail. You'll see blackened stumps and acres of burned trees.

It's a 3-mile downhill slope from Straight Creek Pass to the Green Fork Guard Station. Leaving the burned areas behind, you'll pass intersections with several side trails, including Trail 216, an opportunity for another side trip that is a scenic loop through the Halfmoon Park area.

Horse traffic increases dramatically north of Green Fork, so the trail is churned up and muddy at stream crossings and in every boggy area.

Another 3.3 miles brings you to the intersection with Trail 248 at mile 53.3 for this segment, where the CDT turns west to go over Elbow Pass. Although the official route goes over Elbow Pass, it is possible to continue on the Straight Creek Trail to Benchmark.

The 3.5-mile Elbow Pass Trail 248 was reconstructed in 1987, so it doesn't follow exactly the line of the pack trail as shown on the topo. A steep climb takes hikers from 5,760 feet to 6,560 feet at the top of the pass. From there, it is downhill to an intersection with Trail 202, which parallels the South Fork of the Sun River flowing northward between the steep cliffs of the Divide on the west and the rocky ridges of Patrol Mountain on the east.

The CDT follows the South Fork of the Sun River for 8.5 miles to Benchmark, an easy walk that drops only 600 feet in elevation. Hikers may see a lot of wildlife along this portion of the Sun River, which is in the Sun River Game Preserve, where hunting is prohibited.

Segment 23
1:100,000 MAPS:
DEARBORN RIVER and CHOTEAU
5/8
SCALE: 5/8 INCH = 1 MILE
1 CM = 1 KM
Continental Divide
Continental Divide Trail (current segment)
Continental Divide Trail (previous and next segments)
River or stream
Lake or pond
Marsh or swamp
Primary highway
Secondary highway
Light duty road
Unimproved road
Trail
Quarry or open mine pit
USGS: CHOTEAU
USGS: DEARBORN RIVER
SHOWN HERE: NORTHERN PORTION OF SEGMENT 23. SEE PAGES 236-237 FOR SOUTHERN PORTION.
SCAPEGOAT
LEWIS AND CL
GAME PRESERVE
Benchmark
Benchmark Airport
Fairview Mountain
Red Hill
Patrol Mountain
Cyanide Mountain
Crown Mountain
Elbow Pass
Bunyan Point
Cigarette Rock
Straight Creek Pass
Red Slide Mountain
Halfmoon Peak
Welcome Pass
Observation Pass
Observation Point
Flint Mtn
Renshaw Mountain
Burnt Top Mountain
Sheep Sheds
Sugar Loaf
Lime Ridge
Lime Gulch
Roost Hill
Black Butte
McCarty Hill
Gravel Pit
Haystack Butte
Swallow Canyon
Smith Lake
NATIONAL FOREST BOUNDARY

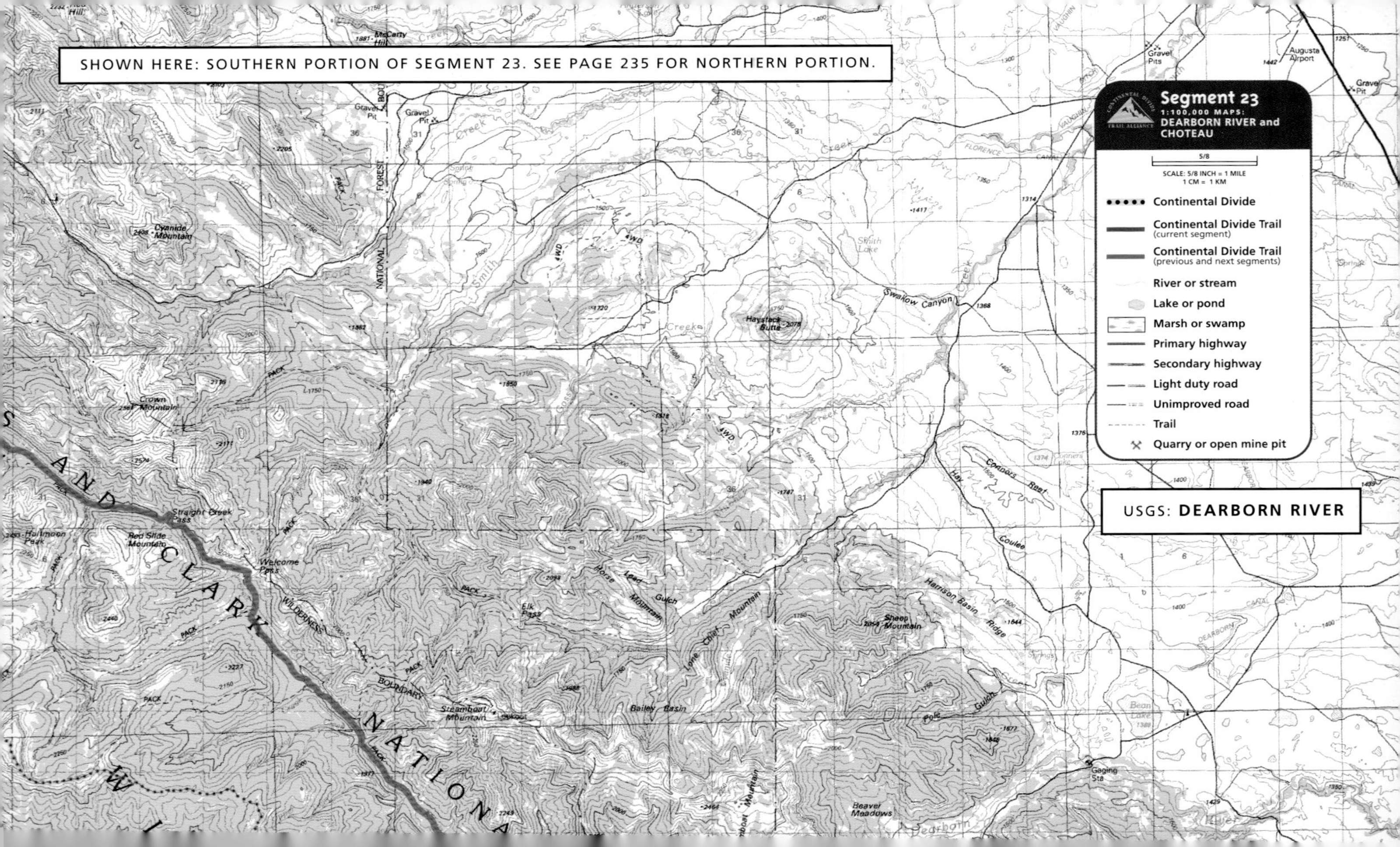

SHOWN HERE: SOUTHERN PORTION OF SEGMENT 23. SEE PAGE 235 FOR NORTHERN PORTION.
Segment 23
1:100,000 MAPS:
DEARBORN RIVER and CHOTEAU
SCALE: 5/8 INCH = 1 MILE
1 CM = 1 KM
Continental Divide
Continental Divide Trail
(current segment)
Continental Divide Trail
(previous and next segments)
River or stream
Lake or pond
Marsh or swamp
Primary highway
Secondary highway
Light duty road
Unimproved road
Trail
Quarry or open mine pit
USGS: DEARBORN RIVER
Augusta Airport
Gravel Pits
Gravel Pit
McCarty Hill
Cyanide Mountain
Crown Mountain
Haystack Butte
Smith Lake
Swallow Canyon
Connors Reef
Hay Coulee
Harrison Basin Ridge
Sheep Mountain
Lone Chief Mountain
Horse Mountain
Lead Gulch
Elk Pass
Bailey Basin
Steamboat Mountain
Pole Gulch
Beaver Meadows
Gaging Sta
Bean Lake
Welcome Pass
Straight Creek Pass
Red Slide Mountain
Halfmoon Peak
WILDERNESS
BOUNDARY
NATIONAL FOREST
LEWIS AND CLARK NATIONAL

HELENA NATIONAL FOREST
LEWIS AND CLARK NATIONAL FOREST
CONTINENTAL DIVIDE
WILDERNESS BOUNDARY
Olson Peak
Red Ridge
Galusha Peak
Pyramid Peak
Monitor Mountain
Bear Den Mountain
Table Mountain
Skull Gulch
Sugarloaf Mountain
Creek Ridge
Blowout Mountain
Caribou Peak
Burned Point
Red Mountain
Sunset Hill
Alice Creek Basin
Lewis and Clark Pass
Wildcat Gulch
Alice Mountains
Telephone Gulch
Green Mountain
Silver King Mountain
Lookout
Lone Mountain
Indian Meadows
F S Station
F S Sta
Evergreen Cabins
Cadotte Pass
Rogers Pass
Toms Gulch
Copper Camp
Cotter Mine
INDEFINITE BOUNDARY
HNF
PACK

Segment 24
Benchmark / South Fork TRHD to Badger Pass

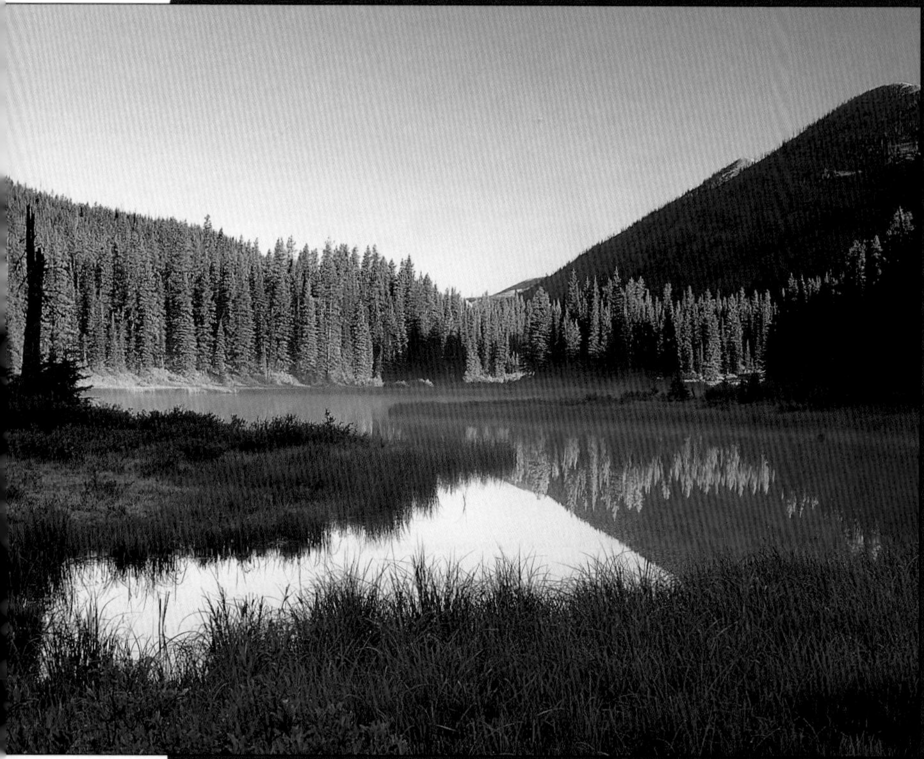

Beaver Lake in the Bob Marshall Wilderness, south of Muskrat Pass

88.3 miles
Difficulty: Strenuous

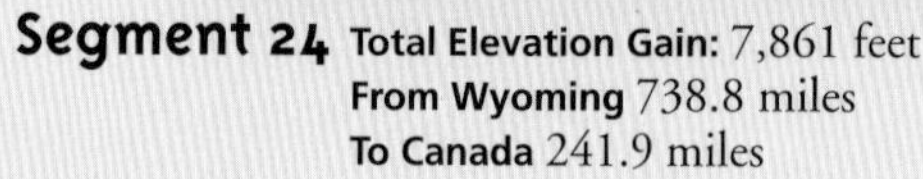
Segment 24 **Total Elevation Gain:** 7,861 feet
From Wyoming 738.8 miles
To Canada 241.9 miles

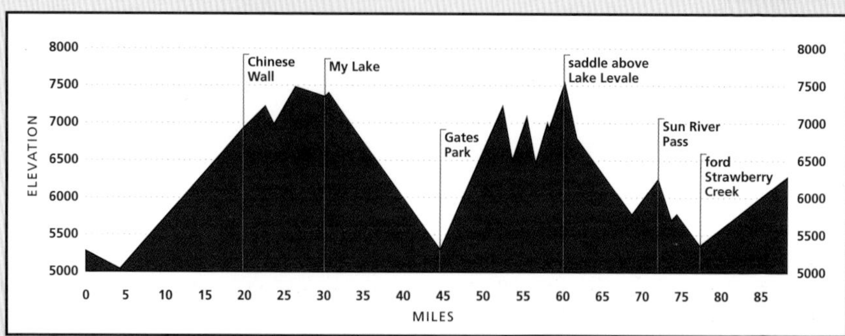

TRAIL OVERVIEW No other section of the Idaho/Montana CDT sees as much horse traffic as the Benchmark to Gates Park area of the Bob Marshall Wilderness. If you prefer to hike on trails limited to foot traffic, you may want to choose other sections of the CDT. Of course, through-hikers have to put up with everything from sidewalks to no trail at all, so a few horses should not put you off your game. There are about 1.5 million acres of off-trail hiking opportunities in the Great Bear/Bob Marshall/Scapegoat Wilderness complex, so adventurous souls can escape from everyone, including horses.

Access to the Bob Marshall Wilderness is very limited, so even experienced backpackers will find it a challenge to carry enough food to complete this segment of the CDT. The segment ends at Badger Pass, which is 10.5 miles from the nearest trailhead—so when you're done, you're still not done. Adding that 10.5 miles brings this long-distance trek to 98.8 miles.

Professional outfitters are required to book their trips with the Forest Service, but others, including hikers with pack stock, do not need a permit. Backpackers can hire an outfitter to pack in resupplies at a halfway point. The cost is minimal and the payoff in terms of hiking comfort is high. Resupplies from an outfitter will also give you more options for exploring side trips near the CDT. Gates Park, at mile 44.6, is often used as a resupply point. Badger Pass and Benchmark are also potential resupply points. See the "Supplies, Services, and Accommodations" box for a list of outfitters.

The most well-known destination in The Bob is the "Chinese Wall." The Wall is the ultimate expression of the Continental Divide, a perfect, graphical representation of the curving, wavering line of the backbone of the continent. Hung on the Chinese Wall's steep, eastern side are miniature hanging gardens, swards of grass and trees clinging to the heights on every narrow ledge. The Wall is the home of mountain goats and the precipitator of weather patterns. It kneads moisture from the clouds that pass over it, dumping mass quantities of snow in the tightly folded terrain between the Wall and the Front Range to the east. Be prepared for muddy trails, bogs, and frequent stream crossings.

Compared to Glacier National Park, the topography of The Bob is mild. The Wall is a tourist magnet and heavily visited along the southern portion, but you're likely to have the North Wall all to yourself as it is too far for most hikers to venture—even outfitters and trail crews are infrequent visitors to the North Wall.

The Chinese Wall definitely has an impact on the trail system. The thousand-foot-high escarpment is seldom crossed by the trail system, and it drives the CDT down into the eastern valleys several times. As a result, the route looks like a saw blade or the teeth of a comb laid flat, with zigzagging departures from, and returns to, the Divide.

Most of the trail intersections in the Bob Marshall are well-signed. Because the trails are so well marked, it is not necessary to mention every intersection in the trail description for this segment of the CDT. The intersections that are noted in this guide affect the route of the CDT, are of particular interest for side trips or access, or could cause confusion in route-finding. Unsigned intersections are either "passing lanes" formed by pack trains, or spur trails to outfitters' camps. If it is not signed, you can ignore it. When we did The Bob, there were no CDT signs, but new signs have since been added.

Once you enter the Bob Marshall Wilderness, the only water problem you'll have is too much of it. Frequent river and stream crossings are the norm, and your emphasis is more likely to shift to finding a dry spot to set up your tent. If you are hiking The Bob earlier in the season, a pair of overshoes or other waterproof footgear is worth carrying. For most of this segment, the trail parallels the Sun River or other major streams.

By late August, the insects have abated, but if you "Do The Bob" earlier, take plenty of repellent to ward off mosquitoes and black flies.

Review the precautions and safety guidelines for hiking and camping in bear country. This trail passes through prime grizzly bear habitat. Both grizzly and black bears are common. Pepper spray is recommended. Review the section on "Safety Concerns."

MOUNTAIN BIKE NOTES: This segment lies entirely within the Bob Marshall Wilderness, where mountain bikes are prohibited.

LAND ADMINISTRATORS (SEE APPENDIX A)

Lewis & Clark National Forest, Rocky Mountain Ranger District
Flathead National Forest, Spotted Bear Ranger District

MAPS

USGS QUADRANGLES: Benchmark, Pretty Prairie, Prairie Reef, Slategoat Mountain, Amphitheater Mountain, Three Sisters, Gates Park, Porphyry Reef, Pentagon Mountain, Gooseberry Park, Morningstar Mountain, Crescent Cliff, Hyde Creek

USFS: Bob Marshall, Great Bear, and Scapegoat Wilderness Complex. This map is a 1:100,000 scale topographical map and is good enough that it may be substituted for USGS topos if your budget is tight.

BEGINNING ACCESS POINT

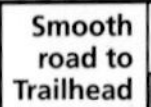

BENCHMARK/SOUTH FORK TRAILHEAD: From Augusta, Montana, on Hwy. 287, go west on Ranger Station Road (to Nilan Reservoir) for about 17 miles. The road is paved for a few miles, then gravel for the remainder. Watch out for horse trailers and trucks on the curves. Turn southwest at the intersection with Road 235 (signed "Benchmark"). It is about 18 miles on Road 235 to the South Fork Trailhead. Benchmark consists of multiple parking lots for horse trailers, an airstrip, and other amenities, all of which can be a little confusing. The trailhead for this segment is at the end of the road.

ENDING ACCESS POINT

SWIFT DAM TRAILHEAD AT SWIFT RESERVOIR: Badger Pass, where this segment ends, is 10.5 miles from the nearest trailhead. Hike easterly on North Fork Birch Creek Trail 121. The trail crosses Blackfeet Indian Reservation lands, and the tribe requests that hikers ask for permission to use the trail. (See Appendix A for tribal contact information.) The trail rounds the northern shore of the reservoir, and shuttle or support crews can drive about 2 miles uphill past the reservoir before the foot/horse path is closed to motorized vehicles. There is limited traffic on the Swift Dam Road. The nearest town is Choteau, Montana, an additional 36 miles south on Hwy. 89. The city of Browning, on the Blackfeet Indian Reservation, is 38 miles to the north on Hwy. 89.

ALTERNATE ENDING ACCESS POINT It is possible to cut this long segment in half by exiting the wilderness from Gates Park via Trail 165 over Headquarters Pass to the South Fork Teton Trailhead. The hiking/driving distance is about the same, but there are serious quagmires to get through on the Headquarters Creek Trail. Some of the bogs are deep enough to swallow a pack mule. Access is north of Choteau, from Canyon Road.

ALTERNATE ENDING ACCESS POINT Strong, experienced backpackers may choose to go on to Marias Pass (see Segment 25), which adds 34 miles to an already long hike. The advantage is that Marias Pass is on a paved highway, and no extra hiking miles are required to reach the trailhead.

TRAIL DESCRIPTION The South Fork Trailhead is near where the access road ends. Look for the area signed as "Hiker Parking." Horse traffic is heavy and the trails look like roads as they near the Benchmark area. To continue north on the CDT, look for the trail signed as "South Fork Sun River 202." Trail 202 has been improved with bog bridges and other trail work, some in cooperation with the Professional Wilderness Outfitters Association. Hikers will still have some boulder-hopping to do at frequent crossings of small, feeder streams on this trail. Pack bridges, built for horse traffic, cross the deeper channels.

The Bob Marshall Wilderness boundary sign is reached at 4.3 miles from the Benchmark/South Fork Trailhead. Review the "Wilderness Alert" information in Segment 14 for regulations pertaining to camping and hiking. There are additional regulations for stock use in The Bob. Check with the Rocky Mountain Ranger District of the Lewis & Clark National Forest for details (see Appendix A).

Past the entrance to the Bob Marshall Wilderness, the route of the CDT turns west on Trail 203 to follow the West Fork of the South Fork of the Sun River. (I know, the names alone will slow you down. We'll abbreviate that to WFSFSR.) There's a "Low Water Trail" across the WFSFSR for hikers simply dying to wade in the Sun River, but it is much easier to take the pack bridge.

Cross a pack bridge at mile 5.4. There are "no camping" signs near this pack bridge—and most other pack bridges in the wilderness are off limits to campers. Continue upstream on Trail 203 through the beautiful and relatively open WFSFSR valley. We saw our first grizzly, a blond yearling, in this area.

Aspen trees, grassy meadows, and willows add some variety to these lower elevations (5,000 to 6,000 feet), and the fall colors are magical in late September. A few miles up Trail 203, at the top of a small rise, views of Red Butte, which really is red, frame the horizon.

WILDERNESS ALERT

In 1940, three primitive areas were combined to form the Bob Marshall Wilderness Area. In 1964, Congress gave official wilderness status to the area. The name commemorates Robert Marshall, a legendary Forest Service Ranger who advocated the protection of "primeval" wilderness. Marshall, known for his long-distance hiking capabilities, routinely covered 35 miles a day in the wilderness that was to become his namesake. In the 1970s, the Scapegoat and Great Bear areas were added to the wilderness system. These contiguous lands, known to the locals as "Bob Marshall Country" or "The Bob," form an extension of public lands that includes Glacier National Park in a long "grizzly corridor" that has played a large part in restoring the endangered species.

The trail to Prairie Reef Lookout, at mile 10.4, is a worthwhile side trip, climbing 4 miles to a manned lookout tower at elevation 8,858 feet. The views are magnificent and you pay for them with an extremely steep climb. Local outfitters take tourists up on horseback, so don't expect solitude.

There are multiple trail intersections and signs at Indian Meadows. CDT trekkers stay on Trail 203, which is also signed as "Chinese Wall." There is good camping here, just off the trail, near Ahorn Creek, at mile 11.4 for this segment. The Indian Point Guard Station is nearby.

Another side trip is offered at mile 12.7, where Trail 211 goes up Indian Creek to Whiteriver Pass. This trail actually crosses the Divide below the Chinese Wall after skirting Red Butte. If cliffs, rocks, and mountain goats are your idea of a good time, this side trip is for you. Trail intersection signs at Indian Creek give CDT trekkers the distance of 13 miles to Larch Hill Pass, which I judge to be about 1 mile short of true. The claim for 20 miles to Gates Park is also short, by about 1.9 miles. Trail 203 (the CDT) turns north at this intersection.

Trail 203 turns west again at Burnt Creek and follows that drainage up to the Chinese Wall. The trail becomes "Chinese Wall Trail 175" where it turns north to skirt this impressive line of cliffs that mark the Continental Divide. "No Camping" signs at the base of the Chinese Wall, mile 19.8, restrict use of the delicate alpine environment. Plan to camp before or after the Wall. The camping closure is about 3 miles long, ending at Salt Mountain.

Just south of Larch Hill Pass, at mile 26.4, Trail 175 intersects Trail 194. When we hiked this section, the intersection was not signed. Whether it's signed or not, CDT trekkers turn briefly southeast (right), and then north again on Trail 194 to My Lake. Do not go all the way to Larch Hill Pass.

Trail 194 is 4.2 miles long. It passes My Lake at mile 30.1 for this segment. The small lake sits in the eastern lee of the Divide, surrounded by grass and conifers.

Half a mile past My Lake, Trail 194 becomes Rock Creek Trail 111. Near the top of Rock Creek Trail, at Spotted Bear Pass, a very short excursion to the ridge top leads to excellent views of the Three Sisters peaks and of Redhead Peak.

After some initial switchbacks, the Rock Creek Trail proceeds steadily downhill, southeast, then northeast. The trail passes the unmanned Rock Creek Guard Station. Near here new construction of a spur trail to the Moose Creek Lookout was planned but not yet completed when we hiked The Bob.

The Rock Creek Trail is 14 miles long, terminating at Gates Park and the Gates Park Guard Station. This 14-mile excursion away from the Divide is the first and the longest of several zigzags in the route of the CDT. Hiking so many extra miles away from and then returning to the Divide may tempt some trekkers to stay up on the Divide and work cross-country to the next trail. However, only an experienced rock climber could be assured of finding a place to descend the cliffs to intercept the continuation of Trail 175. Snow also lingers into late July and early August in some locations. Still, I was tempted to lobby the Forest Service for a connecting trail closer to the Divide, especially when the trails up and down the creek drainages were hopelessly mired in mud, bogs, swamps, and quagmires. There is a virtue to everything—the mud held many grizzly prints, both sow and cub, and also told the stories of other wildlife that use these trails.

At Gates Park (mile 44.6), the route of the CDT makes a U-turn to follow Red Shale Creek northeasterly to the Divide. Gates Park is a good camping spot, with multiple water sources and a Guard Station built around an old homesteader's cabin. A resident herd of elk can often be seen grazing in the large meadow. Multiple pack trails lead into the Gates Park area and it is heavily used by outfitters, making it a likely drop-off point for resupplies.

Of the many trails leading into Gates Park, the one side trip that I would recommend is the hike up to Beartop Lookout on Trail 129. From the Park, go easterly, crossing the Sun River on a pack bridge. It is 5.2 miles to the seldom visited lookout, which offers a panoramic vista of surrounding peaks and valleys, including Rocky Mountain and Old Baldy. Rocky Mountain, elevation 9,392 feet, is the tallest peak in the Bob Marshall Wilderness.

Red Shale Creek Trail 130 is the next access route to the Divide for northbound hikers. The infamous 1988 fire started along this trail. The landscape is still dotted with burned stumps, and standing but burned trees. Deadfall can be a problem when winds blow the burned trees onto the trail. Despite the burn, there are few views along the trail due to intervening, low hills. But closer to the Divide, open areas offer intermittent views of Lookout Mountain to the south, an impressive massif that looks like the back of a reddish whale surfacing from a sea of vegetation. The trail fords Red Shale Creek about a mile below the intersection with Trail 175 along the North Wall. Here the burned area ends and the intact trees, grasses, and flowers below Sock Lake are a welcome sight.

Sock Lake is not visible from the trail, but is accessible via a steep, 800-foot climb to a hanging cirque. Lake Levale to the north is easily accessible and the setting is

SUPPLIES, SERVICES, AND ACCOMMODATIONS

AUGUSTA, MT, is on Highway 287.

Distance from Trail: 31.5 miles

Zip Code: 59410

Bank:	None (See Choteau, Segment 25)	
Bus:	None	
Camping:	Wagons West Campground, 76 Main St., $10 per night	406-562-3295
Dining:	Mel's Diner, Main Street	406-562-3408
	The End of the Trail, Wagons West Motel, 76 Main St.	406-562-3611
	Espresso at Latigo & Lace, Main Street	406-562-3665
	Sun Canyon Cafe, Sun River Road	406-562-3654
Gear:	Allen's Manix General Store and Trading Post, Main St.	406-562-3333
Groceries:	Allen's Manix General Store and Trading Post, Main St.	406-562-3333
Information:	Augusta Information Station Office, 405 Manix St.	406-562-3347
Laundry:	Augusta Laundromat, Main Street	
Lodging:	Sun Canyon Lodge, Sun River Road, $35–$75	406-562-3654
	Wagons West Motel, 76 Main Street, $35–$65	406-562-3295
Medical:	None (See Choteau, Segment 25)	
Outfitters:	A Lazy H Outfitters, P.O. Box 729, Choteau, MT 59422	800-893-1155
	Sun Canyon Outfitters, Sun River Road, Augusta, MT	406-562-3603
	7 Lazy P Guest Ranch, P.O. Box 178, Choteau, MT 59422	406-466-2044
	Montana Safaris, P.O. Box 1004, Choteau, MT 5942	406-466-2044
	Ford Creek Guest Ranch, P.O. Box 329 (12 miles from Benchmark) Augusta, MT 59410	406-562-3672
	Benchmark Wilderness Guest Ranch (about 4 miles from Benchmark)	406-562-3336
	(Ford Creek Ranch and Benchmark Wilderness Ranch also offer lodging, food, and resupply delivery services.)	
Post Office:	U.S. Post Office, 129 Main Street, Augusta, MT 59410	406-562-3370
Showers:	Wagons West Campground, 76 Main Street	406-562-3295
	$3.00 for non-campers, otherwise included in camping fee	

beautiful. The hike along the North Wall is much more strenuous than its counterpart to the south along the Chinese Wall. A series of four spur ridges must be crossed, with 500- to 600-foot climbs and descents marking each ridge. The trail is also steeper, with rocky switchbacks that aren't up to the usual Bob Marshall standards for trail construction.

Avalanche chutes are numerous south of the North Fork of Lick Creek, and one can see that travel along the North Wall would be dangerous when snow blankets the Divide. A long ascent through open parklands leads to the intersection with Spur Trail 132 to Moonlight Peak at mile 58.2.

At 7,535 feet in elevation, the saddle on the ridge south of Lake Levale is the high point on the North Wall Trail. From the saddle, the trail turns northwesterly to descend to the lake. There are good views through whitebark pine trees of Signal Mountain to the east and of the Divide to the west. A nest of trails surrounds the eastern shore of Lake Levale. This lake was stocked with arctic grayling in the past, and a fellow backpacker said that the fish population was still plentiful. Glacial silt gives Lake Levale's waters its milky turquoise color. This is the best spot to camp before descending along Open Creek, but remember to camp at least 200 yards from the shore.

From Lake Levale to Open Creek Trail 116, hikers cross below frequent avalanche chutes and just above the timberline. The mixture of boulders and flowers makes for an interesting rock garden to which Open Creek adds two waterfalls. It is possible to continue north for a short but brutal climb to Kevan Mountain, which looks much higher than its 8,412-foot elevation thanks to several cliffy arms that dominate the northern horizon.

CDT trekkers turn eastward to descend along Open Creek on Trail 116, at mile 61.7. Open Creek belies its name by not being very "open." The drainage is narrow and enclosed in thick forest, which did not burn in the '88 fires. Mud holes, bogs, and rotted bridges will slow your descent.

About 7 miles of steady descent brings you to Round Park, an excellent campsite in drier years. Near the intersection with North Fork Sun River Trail 110, "Signboard Park" 0.5 mile east of Round Park, is also a good camping spot. The route of the CDT makes a 90° turn to the north (left for northbound hikers) at Signboard Park to follow Trail 110 to Sun River Pass.

"Mega mud holes" are noted in my travel diary for the trail north to Sun River Pass. The north side of Sun River Pass differs so dramatically in character that you'll think you've entered a new land. Crossing the Divide at Sun River Pass puts you in a drier zone. Although it makes no sense, the trail number changes from 110 to 177 when you cross the Divide. Trail 177 is short-lived—you'll intersect Trail 324 and follow it north to Strawberry Creek.

Grizzly Park is an excellent camping area, despite the scary name. At mile 73.7 (about 1.7 miles north of Sun River Pass), the trail passes through open meadows, cinquefoil shrubs, and ample water from Bowl Creek. Relatively new trail construction above Bowl Creek takes hikers out of the boggy creek bottom and up onto the northeastern slopes, eliminating stream crossings but also limiting access to water.

The Strawberry Creek ford at mile 77.3 is the next best water source. This wide, shallow ford is pretty and pleasant in August, but can be very dangerous earlier in the season when snowmelt swells the creek to a river-sized flood. On the north side of the ford, the trail forks, with the left fork leading west past Gooseberry Park to the Middle Fork of the Flathead River. The Flathead is famous for fishing, kayaking, and rafting. Some outfitters bring rafters to this junction for a long float north through the Great Bear Wilderness. The right fork, now Trail 161, leads east, then north along Strawberry Creek, and this is the route of the CDT.

It is a gentle, 11-mile climb up Strawberry Creek to Badger Pass. Water is plentiful to within about 0.5 mile of the pass and camping opportunities are numerous. Black bear and elk are common in this area, and we saw white-tail deer near Whiskey

Ridge. Whiskey Ridge to the east and Cap Mountain to the west can be glimpsed through the trees as the trail makes its way north. Both massifs just top 7,000 feet, but are as bare and alpine-looking as an 11,000-foot peak would be in more southerly latitudes. Seeing the timberline at 6,000 to 7,000 feet reminded us of how far north we'd come since our start at the border of Yellowstone National Park. We could practically smell those Canadian snowfields and the glaciers in Glacier National Park.

The trail crosses the Divide at Badger Pass (elevation 6,280 feet, mile 88.3), and briefly leaves the wilderness. This segment ends at Badger Pass, where hikers can exit the wilderness by hiking eastward for 10.5 miles to Swift Reservoir and the Swift Dam Trailhead. The hike to the trailhead is quite scenic as it skirts rocky Family Peak, and cliff-walks above the North Fork of Birch Creek. The trail is unusually dry by Bob Marshall standards, but there are enough creek crossings to provide water to filter for drinking.

OTHER EXCURSIONS

PRETTY PRAIRIE/SUN RIVER

DIFFICULTY: Easy
DISTANCE: About 18.3 miles

Throughout the trail description for this segment, recommended side trips are noted. In addition to these, add a loop through the Pretty Prairie area to your list. This trip also begins at the South Fork Trailhead, following Trail 202 up the South Fork of the Sun River. Instead of turning west on the CDT at the intersection with Trail 203, continue north to Prairie Creek Trail 262. Trail 262 makes a 4-mile loop through Pretty Prairie to join Goat Creek Trail 249. The trail follows Goat Creek for 5 miles back to the Sun River, where you can pick up Trail 202 again and return to the South Fork Trailhead. This mellow hike is mostly meadows, creeks, and rivers—a good choice for hikers who want just a taste of "The Bob."

CROWN MOUNTAIN

DIFFICULTY: Moderate
DISTANCE: About 8.7 miles

On the approach route to Benchmark, off Road 235, watch for the Crown Mountain Trail sign. A dirt road crosses Ford Creek to the trailhead. For 2.7 miles, the trail winds through scattered lodgepole pines near Whitewater Creek. It tops out on the southern slopes of Crown Mountain, which earns its name by presenting a king's crown of rocks that tower above the trail. Views are excellent in all directions, including toward the Front Range, which rises like an arrested wave of rock over the Great Plains; and Haystack Butte, the lone pyramid on the plains to the east. At 2.7 miles there is a junction with Petty-Crown Trail 232, where you have the option of hiking into the Scapegoat Wilderness, or turning northeasterly to return to Road 235. The return route follows Petty Creek downhill for 3 miles to an intersection with Trail 244, Petty Ford Creek, which in turn leads back to Road 235 (2 miles). You'll have about a 1-mile hike west on the road to get back to the Crown Mountain Trailhead.

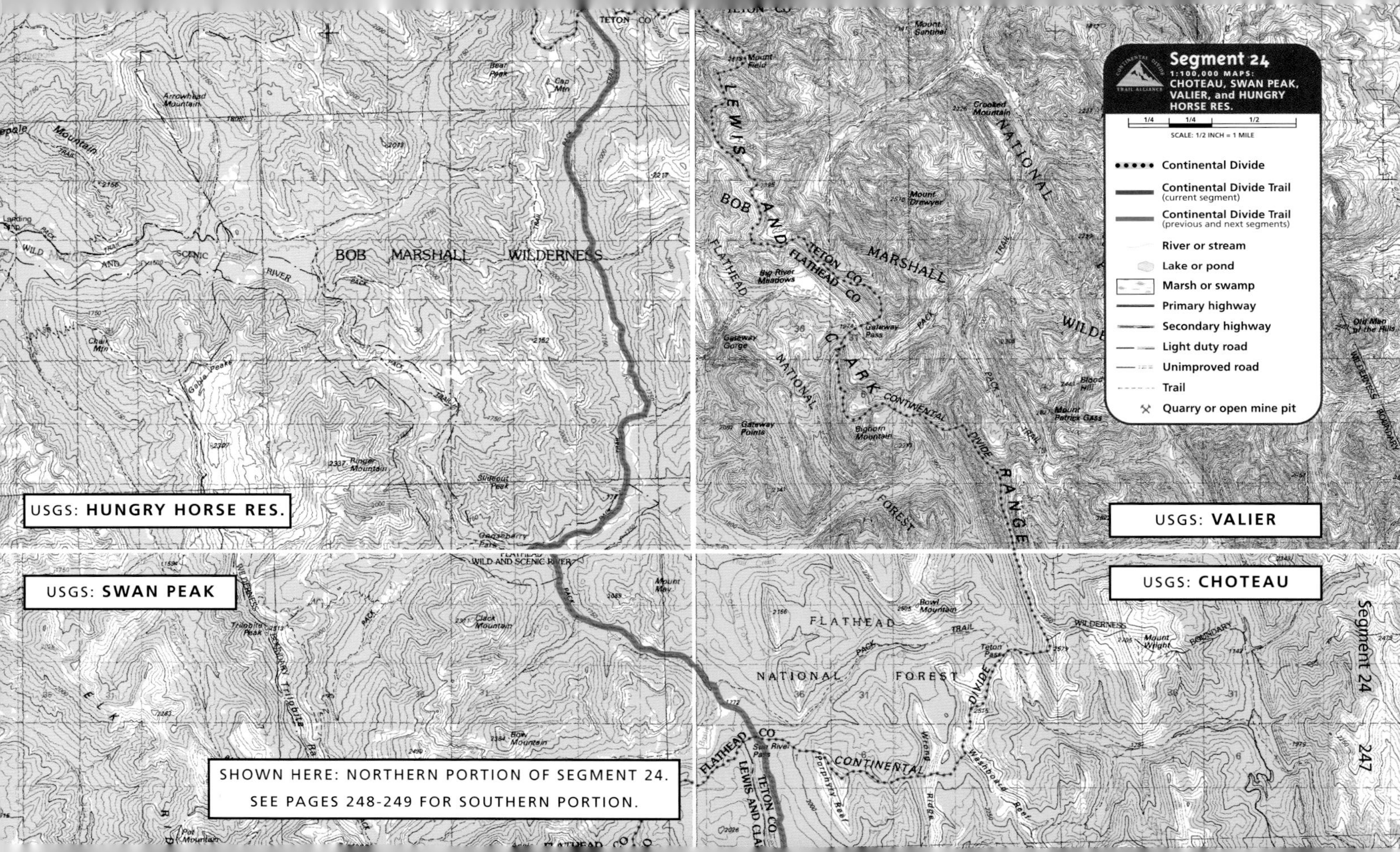

SHOWN HERE: NORTHERN PORTION OF SEGMENT 24.

SEE PAGES 248-249 FOR SOUTHERN PORTION.

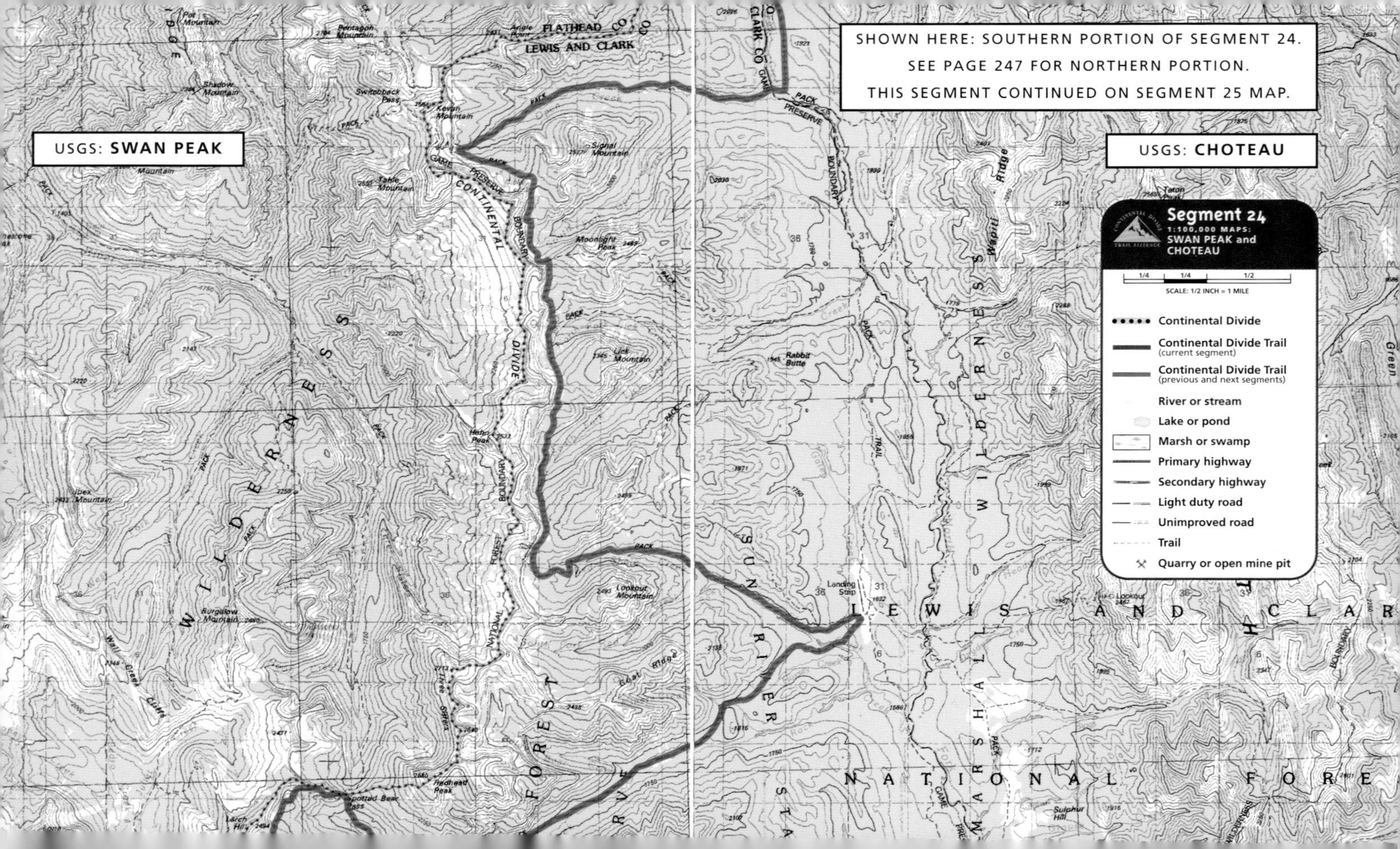

SHOWN HERE: SOUTHERN PORTION OF SEGMENT 24.
SEE PAGE 247 FOR NORTHERN PORTION.
THIS SEGMENT CONTINUED ON SEGMENT 25 MAP.
USGS: SWAN PEAK
USGS: CHOTEAU
Segment 24
1:100,000 MAPS: SWAN PEAK and CHOTEAU
SCALE: 1/2 INCH = 1 MILE
Continental Divide
Continental Divide Trail (current segment)
Continental Divide Trail (previous and next segments)
River or stream
Lake or pond
Marsh or swamp
Primary highway
Secondary highway
Light duty road
Unimproved road
Trail
Quarry or open mine pit
FLATHEAD CO
LEWIS AND CLARK CO
CONTINENTAL DIVIDE
GAME PRESERVE
Pentagon Mountain
Switchback Pass
Kevan Mountain
Table Mountain
Signal Mountain
Moonlight Peak
Lick Mountain
Hahn Peak
Lookout Mountain
Three Sisters
Redhead Peak
Spotted Bear Pass
Larch Hill
Ibex Mountain
Burgalow Mountain
Wall Creek Cliffs
Shadow Mountain
Rabbit Butte
Landing Strip
Wapiti Ridge
Teton Peak
Sulphur Hill
WILDERNESS
SUN RIVER
LEWIS AND CLARK NATIONAL FOREST
NATIONAL FOREST
MARSHALL

RANGE
Mortimer Gulch
Big George Gulch
INDEF BDY
Allan Mountain
Sheep Sheds
Renshaw Mountain
Basin
Black Reef
Patricks
PACK TRAIL
Elephant Head
Medicine Springs
Sun Butte
Sheep Reef
Elk Hill
PACK TRAIL
BOB
Sheep Mountain
GAME PRESERVE
Slategoat Mtn
GAME PACK BDY TRAIL
BOUNDARY
WILDERNESS
Deadman Hill
PACK TRAIL
Slategoat Mtn
Prairie Reef
Lookout
SUN RIVER GAME
LEWIS AND CLARK NATI
Grizzly Gulch
No Name Gulch
PACK
Red Butte
BOUNDARY
FOREST
LEWIS AND CLARK CO
BOUNDARY
POWELL CO
Junction Mountain
GAME PRESERVE
NATIONAL
White River Pass
CHINESE WALL
CONTINENTAL DIVIDE
Sphinx Peak
Haystack Mountain
Gladiator Mountain
Amphitheatre Mountain
FLATHEAD CO
POWELL CO
Moccasin Butte
Fault Peak
Sabre Peak
Flathead Alps
River

Segment 25
Badger Pass to Marias Pass

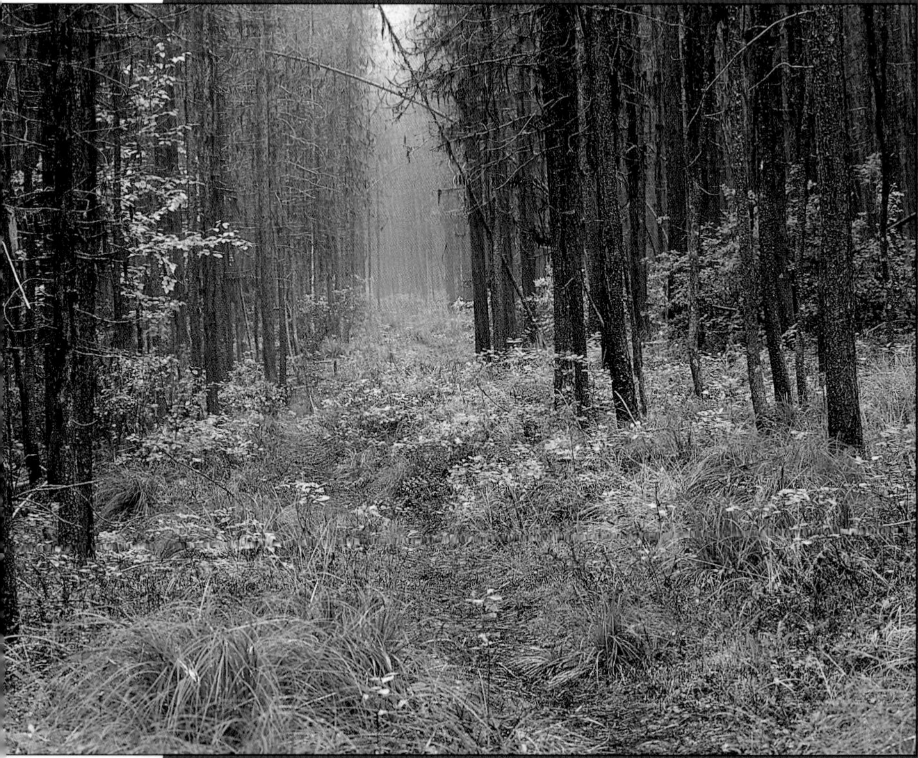

Footpath through a lodgepole pine forest near the Two Medicine River, southeast of Glacier National Park

34.3 miles
Difficulty: Moderate

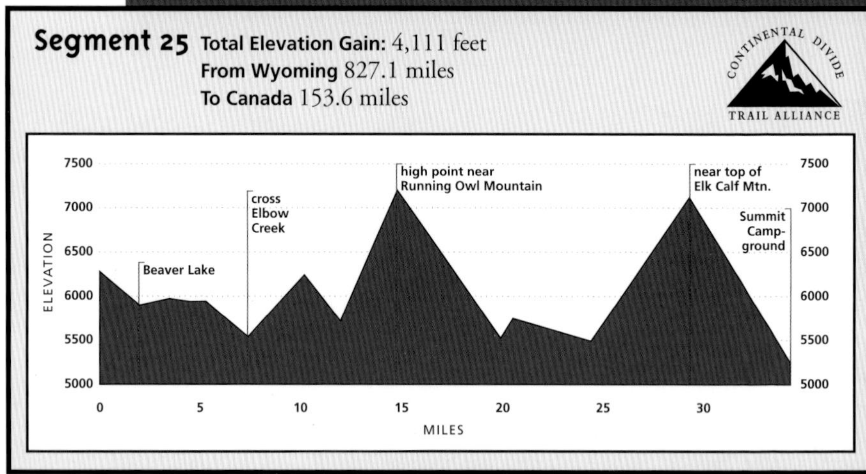

TRAIL OVERVIEW This segment begins at Badger Pass, near the northern border of the Bob Marshall Wilderness. The trail briefly leaves the wilderness, enters the Lewis & Clark National Forest at Badger Pass, then reenters the wilderness on the trek down to Beaver Lake. Northbound hikers leave the Bob Marshall Wilderness for good at Muskrat Pass. This area is seldom-visited and hikers are not likely to meet others on the trail except during hunting season. Portions of this segment, including Elk Calf Mountain, are considered sacred by the local Blackfeet Indians. Blackfeet Indian Reservation lands lie to the north and east, and the peaks of Glacier National Park loom to the northwest.

Marias Pass on Highway 2, at 5,216 feet above sea level, is the lowest pass on Montana's Continental Divide.

This trail passes through grizzly and black bear habitat. Pepper spray is recommended and food should be hung according to the guidelines in "Safety Concerns." By late August, the insects have abated, but if you hike the trail earlier, take plenty of repellent to ward off mosquitoes and black flies.

Water is plentiful all along this segment, with frequent stream crossings and trails that parallel streams and rivers for many miles.

WILDERNESS ALERT

Please note that special rules pertain to wilderness travel. See the Wilderness Alert information in Segment 14 for details.

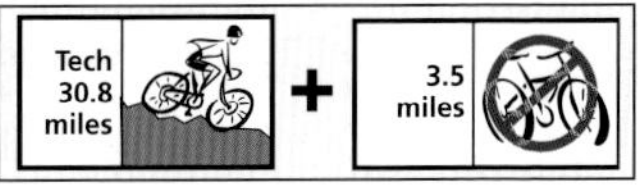

MOUNTAIN BIKE NOTES: This segment can be ridden from Muskrat Pass to Marias Pass, but the access route and the section around Beaver Lake are in the Bob Marshall Wilderness, where mountain biking is prohibited. The remainder of the segment is open to mountain bikes, but some sections, such as the new trail around Running Owl Mountain, are technically difficult. Bikes may have to be carried over deadfall, bogs, and streams. Mountain bikers have access at Marias Pass, via Hwy. 2.

LAND ADMINISTRATORS (SEE APPENDIX A)

Lewis & Clark National Forest, Rocky Mountain Ranger District
Flathead National Forest, Spotted Bear Ranger District

MAPS

USGS QUADRANGLES: Morningstar Mountain, Crescent Cliff, Hyde Creek, Summit
USFS: Bob Marshall, Great Bear, and Scapegoat Wilderness Complex

BEGINNING ACCESS POINT

SWIFT DAM TRAILHEAD AT SWIFT RESERVOIR: Take Hwy. 89 north from Choteau, Montana. It is about 36 miles from Choteau to the Swift Dam Road.

Go west on the Swift Dam Road to Swift Reservoir, about 20 miles. North Fork Birch Creek Trail 121 begins on the northern shore of the reservoir and it is possible to drive about 2 miles uphill past the reservoir before the foot/horse path is closed to motorized vehicles. Hike 10.5 miles on Trail 121 toward Badger Pass. Trail 121 crosses Blackfeet tribal lands and the Blackfeet Nation requests that hikers ask for permission before using the trail (see Appendix A). Intercept Trail 147, the Continental Divide Trail, near Badger Pass.

ENDING ACCESS POINT

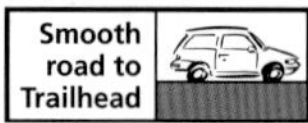

MARIAS PASS: On Hwy. 2, at the Summit Campground near the Roosevelt Memorial.

TRAIL DESCRIPTION Trail 147 descends 380 feet from Badger Pass to Beaver Lake. When we were there, the trail was very muddy and boggy, but Spotted Bear Ranger District crews have since made some improvements. There were no CDT signs on this trail, but rangers plan to sign the CDT.

Good camping spots are limited around Beaver Lake due to marshy conditions, but there is one beautiful area near the southeastern shore with views of the surrounding tree-covered hills. The physical Divide runs north of the lake. Drinking water can be filtered from the outlet stream.

The route of the CDT rounds the southern edge of Beaver Lake to continue northwesterly to Muskrat Pass. The topographical map shows a trail rounding the northern edge of Beaver Lake also, but the official and better-maintained trail is the southern route. The trail sign for Muskrat Pass was broken in two when we were there, but route-finding was not difficult. There is a trail leading southward along Cox Creek, but CDT trekkers will know to turn northward here.

SOUTHBOUND HIKERS: A left-hand (northeasterly) turn will put you on the correct trail from the southern end of Beaver Lake to Badger Pass.

Muskrat Pass is low, wide, and boggy. At 5,974 feet, it offers limited views of the Muskrat Creek basin and of the rocky ridges to the northeast. Unnamed peaks rise to about 7,500 feet on the horizon, their relatively low elevation belied by treeless, rocky slopes that make them look much higher.

From Muskrat Pass (mile 3.5) the trail descends toward Blue Lake (mile 4.5), a marshy pond that is too wet for camping. The trail stays about a hundred feet above the marsh and is almost flat as it follows Muskrat Creek in a northwesterly direction. At mile 5.3, there is an intersection with the trail along Crucifixion Creek, but CDT trekkers remain on the main track (Muskrat Creek Trail 147).

Cross Elbow Creek at mile 7.4, near the confluence of Muskrat and Elbow creeks. The creek is lined with willows and brush for the most part, but there is reasonably good camping in the flat spot near the creek confluence, or climb to a bench slightly above Muskrat Creek in wetter weather. Elbow Mountain is the peak to the southeast.

At Elbow Creek, the trail number changes to 145. This trail skirts the southwestern edge of the Bruin Peaks, whose rocky slopes rise to 7,728 feet above the trail. Water is still plentiful as the trail parallels a tributary of Elbow Creek.

A pleasant meadow and excellent camping are reached at mile 11. North Badger Creek runs along the eastern edge of the meadow, which is also the intersecting point with Trail 103, North Fork Badger Trail. There is a hitching rail and other evidence of light use by horsemen.

S **SOUTHBOUND HIKERS:** Trail 145 to Badger Pass looks like a faint two-track in the grass at the intersection of trails 103 and 145. At this intersection, there is also a sign that says if you kept going south on 103 you would reach the Continental Divide in 3 miles. That, of course, is not the official route of the CDT. The official trail takes a southeasterly course to the Beaver Lake/Badger Pass area.

From the meadow, Trail 103 takes hikers northeast on a jeep track to an intersection with Trail 141 at mile 12. Newly constructed tread departs the jeep track to climb around Running Owl Mountain. This trail was incomplete when we were there, so we did some bushwhacking to the completed portion near Lee Creek. Trail crews have since constructed switchbacks across the steeper terrain above Kip Creek.

Running Owl Mountain can be glimpsed intermittently through scattered trees as the trail climbs to 7,200 feet on the western shoulder of the mountain. Bullshoe Mountain raises its 8,000-foot head to the west. Bullshoe Mountain is on the route of proposed trail construction that will take future hikers along a more direct route (closer to the physical Divide) from Elk Calf Mountain to Bullshoe, with a tie-in trail to Running Owl Mountain.

There is ample water along the loop around Running Owl Mountain as hikers follow first one creek drainage and then another. The entire loop of Trail 141 is 7.4 miles long. Information from the Rocky Mountain Ranger District gives its length as 6 miles, but I think they underestimated the distance. It is considerably shorter, only 4.9 miles, to stay on Jeep Track 103 to the Badger Ranger Station, but you'll miss some good views and the pleasure of being on a foot/horse path instead of a 4WD road.

Lee Creek Trail 141 comes back into North Fork Badger Trail 103 at mile 19.4 for this segment. From here it is only 0.5 mile to the Badger Ranger Station. For northbound hikers, the trail bends west/northwest to follow the South Fork of the Two Medicine River. You'll encounter aspen trees and grassy meadows filled with wild flowers in late June and July. Wild strawberry plants are abundant. The trail becomes 101/Two Medicine at the ranger station.

Various trails and 4WD roads enter Trail 101 from the northeast, including Whiterock Trail 102, but none of these are part of the CDT trail system. These trails can be used, however, as access points to the CDT from the northeastern border of the Lewis & Clark National Forest. There is also a signed intersection with Woods Creek Trail 140, East Fork of Woods Creek Trail 170, and Two Medicine Ridge (3 miles to the north/northwest); CDT trekkers stay on Trail 101, the South Fork Two Medicine Trail.

SUPPLIES, SERVICES, AND ACCOMMODATIONS

CHOTEAU, MT, is on Highway 89, and provides all services. The city of Browning, on the Blackfeet Indian Reservation, is 38 miles north of Swift Dam Road, on Hwy. 89. There are no supplies and services near the trail, and none near the Swift Dam Trailhead.

Distance from Trail: 56 miles (20 miles on Swift Dam Road, and 36 miles on Hwy. 89)

Zip Code: 59422

Bank:	Citizens State Bank, 201 Main Avenue N.	406-466-5743
Bus:	None	
Camping:	KOA Kampgrounds, East of Choteau (sign on Hwy. 89)	406-466-2615
	Eureka Reservoir, on Canyon Road, north of Choteau, toilets and tables, no showers	
Dining:	The Buckaroo, 202 Main Avenue N.	406-466-2667
	Choteau Seafood & Steakhouse, 210 Main Avenue	406-466-5233
	Outpost Deli, 819 7th Ave. N.W.	406-466-5330
	John Henry's, 215 Main Avenue N.	406-466-5642
Gear:	Coast to Coast, 406 Main Avenue S.	406-466-2191
Groceries:	Neighborhood Grocery, 415 2nd Avenue N.W.	406-466-2776
	Rex's Market, 29 1st Street N.E.	406-466-2927
Information:	Visitors Center on Hwy. 89 (no phone); or the combination Mayor's Office/ Chamber of Commerce/Main Connection Tourist Travel; also see Best Western Stage Stop Inn.	406-466-5316
Laundry:	Next door to Western Star Motel, on Main Ave., has no name. Also, see KOA Kampground.	
Lodging:	Best Western Stage Stop Inn, 1005 Main Avenue N., $55, complimentary breakfast, hot tub, indoor pool, guest laundry, tourist information,	406-466-5900
	Bella Vista Motel, 614 Main Avenue N., $35	406-466-5711
	Western Star Motel	406-466-5737
Medical:	Teton Medical Center, 915 4th Street N.W.	406-466-5763
Outfitters:	A Lazy H Outfitters, P.O. Box 729, Choteau, MT 59422	800-893-1155
	7 Lazy P Guest Ranch, P.O. Box 178, Choteau, MT 59422	406-466-2044
	Montana Safaris, P.O. Box 1004, Choteau, MT 59422	406-466-2004
	JJJ Outfitters, P.O. Box 509, Choteau, MT 59422	406-466-2245
Post Office:	U.S. Post Office, 103 1st St. N.W., Choteau, MT 59422	406-466-2362
Showers:	See KOA Kampground	

The South Fork of the Two Medicine River runs below the jeep track that serves as a trail from the Badger Guard Station to the intersection with Elk Calf Mountain Trail 137. In some spots, the river is constricted to a frothing spill of white water as it runs through a rocky gorge. Views to the northwest and upstream include the higher points of the Lewis Overthrust that created the peaks of the Front Range of the Rocky Mountains in Glacier National Park.

The intersection that northbound hikers must watch for is at mile 24.4 (4.5 miles northwest of the Badger Guard Station). When we were there, this intersection was signed, showing Elk Calf Mountain Trail 137 crossing the South Fork of the Two Medicine River and then climbing southwesterly toward the Divide. We saw some black bear sign in this area.

Northbound Hikers will leave Trail 101 at the intersection with Trail 137. Elk Calf Mountain Trail 137 was crisscrossed with deadfall, and difficult to find in places when we were there, but it has since been improved by trail crews. The trail is steep in places as it nears Elk Calf Mountain and climbs toward the Divide. There is a spur trail to the top of Elk Calf Mountain, but the CDT stays just below the summit. In the summer of 1998, about 5,000 acres burned in the Challenge Creek area on the south side of the Divide, near Elk Calf Mountain. The burn can be seen from the CDT.

We hiked this portion of the trail in a combination snow and rain storm, which may explain why we missed the intersection with Trail 133 to the Summit Campground. We knew the CDT should make a turn in order to take hikers to the campground, but we apparently turned too soon. Embarrassingly enough, rangers assure me that the correct turn was not only signed, but that new "turnpiking" (log sills covered with filter cloth and then topped with gravel) and new tread had been constructed to lead hikers to the campground.

Bad weather can play havoc with route-finding. If you get lost in bad weather, just walk toward the train sounds and you'll end up at Hwy. 2. Burlington Northern trains can be heard for about the last 5 miles of the trail. We ended up on the Pike Creek 4WD road that intersects Hwy. 2 just south of the Roosevelt Memorial. From there, it is a short hike northeast on the highway to the campground. At the Summit Campground, I looked for the correct trail again, but could not find it.

SOUTHBOUND HIKERS: Here's hoping the signing at Summit is improved in the future. More signing is planned.

The Summit Campground closes early in the season. It was closed when we were there again on September 3. Freezing temperatures come early this far north and rangers shut down the water system to keep it from bursting. However, backpackers with tents are welcome to cross the closure barriers and camp. Drinking water can be filtered from nearby Summit Creek.

Segment 25
1:100,000 MAP: HUNGRY HORSE RESERVOIR
5/8
SCALE: 5/8 INCH = 1 MILE
1 CM = 1 KM
Continental Divide
Continental Divide Trail (current segment)
Continental Divide Trail (previous and next segments)
River or stream
Lake or pond
Marsh or swamp
Primary highway
Secondary highway
Light duty road
Unimproved road
Trail
Quarry or open mine pit
CONTINENTAL DIVIDE
PASS
137 / 133
Campground
Summit
137 Two Medicine
GLACIER CO
PONDERA CO
FLATHEAD CO
Elk Calf Mtn
137
101
141
Trail under construction, route is approximate
Badger Guard Station
LEWIS AND CLARK NATIONAL FORES
Two Medicine Ridge
Lubec Ridge
RESERVATION BOUNDARY
INDEFINITE BOUNDARY
False Summit
Bison
Mount Baldy
Half Dome Crag
Lookout
T 29 N

Goat Mtn
Square Mountain
Running Owl Mtn
Bruin Peaks
Curly Bear Mountain
Murningstar Mountain
Spotted Eagle Mountain
Patrol Ridge
Slippery Bill Mountain
CONTINENTAL DIVIDE
145
Elbow Mtn
Crescent Cliff
Red Plume Mountain
Lookout
PONDERA CO
FLATHEAD CO
TETON CO
T 28 N
T 27 N
Three Forks
Bear Peak
Cap Mtn
Arrowhead Mountain
Lodgepole Mountain
Wildrose Mtn
Landing Strip
FLATHEAD WILD AND SCENIC RIVER
BOB MARSHALL WILDERNESS
PACK TRAIL

Segment 26
Marias Pass to East Glacier Park

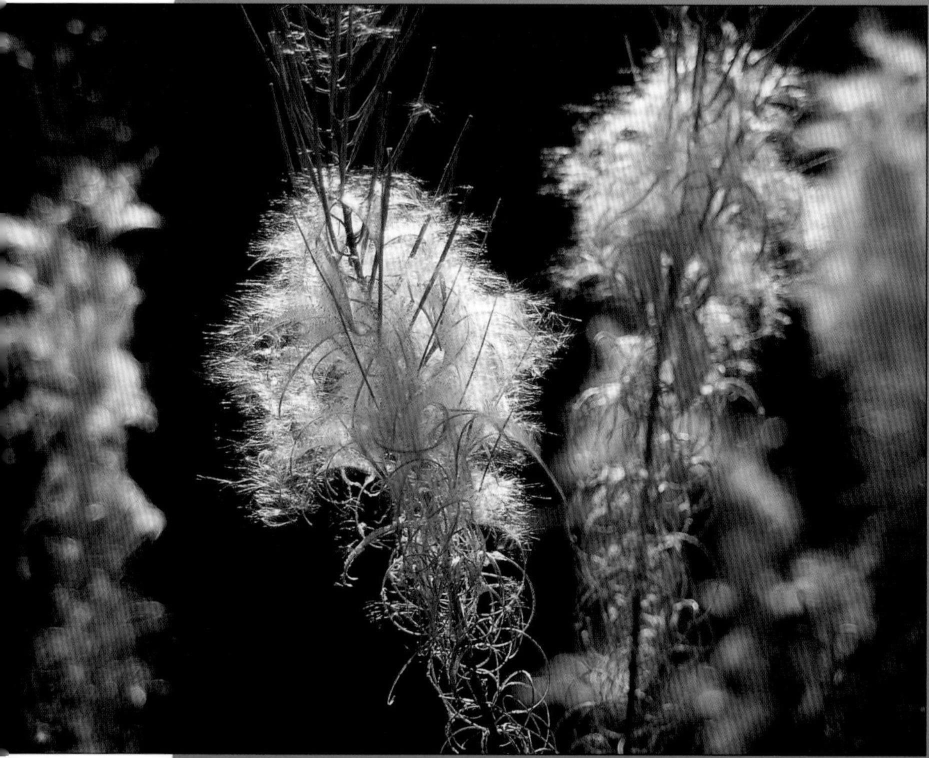

Fireweed in autumn, found along the trail from Marias Pass to East Glacier

15.2 miles, 24.5 km
Difficulty: Easy

Segment 26 **Total Elevation Gain:** 1,190 feet, 362.8 meters
From Wyoming 861.4 miles
To Canada 119.3 miles

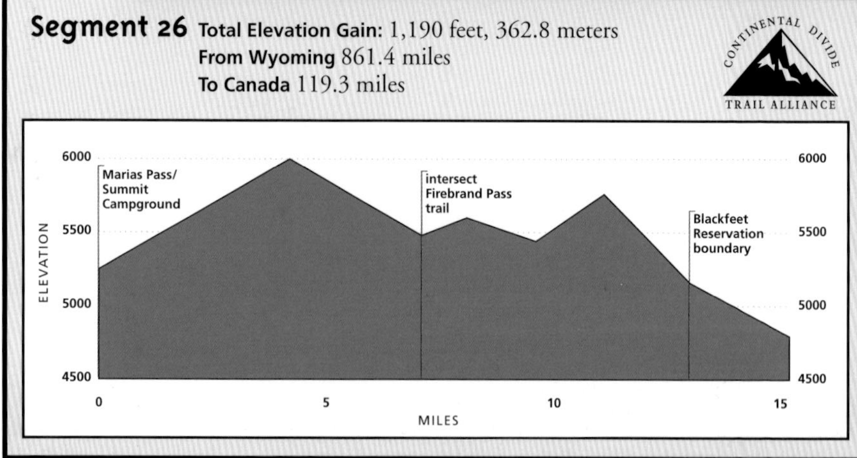

TRAIL OVERVIEW Yikes! You mean I have to have a permit? In this segment, northbound hikers enter Glacier National Park for the first time. Read the National Park Alert below before you hike any farther. Of utmost importance to long-distance trekkers is the requirement for backcountry permits. The Summit/Autumn Creek Trail to East Glacier is in a little-used section of the park, so there is no ranger station nearby. Hopefully, you will have arranged far in advance for your backcountry permit. If not, you're faced with how to reach the nearest ranger station, which is at Two Medicine, some 25 highway miles away. Here is the best plan:

1. Northbound hikers should begin the Marias Pass to East Glacier segment early in the morning so you can complete the 15.2-mile (24.5-km) hike in one day. No permits are required for dayhiking. You end up in East Glacier at the end of the day, a small burg with an astounding array of eateries, espresso shops, lodging options—and a post office where you can pick up resupplies that you mailed to yourself.
2. Eat yourself into a pleasant stupor and find cheap lodgings.
3. East Glacier is an excellent place from which to catch a ride to Two Medicine. There are also buses from Glacier Lodge to Two Medicine. Pick up your permit at the Two Medicine ranger station, allowing time to watch the mandatory instructional video.
4. Take the bus back to East Glacier, pick up your belongings, and dayhike 10.4 miles to the Two Medicine Campground via the official route of the CDT, the Scenic Point Trail.
5. Pitch your tent at the Two Medicine Auto Campground. You are now in the Park to Beat all Parks, you have a license to hike, and the scenery beckons like your best dreams.

When we hiked the trail, this segment did not entirely live up to Glacier National Park standards. Intersections were well-marked, but the trail itself was little-used. Stream crossings were not bridged, so the trail dipped into muddy ravine after muddy ravine, and was overgrown in places. But if you've already hiked hundreds of miles on the CDT, it's not bad. Any trail is better than none.

Since we hiked the trail, Glacier's trail crews have cleared the brush from Marias Pass to the Firebrand Pass Trail intersection. Extensive tread work was also done. Additional upgrades were planned.

From Marias Pass to East Glacier, look for the metal cross-country ski trail tags hung on trees. Some of these metal markers have been in place since the 1930s and are faded, but they may be your only guide to finding the trail.

The trail stays in the low country on the east side of the Front Range of the Rocky Mountains, so the scenery here is pedestrian compared to the rest of the CDT in the park.

I normally don't carry a groundcloth for my tent, but I recommend that you do so in Glacier National Park, as the assigned campsites are often rocky and muddy. Glacier's literature claims that each campsite is large enough for four people, but we found that most sites could not accommodate two of our two-person tents. Getting an early start to reach a campground in the afternoon results in a better selection of campsites. Be prepared for enforced social activity in the "food preparation" areas of each campsite. You need a good backpacking stove for trekking in the park.

In almost every way imaginable, Glacier National Park is an exception to the rest of the Montana/Idaho Continental Divide Trail:

- The trails are marked with indestructible signs that also give the distance to every conceivable destination. Paved highways provide access to the trailheads.
- A system of seasonal and permanent bridges crosses the major streams and rivers, eliminating most fords.
- There are actually other human beings, not just animals, on the trail.
- Glacier National Park has gone metric, so switch your mind and your hiking time estimates to kilometers. (Ten kilometers equals 6.21 miles.)

RESERVATION LAND USE ALERT

The CDT crosses about 5 miles of Blackeet Tribal Lands near East Glacier, on the Autumn Creek and the Scenic Point trails. A Blackfeet Tribal Conservation/Recreation Use Permit is required for all recreational uses, including backpacking. The fee is $5 annually (good for one year). The permit can be obtained at most shops in East Glacier Park, as well as the grocery store on Hwy. 2. For further information, contact Blackfeet Fish and Wildlife, 406-338-7207.

MOUNTAIN BIKE NOTES: This segment lies mostly within Glacier National Park, where mountain bikes are prohibited.

LAND ADMINISTRATORS (SEE APPENDIX A)

National Park Service, Glacier National Park
Blackfeet Tribal Council, Browning, MT

MAPS

USGS QUADRANGLES: Summit, Squaw Mountain, East Glacier Park

TRAILS ILLUSTRATED: Glacier National Park/Waterton Lakes National Park, Montana and Alberta

U.S. PARK SERVICE: Glacier National Park Visitors' Map

BEGINNING ACCESS POINT

MARIAS PASS ON HIGHWAY 2

ENDING ACCESS POINT

EAST GLACIER PARK, intersection of highways 2 and 49

NATIONAL PARK ALERT

In Glacier National Park, the vast complex of the Rocky Mountains narrows as if a tightly cinched belt were pulled across its girth. From high points along the Continental Divide Trail, hikers can look down on the nearby western prairies. The Livingston Range to the west and the Lewis Range to the east run roughly north/south through the park, with only about 5 miles separating the two parallel spines of rock. These ranges exacerbate sudden, drastic changes in the weather, so hikers must be prepared for cold temperatures at any time of year. Yellowstone National Park is twice as big as Glacier, but Glacier's vastly differing ecozones result in greater plant diversity. Glacier boasts naturally occurring populations of grizzly bears, mountain lions, and wolves. Read the animal avoidance tips in "Safety Concerns" before you hike in Glacier, and see the history, natural environment, planning, climate, and geology sections at the beginning of this book for more information on Glacier National Park.

To obtain a copy of Glacier National Park's Backcountry Camping Policies, call 406-888-7800, or write to National Park Service, Glacier National Park, West Glacier, Montana 59936. Web: www.nps.gov/glac

Here is a brief summary of Glacier's policies:

- Camping is restricted to designated and assigned campsites.
- Advance reservation forms are processed beginning on May 1 of each hiking season. Forms must be accompanied by payment of applicable fees ($20 per itinerary).
- Noncontiguous itineraries are not permitted. (If you have rest breaks or other excursions planned that will cause your CDT trek to be non-contiguous, you can file for two or more separate itineraries.)
- Wood fires are prohibited in most backcountry campsites.
- All food and other attractants must be hung beyond the reach of bears. Bring 25 feet of rope.
- Stock use is limited and special restrictions apply. Request the "Private Stock Use" pamphlet.
- Pets are not allowed on backcountry trails and must be leashed in auto campgrounds.
- There are vehicle size/length limits on Going-to-the-Sun Road.

SUPPLIES, SERVICES, AND ACCOMMODATIONS

EAST GLACIER PARK, MT, is on highways 2 and 49. It is a small town, but has most of the services you will need.

Distance from Trail: 12 miles from Marias Pass

Zip Code: 59434

Bank:	None, ATM machine at the Exxon Station on Hwy. 2, and in Glacier Park Lodge	
Bus:	None, but Amtrak has a train station, 400 Hwy. 49 N.	406-226-4452
Camping:	Y Lazy R Campground and Laundromat, southwest side of town on Hwy. 2	406-226-5573
	Firebrand Campgrounds/Laundromat, milepost 206, Hwy. 2 (3 miles southwest of town)	
	Red Eagle Campground, Lower Two Medicine Lake (4 miles north of town)	
Dining:	Two Medicine Grill, 314 Hwy. 2	406-226-5572
	Serranos Mexican Restaurant, 29 Dawson Avenue	406-226-9392
	Blondies, 33 Dawson Avenue	406-226-9200
	Summit Station Restaurant, Hwy. 2	406-226-4428
	Whistle Stop Restaurant, 1020 Hwy. 49	406-226-4426
Gear:	Limited gear is available at the grocery store.	
Groceries:	Glacier Park Trading Company (also has USGS maps, Avis rental cars, espresso), 316 Hwy. 2, www.glacierrepublic.com	406-226-4433
Information:	The Mountain Pine Motel, P.O. Box 260, Hwy. 49, north of Glacier Lodge	406-226-4403
Laundry:	See Y Lazy R Campground and Firebrand Campground	
Lodging:	Backpackers Motel, behind Serranos Restaurant, Hwy. 2, $10	406-226-9392
	Mountain Pine Motel, Hwy. 49 (north of Glacier Park Lodge), $50	406-226-4403
	Glacier Park Lodge (closes 9/26), Hwy. 49, $114–$206	602-207-6000
	Glacier Park, Inc., Central Reservations, Phoenix AZ	602-207-6000
Medical:	None; call Park Service in case of emergencies.	406-888-7800
Outfitters:	Montana Raft Company and Glacier Wilderness Guides (sherpa and guide services in the Park), Box 535, West Glacier, MT 59936,	
	E-mail: glguides@cyberport.net	1-800-521-RAFT
	Web: www.travelfile.com/get?glguides	406-387-5555
Post Office:	U.S. Post Office, P.O. Box 9998, 34 Dawson Avenue, 59434-9998	406-226-5534
Showers:	See Camping	

TRAIL DESCRIPTION The beginning of this trail is directly across from the Roosevelt Memorial and Summit Campground at Marias Pass. Cross Hwy. 2 and then cross the Burlington Northern Railroad tracks. Look for a little-used vehicle crossing, a large antenna pole, and a small, wooden footbridge crossing the stream. The trail is definitely not obvious at this point, being mostly overgrown. Orange metal markers on the trees indicate that this trail is also a cross-country ski trail. There is a white, snow-depth marker near the trail's beginning.

Hike southwest (parallel to the railroad tracks) for a short distance, following the yellow and orange markers. Tread improves in the trees. The character of the trail changes dramatically at the border of Glacier National Park, where it becomes quite clear and hikers see the first of many high-quality trail signs, typical of the national park. Here also is your first example of many regulation signs to come: "Camping permit required, bicycles not permitted, horses permitted, dogs and motorcycles not permitted, firearms not permitted, grizzly bear warning," and so forth. A rare, blue-and-white Continental Divide Trail sign is posted where the trail enters the park.

Just beyond the park boundary, there is an intersection with a cross-country ski trail that parallels the railroad track. The CDT continues west on the Summit Trail, crossing the southern end of Three Bears Lake on a manmade dike.

At 1.5 km, a signed intersection shows the southern loop that goes back to Hwy. 2. CDT hikers turn north (right) here on the Autumn Creek Trail. From this intersection, it is 23 km (14.3 miles) to East Glacier. The many stream crossings were relatively easy in September, but we could see from the eroded banks that snowmelt would swell the streams to serious obstacles for early-season hikers.

Hikers reach the highest point (if "highest" can be used to describe this nearly flat trail) at mile 4.2 (6.8 km) below Summit Mountain, an 8,770-foot peak west of the trail. The trail also crosses a closely spaced series of five minor tributaries of Summit Creek in the same area.

At 11.5 km (7.1 miles) from Marias Pass, the Autumn Creek Trail intersects the Firebrand Pass Trail. For a short distance, the quality of the trail improves markedly, showing the effects of hikers who use the Lubec Trailhead to access the Firebrand Pass/Ole Lake area. Hikers are now 13 km from East Glacier. The Autumn Creek Trail and the Firebrand Pass Trail are one and the same here, so northbound hikers turn left (north-westerly) on the Firebrand Pass Trail.

The trail to East Glacier soon diverges from the Firebrand Pass Trail (at mile 8.1). Northbound hikers keep right (north) on the Autumn Creek Trail. The forest is less dense along this section of trail. Scattered trees and open meadows offer pastoral views to the east. From this intersection northward, the trail was so faint that it was just like old times back on the Montana/Idaho border, where we regularly had to scout for the trail. Since we hiked this area, the rangers have planned improvements, so the trail should be easier to find for future hikers.

Elevation changes are minor for the rest of the hike, with a gentle descent to cross Railroad Creek and a 300-foot climb to a bench below Squaw Mountain. The last 4 miles of this segment are all gently downhill.

At the Glacier National Park/Blackfeet Indian Reservation boundary (mile 13) near East Glacier, the trail is signed with a CD symbol. That makes two CD signs, one at each end of the portion of the trail that passes through the park. Signs here say, "East Glacier Ranger Station, 3.5 km; 21 km to Marias Pass." When we were there, the East Glacier Ranger Station was not manned. It is not a permit-issuing station. We saw quite a bit of black bear sign in this area, about 2 miles from town, and the aspen parklands were full of ruffed grouse.

On Blackfeet Indian Reservation lands, the trail becomes a two-track and then a road, with the quality of the road improving as you near the town of East Glacier. There is a Y-shaped intersection on the road that will not bother northbound hikers, but southbound hikers will have to remember to keep left (southwesterly), as the intersection is not signed. Cross-country ski trail markers can also be used to choose the correct route.

The route of the CDT passes behind (west) of the biggest hotel in East Glacier, the Glacier Park Lodge, on Hwy. 49. The trail first crosses a bridge over Midvale Creek, then goes gently uphill toward a golf course behind the lodge. Midvale Creek Road becomes 4th Avenue, which passes along the golf course behind the hotel. From this point, hikers can see the town and can make their way through the streets to the main street (Hwy. 49). More grocery stores, restaurants, gas stations, and motels are located east of the lodge at the intersection of highways 49 and 2. Glacier Lodge is reached at mile 15.2 (24.5 km).

S **SOUTHBOUND HIKERS:** Finding the Autumn Creek Trail near East Glacier Park is difficult. The Glacier Park Lodge or the Mountain Pine Motel can be used as a landmark. Go behind the lodge and west of the golf course. As you go south on 4th Avenue, it becomes Midvale Creek Road. Cross the bridge over Midvale Creek and proceed gently uphill for a short distance. Watch carefully on your right (west) for a single orange marker on a rough road. This is the first right-hand turn south of the bridge. You are still on reservation land here, so the trail is an unsigned road.

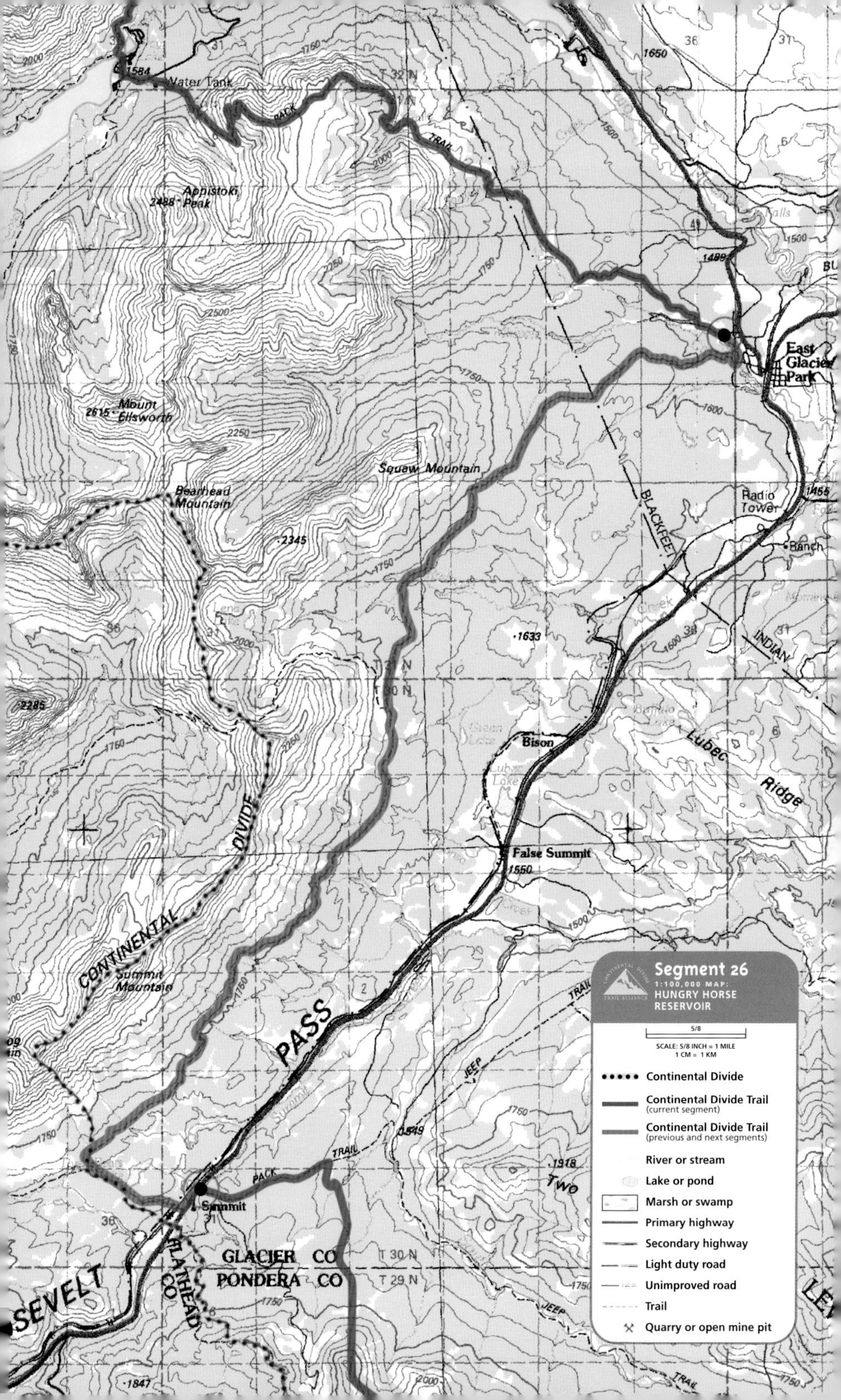

Segment 26
1:100,000 MAP:
HUNGRY HORSE
RESERVOIR
SCALE: 5/8 INCH = 1 MILE
1 CM = 1 KM
Continental Divide
Continental Divide Trail (current segment)
Continental Divide Trail (previous and next segments)
River or stream
Lake or pond
Marsh or swamp
Primary highway
Secondary highway
Light duty road
Unimproved road
Trail
Quarry or open mine pit
Water Tank
Appistoki Peak
Mount Ellsworth
Squaw Mountain
Bearhead Mountain
East Glacier Park
Radio Tower
Ranch
BLACKFEET
INDIAN
Lubec Ridge
Bison
False Summit
CONTINENTAL
DIVIDE
Summit Mountain
PASS
Summit
GLACIER CO
PONDERA CO
FLATHEAD CO
T 30 N
T 29 N
T 32 N
T 31 N
Two
PACK TRAIL
JEEP

Segment 27
East Glacier Park to Two Medicine Campground: Glacier National Park

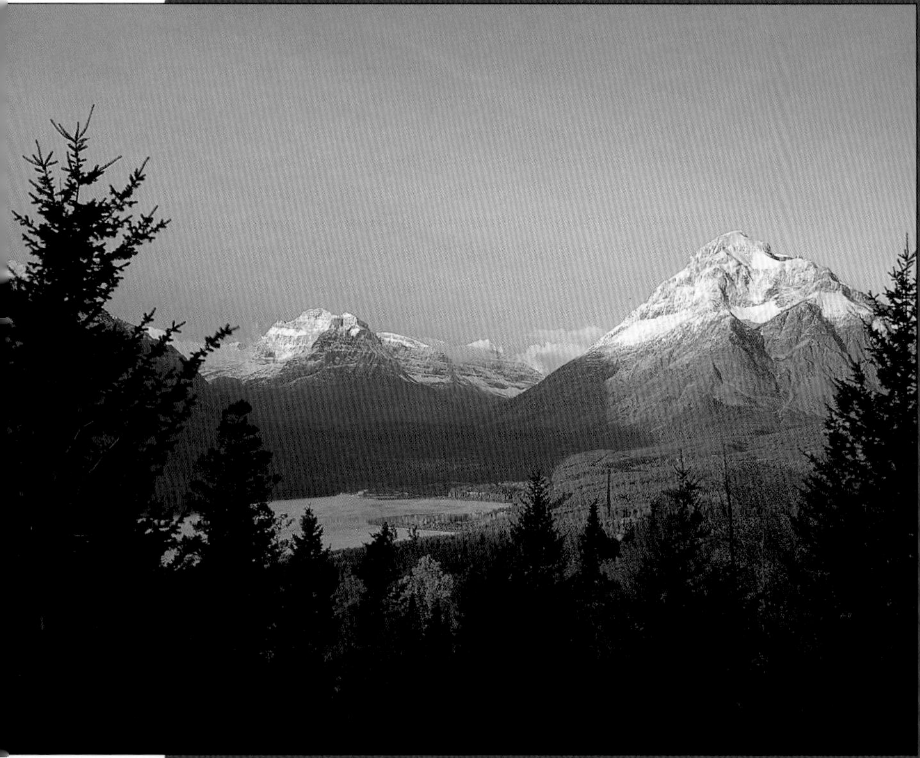

Lofty peaks surround Two Medicine Lake in Glacier National Park.

10.5 miles, 12.31 km
Difficulty: Moderate

Segment 27 **Total Elevation Gain:** 2,605 feet, 794 meters
From Wyoming 876.6 miles
To Canada 103.3 miles

CONTINENTAL DIVIDE TRAIL ALLIANCE

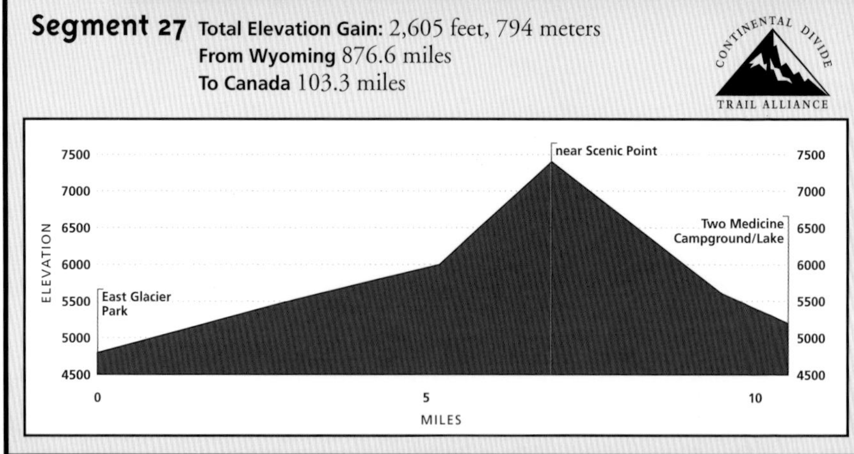

TRAIL OVERVIEW The Scenic Point/Mount Henry Trail climbs from 4,795 feet in East Glacier Park to 7,400 feet on the shoulder of Scenic Point. From the Point, the trail crosses a high saddle and then descends to the trailhead on the highway east of the Two Medicine Ranger Station. Lower Two Medicine Lake and Two Medicine Lake can both be seen from high points along this trail, and the view of Rising Wolf Mountain, Appistoki Peak, and a ring of other peaks is the first taste of Glacier's grandeur for northbound hikers. To the west, hikers can see all the way to Dawson Pass. To the east, the town of Browning on the Blackfeet Reservation is visible. As you near your destination at the Two Medicine Campground, Appistoki Falls is a short side trip worth taking.

Dry winds literally roar like jet planes as they sweep over the arid, alpine zone of barren Scenic Point. When we hiked across the saddle west of the point, gusty winds blew so strongly that we almost resorted to crawling. The danger of being blown over the cliffs on the north face was real. These winds are frequent and have shaped the vegetation below the point into twisted, ground-hugging krummholz that offers little protection to hikers. Winds of 80 miles per hour have been recorded on this ridge.

Proterozoic algae that pumped oxygen into the earth's oxygen-poor atmosphere half-a-billion years ago left their imprint in the Altyn dolomite along this section of trail. Extraordinarily well-preserved fossils of this algae can be seen in the cream-colored rocks east of Scenic Point. These "stromatolites" look like faded versions of the mad swirls in a Van Gogh painting. Algae accumulates in mats and the resultant fossils look like swirls, domes, fans or branches. The stromatolites east of Scenic Point are the swirled variety. You can walk up to them and put your hand on the signature of the algae that made all other forms of life on earth possible.

Water sources are adequate, but not plentiful in this segment. Fortymile and Fortyone Mile Creeks are crossed in the first 5 miles, and Appistoki Creek is near the end of the segment.

Be sure to review the rules and regulations that apply to hiking in Glacier National Park (see Segment 26).

MOUNTAIN BIKE NOTES: This segment lies mostly within Glacier National Park, where mountain bikes are prohibited.

LAND ADMINISTRATORS **(SEE APPENDIX A)**

National Park Service, Glacier National Park
Blackfeet Tribal Council, Browning, MT

MAPS

USGS QUADRANGLES: East Glacier Park, Squaw Mountain
TRAILS ILLUSTRATED: Glacier National Park/Waterton Lakes National Park, Montana and Alberta
U.S. PARK SERVICE: Glacier National Park Visitors' Map

BEGINNING ACCESS POINT

EAST GLACIER PARK, intersection of highways 2 and 49

ENDING ACCESS POINT

TWO MEDICINE CAMPGROUND

SUPPLIES, SERVICES, AND ACCOMMODATIONS

See **EAST GLACIER PARK, MT**, Segment 26.

TRAIL DESCRIPTION The trailhead near East Glacier is difficult to find. From Highway 49, go west on Midvale Creek Road to an intersection with Clark Drive. Clark Drive leads directly to the boundary of Glacier National Park. There are no trail signs in or near the town proper. Where you exit the Blackfeet Indian Reservation lands and enter Glacier National Park, the trail is well-signed. The only CDT sign in this segment is at the Glacier National Park/Blackfeet Reservation border. The trail is also signed as "Mount Henry."

The first few miles of trail are through grass, aspen parklands, and scattered trees. We saw ample evidence of bear activity. (Review the bear avoidance tips.)

The first available water is in Fortyone Mile Creek at mile 4.2. Fortymile Creek is crossed, as you might expect, at mile 5.2. The remainder of the hike is dry until you arrive at Appistoki Creek.

Once you gain some elevation, the dangers of getting lost are nil. Hikers can see Glacier Lodge, their departure point for this section, and the northern end of the Bob Marshall Wilderness. Closer to the terminus of the segment you can even see the flag on the ranger station at Two Medicine. Orienteering is not a factor.

The trail climbs steadily through drier and rockier terrain. Switchbacks lead up the eastern slopes of Scenic Point. A long ridge-walk along the curving massif of Scenic Point provides spectacular views, eventually bringing Rising Wolf Mountain and Two Medicine Lake into view.

Steeper terrain above Appistoki Creek requires another set of switchbacks. The short spur trail to Appistoki Falls is signed, so you can't miss it. Near the highway, the trail descends through trees that limit the view, reaching the Mount Henry/Scenic Point Trailhead at mile 10. From the trailhead, walk 0.5 mile west on the highway to the Two Medicine Ranger Station, and beyond that, to the Two Medicine Campground.

Segment 27
1:100,000 MAP:
HUNGRY HORSE RESERVOIR
5/8
SCALE: 5/8 INCH = 1 MILE
1 CM = 1 KM
Continental Divide
Continental Divide Trail (current segment)
Continental Divide Trail (previous and next segments)
River or stream
Lake or pond
Marsh or swamp
Primary highway
Secondary highway
Light duty road
Unimproved road
Trail
Quarry or open mine pit
Water Tank
Appistoki Peak
2488
Mount Ellsworth
2615
Squaw Mountain
Bearhead Mountain
2345
BLACKFEET
INDIAN
Radio Tower
East Glacier Park
Bison
False Summit
1550
Lubec Ridge
CONTINENTAL
DIVIDE
Summit Mountain
PASS
JEEP
PACK
TRAIL
Summit
Two
GLACIER CO
PONDERA CO
T 30 N
T 29 N
T 32 N
T 31 N
INDEFINITE
2164
1918
1489
1650
1584

Segment 28 Two Medicine Campground to St. Mary Falls: Glacier National Park

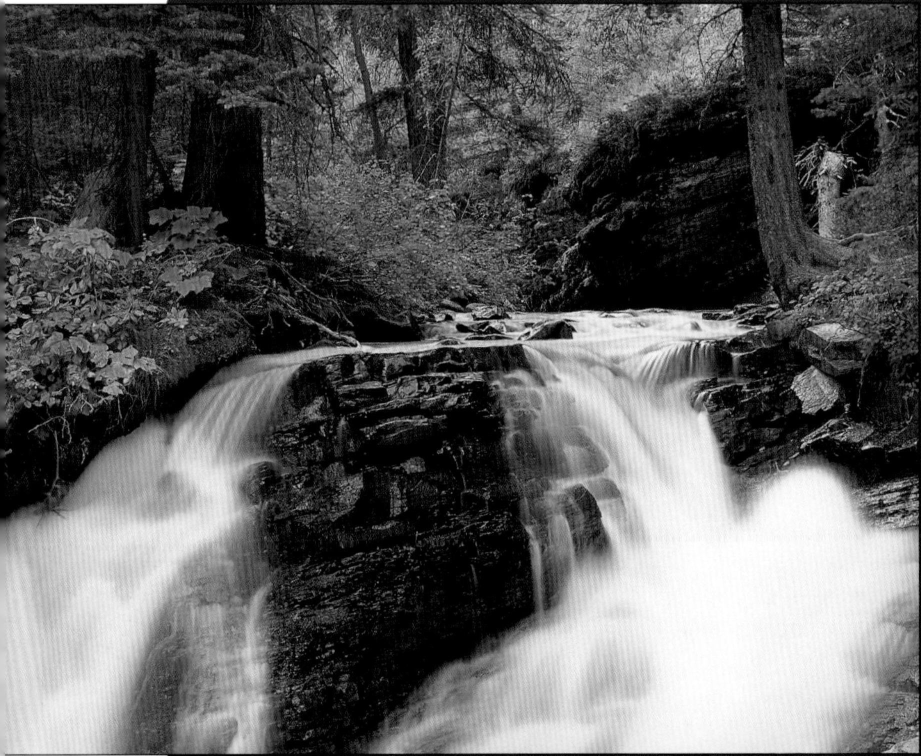

The CDT crosses Virginia Falls on wooden bridges in Glacier National Park.

38.7 miles, 62.28 km
Difficulty: Strenuous

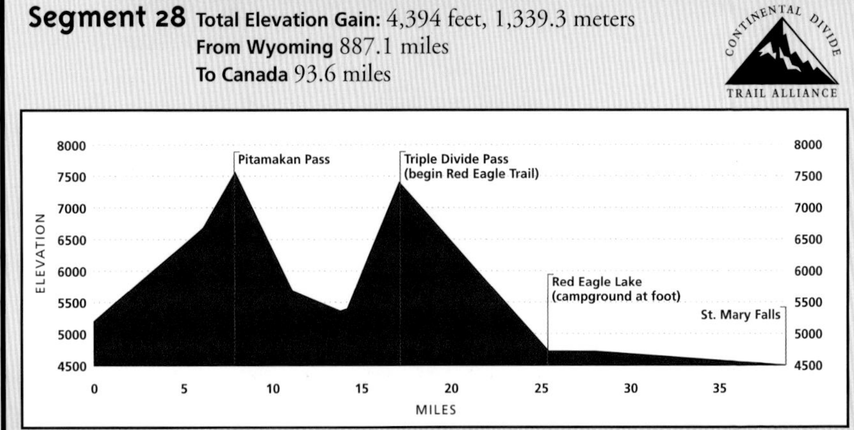

TRAIL OVERVIEW When we checked in at the Two Medicine Ranger Station, we discovered that one of the campgrounds on our itinerary, Morning Star, was closed due to grizzly bear activity. We could hike through the area, but couldn't camp. Volunteer staff at the station helped us reorganize the hike to include Oldman Lake as an alternative. Grizzly activity can force trail and campground closures at any time.

In sparse vegetation above the Triple Divide Pass Trail, we almost collided with a sow grizzly and cub. Strong winds from the pass blew away the sound of our approach. We rounded a corner of the trail and there she was. Luckily, she decided we were of no interest and ambled on. The spur trail to Medicine Grizzly Lake was closed due to bear activity and the entire area around Morning Star Lake had been rototilled by bears rooting for rodents. When we arrived at Red Eagle Lake Campground, two rangers greeted us with "Well, I see you made it out alive." (Be sure to review bear avoidance techniques.)

Backcountry permits are required in Glacier National Park. Permits must be picked up in person, no sooner than the day before your departure date. Permits not picked up by 10:00 a.m. are deleted from the system. See Segment 27 for tips on arranging permits.

"Dry Fork" was not dry when we were there, but even when its lower reaches are dry, numerous waterfalls still decorate the cliffs that hold the trail in a tight embrace. Long waterfalls from Boy Lake and Young Man Lake stream from the flanks of Rising Wolf Mountain. The trail frequently crosses streams from the massif of Red Mountain and Spot Mountain to the north. Oldman Lake provides both drinking water and fishing opportunities. Farther north, the trail parallels Hudson Bay Creek and Red Eagle Creek. Remember to fill water bottles before you tackle Pitamakan Pass and Triple Divide Pass.

The panoramas are breathtaking. Plan for fewer miles per day so that you have time to admire the awesome terrain.

Triple Divide Pass is more than a scenic wonder—it is a geological marvel. Waters from this pass drain indirectly to the Pacific Ocean, the Atlantic Ocean, and Hudson Bay. That mention of Hudson Bay should remind you how far north you have come. Be prepared for cold weather, including snow.

MOUNTAIN BIKE NOTES: This segment lies entirely within Glacier National Park, where mountain bikes are prohibited.

LAND ADMINISTRATORS (SEE APPENDIX A)

National Park Service, Glacier National Park

MAPS

USGS QUADRANGLES: Squaw Mountain, Kiowa, Cut Bank Pass, Mount Stimson, Rising Sun, Logan Pass

TRAILS ILLUSTRATED: Glacier National Park/Waterton Lakes National Park, Montana and Alberta

U.S. PARK SERVICE: Glacier National Park Visitors' Map

BEGINNING ACCESS POINT

OLDMAN LAKE/NORTH SHORE TRHD: Drive west on Two Medicine Road from Hwy. 49.

ENDING ACCESS POINT

ST. MARY FALLS: Look for the signed, paved parking lot south of Going-to-the-Sun Road, at the head of St. Mary Lake.

SUPPLIES, SERVICES, AND ACCOMMODATIONS

See Segment 26 for **EAST GLACIER PARK, MT.**

Distance from Trail: 13 miles

Special Notes: The Two Medicine Campstore & Campground is on Two Medicine Road, near the Ranger Station, 0.2 mile from the trailhead. The camp store offers groceries, fishing tackle, camping supplies, sundries, and a snack bar.

TRAIL DESCRIPTION

The Oldman Lake/North Shore Trailhead is at the end of the parking lot below Rising Wolf Mountain at Two Medicine Campground. Cross a bridge over the stream that connects Two Medicine Lake and tiny Pray Lake. Trails to Upper Two Medicine Lake, Dawson Pass, and other destinations also begin at the North Shore Trailhead.

The first mile of trail is through spruce and pine forest, with occasional views of Lower Two Medicine Lake. An easy, mostly flat walk on a trail kept in excellent condition leads to the Dry Fork Creek drainage. The first of many waterfalls in this segment is an outlet from Sky Lake on Rising Wolf Mountain, at mile 1.5.

At mile 2.4, a junction with Dry Fork Trail is well-signed with the usual Glacier Park thoroughness, giving the distance in kilometers to all conceivable destinations. Stunted aspen trees add variety to the terrain in the open area around the trail junction. The route is marked with stone cairns, although the tread is still visible.

At mile 6.1, a spur trail leads 0.3 mile to Oldman Lake and the campground. The lake sits in a nicely rounded cirque below Mount Morgan. We thought the tent sites at Oldman Lake were too small for two tents, but we found sites even smaller at Atlantic Falls further north.

The next morning, as we climbed to Pitamakan Pass, a minuscule round break in the clouds allowed the sun to spotlight the cliffs above the lake, the light moving with the shifting clouds until it came to rest on a band of grazing bighorn sheep near Pitamakan Overlook.

From Pitamakan Pass, mile 7.9, hikers get a view that includes the sources of most of the waterfalls and four layers of mountains marching to the north. The pass is signed right, left, and straight ahead, so you can't get lost. Dawson Pass Trail, Cut Bank Pass, and Pitamakan Overlook are other options. The overlook is worth a look as it is the highest point offered near the CDT route. This serene, alpine environment is only 8,248 feet high, but looks and feels like a 12,000-foot peak.

Below Pitamakan Lake, the trail enters stands of stunted spruce and subalpine fir. The meadows sport "spring" flowers into September. The forest is thicker and trees are back to normal size when you reach Morning Star Lake at mile 11.1. Above this lake, a strong expression of the Continental Divide as an unbroken line of cliffs makes it hard to tell where Razor Edge Mountain ends and Tinkham Mountain begins.

When we were there in early September, trail crews had already removed the seasonal bridge across the outlet below Morning Star Lake. Luckily, the ford was shallow, but still no fun on a cold day. North of Morning Star Lake, as the trail continues to descend along the North Fork of Cut Bank Creek, a 1,200-foot waterfall pours down the cliffs on the east side of the Divide.

At mile 13.8, the CDT intersects the Triple Divide Trail, 0.4 mile from the Atlantic Creek campground. From this intersection, it is 3.3 miles to Triple Divide Pass to the west, and Red Eagle Lake Campground is 11.6 miles. The distance from Atlantic Creek to Red Eagle Lake makes for a perfect day's hike, with time to admire the view from Triple Divide Pass.

From the trail up to Triple Divide Pass, Medicine Grizzly Peak can be viewed in all its glory, with Medicine Grizzly Lake below. As usual, multiple waterfalls streak the cliffs leading down into the cirque that holds the lake. The trail is one long incline all the way up, with no switchbacks and few bends, reaching the pass at mile 17.1.

On the north side of Triple Divide Pass, snowdrifts linger all year long. Waterfalls and streams cut under them so that it looks like blue, glowing lights have been set up under the water-carved drifts. Small glaciers wink white on Norris Mountain.

Once down off the pass, water is plentiful. Thick brush and grass almost cover the trail as it descends the Hudson Bay Creek valley east of Split Mountain. The thick brush can screen bears and hikers from each other, so remember to make some noise on the descent. This section of the trail is little-used. We were the only hikers on the trail and the only campers at Red Eagle Lake.

At lower elevations near Red Eagle Lake, we passed through some old-growth forest. In the shade of the big trees were watermelon berries, raspberries, and thimble berries, which made for good trailside snacks. The stand of dense, moss-hung trees is only about 0.5 mile long and soon gives way to more open country near the confluence of Hudson Bay Creek and Red Eagle Creek. A log bridge crosses Red Eagle Creek and the trail descends into a stand of deciduous trees at elevation 4,800 feet.

Downstream, a suspension bridge crosses the rushing water at the confluence of the two creeks, both of which looked more like rivers. With the seasonal bridge removed, the ford would be dangerous. The force of the water has eroded the rocks into ribbon-candy shapes reminiscent of slot canyons in Utah.

A campground at the head of Red Eagle Lake is open to stock use. The campground at the foot is roomier and the setting is beautiful. Red Eagle Mountain dominates the western horizon, with Mahotopa Mountain, Little

Chief Mountain, and Almost a Dog Mountain backing it up in succeeding waves of high, bare ridges. To the southwest, looking past the head of the lake, Logan and Red Eagle glaciers gleam on the slope of Mount Logan. When we hiked out the next morning, there were fresh black bear prints overlaying the prints of the rangers who had come to check on us.

There is a horse ford and a suspension bridge at the St. Mary Falls trail intersection, mile 28. The continuation of the CDT northwesterly on the St. Mary Trail is faint, nearly disappearing in tall grass. The tread improves where the trail climbs to top a glacial moraine, but is not well-used and clear of brush until hikers emerge into touristville near Virginia Falls. Look back over your shoulder to see the last good views from the top of the moraine—Curly Bear Mountain and Triple Divide Pass. The trail descends into lodgepole pine forest as it approaches the St. Mary Lake shore.

Droves of tourists provide culture shock from Virginia Falls to the intersection with the Piegan Pass Trail (mile 38.7). It is only 1.8 miles from the Going-to-the-Sun Road to Virginia Falls, so tourists hike the pleasant trail past multiple waterfalls on Virginia Creek and St. Mary River.

Reynolds Creek Campground, near Deadwood Falls, is reserved for CDT and other long-distance trekkers who need an intermediate stop between Red Eagle Lake and Many Glacier. It cannot be used on the first or last night of an extended itinerary.

OTHER EXCURSIONS

THE GOING-TO-THE-SUN ROAD is an experience not to be missed. This engineering marvel is narrow and twisting as it passes over "The Crown of the Continent" at Logan Pass. Vehicle length and width restrictions apply. The road closes, usually in late September, before the winter snows begin their annual procedure of burying it under 80 feet of the white stuff. Hiking, skiing, or mountain biking the road in October is a great trip—no cars, and all that gorgeous scenery. The 50-mile road crosses the park from east to west and is accessible via paved highways at both ends.

A waterfall on an outlet stream from Sky Lake cascades near the CDT as the trail travels north from Two Medicine Lake to Oldman Lake. There are multiple waterfalls on this route, marking the outlets from cirque lakes.

Segment 28
1:100,000 MAPS:
HUNGRY HORSE RES.
and SAINT MARY
CONTINENTAL DIVIDE TRAIL ALLIANCE
5/8
SCALE: 5/8 INCH = 1 MILE
1 CM = 1 KM
Continental Divide
Continental Divide Trail
(current segment)
Continental Divide Trail
(previous and next segments)
River or stream
Lake or pond
Marsh or swamp
Primary highway
Secondary highway
Light duty road
Unimproved road
Trail
Quarry or open mine pit
2708 Red Eagle Mountain
2908 Little Chief Mountain
Almost-a-Dog Mountain
2469 Curly Bear Mountain
White Calf Mtn
2710
2390 Kakitos Mtn
2681 Kupunkamit Mountain
2306
Medicine Owl Peak 2524
Mount James
Norris Mtn
Red Eagle Pass
2556
2816
CONTINENT
2545 Bad Marriage Mountain
2542 Mad Wolf Mountain
INDIAN
Cut
Bank
RESERVATION
T 33 N
T 32 N
1500
1750
2000
2250
36
31
6

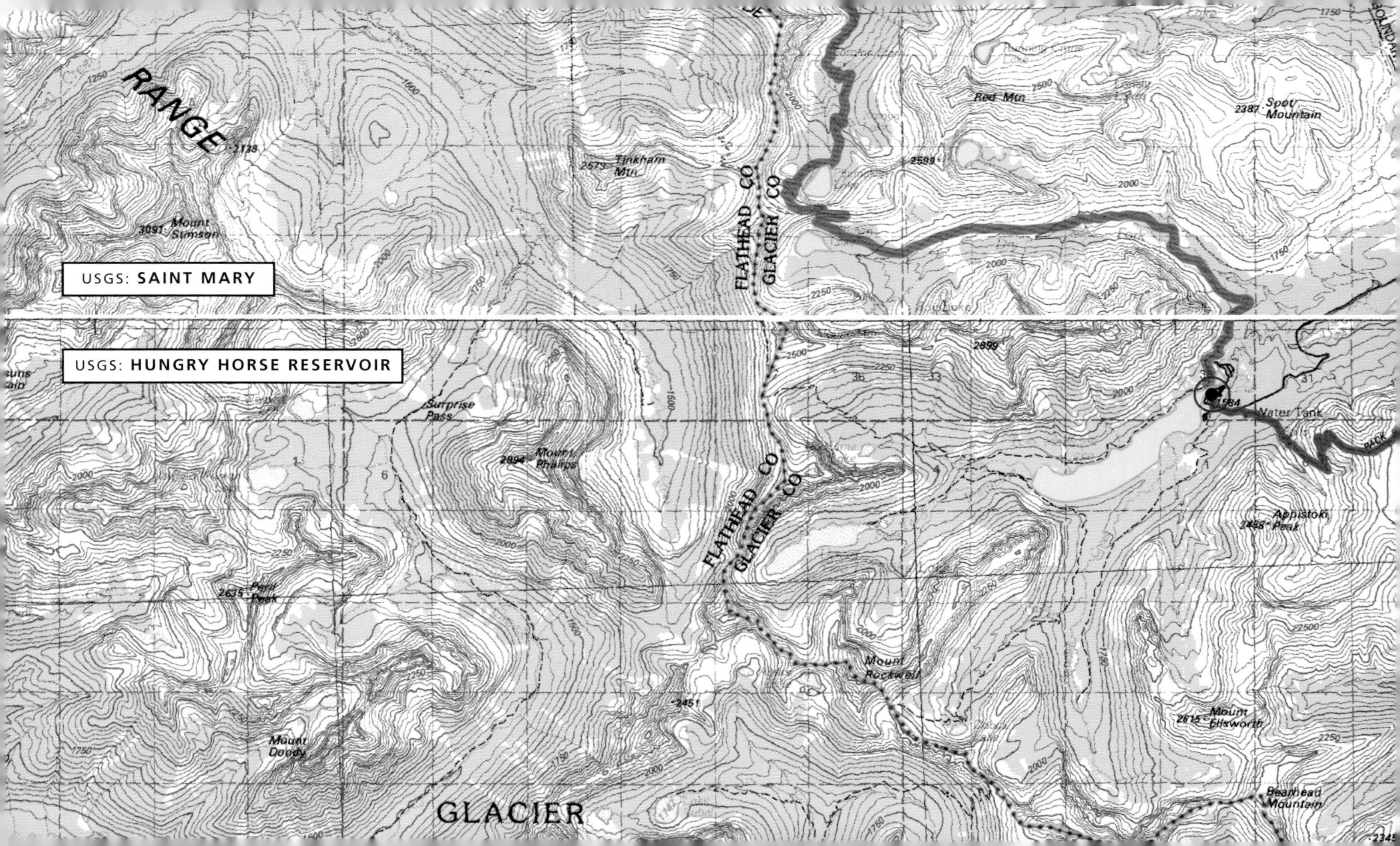
USGS: SAINT MARY
USGS: HUNGRY HORSE RESERVOIR
RANGE
3091 Mount Simpson
2573 Tinkham Mtn
FLATHEAD CO
GLACIER CO
Red Mtn
2387 Spot Mountain
2899
Surprise Pass
2894 Mount Phillips
2635 Peril Peak
Mount Doody
Mount Rockwell
2451
Water Tank
2488 Appistoki Peak
2815 Mount Ellsworth
Bearhead Mountain
GLACIER

Segment 29
St. Mary Falls to Many Glacier: Glacier National Park

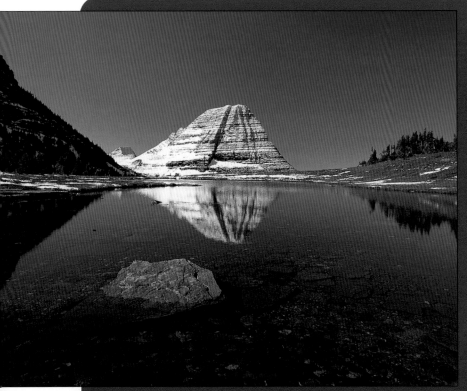

Bearhat Mountain, as seen from Logan Pass

15.6 miles, 25.12 km
Difficulty: Strenuous

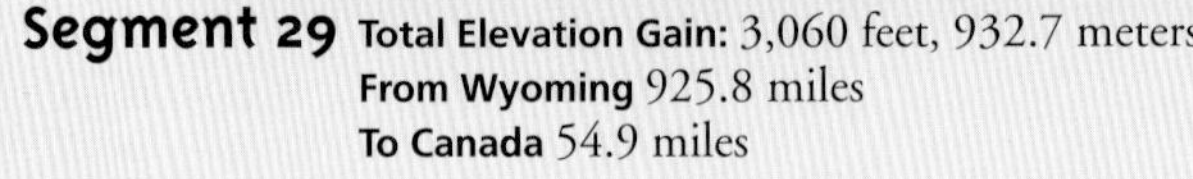

Segment 29 **Total Elevation Gain:** 3,060 feet, 932.7 meters
From Wyoming 925.8 miles
To Canada 54.9 miles

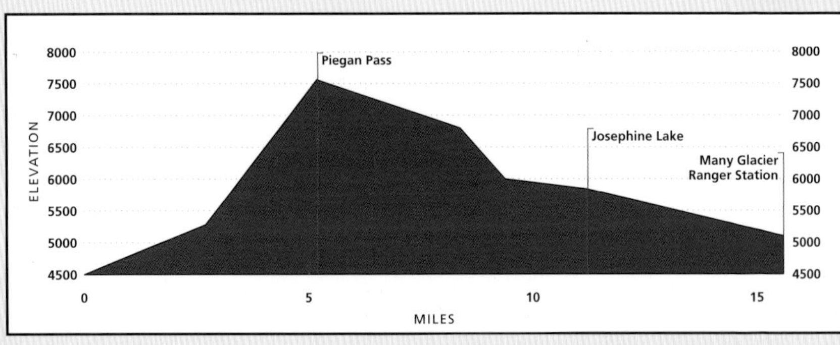

TRAIL OVERVIEW Don't let the proximity of roads and other outposts of civilization lull you into complacency about possible encounters with bears. We were forced off the trail near Swiftcurrent Lake by a black bear with two cubs. Review the bear avoidance tips.

This short but strenuous hike begins near the Going-to-the-Sun Road and ends at the highway, Glacier Route Three. Hikers should plan to complete the hike in one day as there are no officially sanctioned campgrounds along the route.

Two separate routes intersect the highway near the end of this segment. Which trail you take depends on where you want to end up. To finish at the Many Glacier Lodge on Swiftcurrent Lake, northbound hikers keep right to take the route on the east side of Lake Josephine and Swiftcurrent Lake. This trail has the advantage of intersecting the highway closer to the Appekuny Falls Trailhead and the alternate continuation of the CDT on the Red Gap Pass trail (see Segment 31). Disadvantages are limited views, heavy horse use, and more highway-walking to the Many Glacier Campground. To end the hike at the Many Glacier Ranger Station and the Swiftcurrent Inn, keep left on the western-most route around the lakes. This trail is dryer, higher, and more scenic. It intersects the highway closer to the Swiftcurrent Pass Trailhead, a plus if you are continuing north on the designated route of the CDT that terminates at Waterton Lake (see Segment 30).

In this segment, hikers climb steadily for over 3,000 feet to cross Piegan Pass. "Piegan" is the language of the Blood Indians, a branch of the Blackfeet. If Piegan Pass is impassable due to snow, an alternate route takes hikers over Swiftcurrent Pass via the Highline Trail, which begins at Logan Pass. Check with rangers before attempting either route. An ice axe and the ability to self-arrest may be necessary in July. The trail is usually melted out by August 1.

Scenic highlights include the less-visited eastern side of "The Garden Wall," an arête whose knifelike edge hovers over the trail as it wends its way along Cataract Creek; the Bishop's Cap Glacier high on the wall; and Feather Plume Falls. Mountain goats, grizzlies, and black bears are often sighted on this route.

Water is plentiful on both sides of Piegan Pass.

MOUNTAIN BIKE NOTES: This segment lies entirely within Glacier National Park, where mountain bikes are prohibited.

LAND ADMINISTRATORS (SEE APPENDIX A)

National Park Service, Glacier National Park

MAPS

USGS QUADRANGLES: Rising Sun, Logan Pass, Many Glacier

TRAILS ILLUSTRATED: Glacier National Park/Waterton Lakes National Park, Montana and Alberta

U.S. PARK SERVICE: Glacier National Park Visitors' Map

BEGINNING ACCESS POINT

ST. MARY FALLS: Look for the signed, paved parking lot south of Going-to-the-Sun Road, at the head of St. Mary Lake.

ENDING ACCESS POINT

Smooth road to Trailhead

SWIFTCURRENT LAKE TRAILHEAD: Take Glacier Route Three to the picnic area near Many Glacier Ranger Station.

SUPPLIES, SERVICES, AND ACCOMMODATIONS

RISING SUN is an Inn/Campground complex on the Going-to-the-Sun Road.

Distance from Trail: 5.1 miles

Zip Code: 59434

Bank: None. ATM in St. Mary at St. Mary Lodge and at Park Cafe Store

Bus: One-way tours from the inn to various points along Going-to-the-Sun Road, but no public transportation system.

Camping: Rising Sun Campground

Dining: Two Dog Flats Mesquite Grill

Gear: Limited gear at camp store

Groceries: Rising Sun Camp Store

Information: Glacier Park, Inc., Viad Corp. Center, Phoenix, AZ 85077-092 602-207-6000

Laundry: None

Lodging: Rising Sun Motor Inn, P.O. Box 147, East Glacier Park, MT 59434 Open June 8 to September 23, motel and cabins, $64–$81. For advance reservations call 602-207-6000 in the U.S.; 403-236-3400 in Canada; for same-day reservations call 406-732-5523.

Medical: None. Call Park Service in case of emergencies. 406-888-7800

Post Office: None

Showers: Rising Sun Motor Inn. Get shower tokens at the camp store or front desk.

Special Notes: St. Mary is on Hwy. 89, 12 miles from the trailhead. It is a small town, but has most of the services you will need, including a gear shop.

TRAIL DESCRIPTION Northbound hikers turn west on the Piegan Pass Trail near St. Mary Falls. The hike is through trees below the Going-to-the-Sun Road on a wide trail that parallels Reynolds Creek for about 1.5 miles. The Reynolds Creek Campground, near Deadwood Falls, was established to provide an intermediate stop between the Red Eagle Valley and Many Glacier for long-distance hikers. To use this campground, you must have an extended itinerary (three or more nights).

1.2 miles south of the Going-to-the-Sun Road, a signed intersection gives hikers the opportunity for a side trip to Gunsight Pass and other destinations. Many of the trails in Glacier are interconnected. This particular intersection even offers a trail to Lake MacDonald Lodge, 30 km distant on the western edge of the park.

The trail gets steeper as it climbs to the highway and then continues to climb toward Piegan Pass. Northbound hikers actually cross under the highway, wading in a small creek that flows through a large culvert. Climb up and cross the highway if too much water or ice makes the culvert tricky. It is not easy to see the sign for the trail where it is hidden in trees north of the highway. Look for the path where it emerges from the culvert.

As the trail climbs higher, pause for a view to the south of Jackson Glacier. A junction with the Siyeh Pass Trail is reached at mile 3.4. The Siyeh Trail makes a loop from Siyeh Bend to Baring Falls on the highway, sharing the Piegan Pass Trail for about 1.5 miles. "Siyeh," which means "Mad Wolf," was the name of a Blackfeet Indian warrior who fought a famous battle with Kootenai Indians near Cut Bank Pass. The Siyeh Pass Trail diverges at mile 4.9.

Piegan Pass, the notch between Cataract Mountain and Pollock Mountain, is reached at mile 5.2, elevation 7,560 feet. The Piegan Glacier, and the waterfall rushing from the cliff below it, are visible to the southwest. North of the pass, the whole Cataract Creek valley is open to view. As you descend, Morning Eagle Falls comes into view. Snowdrifts at the base of The Garden Wall seldom melt out, shielding the final descent of more waterfalls from Bishops Cap and Grinnell Glaciers.

We saw a lot of bear sign in this section of trail, including one distinct bear trail that told a story of berry-eating orgies and stalking mountain goats. South of Feather Plume Falls we saw mountain goats on the hillside; haughty billies and bouncing youngsters, all of them living on the edge. In addition to all the goats and bears, we heard elk bugling in the valley when we were there in September.

From Feather Plume Falls north to Many Glacier, there was quite a bit of tourist traffic, but in the wild valley between Piegan Pass and the falls, there were no humans.

At the junction with the Grinnell Lake Trail (mile 9.4), pull out your map and decide which of the two options offered will take you where you want to go. (See the "Trail Overview" at the beginning of this segment.) We opted for the left (west) turn that took us by Grinnell Lake and along the western edge of Lake Josephine. It is 3.1 miles from Grinnell Lake to Glacier Route Three.

Hidden Falls is a worthwhile side trip on the Josephine Lake trail (mile 11.2). The falls is only 0.5 km off the trail and is actually two falls plunging into aquamarine pools in a very narrow gorge.

Glacier Route Three is reached at mile 15.6. The ranger station, Swiftcurrent Inn, and the Swiftcurrent Pass TRHD are to the west on the highway. Many Glacier Lodge and the Appekuny Falls TRHD (Red Gap Pass Trail) are to the east. See Segment 30 for details on the alternate routes leading to the Canadian border.

SOUTHBOUND HIKERS: This segment of trail begins in the picnic area east of the Many Glacier Ranger Station.

OTHER EXCURSIONS

LOGAN PASS
DIFFICULTY: Easy
DISTANCE: 6 miles round trip

LOGAN PASS, "The Crown of of the Continent," is west of the route of the CDT, on the Going-to-the-Sun Road. Displays at the large visitor center feature the history, flora, and fauna of Glacier National Park. A trail that begins as a boardwalk near the visitor center leads southwest to Hidden Lake. This is the shortest route to Glacier's highcountry near Bearhat Mountain. The setting earns all the hyperbole penned by writers past and present.

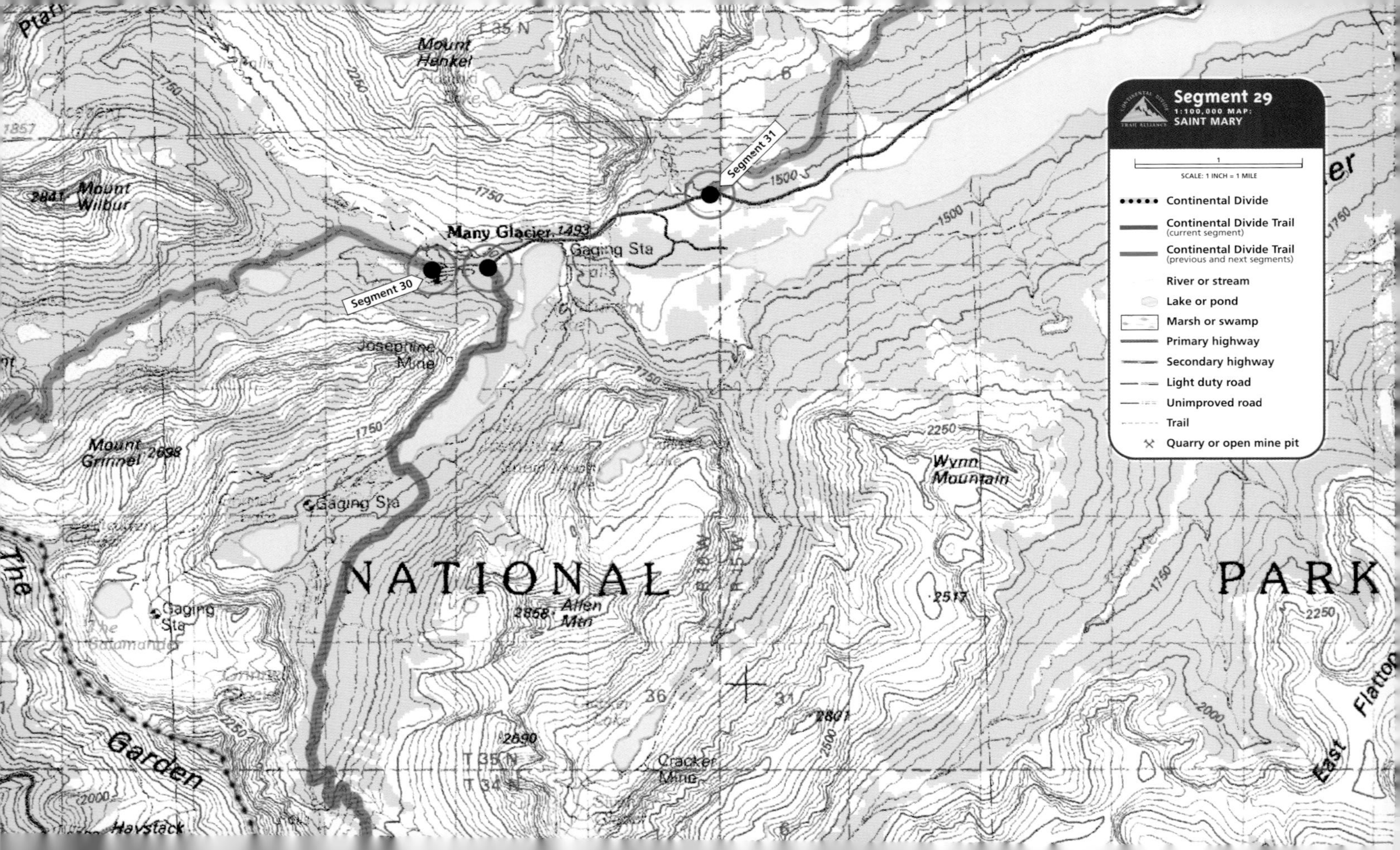
Segment 29
1:100,000 MAP:
SAINT MARY
SCALE: 1 INCH = 1 MILE
Continental Divide
Continental Divide Trail
(current segment)
Continental Divide Trail
(previous and next segments)
River or stream
Lake or pond
Marsh or swamp
Primary highway
Secondary highway
Light duty road
Unimproved road
Trail
Quarry or open mine pit
Segment 30
Segment 31
Many Glacier 1493
Gaging Sta
Mount Henkel
Mount Wilbur
2841
Mount Grinnel 2898
Josephine Mine
Wynn Mountain
2517
NATIONAL
PARK
2858 Allen Mtn
Cracker Mine
2690
2801
The
Garden
Haystack
East
T 35 N
T 34 N
R 16 W
R 15 W

Wall
Mount Oberlin
Clements Mtn
1783
Matahpi Peak
Going-to-the-Sun Mountain
1968
2250
2000
1500
1750
Saint Mary Lake
1943
Heavy Runner Mountain
Reynolds Mountain
36
31
6
T 34 N
T 33 N
2708 Red Eagle Mountain
2908 Little Chief Mountain
2667 Fusillade Mountain
2762 Citadel Mountain
2500

Segment 30
Swiftcurrent Pass Trailhead to Waterton Townsite: Glacier National Park

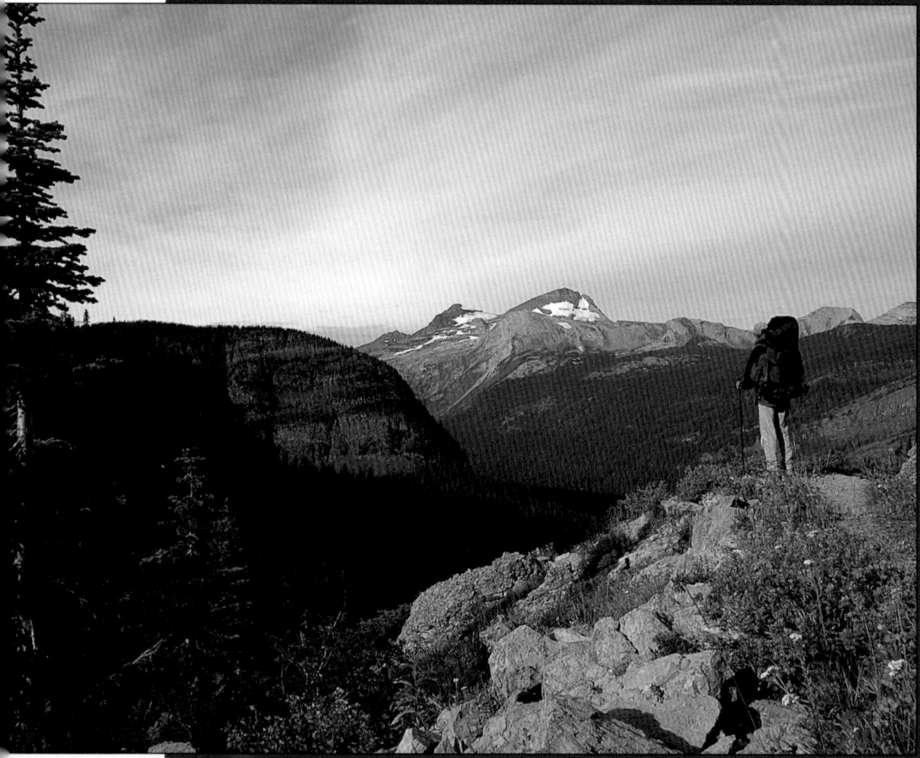

On the Waterton Lake Trail, north of Fifty Mountain in Glacier National Park

39.3 miles, 63.25 km
Difficulty: Strenuous

Segment 30 **Total Elevation Gain:** 4,027 feet, 1,277.43 meters
From Wyoming 941.4 miles
To Canada 35.1 miles (39.3 miles to Waterton Townsite)

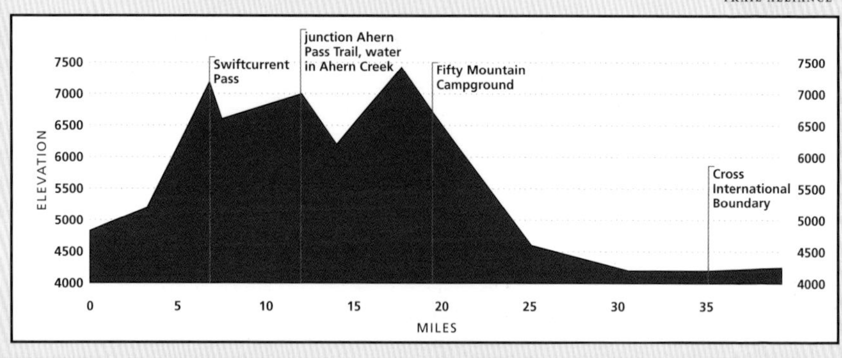

TRAIL OVERVIEW When northbound hikers reach Many Glacier, they have two options for continuing north to Canada. The alternate route of the CDT begins at Appekuny Falls Trailhead and ends at Chief Mountain Customs Station. The designated and traditional route is described in this segment. This traditional route crosses Swiftcurrent Pass to intercept the Highline Trail, which closely parallels the physical Divide to Fifty Mountain, then drops into Waterton Valley for a long hike to Waterton Lake. At Goat Haunt on Waterton Lake, hikers are still about 4 miles from the Canadian border. The border can be crossed by hiking along the western shore of the lake, or by catching the Waterton Shoreline boat to the townsite.

Why two routes? The reasons are primarily legal. Chief Mountain is an official Customs Station. Goat Haunt is not a customs station, but U.S. Forest Service rangers trained for customs duties will look you over, ask a few questions, and generally uphold international border-crossing laws. It is simpler for hikers to stop where one does not have to cross the border, and the border can be crossed legally if hikers wish to do so—at Chief Mountain Customs.

The question of which route to choose becomes more critical later in the season. The Goat Haunt Ranger Station closes in late September. Hikers that cross into Canada in October and do not check in with Customs in Waterton are breaking the law. Late season hikers should opt for the alternate route (see Segment 31).

Which route is better? You can't go wrong in Glacier National Park. Both routes offer splendid scenery. We hiked them both and I preferred the route that ends at Chief Mountain Customs. There were fewer hikers on the trail and in the campgrounds. This route actually climbs higher to cross Red Gap Pass than the traditional route does to cross the Divide, and it is 13 miles shorter. Choose the hike that suits you best and that complies with the legal requirements at the time of your trek. Remember to apply for your selected itinerary well ahead of time (see "National Park Alert" in Segment 26).

More than one-third of Glacier National Park is alpine. In this segment, hikers spend a lot of time above treeline. Sheer cliffs, talus slopes, and snowfields predominate from Swiftcurrent Pass to Fifty Mountain. After crossing the Divide, the trail descends more than 3,000 feet to reach Waterton Lake at elevation 4,200 feet. Ironically, this is the lowest point on the Idaho/Montana CDT. You may have felt like you were climbing all the way from Yellowstone National Park to Canada, but you've been heading downhill as you worked your way north.

Don't let the low elevations fool you. The mountain peaks are of the rough, raw, recently glaciated genre; the absolute elevation change from valley floors to mountain summits is dramatic; and the timberline struggles to top 6,000 feet.

Water sources are less frequent along the Highline Trail. Ahern Creek and Cattle Queen Creek are the best stops between Swiftcurrent Pass and Fifty Mountain. Water is plentiful on the Waterton Valley Trail.

MOUNTAIN BIKE NOTES: This segment lies mostly within Glacier National Park, where mountain bikes are prohibited.

LAND ADMINISTRATORS (SEE APPENDIX A)

National Park Service, Glacier National Park
Waterton Lakes National Park, Canadian Parks Service

MAPS

USGS QUADRANGLES: Many Glacier, Ahern Pass, Mount Geduhn, Porcupine Ridge
TRAILS ILLUSTRATED: Glacier National Park/Waterton Lakes National Park, Montana and Alberta
U.S. PARK SERVICE: Glacier National Park Visitors' Map
CANADIAN PARKS SERVICE: Waterton Lakes National Park, 1:50,000

BEGINNING ACCESS POINT

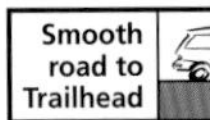

SWIFTCURRENT PASS TRAILHEAD: The trailhead is located at the west end of the Swiftcurrent Inn parking lot, and is accessible via Glacier Route Three (Many Glacier Road).

ENDING ACCESS POINT

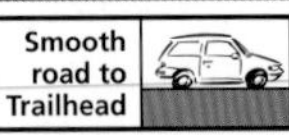

WATERTON TOWNSITE, CANADA: Cross the Canadian border on Chief Mountain International Highway 17; then Canadian Highway 6 to Highway 5; and southwest on Hwy. 5 to Waterton Park.

TRAIL DESCRIPTION

This segment begins at the west end of the Swiftcurrent Inn parking lot. Look for the "Swiftcurrent Pass Trail" sign. The trail skirts several small lakes, strung like beads below the pass, including Fishercap Lake, Redrock Lake, and Bullhead Lake. Fill water bottles where the trail crosses the creek at the head of Bullhead Lake before climbing to the pass.

The climb up the many switchbacks to Swiftcurrent Pass rewards hikers with views of yet more waterfalls, and one can also see beyond the Rocky Mountain Front into the vast Great Plains to the east.

At Swiftcurrent Pass (mile 6.8), a spur trail leading to Swiftcurrent Lookout is signed. A small chalet that tops the lookout can be seen from the trail. Cross the pass and intersect the Highline Trail. The Highline Trail comes up from Logan Pass and can be used as an alternate route to access this traditional hike to the Canadian border—useful when Swiftcurrent Pass is still snowed in. Fifty Mountain Campground is 11.7 miles to the north and Goat Haunt Ranger Station is 22.2 miles (35.7 km) distant. There is a sign and a direction for everything but the Granite Park Campground, which is the CDT trekker's next destination.

Another intersection 0.1 mile to the north shows once more the direction to everything mentioned above, but also finally points the way to the Granite Park Campground. The Granite Park Campground is well below the Highline Trail. A tributary of Mineral Creek provides water at the campground.

Nearby Granite Park Chalet sells snacks and beverages. This historic chalet was built in 1913 and closed in 1992 due to numerous health and safety problems.

An organization called "Save the Chalets" is fund-raising to restore Granite Park and Sperry Chalets to their former glory (see Appendix E). In the meantime, hikers can arrange to stay in the no-frills "stone tent" for $60/night. We opted for a one-night stay to experience a bit of living history.

Four grizzly bears in "Mauling Meadows" (local black humor) below the chalet hastened our decision. We felt justified in spending the money when two other hikers, scared by the bears, joined us in the chalet.

The Highline Trail offers big views as the well-constructed route stays high on the west side of "The Garden Wall," an arête formed when two glaciers gnawed at the ridge from both sides, leaving a narrow rim of rock running north/south along the Continental Divide—in this case creating an image that lives up to the Blackfeet Indian name for the Divide as the "Backbone of the World."

When we hiked the trail in September, we crossed an old snowfield below Iceberg Peak. Trekking poles were sufficient to cross the ice so late in the hiking season, but recommendations for proficiency with an ice axe are not to be taken lightly.

The Highline Trail crosses two tributaries of Ahern Creek, a good water source, near the intersection to Ahern Pass Trail at mile 12, about 5 miles north of Granite Park. The trail then descends, losing a few hundred feet in elevation, to cross Cattle Queen Creek at mile 14. Hikers cross the Divide at mile 17.7, elevation 7,420 feet. From the Divide, Flattop and West Flattop Mountains form the foreground of the view to the west, with the higher peaks of the Livingston Range dominating the horizon. A group of glaciers can be seen below Vulture Peak and another group below Mount Carter.

At the pass south of Fifty Mountain Campground, hikers and the physical Divide part company. The Divide leaves the Lewis & Clark Mountains, crosses West Flattop, and turns north to follow the Livingston Range. The trail takes a saner route, east of all those glaciers.

Fifty Mountain (mile 19.5) is a busy campground, the hub for many other trails. The food preparation area is usually humming with backpackers and conversations center around gear and blister remedies.

From Fifty Mountain, it's all downhill to Waterton Lake, following the Waterton Lake Trail. The descent brings hikers out of the alpine zone, through subalpine krummholz, and into thick forest and shrubs. There are still some excellent views from occasional open areas, including small glaciers, cirques, and waterfalls. Looking north toward Canada, there are fantastic glacier-sculpted horns, spires, and arêtes.

Where the trail flattens at the bottom of a steep descent, we saw several bear trails intersecting the human trail. There were claw marks on the trees, one bear "bed" on a rock ledge next to the trail, and bear prints in the trail. All looked to be the work of black bears, not grizzlies.

The trail from Stoney Indian Pass comes in from the east at mile 25.1. If you have the time and your knees will still function after the steep descent, Stoney Indian Pass is an excellent side trip, 6 km (3.7 miles) east of this intersection.

SUPPLIES, SERVICES, AND ACCOMMODATIONS

MANY GLACIER, MT, is a hotel/campground/inn complex at the western end of Glacier Route Three.

Distance from Trail: 0.2 mile

Zip Code: 59417

Bank: ATM machine in the Many Glacier Hotel

Bus: Tours from the Inn to various points along Glacier Route Three, but no other transportation system. Inquire at the inn or hotel.

Camping: Many Glacier Campground. There are two sites that are reserved for backcountry travelers on extended trips such as the CDT.

Dining: Many Glacier Hotel, Ptarmigan Dining Room
Swiftcurrent Motor Inn, Italian Garden Ristorante

Gear: Swiftcurrent Campstore, next to Swiftcurrent Inn

Groceries: Swiftcurrent Campstore

Information: Glacier Park, Inc., Viad Corp. Center, Phoenix, AZ 85077 602-207-6000

Laundry: Swiftcurrent Motor Inn, tokens at camp store and front desk

Lodging: Many Glacier Hotel, June 7 to September 8, \$91–\$174, advance reservations: 602-207-6000, same-day reservations: 406-732-4411
Swiftcurrent Motor Inn, June 7 to September 23, \$75, advance reservations: 602-207-6000, same-day reservations: 406-732-5531
Pinetop Motor Inn, cottages with and without bath, \$29–\$49

Medical: Glacier County Medical Center, 892 2nd St. E., Cut Bank, MT 406-873-2251

Post Office: See Swiftcurrent Motor Inn above

Showers: Swiftcurrent Motor Inn, tokens at camp store or front desk

Special Notes: Waterton Townsite, Canada, is a full-service town. Call 403-859-2224 or 1-800-215-2395 for more information. Hikers can opt to ride a boat from Goat Haunt to Waterton Townsite instead of hiking the last 8.7 miles of this segment. Waterton Inter-Nation Shoreline Cruises operates May to September, weather permitting, tickets \$8/person payable at Goat Haunt, 403-859-2362.

As you near Waterton Lake, spur trails lead to Kootenai Lakes (mile 27.5) and to Rainbow Falls. The Waterton Lake Trail becomes a 4WD road where hikers pass the electronic components of a weather alert system. You are back in civilization.

Another "Waterton Valley Trail" sign reassures southbound hikers 2.3 miles north of Kootenai Lakes. For northbound hikers, the nest of trails and roads at the southern end of the lake can be confusing. The ranger station is dead ahead, at mile 30.6 for this segment. The Goat Haunt Campground is to your left (west), and the boat dock/shelter area is to the right (east). Signs do show the direction and distance to Waterton Townsite.

To cross the international boundary into Canada, hikers have a choice of hiking the trail around the western side of the lake, or taking the boat to Waterton Townsite. From the ranger station on the shore, it is an 8.7-mile hike to the town.

About halfway, the trail crosses the border, which looks like a bulldozer cut that has long since been neglected. Elevation changes are slight as the trail crosses several creeks and climbs to make its way through the trees on the lake shore. At the townsite, the trail emerges on a road south of Cameron Falls Bridge, at mile 39.3 for this segment. If you opt to ride the boat, it offers excellent views of the surrounding mountains. To the southeast, Mount Cleveland, the highest peak in Glacier National Park, presides over a seemingly endless array of lesser peaks. At 10,466 feet, the mountain doesn't sound very impressive to visitors from Colorado, but its northern face rises 5,500 feet above the valley, and that is extreme in anyone's book.

Waterton Townsite operates a 238-site campground adjacent to the trailhead. Showers and camp kitchens are available. The town proper is full of restaurants and shops. Our finely tuned backpacker olfactory mechanisms could smell the food half a mile away. Welcome to Canada.

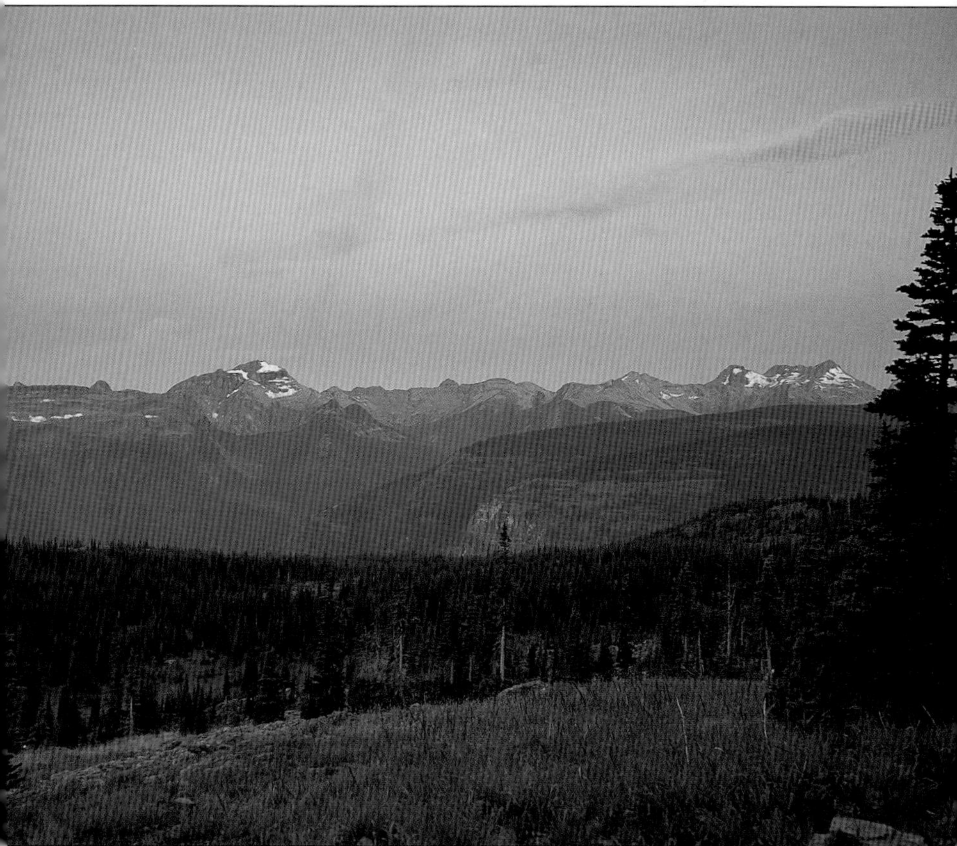

Sunrise from the Granite Park Chalet on the Highline Trail, Glacier National Park

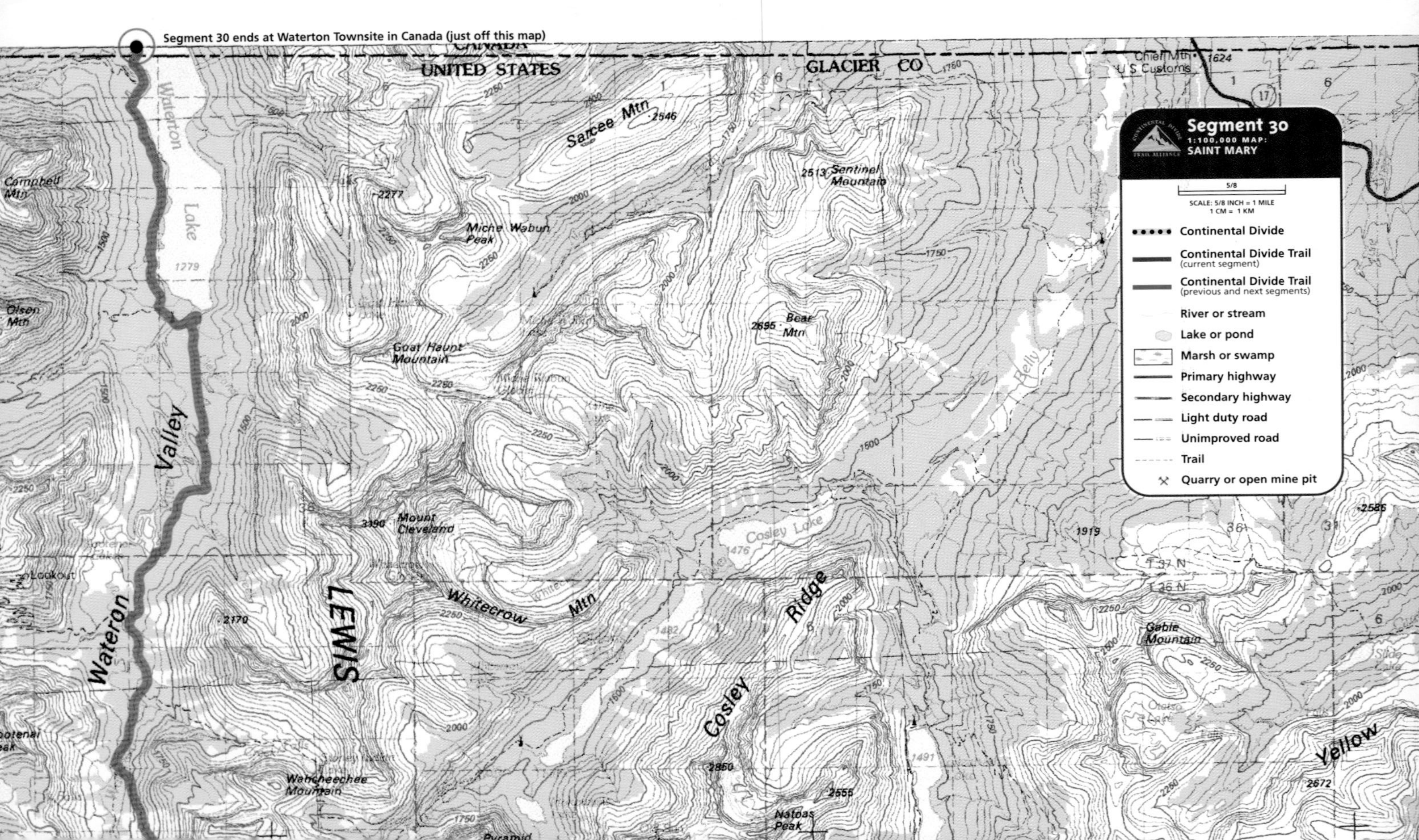
Segment 30 ends at Waterton Townsite in Canada (just off this map)
Segment 30
1:100,000 MAP: SAINT MARY
SCALE: 5/8 INCH = 1 MILE
1 CM = 1 KM
Continental Divide
Continental Divide Trail (current segment)
Continental Divide Trail (previous and next segments)
River or stream
Lake or pond
Marsh or swamp
Primary highway
Secondary highway
Light duty road
Unimproved road
Trail
Quarry or open mine pit
UNITED STATES
GLACIER CO
Chief Mtn 1624
U S Customs
Waterton Lake
Waterton Valley
Sarcee Mtn
Miche Wabun Peak
Sentinel Mountain
Bear Mtn
Goat Haunt Mountain
Mount Cleveland
Whitecrow Mtn
LEWIS
Cosley Lake
Cosley Ridge
Gable Mountain
Natoas Peak
Wahcheechee Mountain
Campbell Mtn
Olsen Mtn
Lookout
Yellow

West Flattop Mtn
GLACIER CO
FLATHEAD CO
Ipasha Peak
Helen Lake
Ptarmigan Wall
Crowfeet Mountain
Apikuni Mountain
Mount Henkel
CONTINENTAL DIVIDE
RANGE
Flattop Mountain
Iceberg Peak
Mount Wilbur
Designated (traditional)
Gaging Sta
Josephine Mine
Swiftcurrent Mountain
Lookout
Mount Grinnel
The Garden
Haystack Butte
GLACIER NATIONAL
Allen Mtn
Cracker Mine
Longfellow Peak

Segment 31
Many Glacier to Chief Mountain: Glacier National Park

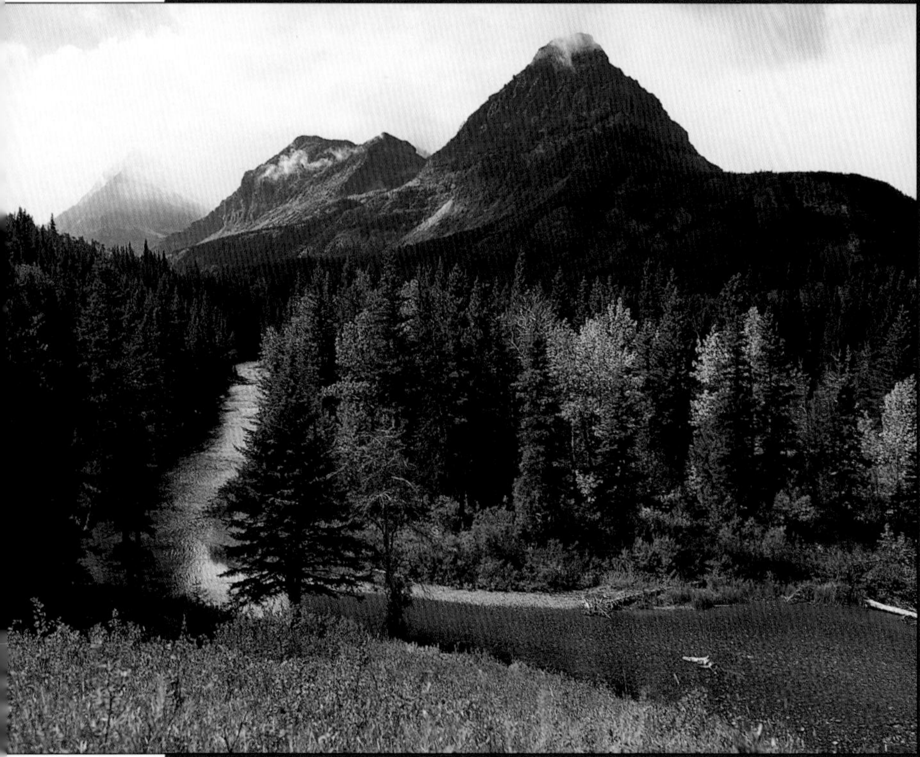

The Belly River and surrounding peaks in Glacier National Park, as seen from the alternate CDT route as it crosses the meadows near the Belly River Ranger Station

26.1 miles, 42 km
Difficulty: Strenuous

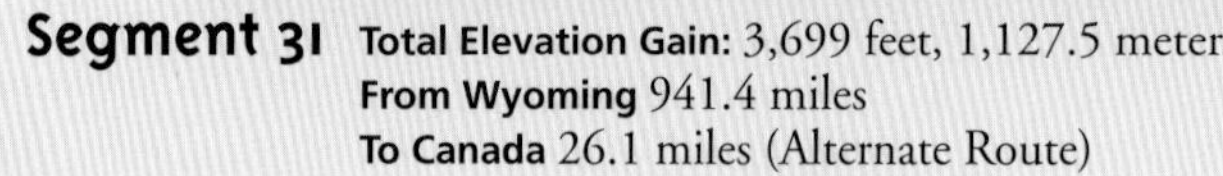

Segment 31 **Total Elevation Gain:** 3,699 feet, 1,127.5 meters
From Wyoming 941.4 miles
To Canada 26.1 miles (Alternate Route)

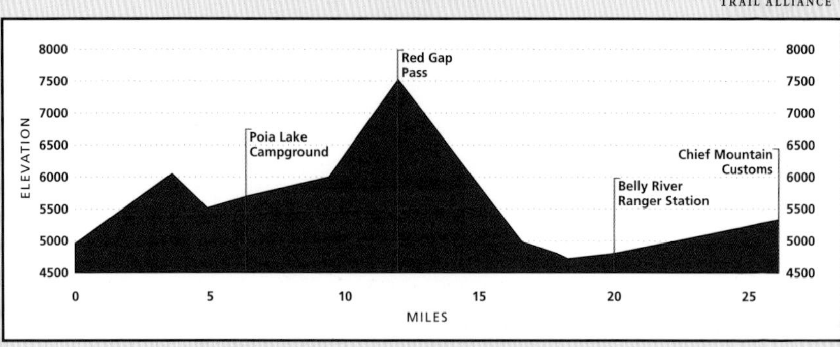

TRAIL OVERVIEW In this segment, the alternate route of the CDT ends at the Canadian border. In many ways, it is a fitting last hurrah. Glacier National Park works its magic one last time in a display of scenic wonders that range from aspen trees along the Belly River to enough alpine splendor to make you dizzy.

The Belly River adds its own touch with Dawn Mist Falls, elk meadows and spruce forests. Ahern, Old Sun, and other nameless glaciers feed the river. It is one cold, dangerous, beautiful stretch of water—and if you don't make it through this section before the end of September, you'll find yourself faced with fording the river. Trail crews remove seasonal bridges at three crossings in this segment.

The "Belly" refers to the translation of Gros Ventre, "Big Belly," a Native American tribe of the northern plains. The cold waters that bear their name flow north to Hudson Bay. Arctic grayling, a fish that is rare in Montana, still exist in both Elizabeth Lake and the Belly River. Elk, deer, mountain lions, wolves, and bears are the locals.

This route takes hikers through a section of the park that doesn't receive as many visitors as the Highline Trail (see Segment 30). It is about 10 miles east of the physical Divide, but the terrain is still impressively rough. The Red Gap Pass and Belly River Trails were chosen as the alternate route of the CDT to provide a manned customs station at its terminus.

Read the "National Park Alert" in Segment 26 for regulations that apply to backcountry users in Glacier National Park. Also review the bear avoidance techniques. Both grizzly and black bears may be encountered in this segment.

Water sources are frequent and easy to access throughout the hike.

MOUNTAIN BIKE NOTES: This segment lies entirely within Glacier National Park, where mountain bikes are prohibited.

LAND ADMINISTRATORS (SEE APPENDIX A)

National Park Service, Glacier National Park

MAPS

USGS QUADRANGLES: Many Glacier, Lake Sherburne, Gable Mountain, Chief Mountain
TRAILS ILLUSTRATED: Glacier National Park/Waterton Lakes National Park, Montana and Alberta
U.S. PARK SERVICE: Glacier National Park Visitors' Map

BEGINNING ACCESS POINT

APPEKUNY (APIKUNI) FALLS TRAILHEAD: The trailhead for Appekuny Falls and the Red Gap Pass Trail is on Glacier Route Three (Many Glacier Road), about 1.5 miles east of the Glacier Hotel.

ENDING ACCESS POINT

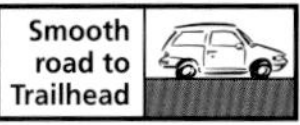

CHIEF MOUNTAIN CUSTOMS: The Canadian border, on Chief Mountain International Highway 17.

SUPPLIES, SERVICES, AND ACCOMMODATIONS

(See Segment 30.)

TRAIL DESCRIPTION The trailhead sign that can be seen from the highway says only "Appekuny Falls" but this is also the trailhead for the Red Gap Pass Trail. As soon as one leaves the small parking lot at the trailhead, Glacier Park's mania for signing takes over and hikers are presented with the distance in kilometers to the Belly River Ranger Station and all points between. This trail was open to horses when we were there, but we saw little horse use until we reached the ranger station.

Red Gap Pass Trail skirts the eastern edge of Apikuni Mountain, climbing gently through small meadows, aspen trees, and shrubs. Swiftcurrent Ridge Lake, at mile 3.6 (6 km), is a pretty, oval mirror of water. Views across the lake include a group of high peaks south and southwest of Lake Sherburne.

Hikers pass through stands of lodgepole pine, spruce, and fir north of the lake. We heard elk bugling several times when we reached the more open area around Kennedy Creek. A band of forest grouse strutted in front of us, too lazy to hide or fly, which was surprising considering the fact that a wolf or coyote had recently dined on a member of the flock.

From Swiftcurrent Ridge Lake, the trail descends to Kennedy Creek. There are a few switchbacks on this section as hikers lose 500 feet of elevation. Avalanche chutes add to the debris along the trail. Altyn limestone gives Yellow Mountain, seen to the north, its sallow color. After the more ordered appearance of other trails in the park, this area looks relatively wild and has its own desolate beauty.

The trail climbs again to reach Poia Lake at mile 6.5. "Poia" is a name from Blackfeet Indian legends. A close translation is "Star Boy," a half mortal who saved the life of Morning Star. Morning Star Lake, also named from the same story, is near Pitamakan Pass to the south. The Poia Lake Campground is on a forested knoll at the southeastern edge of the lake.

The trail crosses the Poia Lake outlet on a log bridge. Fill water bottles here before climbing to Red Gap Pass. The trail parallels Kennedy Creek again as it continues west to the head of the narrow valley. The climb is mellow until mile 9.4, where the trail turns northwest and starts up a series of steep switchbacks. Where the trail crosses small waterfalls, exercise caution. Several accidents, one fatal, have occurred when hikers slipped on the smooth rocks and fell down the falls. When we hiked the trail, mountain goats were visible on the ledges along Crowfeet Mountain's eastern face. They looked like they had been flown in by helicopter and deposited at varying elevations.

The Grinnell argillite stone of Red Gap Pass (mile 12) is truly red. Rain, fog, stormy winds, ice, and sleet heightened the red colors when we crossed the pass in late September. We had to concentrate to keep from slipping on the ice where the switchbacks started down toward Elizabeth Lake. Northbound hikers must descend over 2,000 feet in 4.6 miles. The park rangers gave us an "elevation advisory" with our permit for this section.

The trail winds downhill to a line of stunted trees, and water becomes available again in rivulets that course through the twisted trees and ground-hugging vegetation. I was feeling like hugging some ground myself, but there is no real shelter on the rocky slope above Helen and Elizabeth Lakes.

The valley that shelters Elizabeth Lake is two-tiered, with the top tier holding the murky, shallow Helen Lake and looking as if the glacier that carved it melted yesterday. Elizabeth Lake is a long, thumb-shaped body of water, with campgrounds at both its head and foot. The campground at the foot of the lake is provided with buckets for hanging food, a device meant to foil the flying squirrels.

More downhill trekking through thicker trees leads hikers from Elizabeth Lake to the Belly River Ranger Station. The head of Dawn Mist Falls can be seen from the trail and a short detour takes you to the foot of the falls. The detour is well worth the time as the falls is very appealing, even by Glacier Park standards. Near the station, trails leading to Stoney Indian Pass and to Gable Pass intersect the Belly River Trail. CDT hikers stay on the Belly River Trail, where signs direct you to Chief Mountain Customs.

The Belly River Ranger Station sits in an open meadow with excellent views southward up the river valley. The domestic scene of cabin and horse corrals is a sharp contrast to the wild valley and the glacier-strewn peaks above it. Near the ranger station there are two campgrounds, Belly River Campground and Gable Creek Campground. Gable Creek Campground is north of the station and campfires are allowed there, a fact to remember in cold weather.

The trail from the station to the Canadian border was muddy and chewed up from stock use when we were there. It passes through a lot of open meadows and aspen groves. Hikers have left the high mountains behind, but face one last climb as the trail switchbacks up to Chief Mountain Trailhead next to the customs station, mile 26.1 for this segment, and mile 967.5 for the Idaho/Montana Continental Divide National Scenic Trail.

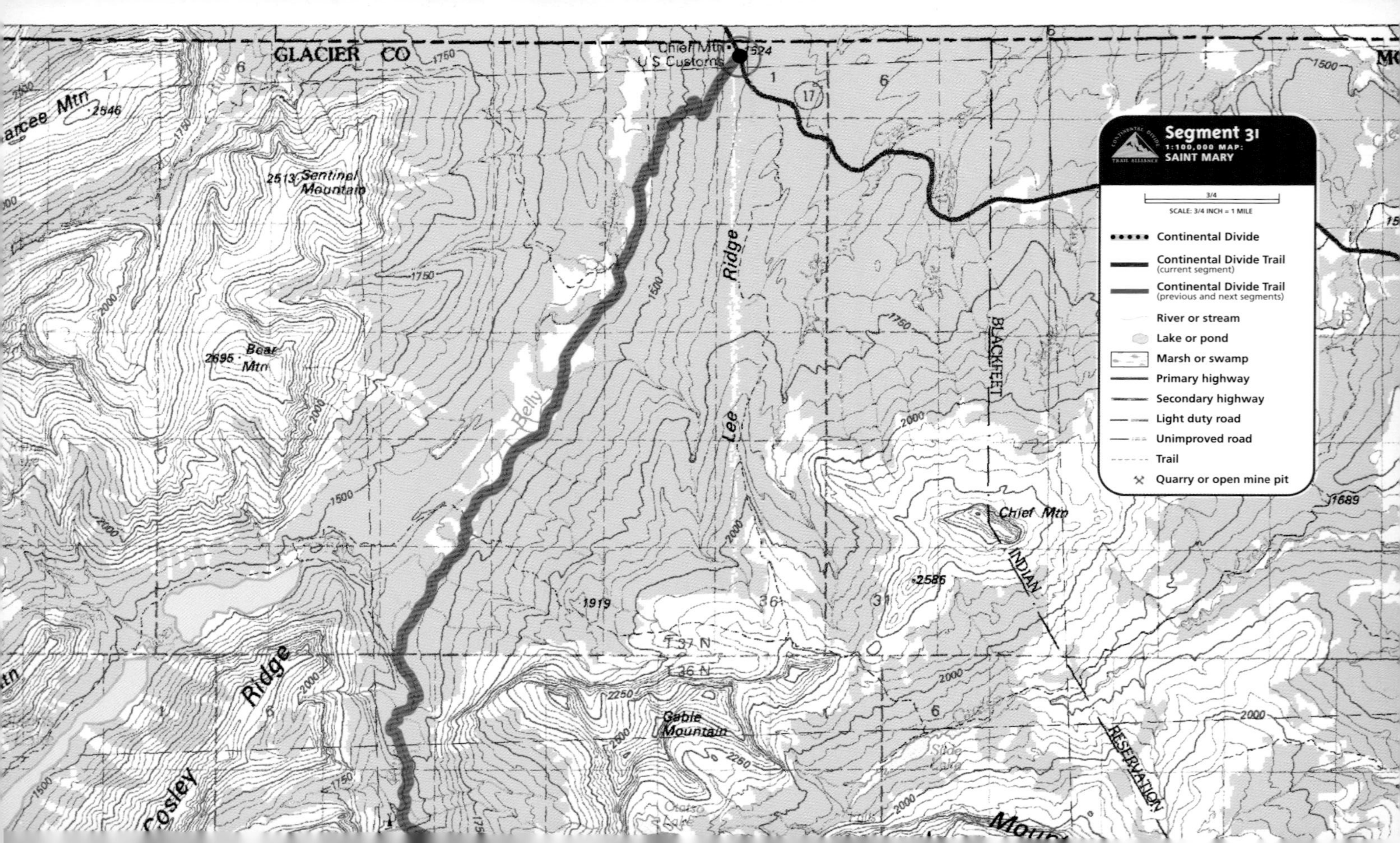

Segment 31
1:100,000 MAP:
SAINT MARY
CONTINENTAL DIVIDE TRAIL ALLIANCE
3/4
SCALE: 3/4 INCH = 1 MILE
Continental Divide
Continental Divide Trail
(current segment)
Continental Divide Trail
(previous and next segments)
River or stream
Lake or pond
Marsh or swamp
Primary highway
Secondary highway
Light duty road
Unimproved road
Trail
Quarry or open mine pit
GLACIER CO
Chief Mtn
U S Customs
1524
17
Sentinel Mountain
2513
Bear Mtn
2695
Lee Ridge
Belly
BLACKFEET
INDIAN
RESERVATION
Chief Mtn
2586
1919
1689
T 37 N
T 36 N
Gable Mountain
Cosley Ridge

Natoas Peak
Seward Mtn
BOUNDARY
2382
Ipasha Peak
2784
Swiftcurren
Wall
Crowfeet Mountain
2460
2764
Apikuni Mountain
CONTINENTAL
Ptarmigan
36 N
35 N
Mount Henkel
Lake Sherburne
Iceberg Peak
Designated Route
Mount Wilbur
2841
Many Glacier 1493
Gaging Sta
Alternate Route
Bould
1818
DIVIDE
Josephine Mine
Swiftcurrent Mountain
Mount Grinnel
2638
Wynn Mountain

Appendix A: Land Administrators

These agencies oversee land along the Continental Divide National Scenic Trail, Montana/Idaho portion. The agencies are arranged in order from south to north. Trail development and maintenance responsibilities do not always correspond with maps. The Continental Divide itself is often the boundary line between states and between jurisdictional agencies. When the trail meanders back and forth over those boundaries, land administrators make agreements as to which agency will construct and maintain the CDT.

Western border of Yellowstone Park to Targhee Pass

Targhee National Forest
Island Park Ranger District
Island Park, ID 83429
208-558-7301

Gallatin National Forest
Hebgen Lake Ranger District
P.O. Box 520
West Yellowstone, MT 59758
406-646-7369

Targhee Pass to Antelope Basin Road — Henrys Lake Mountains

Gallatin National Forest — as above

Antelope Basin Road to Red Rock Pass — Henrys Lake Mountains

Beaverhead National Forest
Madison Ranger District
5 Forest Service Road
Ennis, MT 59729
406-682-4253

Red Rock Pass to Dry Creek — Centennial Mountains

BLM (Special Recreation Management Area)
Dillon Resource Area
1005 Selway Drive
Dillon, MT 59725
406-683-2337

Dr. Harvey Blackburn
U.S. Sheep Experiment Station
HC 62, Box 2010
Dubois, ID 83423
208-374-5306

Dry Creek to Divide Creek — Centennial Mountains to 4 miles west of Bannack Pass in the Beaverhead Mountains

Targhee National Forest
Dubois Ranger District
P.O. Box 46
Dubois, ID 83423
208-374-5422

Big Beaver Creek (Divide Creek) to Morrison Lake — Beaverhead Mountains of the Bitterroot Range

Beaverhead/Deerlodge National Forest
Dillon Ranger District
P.O. Box 1258
Dillon, MT 59725
406-683-3900

One of the many waterfalls visible from the CDT south of Feather Plume Falls in Glacier National Park

Morrison Lake to Bannock Pass — Beaverhead Mountains of the Bitterroot Range

Salmon National Forest
Leadore Ranger District
P.O. Box 180
Leadore, ID 83445
208-768-2371

Bannock Pass to Lemhi Pass — Beaverhead Mountains of the Bitterroot Range

BLM, Lemhi Resource Area
Salmon Field Office
RR 2, Box 610
Highway 93 South
Salmon, ID 83467
208-756-5400

Lemhi Pass to Goldstone Pass — Beaverhead Mountains of the Bitterroot Range

Salmon National Forest
Leadore Ranger District
(see Morrison Lake above)

Goldstone Pass to saddle north of Big Lake Creek on Shewag Lake quadrangle — Beaverhead Mountains of the Bitterroot Range

Beaverhead/Deerlodge National Forest
Wisdom Ranger District
P.O. Box 238
Wisdom, MT 59761
406-689-3243
Web: http://www.fs.fed.us/r1/bdnf

Saddle north of Big Lake Creek on Shewag Lake quadrangle to Chief Joseph Pass— Beaverhead Mountains of the Bitterroot Range

Salmon National Forest
North Fork Ranger District
P.O. Box 780
North Fork, ID 83466
208-865-2383

Chief Joseph Pass to Schultz Saddle — Beaverhead Mountains of the Bitterroot Range and Anaconda Range

Bitterroot National Forest
Sula Ranger District
7338 Hwy. 93 S.
Sula, MT 59871
406-821-3201

Schultz Saddle to Pintler Creek — Anaconda-Pintler Wilderness Area

Beaverhead/Deerlodge National Forest
Philipsburg Ranger District
P.O. Box H
Philipsburg, MT 59858
406-859-3211

(continued on page 300)

Appendix A: Land Administrators (continued)

Pintler Creek to Cutaway Pass — Anaconda-Pintler Wilderness
Beaverhead/Deerlodge National Forest
Wise River Ranger District
Box 100, Wise River, MT 59762
406-832-3178

Cutaway Pass to Continental Divide on Goat Flat — Anaconda-Pintler Wilderness
Beaverhead/Deerlodge National Forest
Philipsburg Ranger District
(see Schultz Saddle on p. 299)

Goat Flat to western border of Mt. Haggin Wildlife Management Area
Beaverhead/Deerlodge National Forest
Wise River Ranger District
(see Pintler Creek above)

Mt. Haggin Wildlife Management Area
State of Montana
Department of Fish, Wildlife and Parks
1820 Meadowlark Lane
Butte, MT 59701
406-494-1953

Eastern border of Mt. Haggin Wildlife Management Area to Burnt Mountain — Fleecer Mountain Range
Beaverhead/Deerlodge National Forest
Wise River Ranger District
(see Pintler Creek above)

Burnt Mountain to crest of Divide in Highland Mountains
Beaverhead/Deerlodge National Forest
Butte Ranger District
1820 Meadowlark Lane
Butte, MT 59701

Crest of Divide in Highland Mountains to Pipestone Pass
Beaverhead/Deerlodge National Forest
Jefferson Ranger District
3 Whitetail Road
Whitehall, MT 59759
406-287-3223

Pipestone Pass to county line north of Lowland Campground — crosses I-15 to enter the Boulder Mountains
Beaverhead/Deerlodge National Forest
Butte Ranger District
(see Burnt Mountain above)

County Line north of Lowland Campground to just south of Bison Mountain
Beaverhead/Deerlodge National Forest
Jefferson Ranger District
(see Crest of Divide in Highland Mountains above)

South of Bison Mountain to Nevada Mountain (except Marysville area)
Helena National Forest
Helena Ranger District
2001 Poplar Street, Helena, MT 59601
406-449-5490

Marysville Area
BLM, Butte District Office
Headwaters Resource Area
P.O. Box 3388, Butte, MT 59702
406-494-5059

Nevada Mountain to southern border of Scapegoat Wilderness — Lewis and Clark Range
Helena National Forest
Lincoln Ranger District
7269 Highway 200, Lincoln, MT 59639
406-362-4265

Scapegoat Wilderness southern border to Sun River Pass in the Bob Marshall Wilderness
Lewis and Clark National Forest
Rocky Mountain Ranger District
P.O. Box 340, Choteau, MT 59422
406-466-5341

Sun River Pass to Muskrat Pass — Bob Marshall Wilderness
Flathead National Forest
Spotted Bear Ranger District
P.O. Box 190340, Hungry Horse, MT 59919
406-758-5376 or 406-387-5243

Muskrat Pass to Marias Pass
Lewis and Clark National Forest
Rocky Mountain Ranger District
(see Scapegoat Wilderness above)

Glacier National Park to Canada
Backcountry Trails Manager
Glacier National Park
West Glacier, MT 59936
406-888-7800, 406-888-7801
Web: http://www.nps.gov/glac

Canadian border to Waterton Townsite (Waterton Lake)
Waterton Lakes National Park
Canadian Parks Service
Waterton Park, Alberta T0K 2M0
403-859-2224

Portions of Autumn Creek and Scenic Point Trails near East Glacier Park
Blackfeet Tribal Business Council
Browning, MT, 406-338-7521
Blackfeet Fish and Wildlife, 406-338-7207

Glacier National Park Backcountry Reservations (accepted after May 1 each year)
P.O. Box 395, Glacier National Park
West Glacier, MT 59936
406-888-7800

Appendix B: Equipment Checklist

ALWAYS CARRY THE TEN ESSENTIALS

matches and lighter
knife
emergency shelter (tarp or groundcloth)
food and water
mirror or whistle for signaling
extra clothes
headlamp or flashlight with extra batteries
compass and maps
first aid kit
sunglasses and sunscreen

CONSIDER ADDING THESE ITEMS FOR DAYHIKES

pepper spray (bear deterrent)
daypack
moleskin
insect repellent
cord or rope
trowel for catholes (a metal trowel is shiny enough to use as a mirror)
lightweight hat and gloves
extra socks
insulating layer, top and bottom (fleece, wool, etc.)
rain gear
camera and film

FOR OVERNIGHT OR THROUGH-HIKES

sleeping bag
insulating ground pad
tent or shelter
stove, fuel, and eating/cooking utensils
bag for garbage
food bag (preferably waterproof, for hanging food)
extra clothing
long underwear
light shoes for around camp (water sandals serve two purposes)
water filter or iodine tablets
toiletries and personal hygiene kit (no scented or perfumed toiletries)
repair kits for tent, stove, water filter, etc.
pack cover

OPTIONAL

water bag
chair
pillow
journal
reading material
watch
fishing gear
groundcloth for tent
binoculars
candle lantern
walking stick or trekking poles
radio
kitchen sink

Appendix C: Map Sources

U.S. GEOLOGICAL SURVEY

Denver Federal Center
P.O. Box 25286
Denver, CO 80225-9916
1-800-USA-MAPS
Fax: 303-202-4693
e-mail: infoservices@usgs.gov
Web: http://edcwww.cr.usgs.gov/webglis/

Rocky Mountain Mapping Center
1-800-435-7627

TRAILS ILLUSTRATED

P.O. Box 3610
Evergreen, CO 80439
1-800-962-1643
Web: http://www.trailsillustrated.com

DELORME MAPPING

Montana Atlas and Gazetteer
Idaho Atlas and Gazetteer
P.O. Box 298
Freeport, ME 04032
207-865-4171

Forest Service maps are available at the district offices in Idaho and in Montana. See Appendix A for more information.

Appendix D: Map Lists

Alphabetical List: USGS Topographical Maps for the Continental Divide National Scenic Trail route for Idaho and Montana. These are all 7.5-minute maps.

Ahern Pass
Amphitheater Mtn.
Bannock Pass (ID, MT)
Benchmark
Bender Point
Big Hole Pass (ID, MT)
Big Table Mountain (ID, MT)
Bison Mountain
Blowout Mountain
Buffalo Lake NE (ID, WY, MT)
Burnt Mountain
Buxton
Cadotte Creek
Caribou Peak
Carpp Ridge
Chief Mountain
Corral Creek (ID, MT)
Cottonwood Creek (ID, MT)
Crescent Cliff
Cut Bank Pass
Deadman Lake (ID, MT)
Deadman Pass (ID, MT)
Delmoe Lake
Dickie Peak
Earthquake Lake (ID, MT)
East Glacier Park
Edie Creek (ID, MT)
Eighteen Mile Peak (ID, MT)
Elk Park Pass
Esmeralda Hill
Fritz Peak (ID, MT)
Gable Mountain
Gallagher Gulch (ID, MT)
Gates Park
Gibbonsville (ID, MT)
Goat Mtn. (ID, MT)
Goldstone Mountain (ID, MT)
Goldstone Pass (ID, MT)
Gooseberry Park
Grace
Granite Butte
Greenhorn Mountain
Heart Lake
Hidden Lake Bench (ID, MT)
Homer Youngs Peak
Homestake
Hyde Creek
Jakie Creek
Jumbo Mountain (ID, MT)
Kelly Lake
Kiowa
Kitty Creek (ID, MT)
Lake Sherburne
Latham Spring (ID, MT)
Lemhi Pass (ID, MT)
Lima Peaks
Lincoln Gulch
Lockhart Meadows
Logan Pass
Lost Trail Pass (ID, MT)
Lower Seymour Lake
MacDonald Pass
Madison Arm (ID, MT)
Many Glacier
Medicine Lodge Peak (ID, MT)
Miner Lake
Monida (ID, MT)
Morningstar Mountain
Morrison Lake (ID, MT)
Mount Evans
Mount Geduhn
Mount Humbug
Mount Jefferson (ID, MT)
Mount Stimson
Mussigbrod Lake
Nevada Mountain
Ophir Creek
Paul Reservoir (ID, MT)
Pentagon Mountain
Pipestone Pass
Porcupine Ridge
Porphyry Reef
Prairie Reef
Pretty Prairie
Reas Pass (ID, MT)
Rising Sun
Rogers Pass
Scapegoat Mountain
Schultz Saddle
Selway Mountain
Sheepshead Mountain
Shewag Lake (ID, MT)
Slategoat Mountain
Slide Mtn (ID, MT)
Snowline (ID, MT)
Squaw Mountain
Steamboat Mountain
Stemple Pass
Storm Lake
Sugarloaf Mountain
Sula
Summit
Swede Gulch
Targhee Pass (ID, MT)
Targhee Peak (ID, MT)
Tepee Draw (ID, MT)
Tepee Mountain (ID, MT)
Three Brothers
Three Sisters
Thunderbolt Creek
Tucker Creek
Upper Red Rock Lake (ID, MT)
Warren Peak
Whitetail Peak
Wilborn
Winslow Creek (ID, MT)
Wood Lake

Maps recommended for hard-to-find approach routes, or recommended because the CDT passes so close that trekkers could easily wander into the next map area. In alphabetical order:

Agency Creek (ID)
Ajax Ranch (ID, MT)
Antelope Valley (ID)
Big Hole Battlefield
Bohannon Spring (ID, MT)
Butte North
Butte South
Elk Creek
Hebgen Dam (ID, MT)
Island Butte
Jackson (MT)
Sawtell Peak (ID, MT)

Maps recommended for hard-to-find approach routes, or recommended because the CDT passes so close that trekkers could easily wander into the next map area. In order from south to north:

Hebgen Dam (ID, MT)
Sawtell Peak (ID, MT)
Antelope Valley (ID)
Island Butte
Agency Creek (ID)
Bohannon Spring (ID, MT)
Ajax Ranch (ID, MT)
Elk Creek
Jackson (MT)
Big Hole Battlefield
Butte South
Butte North

Appendix D: Map Lists (continued)

South-to-North List: USGS Topographical Maps for the Continental Divide National Scenic Trail route for Idaho and Montana. These are all 7.5-minute maps. They are in order, approximately, from south to north. Note that the CDT meanders so much that sometimes the trekker will exit a map only to reenter it later. Each map is listed only once, even though it may appear more than once on the route. In some cases, the CDT only nicks the edge of the terrain shown on the map.

Buffalo Lake NE (ID, WY, MT)
Latham Spring (ID, MT)
Reas Pass (ID, MT)
Madison Arm (ID, MT)
Targhee Pass (ID, MT)
Targhee Peak (ID, MT)
Earthquake Lake (ID, MT)
Hidden Lake Bench (ID, MT)
Mount Jefferson (ID, MT)
Upper Red Rock Lake (ID, MT)
Slide Mtn (ID, MT)
Winslow Creek (ID, MT)
Big Table Mtn (ID, MT)
Corral Creek (ID, MT)
Monida (ID, MT)
Paul Reservoir (ID, MT)
Tepee Draw (ID, MT)
Snowline (ID, MT)
Lima Peaks
Edie Creek (ID, MT)
Fritz Peak (ID, MT)
Gallagher Gulch (ID, MT)
Deadman Lake (ID, MT)
Eighteen Mile Peak (ID, MT)
Cottonwood Creek (ID, MT)
Morrison Lake (ID, MT)
Tepee Mtn (ID, MT)
Medicine Lodge Peak (ID, MT)
Deadman Pass (ID, MT)
Bannock Pass (ID, MT)
Goat Mtn (ID, MT)
Lemhi Pass (ID, MT)
Kitty Creek (ID, MT)
Goldstone Mtn (ID, MT)
Goldstone Pass (ID, MT)
Selway Mountain
Miner Lake
Homer Youngs Peak
Jumbo Mtn (ID, MT)
Shewag Lake (ID, MT)
Big Hole Pass (ID, MT)
Gibbonsville (ID, MT)
Lost Trail Pass (ID, MT)
Sula
Schultz Saddle
Bender Point
Mussigbrod Lake
Kelly Lake
Warren Peak
Carpp Ridge
Storm Lake
Mount Evans
Lower Seymour Lake
Lincoln Gulch
Dickie Peak
Burnt Mountain
Buxton
Tucker Creek
Mount Humbug
Pipestone Pass
Grace
Delmoe Lake
Homestake
Whitetail Peak
Elk Park Pass
Sheepshead Mountain
Lockhart Meadows
Sugarloaf Mountain
Thunderbolt Creek
Bison Mountain
Three Brothers
MacDonald Pass
Greenhorn Mountain
Esmeralda Hill
Ophir Creek
Nevada Mountain
Granite Butte
Stemple Pass
Swede Gulch
Wilborn
Rogers Pass
Cadotte Creek
Blowout Mountain
Caribou Peak
Heart Lake
Steamboat Mountain
Jakie Creek
Scapegoat Mountain
Wood Lake
Benchmark
Pretty Prairie
Prairie Reef
Slategoat Mountain
Amphitheater Mtn
Three Sisters
Gates Park
Porphyry Reef
Pentagon Mountain
Gooseberry Park
Morningstar Mountain
Crescent Cliff
Hyde Creek
Summit
Squaw Mountain
East Glacier Park
Kiowa
Cut Bank Pass
Mount Stimson
Rising Sun
Logan Pass
Many Glacier
Ahern Pass
Mount Geduhn
Porcupine Ridge
Gable Mountain
Lake Sherburne
Chief Mountain

Appendix E: Conservation and Trail Advocacy Groups

Continental Divide Trail Alliance
P.O. Box 628
Pine, CO 80470
303-838-3760
www.cdtrail.org

Continental Divide Trail Society
3704 N. Charles St., #601
Baltimore, MD 21218
410-235-9610

Alliance of the Wild Rockies
415 N. Higgins Avenue
Missoula, MT 59802
406-721-5420

Save the Chalets
704 Birch Street
Helena, MT 59601-9923
888-CHALET1
www.nps.gov/glac/chalets.htm

Montana Wilderness Association
P.O. Box 635
Helena, MT 59624
406-443-7350

Glacier National Park Associates
Box 91, Kalispell, MT 59903
406-888-5241
www.nps.gov/glac/gnpa.htm

The Glacier Institute
P.O. Box 7457
Kalispell, MT 59904
406-756-1211
www.nps.gov/glac/inst.htm

The Glacier National Park History Association
Box 428
West Glacier, MT 59936
406-888-5756
www.nps.gov/glac/gnha1.htm

Leave No Trace
P.O. Box 997
Boulder, CO 80305
800-332-4100
www.lnt.org

Appendix F: Bibliography and Other Reading

Alt, David, and Hyndman, Donald. *Roadside Geology of Montana.* Missoula, MT: Mountain Press Publishing Company, 1995.

Bergon, Frank. *The Journals of Lewis & Clark.* New York: Penguin Books, 1989.

Boone, Lalia. *Idaho Place Names: A Geographical Dictionary.* Moscow, ID: The University of Idaho Press, 1988.

Cheek, Roland. *Learning to Talk Bear.* Great Falls, MT: Northwinds Publishing and Printing, 1997.

Conley, Cort. *Idaho for the Curious.* Cambridge, ID: Backeddy Books, 1982.

Craighead, John; Craighead, Frank; Davis, Ray. *A Field Guide to Rocky Mountain Wildflowers.* NY: Houghton Mifflin Company, 1963.

Fargis, Bykofsy, Gold, et al. *The New York Public Library Desk Reference.* Second Edition. NY: The New York Public Library and The Stonesong Press, Inc., 1993.

Florin, Lambert. *Ghost Towns of the West.* NY: Superior Publishing Company, 1971.

Garcia, Andrew. *Tough Trip Through Paradise.* San Francisco, CA: The Rock Foundation, Comstock Editions, 1967.

Jones, Tom. *Colorado's Continental Divide Trail: The Official Guide.* Englewood, CO: Westcliffe Publishers, Inc., 1997.

Lopez, Tom. *Exploring Idaho's Mountains.* Seattle, WA: The Mountaineers, 1990.

Maley, Terry. *Exploring Idaho Geology.* Boise, ID: Mineral Land Publications, 1987.

Murie, Olaus. *Animal Tracks.* NY: Houghton Mifflin Company, 1974.

Rockwell, David. *Glacier National Park, A Natural History Guide.* Boston, MA: Houghton Mifflin Company, 1995.

Taylor, Ronald. *Sagebrush Country.* Missoula, MT: Mountain Press Publishing Company, 1992.

Thomas, David; Miller, Jay; White, Richard; Nabokov, Peter; Deloria, Phillip. *The Native Americans: An Illustrated History.* Atlanta, GA: Turner Publishing, Inc., 1993.

Tirrell, Norma. *Montana, Compass American Guides.* Oakland, CA: Fodor's Travel Publications, Inc., 1997.

Ward, Geoffrey. *The West: An Illustrated History.* NY: Little, Brown and Co., 1996.

Whitney, Stephen, et al. *Western Forests. The Audubon Society Nature Guides.* NY: Alfred A. Knopf, 1990.

Appendix G: Definitions

2WD: Two-Wheel-Drive; most sedans and highway vehicles are two-wheel-drive.

4WD: Four-Wheel-Drive; a vehicle equipped with a four-wheel-drive transmission. 4WDs with high clearance and a short wheel base are required to access the CDT in many places along the Idaho/Montana border. The verb is "four-wheelin'" to refer to driving over roads that are little better than trodes.

Argillite: Hardened mudstone with an abundant clay content, descriptive of many mountains in Glacier National Park.

Arête: A sharp, high ridge that separates adjacent glaciers or adjacent glacially carved valleys.

ATV: All Terrain Vehicle. A motorized vehicle designed to travel over rough or roadless terrain, such as a four-wheeler or dirt bike.

Bench: A flat but usually narrow stretch of land, often an elevated area that marks an old shoreline above a waterway. Also any elevated terrain that resembles a bench.

Blaze: An axe cut in a tree's bark to mark a trail. Blazes usually take the form of a lowercase "i," with a smaller dot or square over an elongated slash.

BLM: Bureau of Land Management; a Department of the Interior agency that manages 270 million acres of public land in the western states. Along the Continental Divide Trail, the BLM manages most of the land that is not within the jurisdiction of the Forest Service, allotting some lands for grazing, overseeing mineral rights, and establishing an SRMA (Special Recreation Management Area) for scenic sections. The CDT crosses an SRMA in the Centennial Mountains.

Appendix G: Definitions (continued)

Bog bridge: Planking, usually supported by logs, to take the trail over marshy areas.

Bushwhack: To hike (or fight) your way through bushes, deadfall, and other obstacles to reach your destination without having a trail to follow. The opposite of "tread."

Cairn: A man-made pile of rocks, used to mark a trail where visible tread does not or cannot exist, and where there are no trees to blaze.

Cat cut: A swath of ground leveled by scraping with a "caterpillar" type of bulldozer. A cat cut is not finished enough to be called a road.

CDNST: Continental Divide National Scenic Trail

CDT: Continental Divide Trail

CDTA: Continental Divide Trail Alliance

Cirque: A round or U-shaped area at the head of a glaciated valley, normally an ice-cream-scoop shape that holds a lake or a tarn.

Divide: In lowercase, a divide between two drainages; in uppercase, an abbreviation for the Continental Divide.

Drainage: A region drained by a river or creek.

FR: An abbreviation for Forest Road, used to preface Forest Service Road numbers.

FS: Forest Service, an abbreviation (see USFS).

Glacier: A mass of ice that does not completely melt in the summer, formed on land by the compaction and recrystallization of snow. Glaciers move (flow) due to their own weight.

Hiking season: June to September, but may be July to September at higher elevations. Spring is mid-June to late July, with some variations depending on altitude. Summer is mid-July to late August, with the dates varying depending on altitude. Fall is the month of September. Winter is whenever it snows—continual from October to May, intermittent from May to October.

Horn: A sharp peak formed when multiple glaciers grind at the rock until three or more cirques are formed around a narrow pinnacle.

Krummholz: A German word meaning "twisted wood." Refers to the subalpine trees that are forced into twisted and stunted shapes by extreme weather conditions.

Lost: When you know where you are, but you don't know where the damned trail is.

ORV: see ATV.

Park: Not the same as a city park. In the Rocky Mountains, "park" refers to a natural meadow or open area, as in "Gates Park" in the Bob Marshall Wilderness.

Saddle: A lower spot between two mountain peaks or between two high ridges. Refers to the shape of the land that resembles a horse saddle. A "notch" is a narrow saddle that is shaped more like a "V."

Sign: Animal droppings or "scat" that can be read as a sign of which animals are in the area and how recently.

Switchback: A reversal in trail direction that is used to climb or descend steep slopes, usually occurring in a series. Switchbacks are built by trail crews to prevent erosion, and to keep the grade of the trail within standards recommended for hiking and for stock use.

Talus: An accumulation of broken rock (a trail crew's nightmare).

Tarn: A small, shallow mountain lake or pool.

Through-hiker: One who hikes long distances, stopping for supplies or rest infrequently; a hiker who calls food "fuel" and has overcome the desire for comfort; a person of questionable sanity.

Topo: Short for topographical map.

Tread: A visible path, usually made by trail crews with shovels or trail machines. "Visible tread" is the CDT hiker's dream-come-true.

TRHD: Abbreviation for trailhead, where a trail officially begins, often marked with signs, a parking lot, or other amenities.

Trode: A trail that used to be a road, or a path that is almost wide enough to be a road.

Turnpike: Improvements to a trail meant to eliminate muddy or boggy areas. Log sills are covered with a tough but permeable cloth, then topped with gravel.

Two-track: Almost a road. A two-track is usually open to motorized travel, but shows very little use.

USFS: United States Forest Service; a division of the Department of Agriculture that is responsible for managing national forest lands. You may also see "USDA" for United States Department of Agriculture. Land administration is divided into "districts" commonly called "Ranger Districts" within each national forest.

USGS: United States Geological Survey; the federal agency responsible for creating and maintaining topographical maps, including the 7.5-minute quadrangles used to navigate along the CDT.

The Continental Divide Trail Alliance

Protecting a Vital National Resource

How can you help?

By becoming a member of the Continental Divide Trail Alliance (CDTA). Your willingness to join thousands of concerned citizens across the country will make the difference. Together, we can provide the financial resources needed to complete the Trail.

CDTA is a nonprofit membership organization formed to help protect, build, maintain, and manage the CDT. CDTA serves a broad-based constituency and includes people who enjoy recreating on public lands, as well as those concerned about overdevelopment.

As a CDTA member, you will:

- Protect a vital and precious natural resource
- Ensure Trail maintenance and completion
- Improve Trail access
- Support informational and educational programs
- Champion volunteer projects
- Advocate for policy issues that support the CDT

What Does It Take to Help Us? Just One Cent a Mile

We realize there are a lot of demands on your time and budget. That's why we're only asking you to give a little—just one cent a mile to support the Trail. For a modest membership fee of $31, you will help us go so very far, and finish what was courageously started so long ago.

For more information
or to send your contribution, write to:

Continental Divide Trail Alliance
P.O. Box 628
Pine, CO 80470
(303) 838-3760
www.cdtrail.org
Please make checks payable to CDTA.

Index

NOTE: Bold citations denote trail descriptions; citations followed by the letter "p" denote photos; citations followed by the letter "m" denote maps.

About the Author

LYNNA PRUE HOWARD is a writer whose work ranges from technical writing for scientific websites to adventure travel. As "PrueHeart the Wanderer" she has explored much of the western United States. Born in New Mexico and raised in Idaho and Alaska, she has long been an outdoor enthusiast. She's also the author of Westcliffe Publishers' *Along Montana and Idaho's Continental Divide Trail* (2000), which tells the tale of hiking the Divide in stories and pictures. Lynna's other Westcliffe projects include a guidebook for Utah's wilderness areas and a collection of adventure travel stories.

Lynna lives in Idaho and often works with her brother, Leland. She has a hard time holding on to the fact that she is 50 years old, but a grown daughter and son offer proof. Her advice to those who would follow in her footsteps is, "Leave some places wild, including those within your heart—and if you get lost, enjoy it."

About the Photographer

LELAND HOWARD is a professional fine art nature photographer with a lifelong background in wilderness exploration and photography. He resides in Idaho.

His work has appeared in numerous and diverse publications, including those of The National Geographic Society, The Sierra Club, Sierra Publishing, Northwest Publications, *Photographic* magazine, *Outside* magazine, and many others. His work illustrates *Along Montana and Idaho's Continental Divide Trail* (2000) and an upcoming guide to Utah's wilderness areas—both from Westcliffe Publishers.

The official route of the Continental Divide Trail in Montana and Idaho is 980.7 miles long. As photographer, Leland added at least 300 more miles to that tally. He climbed above the trail, hiked into valleys below the route, and returned as many as five times to capture the perspectives and moods that define the Continental Divide Trail experience.